RAIL BOOK BIBLIOGRAPHY
1948-1972

A COMPREHENSIVE GUIDE TO THE
MOST IMPORTANT RAILBOOKS, PUBLICATIONS
AND REPORTS

Cross-Indexed by Subject, Author, Title,
Company, and Many Other Catagories

F. K. Hudson
Editor-In-Chief

SPECIALTY PRESS, INC.

OCEAN, NEW JERSEY

TABLE OF CONTENTS

Introduction   Page 1

Subject Entries—Alphabetical   Page 9

Subject Entries—Major Category

     Biographies   Page 95

     Cars   Page 97

     Companies   Page 100

     Electric Railroads   Page 128

     History   Page 129

     Juvenile Literature   Page 134

     Locomotives   Page 138

     Models   Page 145

     Narrow Gauge   Page 149

     Street Railroads   Page 150

     Transit   Page 152

Author Index   Page 157

Title Index   Page 195

Bibliography   Page 225

Acknowledgements

The editors' basic acknowledgement is for the almost universally complete listing and cataloging of books and publications done at the Library of Congress in Washington D. C. with the cooperation of other libraries throughout the United States and the world and with the American Library Association.

The editors' acknowledge with great appreciation the assistance given us in the background preparation of this bibliography by the cataloging and research staffs of the Library of Congress, and the help given us in the listing of the most recently published books, some of which are not yet cataloged by the Library of Congress, by the editors of the publisher listed in the bibliography.

Special thanks to Mr. Oliver S. Foote and his competent staff at Selectype, Inc. in New York are required for their careful attention to a difficult text and their cheerful cooperation in the many revisions and enlargements. Mr. Jay R. Pinover and Mrs. Kathy Roberts of Kingsport Press, Inc. have been continually helpful in the production of this and other books.

The Editors

SECTION 1

INTRODUCTION

INTRODUCTION

This brief introduction describes how RAILBOOK BIBLIOGRAPHY is organized, and what it contains as well as how it can be most easily used. This introduction covers: content, book entry information, use, organization, alternate entries, duplicate treatment, material not covered, errors and suggestion, and abbreviations. Abbreviations are listed separately for quick future reference.

Content—What RRB is.

RAILBOOK BIBLIOGRAPHY is basically a subject indexing and listing of books, government and industry reports, and other publications issued during the 25 year period from 1948 through 1972. The main source of data is the card catalog of the Library of Congress (L. C.) which includes all United States copyright publications as well as other publications not copyrighted but filed by authors, publishers or other libraries for cataloguing purposes. Within the railroad field, this covers most books. The major exceptions are books published privately, generally in small quantity, by individuals or railfan groups.

RRB has supplimented the Library of Congress information by reviewing trade publications for reports of new books, and by circulating a questionaire on railroad books to known publishers in the railroad field.

RRB follows the format of the L. C. catalog card for two reasons. First, it is a concise means of presenting the information, and, second, many readers will use RRB as a guide to public library sources.

RRB covers, we believe, almost all of the major books and reports on American railroads of the 1948-1972 period. The only items not included are certain duplicate entries and some highly specialized pamphlets or reports that are difficult to obtain or to locate in libraries. Where small papers or reports constitute a main source of information, they have been included as a basic information resource regardless of their location or length.

RRB is extensively cross-indexed by alternate subject headings to aid the reader in locating matters of interest, and is completely indexed by author and by title.

Book Entry Information—How books are described.

Each main entry in RRB follows the same form as the Library of Congress catalog card, that is: short title, subtitle, author, publication information, collation or physical description, and location code within RRB.

Short Title.

The short title is usually the one used on the cover of the book. In rare cases this may have been shortened by the book cataloger for brevity. In L. C. cards, titles are never capitalized except for the first word in the title or where proper names are used.

Subtitle.

Generally, this is the longer additional title or content description information found on the title page of the book being cataloged. Here, it is important to remember that this is the author's or editor's further description of what the book is about and is not the cataloger's description or critical review of the contents. In a few cases where the title page does not supply a subtitle, a cataloger may briefly examine the contents to provide a short description of his own.

Author or Editor

A listing of the book's authors, editors and contributors. Occasionally, where the publication is produced by an editorial staff, the publisher may be listed in place of an individual author.

Publication Information.

A brief entry showing the city where published, the publisher, and the date of publication.

Collation or Physical Description.

A summary of the book's length, content as to text and illustrations, and height.

> **Length.** The number of pages is shown directly, with any preface noted as such in parenthesis. In certain cases where the book is in several sections or volumes, the pages will be shown by consecutive section. For example, 208 p. (pf.—28 p.), means a book of 208 pages preceeded by a preface of 28 pages. A similiar book with an additional section of 110 pages, would be listed 208 p. (pf.—28 p.), 110 p. Books issued in more than one volume are noted by the number of volumes (2 v., 3 v.) preceding the length designation.

> **Content.** A short summary of the nature of the book's physical content, dealing in order with illustrations as a general catagory, and when particular types are important as follows in alphabetical order: charts, facsimiles, forms, maps, plans, plates, portraits and tables. Occasionally, the number of illustrations used are also listed. In RRB this is done in parenthesis following the particular type of illustration. See abbreviations for specific symbols.

> **Height.** The height of the book measured in inches along the spline or bound edge. Where the length (depth along shelf) may be noted, the height is listed first. RRB is nine inches high, and is reported as 9 in. If depth were added, the description would be 9x6 in.

> **Location Code.** A simple means of locating each main entry within RRB. The code follows the alphabetical listing of the letters in the main entry heading.

Use—How to use RRB.

The basic problem of any reader trying to find something listed by someone else is to duplicate, as nearly as possible, that persons thought process in terms of labelling and defining the subject at hand. The easiest way to do this is to try to use the same type of reasoning process as the indexer uses in making the index. This involves first determining the single most descriptive and general subject heading for the item under consideration, and then determining the various alternative headings which might be considered by others as synonymous with or related to the main or general heading.

After doing this with the entries in RRB, and examining the books listed under the main subject headings, the reader should also review the informational (single line) entries found at the end of the main entry sections, and the author and title indexes. Author entries may be particularly useful because many authors specialize in certain subjects, periods or geographical locations.

An example on book location may be helpful. A book dealing with narrow gauge railroads in Colorado would have its main listing under Colorado, but the reader should also examine the entries under the narrow gauge, mountain, and shortline headings as well as those of companies he knows operate in the area, that is, the Denver & Rio Grande Western, the Rio Grande Southern, the Denver, South Park & Pacific, etc.

Organization—How RRB is organized.

Basic entries in RRB are by major subject heading, treated in exact alphabetical order and generally in reverse chronological order. In other words, under the subject heading of History, "All aboard" preceeds "American railroad network," while "American railroad" by John Stover in turn preceeds "American railroad" by John Weaver. If a work has been through several editions, the latest edition is listed first and the earliest edition listed last.

Where several political subdivisions are listed, the order is from the largest to the smallest, that is from state to county to city, and from public body to public agencies such as authorities, commissions and universities. Private organizations, which may take their name from a city or town, follow that location and its agencies in the alphabetical listings. Where organizations take their names from individuals, the individual is listed first and the organization next.

Alternate Entries. Their purpose and use.

The purpose of alternate entries is to ease the readers path to the books of interest to him and to make sure that books which treat several subjects are referenced under each subject. For instance a book dealing with the first transcontinental railway, might have its main entry under history, and informational entries under Union Pacific and Southern Pacific Railways, and, possibly, several additional listings under locomotives, construction, engineering, biographies, and location headings depending on the book's content and catalog description.

Duplicate Treatment. Treatment of a book's duplications, revisions and additions.

No book has more than one main entry in RRB unless it has been substantially revised, enlarged or changed. Where these changes occur, the books are listed separately, with the last edition reported first. Where newer editions of the same work are printed without apparent change, the main entry will show the date of the original issue plus all known (after 1948) later editions.

Material Not Covered. What RRB does not include.

RRB is primarily a listing of copyrighted or publically cataloged works including books from established publishers. RRB does not yet contain certain privately published, narrowly circulated, or uncataloged works simply because we do not know of their existence.

Errors and Suggestions.

While the editors have been careful to ulitize reliable source material and to individually investigate possible sources of error both in the source material and text, we recognize that a book of this scope and complexity is subject to the possibility of error and omission. If any reader observes such an error, we would like to know about it, and will correct it in future editions. We will also work to improve the book's content and format, and to enlarge the coverage, particularly of the more specialized works, as we progress.

Your suggestions, comments and advice will receive our prompt attention. They may be directed to:

The Editor
RAILBOOK BIBLIOGRAPHY
P. O. Box 2187
Ocean, New Jersey 07712

ABBREVIATIONS

Abbreviations used in the collation or physical description of books:

C	Charts
D	Diagrams
(F)	Folded
Fac	Facsimiles
G	Graphs
I	Illustrations
I (IC)	Illustrations, one (or other number) in color
I (PC)	Illustrations, part in color
l	leaf, leaves
M	Maps
MI	Mostly Illustrations
p	pages
P	Portraits
pf	preface
Ph	Photos
PL	Plans
pts	parts
T	Tables
v	volumes

Abbreviations used in title, author and publisher designation:

Associations, Commissions, Organizations, etc:

AAR	Association of American Railroads
AREA	American Railway Engineering Association
ASME	American Society of Mechanical Engineers
ASTM	American Society for Testing and Materials
AWS	American Welding Society
BRT	Brotherhood of Railroad Trainmen
Bu. Acc't. & CF	Bureau of Accounting and Cost Finding
Bu. Ry. Econ.	Bureau of Railway Economics
Bu. Trans. Econ. & Stat.	Bureau of Transportation Economics and Statistics
Comp. Gen.	Comptroller General (U.S.)
GPO	Government Post Office
ICC	Interstate Commerce Commission
NMB	National Mediation Board
RR Ret. Bd.	Railroad Retirement Board
Ry. Sys. & Mgt. Assoc.	Railway Systems and Management Association
Soc. Eng. Ed.	Society for Engineering Education

Abbreviations used in Congressional Committees:

Note: Generally abbreviated by committee title alone without the further designation of committee—for example, House of Representatives, Committee on the Judiciary would be simplified to: House, Judiciary. Subcommittees are designated in a parenthesis following the parent committee. Each Congress is abbreviated by a C (Congress) following the number of the Congress, and a S (Session) following a 1 or 2 for first or second session. For instance, 87C-2S, is the 87th Congress, 2nd session.

Congressional Abbreviations:

C	for Congress, following the numerical designation of the Congress
S	for Session of that Congress
Congress	United States Congress
House	United States Congress, House of Representatives
Senate	United States Congress, Senate

Banking & Cur.	Banking and Currency
Commerce	Commerce
Govt. Ops.	Government Operations
Int. Comm.	Interstate Commerce
Int. & For. Com.	Interstate and Foreign Commerce
Int. & Ins. Affairs	Interior and Insular Affairs
Wash. Metro. Prob.	Washington Metropolitan Problems (Joint Committees)
Judiciary	Judiciary
Labor & Pub. Wel.	Labor and Public Welfare
PO & Civ. Ser.	Post Office and Civil Service

Congressional Subcommittees (in parenthesis after parent):

Exec. Reorg.	Executive Reorganization
RR Ret.	Railroad Retirement
Sur. Trans.	Surface Transportation
Trans. & Aero.	Transportation and Aeronautics

SECTION 2

SUBJECT ENTRIES – ALPHABETICAL

ACCIDENTS
(see also Wrecks)

Down brakes; a history of railroad accidents, safety precautions and operating
practices in the United States of America. Robert B. Shaw. [1st ed.] London,
P. R. Macmillan [c 1961; label: Owen Davies, distributor, Chicago]. 487 p., I,
9 in.   AC-1

Accident reports to ICC. Hearing on S. 1964, a bill requiring carriers to make
reports to the ICC with respect to certain accidents. June 26, 1959, Senate
Int. & For. Comm. Com., 86C-IS. Washington, GPO, 1959. 83 p. (pf.−3p.),
I, 9.4 in.   AC-2

ACCOUNTING

Agenda [of the] annual meeting, railway accounting officers. AAR, Acct.
Div., Washington. 9 in.   ACT-1

Conducting transportation. Acct. Div. AAR, Washington, 1960. 177 p., I, D,
Forms, T, 11 in.   ACT-2

Explanation of rail cost finding procedures and principles relating to the use of
costs. 1948− . ICC, Bur. of Accts., Washington. 11 in.   ACT-3

Interpretations of the uniform system of accounts for railroad companies.
ICC, Bur. of Accts., Washington, GPO [1962]. 47 p. (pf.−14 p.), 10.2 in.
(circular No. 130).   ACT-4

Railroad accounting and statistics; research and fact finding as aids to management. Edward H. Bunnell. Chicago, Watson Publications [1955]. 272 p., I,
9.4 in.   ACT-5

Railroad accounting procedures, prescribed by the Interstate Commerce Commission. Twelfth report by the Committee on Government Operations. House,
85C-IS., Washington, GPO, 1957. 31 p. (pf.−3 p.), T, 9.4 in. (No. 1167).   ACT-6

Railroad accounting procedures prescribed by the Interstate Commerce Commission. Hearings. House, Gov't Ops., 85C-IS., Washington, GPO, 1957. 292 p.
(pf.−5 p.), I, 9.4 in.   ACT-7

Rules governing the separation of operating expenses, railway taxes, equipment
rents, and joint facility rents between freight service and passenger service on
class 1 line-haul railroads. Effective on January 1, 1953. ICC, Washington
[1953]. 20 p. (pf.−5 p.), 9.4 in.   ACT-8

Uniform system of accounts for railroad companies, prescribed by the Interstate
Commerce Commission. ICC, Washington, GPO. 9.4 x 10.2 in.   ACT-9

Uniform system of accounts for railroad companies. Prescribed by the Interstate
Commerce Commission in accordance with section 20 of the Interstate commerce
act. Issue of 1957, as amended to January 1, 1957. ICC, Washington, GPO,
1957. 121 p. (pf.−4 p.), 10.6 in.   ACT-10

Uniform system of accounts for railroad companies. Prescribed by the Interstate Commerce Commission in accordance with section 20 of the Interstate commerce act. Effective Oct. 1, 1952. ICC, Washington, GPO, 1952. 132 p. (pf.–4 p.), 9.4 in.   ACT-11

Uniform system of accounts for persons furnishing cars or protective services against heat or cold. Prescribed by the Interstate Commerce Commission in accordance with section 20 (6) of the Interstate commerce act. Original issue, 1947. Effective Jan. 1, 1947. ICC [Washington, 1946]. 10.6 in.   ACT-12

Working in the shops, enginehouses and dispatching points; maintaining equipment. AAR, Acct. Div., Washington, 1958. 136 p., I, D, J, 11 in.   ACT-13

Working on the tracks. AAR, Acct. Div., Washington, 1956. 82 p., I, Forms, 11 in.   ACT-14

ADDRESSES, ESSAYS, LECTURES

The American railroads–an industry with a challenge. Stuart T. Saunders. New York, Newcomen Society in North America, 1962. 24 p., I, 9 in.   AD-1

ALABAMA

Cleartype colorprint map of Alabama. American Map Co., New York [1950]. 2 M (C), 38 x 25 in. (No. 4401).   AL-1

AMTRACK

Amtrack car spotter; a guide to Amtrack cars and history. New York, Wayner Publications, 1972. 58 p., I, 9 in.   AM-1

Journey to Amtrack; the year history rode the passenger train. Harold Edmonson, ed. Milwaukee, Kalmbach Pub. Co., 1972. 104 p., I (224), M, T.   AM-2

ANALYSIS

Quest for crisis; a world-ranging search for clues to the transport future. James N. Sites. New York, Simmons-Boardman [1963]. 223 p., I, 9.4 in.   AN-1

Railroad trends and prospects; an address before the New York Society of Security Analysts, New York City, June 8, 1951. Julius H. Parmelee. [New York, 1951.] 29 p., I, 9 in.   AN-2

A socio-economic study of forty-five railway operating trainmen's families in Eugene, Oregon. Richard D. Millican. [Eugene] c 1950. 25 l, I, 11 in.   AN-3

ANECDOTES

Will not run February 22nd. Caskie Stinnett. Illus. by Bill Ballantine. New York, Rinehart [1956]. 188 p., I, 7.9 in.   ANE-1

Show me the way to go home; the commuter story. Jerome Beatty. New York, Crowell [1959]. 247 p., I, 8.3 in.   ANE-2

ARKANSAS

Cleartype colorprint map of Arkansas. American Map Co., New York [1950].
M (C), 38.5 x 25 in. (No. 4403). ARK-1

Shortline railroads of Arkansas [by] Clifton E. Hull. [1st ed.] Norman, University
of Oklahoma Press [1969]. 416 p. (pf.–16 p.), I, Fac, M, P, 9 in. ARK-2

ART

Coaches and trains, edited and introduced by John Cadfryn-Roberts. Princeton, N.
J., Van Nostrand [1965]. 12 p., 20 plates (C), 9.8 in. ART-1

Design in transit. Institute of Contemporary Art. [Boston 1967.] I, M (C), PL,
11 in., 32 p. ART-2

ASSOCIATIONS

A. A. R., the story behind a symbol. William T. Faricy. New York, Newcomen
Society in North America, 1951. 28 p., I, 9 in. AS-1

The Association of American Railroads, its organization and activities. AAR
[Washington]. 9 in. AS-2

Summary presentation of the Association of American Railroads to the working
group of the President's Cabinet Committee on Transport Policy and Organization. [Washington, GPO], 1954. 2 v., T, 11.8 in. AS-3

Associations of railroad officers, railroad clubs, and railroad supply organizations
in the U. S. A. and Canada. Bu. of Railway Economics. Washington, 1951. 26 l.,
11 in. AS-4

ATLANTA

Downtown Atlanta railroad transit; a graduate project in complete system
design, submitted by students at the Georgia Institute of Technology. Atlanta,
Georgia Inst. of Technology, 1967. 225 p. (pf.–8 p.), I, M, 11 in. AT-1

BALTIMORE

Baltimore area mass transportation plan, phase II, long range program. Parson,
Brinckerhoff, Quade & Douglas. Baltimore, Metropolitan Transit Authority of
Maryland, 1965. 135 p. (pf.–8 p.), I (PC), M (C), PL (PC), 12.2 in. BA-1

Baltimore region rapid transit system; feasibility and preliminary engineering.
Prepared for the Mass Transit Steering Committee, Regional Planning Council,
Baltimore, Md. [by Daniel, Mann, Johnson & Mendenhall and Kaiser Engineers.
Baltimore] 1968. 116 p. (pf.–9 p.), I (PC), M (C), 11 x 17 in. BA-2

BIBLIOGRAPHY

Bibliography and priced catalogue of early railway books. (1893). Compiled by
S. Cotterell. Clifton, N. J., Augustus M. Kelley, 128, 36 p. BI-1

Bibliography of railroad literature. [5th ed.] AAR, Washington [1954]. 56 p.,
I, 9 x 4 in.   BI-2

Bibliography of railway literature. [4th ed] AAR, Washington [1950]. 48 p.,
I, 9 x 4 in.   BI-3

A tentative check-list of early European railway literature, 1831-1848; with a
prefatory note by Arthur H. Cole. By Daniel C. Haskell. Boston, Baker Library,
Harvard Graduate School of Business Administration [1955]. 192 p., 10.2 in.
                                                                                     BI-4

Nationalization of railways; 1939-1949; a list of references. [Compiled by
Helen R. Richardson, reference librarian. Bu. of Ry. Economics, Washington]
1949. 30 l. (pf.–4), 11 in.   BI-5

Preliminary inventory of the records of the Senate Committee on Interstate
Commerce, Subcommittee to Investigate Interstate Railroads, 1935-43 (Record
group 46). Compiled by Albert U. Blair and John W. Porter. U. S. National
Archives. Washington, 1954. 10 p. (pf. –5 p.), 10.6 in. (No. 55-G, prel.
inventories, No. 75).   BI-6

Rail Book Bibliography: a comprehensive guide and index to railroad books,
reports and publications, Ocean, N. J., Speciality Press, Inc., 1972. 9 in.   BI-7

Railroad books checklist, 1949 to 1969. Ladd Publications. Jacksonville, Ill.,
Ladd Publications, Inc.   BI-8

Railways; a readers guide, by E. T. Bryant. [Hamden, Conn.] Archon Books
[1968]. 249 p., 9 in.   BI-9

Railroads in defense and war, a bibliography, compiled by Helen R. Richardson,
reference librarian. Bu. of Ry. Economics, Washington, 1953. 262 p. (pf.–8 p.),
9 in.   BI-10

Suggestions for books and other material on railroads in the United States for
students of current transportation, by Elizabeth O. Cullen, librarian. Bu. of
Ry. Economics [Washington], 1951. 44 l., 11 in.: also, 1950, 24 l., 11 in. BI-11

BIOGRAPHIES . . . . see Section 2

BOSTON

Air view, rapid transit lines, Metropolitian Transit Authority. [Boston, 1952.]
20.4 x 29 in.   BO-1

PCC cars of Boston, 1937-1967, by Edward A. Anderson. Cambridge, Mass.,
Boston Street Railway Association, 1968. 51 p., I, M, 11 in.   BO-2

The problem of Boston's Metropolitian Transit Authority. Warren H. Deem.
[Cambridge, Bu. for Res. in Mun. Gov't., G. S. of Pub. Adm., Harvard Univ.,
1953.] 70 l., 11.4 in. (No. 20).   BO-3

Rapid transit Boston, by Bradley H. Clarke. Cambridge, Boston Street Railway
Association [1971]. 35 p., I, M, 8.7 x 11 in.   BO-4

Report on alternate program for suburban commuter service. Massachusetts Bay
Transportation Authority. [Boston, 1969.] 3, 78 p., I, M (PC), 11.4 in. Technical
supplement Boston, 1969. I, M, P, L, 11.4 in.   BO-5

Streetcar suburbs: the process of growth in Boston, 1870-1900. Sam B.
Warner. Cambridge, Harvard University Press, 1962. 208 p. (pf.—21 p.), I, M,
T, 9.8 in.   BO-6

Surface cars of Boston, 1903-1963. New England Elec. Ry. Hist. Soc. [Forty
Fort, Pa., H. E. Cox, 1963.] 70 p., I, 11 in.   BO-7

The trackless trolleys of Boston [by Bradley H. Clarke. Cambridge, Boston
Street Railway Association, 1970.] 63 (9 p.), I, M, 11 in. (No. 7).   BO-8

BRAKES

Chalk talks; air brake study course Carl Mac Drennan. New York, Simmon—
Boardman Books [1954]. I, 11 in.   BR-1

The effect of brake show action on thermal cracking and on failure of wrought
steel railway car wheels; a report of an investigation conducted by the Engineering Experiment Station, University of Illinois, in cooperation with the Technical
Board of the Wrought Steel Wheel Industry, by Harry R. Wetenkamp, Omar
M. Sidebottom [and] Herman J. Schrader. [Urbana, 1950.] 104 p., I, D, T,
9 in. (No. 387).   BR-2

BRANCH LINES

Short line junction; a collection of California-Nevada railroads. Jack R. Wagner.
Fresno, Calif., Academy Library Guild, 1956. 266 p., I, 8.7 in.   BR-3

BRIDGES

Least-weight proportions of bridge trusses. Joseph L. Waling. Urbana, University of Illinois [1953]. 56 p., D, T, 9 in. (Eng. Exp. Station, No. 417).   BRI-1

The lateral and longitudinal distribution of loading of steel railway bridges, by
W. W. Sanders and W. H. Munse. Approved by N. M. Newmark. Com., 30;
Impact and Bridge Stresses, AREA, assignment 5. Urbana, 1960. 128 p. (pf.—
8 p.), I, 11 in.   BRI-2

Specifications for welded highway and railway bridges. Prepared by AWS
Conference Committee on Welded Bridges, under the direction of AWS Technical
Activities Committee. Edward A. Fenton, technical secretary. 6th ed. New
York, 1963. 94 p., I, 9 in.

Addenda to D2.0—66: Specifications for welded highway and railway bridges;
and SRI-65 gas metal-arc welding with carbon dioxide shielding. 1967. I, 9 in.
                                                                                 BRI-3

Structural fatigue and steel railroad bridges; proceedings of AREA seminar, by W.
H. Munse, J. E. Stallmeyer [and] F. P. Drew. Chicago, American Railway
Engineering Association [1968]. 152 p. (pref.—4 p.), I, 9 in.   BRI-4

BUILDERS

Locomotive, trolley, and rail car builders; an all-time directory. Ian Arnold
[Los Angeles, Trans-Anglo Books, 1965]. 64 p., I, 8.3 in.   BU-1

CABLE CARS

Aerial tramways and funicular railways. Z. Schneigert. [Translated by Edward
Jakobwiez and Wladyslaw Iwinski.] English translation edited by Zygumunt
Frenkiel. Oxford, New York, Pergamon Press [1966]. 554 p. (pf.–22 p.), I,
9.8 in.   C-1

Angels Flight. Walt Wheelock. Introd. [by] W. W. Robinson. Illus. [by] Ruth
Daly. Glendale, Calif., La Siesta Press, 1961. 36 p., I, 8.7 in.   C-2

The archaeology of the cable car, by W. W. Hanscom. Compiled and edited by
Walt Wheelock. Pasadena, Calif., Socio-Technical Books, 1970. 121 p., I, 9.4 in.
                                                                         C-3

The big heart. Melvin Van. Photography: Ruth Bernhard. [San Francisco, Fearon
Publishers, c 1957.] 77 p., I, 10.2 in.   C-4

Cable car carnival [by] Lucius Beebe and Charles Clegg. Decorations by E. S.
Hammack. [1st ed.] Oakland, Calif., G. Hardy, 1951. 130 p., I, P, M, 11.4 in.
                                                                         C-5

The cable car in America; cable traction explained, history of 62 lines. George W.
Hilton. Berkeley, Howell-North. 484 p., I (684), 11 in.   C-6

The cable cars of San Francisco. Photos, by Phil Palmer. Text by Mike Palmer.
[Berkeley, Calif.] Howell-North [1959]. 64 p., I, 9 in.   C-7

Cableways, tramways and suspension bridges. U. S. Army. [Washington], 1964.
224 p., I, 9.4 in.   C-8

Famous cableways of the world. F. E. Dean. Illustrated by K. E. Carter. London,
F. Muller [1958; stamped: distributed by Sportshelf, New Rochelle, N. Y.]. 144
p., I, 7.5 in.   C-9

International ropeway review. v. 1–, Apr./June 1959–. London, etc. I, 11.4 in.,
quarterly.   C-10

Saint Louis cable railways. [Chicago] Electric Railway Historical Society [c
1965]. 35 p., I, M, 11 in. (No. 44).   C-11

San Francisco Grip. Text and illus. by Jimo Perini. San Francisco, San Francisco
Grip Publishers, 1969. 189 p. (pf.–9 p.), I (PC), P, 11.4 in.   C-12

The system of wire-cable railways; and 1887 prospectus, mainly of San Francisco,
Pacific Cable Railway Co. Felton, Calif., Glenwood Publishers. 80 p., I, M, 11 in.
                                                                         C-13

CALIFORNIA

Bonanza railroads. [4th ed.] Gilbert H. Kneiss. Stanford, Stanford University
Press [1954]. 187 p., I, 10.6 in.   CA-1

Cleartype colorprint map of California. American Map Co. New York [1950]. 2 M (C), 15 x 10 in. (No. 4404).   CA-2

General statewide grade crossing survey, State of California. Calif. P.U.C. San Francisco, 1949. I, T, 11 in.   CA-3

The railroad story of San Diego County. Fiesta del Pacifico ed. Irene Phillips. National City, Calif., South Bay Press, c 1956. 76 p., M, 7.1 in.   CA-4

Redwood railways; a story of redwoods, picnics, and commuters. Gilbert H. Kneiss. Berkeley, Calif., Howell-North, 1956. 165 p. (pf.–18 p.), I, P, M (2F), F, 9.4 in.   CA-5

Report of accidents reported under General orders Nos. 22-A and 93-A. Calif. P.U.C. San Francisco. 11 in., annual.   CA-6

CANADA

General

Canadian guide. [Montreal, International Railway Pub. Co.] 9 in., monthly.
                                                                          CAN-1

Description of a guided automated individual transportation system by L. G. Grimble & Associates, Ltd. Edmonton, 1968. 53 l., 13 I (F), 11 in.   CAN-2

I'll take the train, by Ken Liddell. Saskatoon, Modern Press Prairie Books Service, 1966. 196 p., I, 9 in.   CAN-3

Rapid transit in Canada [by] J. W. Boorse, Jr. Philadelphia, Almo Press [1968]. 104 p. (pf.–7 p.), I, 9.8 in.   CAN-4

Growth and travel, past and present; a study of the basic components of growth in the Toronto centered region, and their relationship to travel characteristics and demand. Metropolitian Toronto and Region Transportation Study. [Toronto, 1966.] 94 p. (pf.–7 p.), I, M, 11 in.   CAN-5

Government

It was never easy, 1908-1958; a history of the Canadian Brotherhood of Railway, Transport and General Workers. Original manuscript and research by W. E. Greening. Additional research and final text by M. M. Maclean. Ottawa, printed by Mutual Press, 1961. 414 p., I, 8.7 in.   CAN-6

Steam railway employees and their compensation, 1926-1951. Ottawa, Bu. of Statistics [1952]. 7 p., 11 in. (No. 38).   CAN-7

Report; Royal Commission on Employment of Firemen (CPR). [Ottawa, E. Cloutier, Queen's Printer, 1958.] 38 p. (pf.–4 p.), 9.8 in.   CAN-8

The federal railway land subsidy policy of Canada. James B. Hedges. Cambridge, Harvard Univ. Press. 151 p. (pf.–3 p.).   CAN-9

Concordance of the Railway act, R. S. C. 1952, c. 234; containing a history of the Railway act, table of parallel sections and expanded analytical index. Also, Transport, Maritime freight rates and Pipe lines acts [and] Rules of practice of the Board of Transport Commissioners. Compiled by legal staff, Board of Transport Commissioners for Canada. Toronto, Canada Law Book Co., 1954. 9.4 in.

CAN-10

Railway operating statistics. Bu. of Statistics, Ottawa. 11 in.   CAN-11

Preliminary inventory: Record group 11, Dept. of Public Works, Record group 12, Dept. of Transport (Marine: Railways and Canals). [Ottawa] 1951. 30 p., 10.2 in.

CAN-12

History

Alphabetical index of Canadian transportation tokens. Joseph M. Kotler. [Glencoe, Ill., 1963.] 3 l., 11.4 in.   CAN-13

Canadian steam! David P. Morgan, ed. [Milwaukee, Kalmbach Pub. Co., 1961.] I, 11.8 in.   CAN-14

Canada's railways [by] R. A. J. Phillips. Toronto, New York [etc.], McGraw-Hill Co. of Canada [1968]. 122 p., I, M, P, 10.2 in.   CAN-15

Farewell to steam in Canada; Canadian steam locomotives in story and pictures, by N. H. Mika. [Illus. prepared by N. Mika, K. Sprackett and R. Lott.] Belleville, Ont., Mika Silk Screening [c 1965]. 68 p., I (PC), M, 10.6 in.   CAN-16

A history of transportation in Canada [by] G. P. de Glazebrook. [2nd ed., Toronto], McClelland and Stewart [c 1964]. 2 v., M, 7.5 in.   CAN-17

A history of transportation in Canada. New York, Greenwood Press [1969, c 1938]. 475 p. (pf.—25 p.), M (F), 9.4 in.   CAN-18

The intercity electric railway industry in Canada [by] John F. Due. [Toronto], Univ. of Toronto Press [1966]. 118 p. (pf.—10 p.), I, M, 10.2 in.   CAN-19

The last broad gauge [by] Robert R. Brown. Rev. [Montreal, Canadian Railroad Historical Association, 1966.] 11 p., I, 9 in.   CAN-20

The national dream: the great railway, 1871-1881. Pierre Berton. Toronto, McClelland and Stewart [c 1970]. 439 p. (pf.—13 p.), M, 9.8 in.   CAN-21

Oil lamps and iron ponies, a chronicle of the narrow gauges, by Frederic Shaw, Clement Fisher, Jr. [and] George H. Harlan. Decoration by E. S. Hammack; maps and lettering by Frederic Shaw. [1st ed.] San Francisco, Bay Books, 1949. 187 p., I, P, M, 10.6 in.   CAN-22

The railway interrelations of the United States and Canada. William J. Wilgus. New York, Russell & Russell [1970]. 304 p. (pf.—16 p.), M, 9.8 in.   CAN-23

Western rail trail. Norman McKillup. London, New York, Nelson [1962]. 190 p., I, 9.4 in.   CAN-24

Provinces

British Columbia. Report, Dept. of Commercial Transport [Victoria] 1960–. I, 10.6 in., annual. CAN-25

Submissions to the August 28 public hearing on the proposed B. C. hydro rail route from Matsqui to Roberts Bank. Lower Mainland Region Planning Bd. [New Westminster, B. C., 1968]. 59 p., M (FC), 8.7 x 11 in. CAN-26

Argument on behalf of the Province of Manitoba to the Royal Commission on Transportation [by] A. V. Mauro, of counsel for the Province of Manitova. [Ottawa] 1961. 313 l., I, 13.8 in. CAN-27

Submissions to the Royal Commission on Transportation. Winnipeg, printed by C. E. Leech, Printer to the King, 1949. 163 p., 10.2 in. CAN-28

Manitoba's submissions in opposition to an increase in freight rates; presented to the Board of Transport Commissioners for Canada during hearings on the application for a 30% increase in freight rates. Winnipeg, printed by C. E. Leech, Printer to the King, 1947. 130 p., 10.2 in. CAN-29

Railroads: steam, street, etc.

Finding list of Canadian railway companies before 1915. Noel G. Butlin. Washington, Library of the Bureau of Railway Economics, Association of American Railroads, 1952. 31 p., 11 in. CAN-30

The railways of Canada for 1870–1, showing the progress, mileage, cost of construction, the stocks, bonds, traffic earnings, expenses, and organization of the railways of the Dominion. Also, a sketch of the difficulties incident to transportation in Canada in the pre-railroad days, by J. M. and Edw. Trout. Toronto, published at the office of the Monetary Times, 1871. [Toronto, Coles Pub. Co., c 1970.] 213 p., 8.7 in. CAN-31

Canadian National Railways. George R. Stevens. With a foreword by Donald Gordon, and an introd. by S. W. Fairweather. Toronto, Clark, Irwin, 1960-62. 2 v., I, 9.4 in. CAN-32

Canadian National Railways. Keeping Track. Montreal [1958]. I, P, D, 11.4 in., 11 a year. CAN-33

PGE, railway to the north. Bruce Ramsey. Vancouver, Mitchell Press [c 1962]. 265 p., I, M, P, 9 in. CAN-34

Pioneer railways of central Ontario, from the past to the present; Rideau area of Canadian National Railways. William Michaud. [Shannonville, Ont., 1964.] 20 p., I, M, 11.4 in. CAN-35

Canadian Pacific staff bulletin. Montreal. I, P, M, 18 in., monthly. CAN-36

The Grand Trunk Railway of Canada. Archibald William Currie. Toronto, Univ. of Toronto Press, 1957. 556 p., I, 9.4 in. CAN-37

History of the Niagara, St. Catharines & Toronto Railway, [by] John M. Mills. [Toronto] Upper Canada Railway Society; Scarborough, Ont., Ontario Electric Railway Historical Association [1967]. 118 p., I (PC), 11.4 in. CAN-38

Traffic

Canadian transportation system and freight classification. Clarence E. Johnston. Serial 5416-2. [Ed. 2] Scranton, International Correspondence Schools, c 1959. 74 p., I, 8.3 in.   CAN-39

Equalization class rate scale; judgment and order of March 1, 1954, together with notes and reasons for the said judgment, issued February 28, 1955. Bd. of Transport Commissioners. Ottawa, E. Cloutier, Queen's Printer, 1955. 56 p., 9.8 in.
                                                                                  CAN-40

Freight rates in Canada, by Duncan H. MacMillan and Gilmer B. Randolph. Serial 6371. [Ed. 1] Scranton, International Correspondence Schools, c 1963. 64 p., 9 in.   CAN-41

Railway freight traffic. Ottawa, Queen's Printer and Controller of Stationery. Bu. of Statistics. 11 in., annual.   CAN-42

Railway revenue freight loadings. Ottawa, Bu. of Statistics. D. T. 11 in., monthly.
                                                                                  CAN-43

Waybill analysis, carload all-rail traffic. Bd. of Transport Commissioners. Ottawa. 11 in., annual.   CAN-44

CARS . . . . see Section 2

CAR FERRIES

Later history [Ann Arbor ferries]. Frederickson.   sCO-9
Early history [Ann Arbor ferries]. Frederickson.   sCO-10

CATALOGS

A list of postage stamps of the world associated with railways, by R. P. Cornish. 2nd ed. Altrincham, Eng., Railway Phitelic Group, 1969. [3], 52 p., I, 10.2 in.
                                                                                  CAT-1

Baldwin [1913 catalog]. Speciality Press.   sCO-27
Baldwin [1881 catalog]. Howell-North.   sCO-28
Locomotive [Dickson Mfg. Co.]. Best.   sCO-104
Lima locomotives, 1911 catalog. Golden West.   sCO-152

CHICAGO

The Chicago Transit Authority: a study in responsibility. R. K. DeCamp. Chicago [Dept. of Photoduplication, University of Chicago Library] 1958.   CH-1

Chicago's mass transportation system. Chicago Transit Authority. [Chicago, 1959.] 22 p., I, 11 in.   CH-2

Methods for estimating trip destinations by trip purpose, prepared by Natalie G. Sato. Chicago, Chicago Area Transportation Study, 1966. 60 p. (pf.–9 p.), I, 11 in.   CH-3

Skokie Swift, the commuter's friend, by Thomas Buck. Chicago Transit Authority, Research and Planning Dept., Chicago, 1968. 65 p., I, M, 11 in.   CH-4

The Skokie Swift: a study in urban rapid transit; a summary of the Chicago Area Transportation Study's role in the Chicago Transit Authority, village of Skokie mass transit demonstration project sponsored by the Housing and Home Finance Agency, 1964-66. Chicago, 1968. 110 p. (pf.—15 p.), I, 9.4 in.   CH-5

Updating the opportunity model for continuing transportation planning, prepared by James P. Curry. Chicago, Chicago Area Transportation Study, 1970. 63 p. (pf.—9 p.), I, 9.4 in.   CH-6

A century of Chicago streetcars, 1858-1958; a pictorial history of the world's largest street railway. Compiled by James D. Johnson. Photos. and other illus. by Thomas Hollister, unless otherwise credited. Paintings: Robert T. Pernau. Wheaton, Ill., Traction Orange Co., 1964. 143 p., I (PC), M (C), 11 in.   CH-7

The great third rail. Central Electric Railfans Assoc. [Chicago], 1970 [c 1961]. 138, 30 p., I, Fac, M (PC), 11.4 in. (105).   CH-8

Official map, Chicago Terminal District. Chicago, Issued under supervision of the Chicago Switching Committee, Illinois Freight Association, c 1950. M (C), 40 x 37 in.   CH-9

South Side consolidated railroad passenger terminal for Chicago. [Chicago], Plan Commission, 1953. 39 p., I, M (C), 8.7 x 11 in.   CH-10

CINCINNATI

Cincinnati streetcars [by Richard M.] Wagner and [Roy J.] Wright. Cincinnati, Wagner Car Co., 1968—. v., I, M, 11 in.   CI-1

Public transit. Cincinnati, City Planning Comm. Cincinnati, 1948. 89 p. (pf.— 7 p.), I, M (PC), 11 in.   CI-2

CLASSIFICATION

Railroad freight classification, by Gilmer B. Randolph and John A. McConnell. Serial 6352. [Ed. 1. Replaces 5401.] Scranton, International Correspondence Schools, c 1959. 64 p., I, 7.9 in.   CL-1

Railroad freight classification, by Gilmer B. Randolph and John A. McConnell. Serial 6352-1. [Ed. 2] Scranton, International Correspondence Schools [1965]. 7 l., 2 p., I, 7.5 in.   CL-2

CLEVELAND

A history of the Cleveland streetcars from the time of electrification, in memory of the cars of my childhood, especially Nos. 9, 19, 416, 813, and 0169. Kenneth S. F. Morse. Baltimore, c 1955. 42 p., I, 11 in.   CLE-1

COLORADO

Urban mass transportation in Colorado; report to the Colorado General Assembly. Colo. Legislative Council. [Denver], 1959. 38 p. (pf.—9 p.), T, 11 in. (No. 31).
                    COL-1

The Argentine Central, a Colorado narrow-gauge. Frank R. Hollenback. Denver, Sage Books [1959]. 80 p., I, 9 in.   COL-2

The cavalcade of railroads in central Colorado, by George G. Everett. [1st ed.] Denver, Golden Bell Press [1966]. 235 p., I, P, 9 in.   COL-3

Colorado's mountain railroads, by R. A. LeMassena, assisted by R. A. Ronzio [and others]. Golden, Colo., Smoking Stack Press, 1963-68. 5 v., I, F, M (PF), 9 in.   COL-4

Colorado rail annual. v. 1—. Golden, Colorado Railroad Museum. I, M, 11 in.
                    COL-5

Cripple Creek Railroads; a quick history of the great gold camp's railroads. Leland Feitz. Denver, Golden Bell Press [1968]. 30 p., I, 8.7 in.   COL-6

The Crystal River pictorial; photographic record of the short lines of the Crystal River district of Colorado. By Dell A. McCoy and Russ Collman. Denver, Sundance, Ltd., 1972. I (300), 11 x 8.5 in.   COL-7

Lettering guide for early Colorado narrow gauge freight cars, by William M. Cohen. [Denver] Rocky Mountain Region of the National Model Railroad Association [c 1970]. 95 p., I, 8.7 in.   COL-8

Little engines and big men. Gilbert A. Lathrop. Caldwell, Idaho, Caxton Printers, 1954. 326 p., I, 8.7 in.   COL-9

Railroads and the Rockies; a record of lines in and near Colorado. Robert M. Ormes. Denver, Sage Books [1963]. 406 p., I, M, 9.4 in.   COL-10

Rails around Gold Hill. [Limited ed.] Morris Calfy. [Denver, Rocky Mountain Railroad Club, 1955.] 463 p. (pf.—14 p.), I (PC), M (6F), 11.4 in.   COL-11

The Silverton train; a story of southwestern Colorado's narrow gauges. Louis Hunt. With photos. by the author. Leucadia, Calif., 1955. 70 p., I, 12.2 in. COL-12

Three little lines: Silverton Railroad, Silverton, Gladstone and Northerly Railroad, Silverton Northern Railroad. Josie M. Crum. [Bert Baker, editor. Limited 3d ed. St. Paul, 1956.] 53 p., I, M, 9 in.   COL-13

Thirty pound rails. Kelly Choda. Aurora, Colo., Filter Press [1956]. 46 p., I, 8.7 in.
                    COL-14

COMPANIES . . . . see Section 2

COMMUNICATION SYSTEMS

Over the railroad air waves (filmstrip). Missouri Pacific Railroad Co., 1952. 71 fr., C, 35 mm.   COM-1

Report to be presented at the annual session of the Communications Section. AAR, Communication Sec. [n. p.]. I, D, 9 in.   COM-2

COMMUTER

Commuter railroads; a pictorial review of the most travelled railroads, by Patrick C. Dorin. [1st ed.] Seattle, Superior Pub. Co. [1970]. 192 p., I, 11 in.   COMM-1

Coordinated bus-rail service: Rockland County—Westchester County—New York City; progress report. No. 1—. Tri-State Transportation Committee (Conn., N. J., and N. Y.), Mar. 1964—. Forms, M, 11 in. COMM-2

Fiscal impacts of commuters on core cities with varying revenue structures [by] Phillip E. Vincent. [Los Angeles, Institute of Government and Public Affairs, Univ. of Calif., 1969.] 39 l., 11 in. (MR-130). COMM-3

Library service for commuting students; a preliminary study of problems in four southeastern New York counties, by Matilda A. Gocek. Poughkeepsie, Southeastern New York Library Resources Council [1970]. 27 p. (pf.—8 p.), M, 11.4 in. COMM-4

Origin-destination survey; park'n ride station and service at New Brunswick, New Jersey on Pennsylvania Railroad, submitted by Research Data Processing Corporation, Traffic Research Corporation [and] R. L. M. Associates, consultants. [New York, Tri-State Transportation Committee (Conn.-N. J.-N. Y.)] 1963. 50 l., I, M (PC), 11 in. COMM-5

Park'n ride rail service; New Brunswick, Newark [and] New York City; a final report on the mass transportation demonstration project, October 27, 1963— April 24, 1965. [Tri-State Transportation Comm, New York] 1967. 39 p., I, 11 in. COMM-6

Park'n ride rail service: New Brunswick-Newark-New York City. Progress report No. 1—. Tri-State Transportation Committee (Conn., N. J. and N. Y.), May 1964—. I, M, 11.4 in. COMM-7

Problems of the railroads. Boston College, Seminar Re. Bu. [Boston] 1959. 51 l. (pf.—3), D, 11 in. COMM-8

Reestablishing the link; a study of the commuter rail station [by] Anthony R. Sloan [and] John W. Blatteau. [Philadelphia] Southeastern Pennsylvania Transportation Authority, 1970. 66 p., I, 8.7 x 11.4 in. COMM-9

Report from W. J. Ronan to Governor Rockefeller on the report by the Institute of Public Administration on New York Central and New Haven Railroad commuter services. [Albany] 1964. 6 l., 13.8 in. COMM-10

Suburban service adjustment experiment: a summary, Harlem Division—New York Central Railroad, Westchester and Putnam Counties; a final report on the mass transportation demonstration grant project: July 1, 1964—October 31, 1966. Tri-State Trans. Comm. [New York] 1967. 8 p., I, M, 11 in. COMM-11

Suburbs to Grand Central; a study of the feasibility of reorganizing the suburban services of the New York Central and New Haven Railroads under a public agency. Institute of Public Administration, New York, 1963. 1 v., I, M, 11.4 in. COMM-12

Transportation needs of the poor, a base study of New York City [by] Oscar A. Ornati, with assistance from James A. Whittaker and Richard Solomon. New York, Praeger [1969]. 127 p. (pf.—16 p.), I, 10.2 in. COMM-13

Effect of railroad mergers on commuter transportation. Hearings on solutions to problems of improved commuter service in mass transportation. March 26, 27, and 28, 1968. Senate, Banking and Currency Com. (Housing and Urban Affairs). 90C-2S. Washington, GPO, 1968. 249 p. (pf.—5 p.), M (F), 9.4 in. COMM-14

The Erie-Lackawanna. N. J., 1965.   sCO-114
Editorial comment [L.I.]. L.I.R.R.   sCO-156
Plan [reorganization]. L.I.R.R.   sCO-158
Plan [for L.I.]. L.I.R.R.   sCO-159
Proposed legislation [L.I.]. L.I.R.R. Comm.   sCO-160
Redwood railways. Kneiss.   sSCA-5

COMPETITION

Competition between rail and truck in intercity freight transportation. Charles
River Associates. Cambridge, Mass., 1969. 70 l., I, 11 in.   COMP-1

Competition and railroad price discrimination; legal precedent and economic
policy. Jordan J. Hillman. Evanston, Ill., Transportation Center at Northwestern
University [1968]. 164 p. (pf.—12 p.), 9.4 in.   COMP-2

The economics of competition in the transportation industries. John R. Meyer,
Morton J. Peck, John Stenason, Charles Zwick. Cambridge, Harvard Univ. Press,
1959. 359 p. (pf.—18 p.), I, T.   COMP-3

Facts and arguments in favor of adopting railways in preference to canals, in the
state of Pennsylvania. New York, Arno Press, 1970. 68 p., I, 9. in.   COMP-4

The Iowa pool, a study in railroad competition, 1870-84. Julius Grodinsky. [Chi-
cago] University of Chicago Press [1950]. 184 p. (pf.—11 p.), M, 9.4 in.   COMP-5

Preservation of competitive through rail routes. Hearing, S. 2129 and H. R. 5384, to
amend the Interstate Commerce Act to provide for the preservation of competitive
through routes for rail carriers. Senate, Int. & For. Comm. (Surface Trans.). 85C-
2S. Washington, GPO, 1958. 2 pts., 147 p. (pf.—3 p.), I, M, 9.4 in.   COMP-6

A productive monopoly; the effect of railroad control on New England coastal
steamship lines, 1870-1916. William L. Taylor. Providence, Brown University
Press [1970]. 323 p. (pf.—16 p.), I, M, 9.4 in.   COMP-7

Railway monopoly and rate regulation. Robert J. McFall. New York, AMS Press,
1916.   COMP-8

The railroad monopoly; an instrument of banker control of the American economy. John G. Shott. Washington, Public Affairs Institute, 1950. 250 p. (pf.—
11 p.), 9.4 in.   COMP-9

The regulation of rail-motor rate competition by the Interstate Commerce Commis-
ion. Ernest W. Williams. Ann Arbor, University Microfilms [1952].   COMP-10

CONDUCTORS

Railway conductors; a study in organized labor. Edwin C. Robbins. New York,
AMS Press [1970, c 1914]. 185 p., 9 in.   CON-1

CONGRESSES, CONVENTIONS, SYMPOSIUMS

Charter of the Association of the Pan-American Railway Congress, approved in the
fourth plenary session of the VI Congress held in Havana in April 1948. Pan-American Railway Congress Association. Buenos Aires, 1948. 9 p., 9.8 in. CONG-1

VIII Pan American Railway Congress, Washington, D. C. and Atlantic City, New Jersey, June 12-25, 1953. Volume I. Proceedings. Pan-American Railway Congress Association. [Washington, GPO, 1955.] 482 p. (pf.–7 p.), P, T, 10.2 in.   CONG-2

Rail transportation proceedings. 1970–. Am. Soc. Mechanical Engineers. New York. I, 11 in., annual.   CONG-3

Symposiums on railroad materials [and] lubricating oils; presented at the second Pacific area national meeting, Los Angeles, Calif., Sept. 18-19, 1956. American Society for Testing Materials. Philadelphia [1957]. 169 p. (pf.–5 p.), I, 9.4 in. (No. 214).   CONG-4

COSTS

Costs–a tool for railroad management. Ernest C. Poole. New York, Simmons-Boardman Pub. Corp. [1962]. 173 p., I, 9 in.   COS-1

Formula for use in determining rail terminal freight service costs. ICC Bu. of Acct., CF, &V. Washington, 1954. T, 12.6 x 20 in. (No. 3-54).   COS-2

"Percent variable" study on class 1 railroads. Part I. "Percent variable" or "out-of-pocket cost." Part II. Yearly increase in efficiency for class 1 railroads. John E. Hansbury. Washington, Association of Interstate Commerce Commission Practitioners, 1951. 20 p., I, 9 in.   COS-3

Rail carload cost scales by territories. Jan. 1, 1948–. ICC Bu. of Accts., Washington. T, 11 x 12.6 in.   COS-4

Separable suburban costs, New York Metropolitan area operations, New York Central Railroad, New York, New Haven & Hartford Railroad; a report to the Institute of Public Administration. Banks (R. L.) & Associates, inc. [New York, Institute of Public Administration, 1963.] 1 v., 11 in.   COS-5

Summary of returns to cost inquiry on railroad freight station costs and other performance factors. Prepared by the Cost Finding Section. ICC, Bu. of Accts. Washington, 1960. 27 p., T, 10.6 in. (No. 1-60).   COS-6

Summary of returns to cost inquiry on railroad freight station costs and other performance factors. ICC, Bu. of Acct., & CF. Washington, 1953. [2], 20 p., P, 9.8 in. (No. 1-53).   COS-7

CROSSINGS

Alaska Railway-highway grade crossings on Federal-aid and State maintenance highways in Alaska. Dept. of Highways [Juneau] 1968. 39 l., I, M, 11 in.   CR-1

The railway-highway grade crossing problem: economic principles. Alexander K. Beggs. Stanford, Calif., Stanford Research Institute [1952]. 55 p., I, 11 in.
CR-2

A study of Minnesota grade crossing collisions; a special study issued by the Office of the Safety Director. John T. St. Martin. St. Paul, 1961. 43 p., I, T, 11 in.
CR-3

DENVER

Mile-high trolleys; a nostalgic look at Denver in the era of the streetcars [by] William C. Jones, F. Hol Wagner, Jr. [and] Gene C. McKeever. [Golden, Colo., Intermountain Chapter, National Railway Historical Society, 1965.] 96 p., I, M (CF), PL, 11.4 in.   D-1

DETROIT

Detroit expressway and transit system. Prepared for Detroit Transportation Board by W. Earle Andrews [and others]. New York, 1945. 39 p., I, M (C), D, PL, 18 in.
DE-1

DEVELOPMENT

American railroads, their growth and development. [1st print.] AAR, Washington, 1948—. I, D, 9 in.   DEV-1

American railroads and the transformation of the antebellum economy. Albert Fishlow. Cambridge, Harvard University Press, 1965 [i. e. 1966]. 452 p. (pf.— 15 p.), M, 8.7 in.   DEV-2

Development of railroad transportation in the United States, by Carlton J. Corliss. A lecture at the University of Baltimore, Baltimore, Maryland, February 5, 1945. Washington, D. C., Association of American Railroads [1945]. 32 p., I, M, 9 in.
DEV-3

The railroad and the space program; an exploration in historical analogy, edited by Bruce Mazlish. Cambridge, M. I. T. Press [1965]. 223 p. (pf.—19 p.), 9.4 in.
DEV-4

Pioneering the Union Pacific. Ames.   sCO-274
Union Pacific. Hogg.   sCO-275
How we built [U.P.]. Carson [Best].   sCO-277
The Union Pacific R.R. Fogel.   sCO-282

DINING CAR SERVICE

Dinner in the diner; great railroad recipes of all time, by Will C. Hollister. Introd. by Spencer Crump. Book design: Hank Johnston. [3d ed. rev.] Los Angeles, Trans-Anglo Books [1970, c 1965]. 144 p., I, Fac, M, P, 11.4 in.   DI-1

DISPATCHERS

Rights of trains. 5th ed. Peter Josserand. New York, Simmons-Boardman Pub. Corp. [1957]. 459 p., I, 7.5 in.   DIS-1

Rights of trains. Revised by Peter Josserand. Harry N. Forman. 4th ed. New York, Simmons-Boardman [c 1951]. 397 p. (pf.—9 p.), I, 7.5 in.   DIS-2

DYNAMICS

An analysis of the dynamics of locomotives and railway cars. G. J. Kamat. Urbana, 1951. 2 p., 9 in.   DY-1

The dynamics and economics of railway track systems (symposium). Chicago, Railway Systems and Management Association [1970]. 175 p., I, P, 11 in. DY-2

EAST

Adirondack railroads, real and phantom. Harold K. Hochschild. Blue Mountain Lake, N. Y., Adirondack Museum, 1962. 21 p., I, 11 in.   E-1

Adirondack steamboats on Raquette and Blue Mountain Lakes. Harold K. Hochschild. Blue Mountain Lake, N. Y., Adirondack Museum, 1962. 34 p., I, 11 in.
     E-2

ECONOMICS

The bituminous coal freight-rate structure, an economic appraisal. Thomas C. Campbell. Morgantown, Bu. of Bus. Res., College of Commerce, West Virginia Univ. [1954]. 47 p. (pf.−7 p.), I, 11 in. (v. 3, No. 3).   EC-1

The economic effects of regulation; the trunk-line railroad cartels and the Interstate Commerce Commission before 1900 [by] Paul W. MacAvoy. Cambridge, Mass., M. I. T. Press [1965]. 275 p. (pf.−9 p.), 9.8 in.   EC-2

Economics of transportation, by D. Philip Locklin. 6th ed. Homewood, Ill., R. D. Irwin, 1966. 882 p. (pf.−12 p.), I, M, 9.4 in.   EC-3

The methods of American railroads in promoting economic development; an historical survey. Roy V. Scott. Stillwater, Oklahoma State University, 1963. 40 p., 9 in.   EC-4

Outlook for the railroads. P. Tyler. New York, Wilson, 1960. 208 p., 8.3 in.
     EC-5

Railroads and American economic growth: essays in econometric history. Robert W. Fogel. Baltimore, Johns Hopkins Press [1964]. 296 p. (pf.−19 p.), I, M (IF), 9.4 in.   EC-6

Railway economy; a treatise on the new art of transport, its management, prospects and relations. D. Lardner. New York, A. M. Kelley, 1968. 442 p. (pf.−23 p.), 8.7 in. Reprint of earlier work.   EC-7

Studies in the economics of transportation, by Martin Beckmann, C. B. McGuire [and] Christopher B. Winsten. With an introd. by Tjalling C. Koopmans. New Haven, published for the Cowles Commission for Research in Economics by Yale University Press, 1956 [c 1955]. 232 p., I, 9.4 in.; also, Santa Monica, Calif., Rand Corp., 1955; D, 11 in. (R-M−1488).   EC-8

Transport and economic integration of South America. Robert T. Brown. Washington, Brookings Institution, 1966. 288 p.   EC-9

The transportation economics of the soybean processing industry. Earl C. Hedlund. Urbana, Univ. of Illinois Press, 1952. 189 p. (pf.−7 p.), M, 10.2 in.
     EC-10

ELECTRIC RAILROADS . . . . see Section 2

EMERGENCY BOARDS

The history and operation of railway emergency boards. Bernard Schurman. Ann Arbor, Mich., University Microfilms [1959].   EM-1

EMPLOYEES

Hours of service of railroad employees. Hearings on S. 1938 . . . September 30, October 13 and 14, 1969. Senate, Commerce Comm. (Suf. Trans.). 91C-1S. Washington, GPO, 1969. 243 p. (pf.–3 p.), F, 9.4 in.   EMP-1

The human side of railroading. Carlton J. Corliss. Washington, Association of American Railroads, 1951. 16 p., I, 9 in.   EMP-2

Life in a railway factory, by Alfred Williams. Reprint, new introd. by Leonard Clark. New York, A. M. Kelly, 1969. 315 p. (pf.–8 p.), 9 in.   EMP-3

Railroad employees' benefits [1952 ed]. Commodity Research Bureau, Inc. New York, c 1952. 8.7 in.; also, 1947.   EMP-4

Railway pension plans supplementary to the railroad retirement system. R.R. Retirement Bd., Chicago, 1949. 26 l., T, 10.6 in.   EMP-5

Railroad wages and labor relations, 1900-1952; an historical survey and summary of results, by Harry E. Jones, chairman, Executive Committee. Bu. of Info., Eastern Rys. New York, 1953. 375 p., D, T, 9.4 in.   EMP-6

Employment Guides

Arco R.R. series. Arco Publishing Co., New York. 10.6 in.   EMP-17
Car maintainer, all grades [for subway systems]. 1950.
Maintainer's helper, group A, group C, by David Turner. 3 ed., 1967. 352, 16 p., I.
Maintainer's helper, group D, by David Turner. 2 ed., 1969. 224 p., I,
Motorman, N.Y.C. transit system; a complete and intensive guide. 1947.
Power maintainer, all groups, N.Y.C. subway system. 1957.
Railroad porter. 1955.
Structure maintainer, all grades. 1948. I.
Towerman: municipal sybway system, by David Turner. 4 ed., 1971. 256 p., I.
Towerman, IRT, BMT, IND Divisions, N.Y.C. transit system; complete course for preparation. 1951. I.
Train dispatcher. 1956
Assistant train dispatcher and train dispatches; complete study guide. 2 ed., 1965. I.
Assistant train dispatcher. 1956. I.
Transit lieutenant and sergeant; a course for preparation [N.Y.C. Transit Police]. 1951.

Civil Service Publishing Series; Brooklyn, Civil Service Publishing Corp. 11 in.
                                                                          EMP-18
How to pass maintainer's helper, group A, and maintainer's helper, Group C: past exams, Q. & A., by Jack Rudman. 1952.
How to pass maintainer's helper, group B; Q. & A. 1963.
How to pass railroad clerk; Q. & A. 1965.
How to pass trackman; Q. & A. 1965.

National Learning Series. Plainview, N. Y.   EMP-19
Passbook for civil service examinations (series); study guide. Plainview, N. Y.,
National Learning Corp: Assistant Train Dispatcher, Conductor, Forman (Watch-
man), Forman (Track), Gang Forman (Track), Motorman, Motorman Instructor,
R.R. Caretaker, R.R. Caretaker, R.R. Clerk, R.R. Inspector, R.R. Porter, R.R.
Signal Specialist, R.R. Stockman, Road Car Inspector, Towerman, Trackman,
Train Dispatch, Trainmaster.

Rights of railroad workers, by Dean A. Robb and John E. Lustig. Detroit, Advocates Pub. Co. [1968]. 417 p., I, P, 6.7 in.   EMP-7

Rules governing the classification of railroad employees and reports of their
service and compensation prescribed by the Interstate Commerce Commission
effective January 1, 1951. Together with List of typical railroad occupations . . .
and Wage statistics inquiries, memorandum of informal instructions. ICC, Bu. of
Tran. Econ. & Stat. [Washington, 1951]. 110 p., 19.4 in.   EMP-8

Subversive influence in the Dining Car and Railroad Food Workers Union. Hearings to investigate the Administration of the Internal Security Act and Other
Internal Security Laws. Senate, Judiciary Com. 82C-1S. Washington, GPO, 1951.
154 p. (pf.–7 p.), 9.4 in.   EMP-9

Working on the railroad; a study of job satisfaction, by Ross Stagner, D. R. Flebbe
and E. V. Wood. [Urbana, Univ. of Illinois, 1953.] 293-306 p., T, 9 in.   EMP-10

Employment

Contributory health plans on class I railroads; estimated membership in predom-
inant plans, employee participation, contribution, and benefits; and supplementary pension plans: contributory and noncontributory plans for supplementing
railroad retirement annuities (appendix B). Brotherhood of Ry. & Steamship
Clerks, Ft. Handlers, Exp. & Stat. Emp., Cincinnati, 1949. 1 v. (various pagings),
M, T, 11.4 in.   EMP-11

Employment outlook in railroad occupations [by Helen Wood, Gloria Count, and
Raymond D. Larson]. Washington, GPO, 1949. 52 p. (pf.–3 p.), I, 9.8 in. (No.
961).   EMP-12

Find a career in railroading, by C. William Harrison. New York, Putnam [1968].
128 p., I, 8.7 in.   EMP-13

Your future in railroading [by] Thomas M. Goodfellow. [1st ed.] New York,
Richards Rosen Press [1970]. 142 p., I, 8.7 in.   EMP-14

List of typical railroad occupations of positions in each reporting division together
with alphabetical list and index to occupational classification and reporting divisions. ICC, Bu. of Trans. Econ. & Stat. Washington, 1951. 104 p., 10.6 in. EMP-15

Maintenance of way employment on U. S. railroads; an analysis of the sources of
instability and remedial measures, by William Haber and [others]. Foreword by
Sumner H. Slichter. [Detroit, Brotherhood of Maintenance of Way Employees,
1957.] 237 p., I, 9.4 in.   EMP-16

Wages, earnings [etc., N.C.&St.L. Ry.], Fels   CO-183

ENGINE MEN

From cab to caboose; fifty years of railroading. Joseph H. Noble. [1st ed.] Norman, Univ. of Oklahoma Press [1964]. 206 p., I, M, 9.8 in.   EN-1

ENGINEERING

American Railway Engineering Association Manual . . . Complete to Mar. 19, 1953. Chicago [1953–]. 2 v. (loose-leaf), I, 9 in.   ENG-1

Mathematical physics and selected papers; includes engineering problems of Britian's railways, and "On Rail-Roads." John Herapath. New York, Johnson Reprint Corp., 1972. 880 p.   ENG-2

Modern railroad structures, by Charles P. Disney and Robert F. Legget. 1st ed. New York, McGraw-Hill Book Co., 1949. 213 p. (pf.–8 p.), I, 10.6 in.   ENG-3

Railroad engineering. William W. Hay. New York, Wiley [1953–]. I, 9.4 in.
ENG-4

Chief Engineers [IC].   sCO-142
How we built [UP]. Dodge.   sCO-279

EXPRESS SERVICE

Early railroad days in New Mexico. Henry A. Tice. Santa Fe, Stagecoach Press, 1965 [c 1932]. 61 p., I, 7.2 in.   EX-1

EXPRESS TRAINS

400,000 miles by rail; 60 years aboard the great name trains. Burt C. Blanton. Berkeley, Howell-North. 184 p., I (200), 11 in.   EXP-1

The Hiawatha story. Scribbins, 1970.   sCO-71
20th Century. Beebe, 1962.   sCO-192
The run of the Twentieth Century. Wayner.   sCO-193
Two trains to remember. Beebe.   sCO-196
Southern Pacific Daylight. Wright.   sCO-261
The Overland Limited. Beebe.   sCO-287

FINANCE

Boston capitalists and western railroads; a study in the nineteenth-century railroad investment process [by] Arthur M. Johnson and Barry E. Supple. Cambridge, Harvard Univ. Press, 1967. 392 p. (pf.–10 p.), M, 9.8 in.   F-1

British investment in American railways, 1834-1898, by Dorothey R. Adler. Edited by Muriel E. Hidy. Charlottesville, published for the Eleutherian Mills-Hagley Foundation [by] University Press of Virginia [1970]. 253 p. (pf.–14 p.), 10.6 in.   F-2

The capacity and capital requirements of the railroad industry. ICC, Bu. of Trans. Econ. & Stat., Washington, 1952. 109 p. (pf.–3 p.), 10.2 in. (No. 5227).   F-3

Railroad capitalization; a study of the principles of regulations of railroad securities. James C. Bonright. New York, AMS Press, 1970.　　　　　　F-4

Recorded depreciation and amortization, class 1 line haul railways, including their lessors and proprietary companies, December 31, 1950. ICC, Bu. of Trans. Econ. & Stat., Washington, 1952. 4 p., T, 10.6 in. (No. 552).　　　　F-5

Railroad equipment financing. Donald M. Street. New York, Columbia Univ. Press, 1959. 177 p., 8.3 in.; also, Ann Arbor, Mich., University Microfilms [1958].　　　　　　　　　　　　　　　　　　　　　　　　　　F-6

The financial community and the railroad treasurer. Railway Systems and Management Association, Chicago [1966]. 91 p., I, P, 11 in.　　　　　　F-7

Railroad financial modifications: the origins, development and scope of section 20b of the Interstate Commerce Act (The Mahaffie Act). Walter J. Chamberlin. Ann Arbor, University Microfilms [1957] (Publication No. 23,308).　　F-8

Holding and investment company ownership of railroad securities. Robert E. Berger. Ann Arbor, University Microfilms, 1951 (Publication No. 2523).　F-9

Investment in transportation. A study of investment and financial problems of railroads and highways; a discussion of proposed solutions to these problems, particularly with reference to possible inequities existing between the two media, and an analysis of potential new sources of railroad venture capital. Harlan A. Harrison. [Albuquerque, N. M., 1950.] 133 l. (pf.—2), T, 11 in.　　　F-10

Loan guaranty authority of the ICC. Hearings on S. 1146, a bill to amend section 510 of the Interstate Commerce Act so as to extend for 2 years the loan guaranty authority of the Interstaet Commerce Commission. March 9 and 10, 1961. Senate, Int. & For. Comm. (Surface Trans.). 87C-1S. Washington, GPO, 1961. 77 p. (pf.—3 p.), T, 9.4 in.　　　　　　　　　　　　　　　　　　　F-11

Guaranteed loans for railroads. Hearings on H. R. 1163, a bill to amend section 510 of the Interstate Commerce Act so as to extend for one year the loan guaranty authority of the Interstate Commerce Commission. March 1 and 2, 1961. House, Int. & For. Comm. Com. 87C-1S. Washington, GPO, 1961. 136 p. (pf.—3 p.), D, T, 9.4 in.　　　　　　　　　　　　　　　　　　　　F-12

Guaranteed loans for common carriers. Hearings on H. R. 11527, a bill to amend the Interstate Commerce Act by adding thereto a new part V, to provide for a temporary program of assistance to enable common carriers subject to such act to finance improvements and developments. House, Int. & For. Comm. 85C-2S. Washington, GPO, 1958. 168 p. (pf.—3 p.), T, 9.4 in.　　　　　　F-13

Voluntary modification of railroad financial structures. Hearings on S. 1253, a bill to amend the Interstate Commerce Act, as amended . . . Senate, Com. on Int. Comm. 79C-1&2S. Washington, GPO, 1946. 2 pts. (750 p., pf.—3 p.), T, D, 9 in.　　　　　　　　　　　　　　　　　　　　　　　　　　F-14

Policy formation in railroad finance: refinancing the Burlington, 1936-1945. John T. O'Neil. Cambridge, Harvard University Press, 1956. 234 p. (pf.—12 p.), I, 9.8 in.　　　　　　　　　　　　　　　　　　　　　　　　　F-15

Rates or return: class 1 line-haul railways of the United States, 1921-1948. An analysis and an appraisal embodying a comparison with other industries regulated and unregulated, by Sidney L. Miller, Virgil D. Cover, and others. Sidney L. Miller. [Pittsburgh] University of Pittsburgh Press, 1950. 211 p. (pf.–14 p.), D, T, 9.4 in.   F-16

A discussion of various ratios used in the analysis of railroad bonds. George M. Grinnell. [n. p., 1951.] 31 p., 9 in.   F-17

Trends and cycles in capital formation by United States railroads, 1870-1950. Melville J. Ulmer. [New York] National Bureau of Economic Research, 1954. 70 p., I, 9 in.   F-18

The Federal valuation of the railroads in the United States. Bowman H. Moore. [Chicago] 1952. 87 p., 9.2 in.   F-19

Index of the Valuation reports, compiled by Herbert William Rice. ICC. Washington, Association of American Railroads [1951]. 128 l., 11 in.   F-20

Selected elements of value of property used in common carrier service, before and after recorded depreciation and amortization, class 1 line haul railways, including their lessors and proprietary companies. Jan. 1, 1952–. ICC, Bu. of Trans. Econ. & Stat., Washington. T, 10.6 in. (No. 5310).   F-21

Improvements in budget presentation [Alaska R.R.].	sCO-4
Report to RFC Adm. [B&O].	sCO-32
RFC loans [B&O].	sCO-33
A case study [balloting]. Masson.	sCO-39
The economic history [C&FI]. Teweles.	sCO-67
Chapters of the Erie. Adams.	sCO-112
High finance in the 60's [Alb.&Sus.]. Adams.	sCO-7
An economic history [Misabe Div.-GN]. Thompson.	sCO-130
Illinois Central. Sunderland.	sCO-143
A financial study [NH]. Edwards.	sCO-197
The New Haven Railroad. Weller.	sCO-198
New shares for old. Masson.	sCO-38
The state, the investor and the railroad. Salsbury.	sCO-37
Throttling the R.Rs. Carson.	sCO-9
History [UP]. Trottman.	sCO-281

FLORIDA

A chronological list on the history of Florida railroads; a list of references, May, 1963. Bureau of Railway Economics, Washington, 1963. 20 p., 11 in.   FLA-1

The story of the Florida railroads, 1834-1903. George W. Pettengill. Boston, Railway & Locomotive Historical Society, 1952. 133 p., I, F, 9 in. (No. 86).   FLA-2

Mass transit study, May, 1965. Parson, Brinckerhoff, Quade & Douglas. [Titusville, Fla.] 1965. 12 l., M, 11.4 in. (E. C. Fla.).   FLA-3

FREIGHT

Commodity flow interconnections within the United States as reflected in the carload waybill analyses of the Interstate Commerce Commission, 1949-1950. Jere W. Clark. Ann Arbor, University Microfilms [1954]. (Publication No. 7957.) FT-1

Contracts between freight forwarders and railroads. Hearings on S. 3714 . . . Sept. 9, 10, and 11, 1968. Senate, Comm Com. (Surface Trans.). 90C-2S. Washington, GPO, 1968. 171 p. (pf.—4 p.), I, 9.4 in. FT-2

Costs and decision making in transportation. Ry. Systems & Management Assoc., Chicago [1965]. 106 p., I, M, P, 11 in. FT-3

Domestic transportation; practice, theory, and policy [by] Roy J. Sampson [and] Martin T. Farris. Boston, Houghton Mifflin [1966]. 464 p. (pf.—16 p.), I, M, 9.8 in. FT-4

The economics and control of road-rail competition; a critical study of theory and practice in the United States, Great Britain and Australia, by H. M. Kolsen. [Sydney] Sydney University Press [New Zealand, Price Milburn; London, Methuen, 1968]. 182 p., D, graphs, T, 9 in. FT-5

Freight train. William H. Bunce. Drawings by Lemuel B. Line. New York, Putnam [1954]. Unpaged, I, 8.3 x 10.6 in. FT-6

Freight transportation in the Soviet Union, including comparisons with the United States [by] Ernest W. Williams, Jr. with the assistance of George Novak and Holland Hunter. A study by the National Bureau of Economic Research. Princeton, N. J., Princeton University Press, 1962. 221 p. (pf.—21 p.), M, D, T, 9.4 in. (No. 76). FT-7

Freight transportation in the Soviet Union: a comparison with the United States [by] Ernest W. Williams, Jr., assisted by George Novak. [New York] National Bureau of Economic Research, 1959. 38 p. (pf.—9 p.), M (F), D, T, 9 in. (No. 65). FT-8

Piggyback transportation for Pacific Northwest cooperatives. William C. Bouser. [Washington] Farmer Cooperative Service, U. S. Dept. of Agriculture, 1960. 32 p. (pf.—4 p.), I, 10.2 in. (report 86). FT-9

Protection of rail shipments of fruits and vegetables, by W. H. Redit. Rev. Washington, Agric. Res. Serv. U. S. Dept. of Agric., GPO, 1969. 98 p. (pf.—4 p.), I, M, 10.2 in. (No. 195); also, 1961, 108 p. FT-10

Railroad transportation: Freight (Filmstrip). Society for Visual Education, 1947. 56 frames, 35mm (b & w), (6). FT-11

Selected special freight statistics; traffic, operating, and other statistics for railroads, motor carriers, and other transportation agencies. Paul L. Ambelang. Washington, ICC, 1952. 64 p. (pf.—7 p.), T, 10.6 in. (No. 524). FT-12

Special railroad freight services. Serial 6355. George L. Wilson. [Ed. 1] Scranton, International Correspondence Schools, c 1962. 56 p., 7.5 in. FT-13

Transportation demand projection and forecasts; projection to 1972 of aggregate ton-miles and modal shares of aggregate ton-miles; reviews of major governmental and extra-governmental demand projection of macro-economic forecasts. Richard Lawson. Prepared for Off. of Policy Review, Dept. of Transportation, Washington, D. of T., 1969. 55 l. (pf.—7), 10.2 in. FT-14

Wheels, wings, and water; the story of cargo transport. Charles I. Coombs.[1st ed.] Cleveland, World Pub. Co. [1963]. 222 p., I, 10.2 in. FT-15

FUTURE

The developing transportation revolution; conference report, September 15-16, 1960, Chicago Illinois. Chicago, Railway Systems and Management Association [1960]. 77 p., I, P, 11 in. FUT-1

Let's look ahead and stay ahead; a ten-year projection of railroad growth potential. Prepared for the Railway Progress Institute, Chicago. Transportation Facts, Inc. [Chicago, 1957]. 98 p., D, T, 8.7 x 11.4 in. FUT-2

The future of rail transport in the United States; guidelines for nationwide policy, by James H. Lemly. Atlanta, Bu. of Bus. and Econ. Res., Georgia State College, 1964. 46 l. (pf.–5), I, 11 in. (Res. No. 28). FUT-3

Super-railroads for a dynamic American economy. John W. Barringer. New York, Simmons-Boardman Pub. Corp. [1956]. 91 p., I, 10.6 in. FUT-4

GAGES (see also narrow gauge, companies, etc.)

The war of the gauges. For the narrow-gauge railway: Gen. Wm. J. Palmer (as told to Samuel Bowles in 1871). For the standard-gauge railway: Lorenzo M. Johnson (in 1878). Together with an introd. by John J. Lipsey and six narrow-gauge photos, never before published. Colorado Springs, priv. print. by J. J. Lipsey, Western Books, 1961. 31 p., I, 9 in. G-1

GOVERNMENT

Administration of Metroliner and Turbo-Train projects [by the] Federal Railroad Administration, Dept. of Transportation; report to Congress by the Comptroller General. [Washington] GAO, 1971. 3, 30 p., I, 10.6 in. GO-1

American railroad politics, 1914-1920; rates, wages, and efficiency [by] K. Austin Kerr. [Pittsburgh] Univ. of Pittsburgh Press [1968]. 250 p. (pf.–8 p.), 9 in. GO-2

Enterprise denied; origins of the decline of American railroads, 1897-1917. Albro Martin. New York, Columbia Univ. Press, 1971. 402 p. (pf.–14 p.), 9 in. GO-3

The Federal interest in railroad passenger service. A report for the Secretary, U. S. Dept. of Commerce. W. B. Saunders & Co. Washington, 1959. 113 l. (pf.–3), T, 11.8 in. GO-4

Government promotion of American canals and railroads, 1800-1890. Carter Goodrich. New York, Columbia University Press, 1960. 382 p. (pf.–10 p.), M, 9.4 in. GO-5

The Granger movement; a study of agriculture organization and its political, economic, and social manifestations, 1870-1880. Solom J. Buck. Lincoln, University of Nebraska Press [1963, c 1913]. 384 p., I, 8.3 in. GO-6

Improved guidance needed for relocating railroad facilities at water resources projects; report to the Congress [on the] Corps of Engineers (civil functions), Department of the Army, by the Comptroller General. [Washington, 1970.] 3, 69 p., I, 10.6 in. GO-7

Preliminary inventory of the records of the Commissioner of Railroads (Record group 193). Compiled by Marion M. Johnson. Washington, 1964. 18 p. (pf.–5 p.), 10.2 in. (Pub. 64-7). GO-8

Throttling the railroads [by] Clarence B. Carson. Indianapolis, published by Liberty Fund, for distribution by the Foundation for Economic Education, Irvington-on-Hudson, N. Y., 1971. 132 p. (pf.–11 p.), I, 9.8 in. GO-9

Transport and national goals; analysis of national goods and transport decisions. Edwin T. Haefele, ed. Washington, Brooking Institution, 1969. 201 p. GO-10

GUIDE BOOKS (DIRECTORIES, ETC.)

Atwood's catalogue of United States and Canadian transportation tokens. Compiled and edited by the Catalogue Committee of the American Vecturist Association: Ralph Freiberg, chairman; Roland C. Atwood [and others]. 2 ed. Boston, American Vecturist Association, 1963. 432 p. (pf.–13 p.), 27 plates, 9.4 in.; also, 1958, 397 p. (pf.–11 p.), 22 plates, 9.4 in. GU-1

Bradshaw's railway manual, shareholders' guide, and directory, 1869. New York, A. M. Kelley, 1969. 459, 118 p. (pf.–26 p.), I, M, 9 in. GU-2

Dictionary of railway slang, by Harvey Sheppard. 2 ed. Ilminster, H. Sheppard, Dillington House [1967]. [2] 12 p., 8.1 in. GU-3

The Official list of inter-line ticket agents and passenger traffic officers of the United States, Canada and Mexico. New York, National Railway Publication Co. 10.2 in., quarterly. GU-4

RPM; rail, postal, motor rate guide. Eastern edition. 1st ed. Chicago, J. P. Cascio, 1960–. I, 12.6 in. GU-5

HANDBOOKS, MANUALS, ETC.

Jane's world railways, 1970-71. New York, McGraw-Hill. I, M, 8.7 x 13 in. [Note: Jane's 1st ed.; 1950-51.] H-1

The Traveling Engineers' Association examination questions and answers. Railway Fuel and Operating Officers Association, Chicago. I, 6.7 in. H-2

HAWAII

Hawaiian railroads; a memoir of the common carriers of the fifieth state. Reseda, Calif., Hungerford Press [c 1963]. 80 p., I, M (PF), 9.4 in. By John B. Hungerford. HA-1

HIGH SPEED TRANSPORTATION

High-speed ground transportation extension, 1971. Hearing, October 13, 1971. House, Int. & For. Comm. (Trans. & Aero.). 92C-1S. Washington, GPO, 1971. 30 p. (pf.–3 p.), 9 in. HI-1

High-speed ground transportation extension. Hearing, Ninety-first Congress, second session, on H. R. 17538 and H. R. 17573 . . . June 11, 1970. House, Int. & For. Comm. (Trans. & Aero.). 91C-2S. Washington, GPO, 1970. 43 p. (pf.–3 p.), 9.4 in. HI-2

High-speed ground transportation. Hearing, Ninety-first Congress, second session. on S. 3730 . . . June 4, 1970. Senate, Commerce (Surface Trans.). 91C-2S. Washington, GPO, 1970. 39 p. (pf.—3 p.), 9.4 in.   HI-3

Extension of High-speed ground transportation act. Hearings on S. 3237 and H. R. 16024 . . . July 16 and 17, 1968. Senate, Comm. Com (Surface Trans.). 90C-2S. Washington, GPO, 1968. 166 p. (pf.—3 p.), I, 9.4 in.   HI-4

High-speed ground transportation. Hearings, June 14, 15, and 16, 1965. Senate, Comm. Com. (Surface Trans.). 89C-1S. Washington, GPO, 1965. 183 p. (pf.—5 p.), 9.4 in.   HI-5

High-speed ground transportation; report to accompany S. 1588. Senate, Comm. Com. 89C-1S. Washington, GPO, 1965. 16 p., 9.4 in. (No. 497).   HI-6

Report and recommendations to Governor Kerner and the 75th General Assembly. High Speed Rail Transit Commission [Springfield] 1967. 62 p. (pf.—10 p.), I, M, 11 in. [Illinois].   HI-7

The Japanese National Railway System and its new Tokaido line; a report. N. J. Div. of R.R. Transportation [Trenton, 1963]. 28 p., I, M (C), 8.7 x 11 in. HI-8

Midwest High Speed Rail Transit Conference, Chicago 1967. Proceedings. [Chicago, 1967.] 74 l. (pf.—2), I, 11 in.   HI-9

HISTORY . . . . see Section 2

ILLINOIS

Geographia Map Co.'s highway and railroad map of Illinois. Alexander Gross. New York, Geographia Map Co. [1954]. M (C), 41.6 x 26 in.   I-1

Report and recommendations [high speed trans.].   sHI-7
Trail of the Zephers. Olmstead, 1970.   sCO-62

INDIANA

Electric railroads of Indiana. Jerry Marlette. Indianapolis, Council for Local History, 1959. 158 p., I, 11.4 in.   IA-1

Ghost railroads of Indiana, by Elmer G. Sulzer. Indianapolis, V. A. Jones [1970]. 267 p., I (PC), M, 11.4 in.   IA-2

Indiana's abandoned railroads. Elmer G. Sulzer. Indianapolis, Council for Local History, 1959—. I, 11.4 in.   IA-3

Industrial potentialities of the lower Wabash River Valley; a report. Arthur Longini, chief economist. Chicago and Eastern Illinois R.R. Co. [Chicago, 1954]. 299, 145 p. (pf.—6 p.), I, M, T, 11.4 in.   IA-4

Public Service Commission laws of Indiana; statutes, decisions, opinions of the attorney general, illustrated cases, rules and regulations, edited by William A. Stuckey assisted by the publisher's editorial staff. Indianapolis, Bobbs-Merrill [1951]. 10.2 in.   IA-5

INSURANCE

Report on examination of the Railroad Insurance Rating Bureau, December 31, 1956 to May 14, 1963. Examiner: Frank Cardi. [New York] New York (State) Insurance Dept, 1964. 57, [19], l., 11.8 in.   I(N)-1

INTERSTATE COMMERCE COMMISSION

General (Non-government sources)

Abstracts of Supreme Court decisions interpreting the Interstate Commerce Act. Assoc. of ICC Practitioners. Washington [1954]. 297 p. (pf.−13 p.), 9.4 in.
                                                                                          ICC-1

Selected reading list of books helpful in the study of the principal laws within the jurisdiction of the Interstate Commerce Commission. 3d and rev. ed. Assoc. of ICC Practitioners. Washington, c 1957. 97 p., 9 in.   ICC-2

The commission and the common law; a study in administrative adjudication, by H. Arnold Bennett. [1st ed.] New York, Exposition Press [1964]. 127 p., 8.3 in.
                                                                                          ICC-3

ICC practice and procedure, by Eugene D. Anderson. Indianapolis, Bobbs-Merrill [1966]. 366 p. (pf.−11 p.), 10.6 in.   ICC-4

The Interstate Commerce Commission; a study in administrative law and procedure, dure, by I. L. Scharfman. New York, Harper & Row [1969]. 4 v. in 5, 8.7 in.
                                                                                          ICC-5

Interstate Commerce Commission jurisdiction over financial statements in reports to stockholders. [Chicago] A. Andersen, 1962. 136 p., I, 10.6 in. (case, v.7).
                                                                                          ICC-6

Manual of practice and procedure before the Interstate Commerce Commission [by] Eugene D. Anderson [and] Joseph D. Feeney. [Washington] Association of Interstate Commerce Commission Practitioners [1967]. 76 p. (pf.−7 p.), 9 in.
                                                                                          ICC-7

Regulation of transport innovation; the ICC and unit coal trains to the East Coast, by Paul W. MacAvoy and James Sloss. New York, Random House [1967]. 143 p., 7.5 in.   ICC-8

Survey of organization and operations of the Interstate Commerce Commission. Report submitted on December 22, 1952, pursuant to S. Res. 332, 82d Congress. Wolf Management Engineering Co. Washington, GPO, 1953. 65 p. (pf.−6 p.), I, M, 9.4 in.   ICC-9

Tedrow's regulation of transportation; practice and procedure before the Interstate Commerce Commission. Joseph H. Tedrow. 6th ed. [rev. by] Marvin L. Fair [and] John Guandolo. Dubuque, Iowa, W. C. Brown Co. [1964]. 445 p. (pf.−11 p.), 9.4 in.   ICC-10

Trade cases. Texts of decisions rendered by Federal and State courts throughout the United States in cases involving antitrust, Federal Trade Commission, and other trade regulation law problems, with table of cases and topical indexes. Commerce Clearing House, Chicago. 10.2 in.   ICC-11

Congress

Amendments to the Interstate Commerce Act. Hearings on S. 755 [and others].
Senate, Commerce (Surface Trans.). 90C-1S. Washington, GPO, 1968. 111 p. (pf.–
4 p.), 9.4 in.   ICC-12

Amending Interstate Commerce Act (certificates of public convenience and necessity–railway property). Hearing on H. R. 4165, a bill to amend the Interstate
Commerce Act, as amended with respect to the issuance of certificates of public
convenience and necessity, and relating to railway property. June 18, 1954. House,
Int. & For. Comm. 83C-1S. Washington, GPO, 1954. 75 p. (pf.–3 p.), 9.4 in.
                                                                                                            ICC-13

Amendment to Interstate Commerce Act (Time lag-rate increase bill). Hearings on
S. 1461, a bill to amend the Interstate Commerce Act, as amended, concerning
requests of common carriers for increased transportation rates. Senate, Int. & For.
Comm. 83C-1S. Washington, GPO, 1953. 245 p. (pf.–5 p.), I, 9.4 in.   ICC-14

Amendments to section 20B of the Interstate Commerce Act, relating to modification of railroad financial structures; report to accompany S. 978. Senate, Int. &
For. Comm. 83C-1S. [Washington, GPO, 1953.] 11 p., 9.4 in. (No. 139).   ICC-15

Hugh W. Cross. Chairman of the Interstate Commerce Commsision. Hearing before
the Permanent Subcommittee on Investigations. Senate, Com. on Gov't. Ops. 84C-
2S. November 15, 1955. Washington, GPO, 1956. 83 p. (pf.–3 p.), 9.4 in. ICC-16

ICC employee boards. Hearing on H. R. 6716, a bill to amend section 17 of the
Interstate Commerce Act to provide for further delegation of duties to employee
boards. June 12, 1961. House, Int. & For. Comm. 87C-1S. Washington, GPO,
1961. 40 p. (pf.–3 p.), 9.4 in.   ICC-17

Judicial review of ICC orders. Hearing on S. 2687 . . . June 25, 1968. Senate,
Commerce (Surface Trans.). 90C-2S. Washington, GPO, 1968. 34 p. (pf.–3 p.),
9 in.   ICC-18

Loan guaranty authority of the ICC. Hearings on S. 1146, a bill to extend for 2
years the loan guaranty authority of the Interstate Commerce Commission. N
March 9 and 10, 1961. Senate, Int. & For. Comm. 87C-1S. Washington, GPO,
1961. 77 p. (pf.–3 p.), T, 9.4 in.   ICC-19

Reorganization plan No. 1 of 1969 (ICC). Hearing, September 26, 1969. Senate,
Gov't. Ops. (Exec. Reorg.). 91C-1S. Washington, GPO, 1969. 135 p. (pf.–3 p.),
9.4 in.   ICC-20

Review of ICC policies and practices. Hearings, June 24 and 25, 1969. Senate,
Commerce (Surface Trans.). 91C-1S. Washington, GPO, 1969. 352 p. (pf.–3 p.),
9.4 in.   ICC-21

Stewardship of the ICC. Hearing on progress made under Public laws 85-625 [and
others]. May 21, 1959. Senate, Int. & For. Comm. (Surface Trans.). 86C-1S.
Washington, GPO, 1960. 51 p. (pf.–3 p.), T, 9.4 in.   ICC-22

Surface transportation: scope of authority of ICC. Hearings on S. 1384 [and
others]. Senate, Int. & For. Comm. 85C-1S. Washington, GPO, 1957. 358 p. (pf.–
7 p.), I, 9.4 in.   ICC-23

Train discontinuances. Hearing on S. 1161, a bill to repeal section 13(a) of the Interstate Commerce Act. October 4, 1963, Providence, R. I. Senate, Comm. Com. 88C-1S. Washington, GPO, 1964. 117 p. (pf.—5 p.), 9.4 in.   ICC-24

ICC (commission reports, papers, etc.)

Exercises in observance of the 75th anniversary of the Interstate Commerce Commission, 1887-1962. Departmental Auditorium, Washington, D. C., April 5, 1962. ICC, Washington, GPO [1962]. 55 p. (pf.—6 p.), P, 9.4 in. (87C-2S, House 492).
                                                                   ICC-25

Consolidated index-digest of reports of the Interstate Commerce Commission involving finance. ICC, Dec. 1957—Apr. 1962—. Washington, GPO. 10.6 in.
                                                                   ICC-26

Some rules of evidence discussed in transportation proceedings. ICC Ref. Serv , Washington, 1962—. 10.6 in.   ICC-27

The Interstate Commerce Act, together with text of certain supplementary acts and related sections of various other acts (with appropriate cross references to the United States code) . . . Published by the Interstate Commerce Commission. Rev. to Jan. 1, 1946. Washington, GPO, 1946. 399 p. (pf.—4 p.), 9 in. Supplement. Rev. to Oct. 15, 1949. Washington, GPO, 1949. 45 p., 9.4 in.
                                                                   ICC-28

Interstate Commerce Commission activities, 1937-1962; supplement to the 75th annual report. ICC, Washington, GPO, 1962. 287 p. (pf.—9 p.), D, T, 9.4 in.
                                                                   ICC-29

Signature reproductions of all commissioners [1887] to February 1958. ICC [Washington, 1958]. 6 l., 10.6 in.   ICC-30

IOWA

Iowa. Statistical report of railroad assessments. Property Tax Div. [Des Moines]. 8.7 in. annual.   IO-1

Statistical report [on] railroad, Pullman, and express companies. Iowa State Commerce Comm. [Des Moines]. 8.7 x 13 in.   IO-2

JUVENILE LITERATURE . . . . see Section 2

KANSAS

Trolley through the countryside. Allison Chandler. Denver, Sage Books [1963]. 384 p., I, M, 11.4 in.   K-1

Kansas City and the railroads; community policy in the growth of a regional metropolis. Charles N. Glaab. Madison, State Historical Society of Wisconsin, 1962. 260 p. (pf.—10 p.), I, P, M, 9.4 in.   K-2

Local railroad promotion in Kansas City, 1855-1880. Charles N. Glaab. Ann Arbor, Mich., University Microfilms [1958]. (No. 58-5250).   K-3

KENTUCKY

Ghost railroads of Kentucy, by Elmer G. Sulzer. Indianapolis, V. A. Jones Co.
[1967]. 257 p., I (PC), M, 11.4 in. Revised, 1968.   KE-1

LABOR

General

Adjustment of retired railroaders; a study of occupational retirement. John W.
Tomlin. Ann Arbor, Mich., University Microfilms [1959]. No. 59-2541.   L-1

The story of "Labor"; thirty-three years on rail workers' fighting front. Edward
Keating. [Washington, 1953.] 305 p., I, 9.4 in.   L-2

Railroad-labor dispute; message . . . President John F. Kennedy. [Washington,
GPO, 1963.] 32 p., T, 9.4 in. (88C-1S. House Doc., 142).   L-3

A socio-economic study of sixty-five railway maintenance workers' families in
Eugene, Oregon. Richard D. Millican. [Eugene] c 1950. 27, 2 l., I, 11 in.   L-4

Labor Relations

The Burlington strike; its motives and methods, including the cause of the strike.
Compiled by Charles H. Salmons. New York, A. M. Kelley, 1970. 480 p., I, P,
8.7 in.   L-5

Chicago to-day; the labour war in America. William T. Stead. New York, Arno
Press, 1969. 287 p. (pf.—8 p.), I, P, 9 in.   L-6

The failure of railway labor leadership; a chapter in railroad labor relations, 1900-
1932. James W. Kerley. Ann Arbor, Mich., University Microfilms [1959]. L-7

The pros and cons of compulsory arbitration; a debate manual. Brotherhood of
R.R. Trainmen, Cleveland, 1965. 194 p. (pf.—6 p.), 11 in.   L-8

The Pullman strike. Leon Stein. New York, Arno, 1969. 1 v. (various pagings),
9 in.   L-9

Railway labor-management negotiations. Hearing on current status of railway labor-
management negotiations. April 24, 1967. Senate, Labor and Pub. Welfare. 90C-
1S. Washington, GPO, 1967. 60 p. (pf.—3 p.), 9.4 in.   L-10

Strike control proposals in the light of railroad industry experience. Michael Marsh.
[Washington] Railway Labor Executives' Association, 1967. 48 p., 8.7 in. L-11

1971 railway labor-management dispute—signalmen. Hearing on H. J. Res . . . May
18, 1971. House, Int. & For. Comm. 92C-1S. Washington, GPO, 1971. 85 p. (pf.—
3 p.), 9 in.   L-12

Railway labor-management dispute, December 1970. Hearing . . . December 9,
1970. Senate, Labor & Pub. Welfare. 91C-2S. Washington, GPO, 1971. 225 p. (pf.—
4 p.), 9.4 in.   L-13

Railroad labor-management dispute. Hearings on H. J. Res. 1112, and H. J. Res.
1124. House, Int. & For. Comm. 91C-2S. Washington, GPO, 1970. 265 p. (pf.—
4 p.), I, 9.4 in.   L-14

The current railway labor-management dispute. Senate, Labor & Pub. Welfare. 91C-2S. [Washington] 1970. 19 p., 9.4 in. L-15

Railway shopcraft dispute. Hearing on S. J. Res. 178, April 2, 1970. Senate, Labor & Pub. Welfare. 91C-2S. Washington, GPO, 1970. 157 p. (pf.−4 p.), I, F, 9.4 in.
L-16

Railway shopcraft dispute, March 1970. Hearing on S. J. Res. 178, March 4, 1970. Senate, Labor & Pub. Welfare. 91C-2S. Washington, GPO, 1970. 132 p. (pf.−4 p.), 9 in. L-17

Digest of Awards [1-5899] of Third Division, National Railroad Adjustment Board. Ray J. Westfall. [St. Louis] c 1952. 2 v., 11.8 in.
Handbook of subjects of Awards [1-5899] of Third Division, National Railroad Adjustment Board. [St. Louis] c 1952. 25 l., 11.8 in. L-18

Collective bargaining in the railroad industry. Jacob J. Kaufman. New York, King's Crown Press, 1954 [c 1952]. 235 p. (pf.−10 p.), 8.3 in. L-19

The great Burlington strike. McMurry. sCO-66
The Pullman boycott. Warne. sCO-231
Pullman. Buder. sCO-232
Strikers [etc.]. Pinkerton. sHT-31

Laws

Due process on the railroads: disciplinary grievance procedures before the National Railroad Adjustment Board, First Division. Joseph Lazar. Los Angeles, Institute of Industrial Relations, University of California [1953]. 38 p. (pf.−9 p.), 24 p.
L-20

Rights of railroad workers, by Dean A. Robb and John E. Lustig. Detroit, Advocates Pub. Co. [1968]. 417 p., I, P, 6.7 in. L-21

Interpretations issued by the National Mediation Board pursuant to section 5, second of the Railway Labor Act, July 1, 1954−June 30, 1961. U. S. National Mediation Board, Washington, GPO, 1961. 170 p. (pf.−7 p.), 9.4 in. L-22

Transcript of proceedings of the Arbitration Board (ARB. Bd. 192, N. M. B. case A-4400) Chicago, Illinois, 1954. Wage increase case. Brotherhood of Locomotive Engineers vs. designated railroads. Nat. Mediation Bd. [New York, 1954]. 39 v. in 2, 11.4 in. L-23

Amend Hours of service act of 1907. Hearings on H. R. 5196 [and] H. R. 8476, and similar bills. House, Int. & For. Comm. [Trans. & Aero.]. 89C-2S. Washington, GPO, 1966. 531 p. (pf.−7 p.), I, 9.4 in. L-24

Hours of service act amendments of 1969. Hearings. House, Int. & For. Comm. 91C-1S. Washington, GPO, 1969. 278 p. (pf.−6 p.), forms, 9.4 in. L-25

Due process on the railroads: disciplinary grievance procedures before the National Railroad Adjustment Board, First Division. Rev. and enl. ed. Joseph Lazar. Los Angeles, Inst. of Ind. Relations, Univ. of Calif. [1958]. 66 p. (pf.−11 p.), 9.4 in.
L-26

Productivity

The measurement of the effect of unionization on wages in the transit industry. Melvin Lurie. Chicago [Dept. of Photoduplication, University of Chicago Library] 1958.   L-27

Report of the Presidential Railroad Commission. Washington, GPO, 1962. 327 p. (pf.–8 p.), 9.4 in.
Appendix volume[s]. Washington, 1962. 4 v., D, T, 11 in.   L-28

Railway Labor Act

Administration of the Railway labor act by the National Mediation Board, 1934-1957. Washington, GPO, 1958. 103 p. (pf.–8 p.), F, T, 9.4 in.   L-29

Twenty years under the Railway labor act, amended, and the National Mediation Board, 1934-1954. Washington, GPO, 1955. 109 p. (pf.–8 p.), T, 9.4 in.   L-30

Fifteen years under the Railway labor act, amended, and the National Mediation Board, 1934-1949. N. M. B., Washington, GPO, 1950. 92 p. (pf.–6 p.), 9 in.
                                                                                  L-31

Amend the Railway labor act. Hearing, Eighty-ninth Congress, second session. H. R. 706. March 11, 1966. Senate, Labor and Pub. Welfare [Labor]. 89C-2S. Washington, GPO, 1966. 317 p. (pf.–4 p.), 9.4 in.   L-32

Railway labor act amendments. Hearings on H. R. 7789, a bill to amend the Railway labor act and to authorize agreements providing for union membership and agreements for deductions from the wages of carriers' employees for certain purposes. House, Int. & For. Comm. 81C-2S. Washington, GPO, 1950. 302 p. (pf.–3 p.), 9.4 in.   L-33

To amend the Railway labor act, providing for union membership and agreements for deduction from wages of carrier employees for certain purposes. Hearings on S. Res. 3295. Senate, Labor & Pub. Welfare. 81C-2S. Washington, GPO, 1950. 323 p. (pf.–5 p.), 9.4 in.   L-34

Retirement (see R.R. Retirement Act)

Unemployment

Causes of unemployment in the coal and other specified industries. Hearings on S. Res. 274, a resolution to investigate the cause of increasing unemployment in certain industries. Senate, Labor & Pub. Welfare. 81C-2S. Washington, GPO, 1950. 512 p. (pf.–6 p.), D, 9.4 in.   L-35

Employment and changing occupational patterns in the railroad industry, 1947-60 [by] Bernard Yabroff and William Kelley with the assistance of Catherine F. Delano. Washington, U. S. Dept. of Labor, GPO, 1963. 32 p. (pf.–5 p.), I, 9.8 in. (No. 1344).   L-36

Experience and problems under temporary disability insurance laws: California, New Jersey, New York, Rhode Island, railroads, prepared in the Unemployment Insurance Service of the Bureau of Employment Security by Margaret Dahm. Washington, 1955. 31 p. (pf.–3 p.), T, 10.6 in.   L-37

Railroad unemployment insurance act. Hearings on S. 2639 . . . March 4, 5 and 6, 1952. Senate, Labor & Pub. Welfare. 82C-2S. Washington, GPO, 1952. 148 p. (pf.—4 p.), 9.4 in.   L-38

LAND GRANTS

The O & C lands [by] Christian O. Basler, land law clerk, Office of Chief of Legislation and Cooperative Relations, Bureau of Land Management. [Washington] 1965. 29 l. (pf.—4), 10.6 in.   LA-1

O & C counties; population, economic development, and finance. Univ. of Oregon, Bu. of Municipal Research and Service. Prepared for the Association of O & C Counties. [Eugene] 1957. 138 l. (pf.—7), M (F), T, 11 in.   LA-2

Oregon and California railroad grant lands. Hearing on S. 2225, a bill relating to the administrative jurisdiction of certain public lands in the State of Oregon, May 4, 1954. Senate, Int. & Ins. Affairs. 83C-2S. Washington, GPO, 1954. 88 p. (pf.—3 p.), 9.4 in.   LA-3

Payment for improvements, Red Rock Reservoir, Iowa. Hearing on S. 931, a bill to authorize the Secretary of the Army to pay fair value for improvements located on the railroad rights-of-way owned by lessees. Senate, Pub. Works. 85C-1S. Washington, GPO, 1963. 29 p. (pf.—3 p.), I, 9.4 in.   LA-4

Railroad coal leases. Hearing 89C-2S. April 26, 1966. Washington, GPO, 1966. 73 p. (pf.—4 p.), 9.4 in.   LA-5

Railroad land grants—transcript of cards in Library, Bureau of Railway Economics. Washington, 1951. 119 l., 11 in.   LA-6

Railroads, lands and politics: the taxation of railroad land grants, 1864-1897, by Leslie E. Desker. Providence, Brown Univ. Press, 1964. 435 p. (pf.—11 p.), I, M, 9.4 in.   LA-7

Use and disposition of railroad right-of-way grants. Hearings on H. R. 6630 [and others]. House, Int. & For. Aff. (Public Lands). 87C-1S. June 29 and 30, 1961. Washington, GPO, 1961. 144 p. (pf.—3 p.), M (PF), 9.4 in.   LA-8

Arid domain [SF]. Greever.   sCO-16
Valuation [Pottawatomie lands—SF].   sCO-19
Illinois Central [colonization]. Gates.   sCO-141
Maryland's influence [land cession]. Adams.   sCO-34

LAWS

Administration of the Railway labor act by the National Mediation Board, 1934-1970. [Washington, for sale by the Supt. of Docs., GPO, 1970.] 203 p. (pf.—9 p.), F, 9.4 in.   LAW-1

ALI-ABA course of study: railroad reorganization; its past, present, and future—Section 77 of the Bankruptcy act and other legislation; study materials. [Philadelphia] Joint Committee on Continuing Legal Education of the American Law Institute and the American Bar Association [1971]. 104 p. (pf.—11 p.), Fac, 11.4 in.   LAW-2

The locomotive engineer, 1863-1963; a century of railway labor relations and work rules. Reed C. Richardson. Ann Arbor, Bu. I. R., Univ. of Michigan [c 1963]. 456 p., D, 9.4 in.   LAW-3

The Granger laws: a study of the origins of state railway control in the upper Mississippi Valley. George H. Miller. Ann Arbor, University Microfilms, 1951.
                                                                                     LAW-4

Railroads and the Granger laws [by] George H. Miller. Madison, University of Wisconsin Press [1971]. 296 p. (pf.—11 p.), M, 9 in.   LAW-5

Railroad decisions of the Interstate Commerce Commission: their guiding principles. David W. Bishop. Washington, Catholic Univ. of America Press, 1961. 193 p. (pf.—11 p.), 9 in.   LAW-6

Law and locomotives; the impact of the railroad on Wisconsin law in the nineteenth century. Robert S. Hunt. Madison, State Historical Society of Wisconsin [1958]. 292 p. (pf.—14 p.), I, P, 9.4 in.   LAW-7

United States regulations for steam and other than steam locomotives; laws, rules, and instructions for inspection and testing of steam locomotives and tenders, and other than steam locomotives; interpretations, rulings and explanations on questions raised relative thereto as prescribed by the Interstate Commerce Commission, Bureau of Locomotive Inspection; also, safety appliance standards for locomotives, as fixed by order of the Commission dated March 13, 1911. Rev. to Dec. 1, 1949. Gibson, Pribble and Company, Richmond [1950, c 1937]. 219 p., I, 6.7 in.
                                                                                     LAW-8

Federal laws, general wage and rule agreements, decisions, awards and orders governing employees engaged in train, yard and dining car service on railroads in the United States. Brotherhood of Railroad Trainmen, Cleveland [1954]. 909 p. (pf.—7 p.), T, 11.4 in.   LAW-9

Merchants, farmers & railroads; railroad regulation and New York politics, 1850-1887. By Lee Benson. New York, Russell & Russell [1969, c 1955]. 310 p. (pf.—10 p.), I, M, 9.4 in.   LAW-10

Principles of inland transportation. 4th ed. Stuart Daggett. New York, Harper [1955]. 788 p., I, 9.8 in.   LAW-11

Railroads and regulation, 1877-1916. By Gabriel Kolkoe. Princeton, N. J., Princeton Universtiy Press, 1965. 273 p. (pf.—7 p.), 8.7 in.   LAW-12

Regulation of railroads, by Frederick W. Denniston. Assisted by Gilmer B. Randolph. [Ed. 3] Scranton, International Correspondence Schools [1965—]. 7.5 in.
                                                                                     LAW-13

A congressional history. Haney.   sHT-9
History of the Grange movement. McCabe.   sHT-18

LOCOMOTIVE ENGINEERS

Life on a locomotive; an engineer on the C&NW in days of steam. Geo. Williams. Berkeley, Howell-North. 300 p., I (12), 9 in.   LO-1

A locomotive engineer's album; the saga of steam engines in America, by George B. Abdill. [1st ed.] Seattle, Superior Pub. Co. [1965]. 190 p., I, 11 in. LO-2

LOCOMOTIVES . . . . see Section 2

LOGGING

Cinders and timber; a bird's-eye view of logging railroads in Northeastern Minnesota yesterday and today [by] Frederick G. Harrison. [n. p. 1967.] 49 p., I, 8.3 x 11 in. LOG-1

Logging railroads of the west; glimpses down the main lines, spurs and incline steel into the old logging days. Kramer Adams. Seattle, Superior Pub. Co. 11 in. LOG-2

Thunder in the mountains, by Hank Johnston: glory days of High Sierra logging with flumes and locomotives. Corona del Mar, Calif., Trans-Anglo Books. 144 p., I, 11 in. LOG-3

They felled the redwoods, by Hank Johnston; the saga of lumber barons logging the Sierra redwoods and how the trees were preserved. Corona del Mar, Calif., Trans-Anglo Books. 96 p., I, 11 in. LOG-4

Logging along [D&RG]. Chappell. sCO-97
Pino Grande. Polkinghorn. sCO-224

LOS ANGELES

City makers. Nadeau. sHT-8

LOUISIANA

Cleartype colorprint map of Louisiana. American Map Co., New York [1950]. 2 M (C), 38 x 25 in. (4416). LOU-1

Louisiana, its street and interurban railways. Louis C. Hennick. Shreveport, La., c 1962–. I, 11.4 in. LOU-2

Louisiana's transportation revolution: the railroads, 1830-1850. Merl E. Reed. Ann Arbor, University Microfilms [1958]. (Publication No. 24,725). LOU-3

MAINE

Maine two-footers; a definitive history. Linwood W. Moody. Berkeley, Howell-North. 350 p., I (213), 9 in. M-1

Railway developments in Maine; an address at Ricker Classical Institute and Ricker College Alumni Association banquet, Houlton, Maine, June 8, 1953. Carlton J. Corliss. [n. p., 1953 or 4.] 19 l., 11 in. M-2

MANAGEMENT

Careers in the American railroad industry. Charles O. Morgret. Cambridge, Mass., Bellman Pub. Co. [1960]. 32 p., I, 9 in. MA-1

Prospects for railfreight statistics as a marketing tool. Prepared by Washington State Dept. of Commerce and Economic Development, Div. of Bus. and Econ. Res. By Malcolm D. McPhee; project director: Keith E. Yandon. Olympia, State Dept. Plant, 1964. 30 p., 9 in.   MA-2

Proceedings. Railway Systems and Management Association [Washington]. I, 11.4 in.   MA-3

Simulation of railroad operations. Railway Systems and Management Association, Chicago [1966]. 208 p., I, M, P, 11.4 in.   MA-4

MANUFACTURERS

Economic analysis of the freight car manufacturing industry of the United States, a thesis in industrial management. Charles R. Marshall. [Philadelphia] 1953. 52 p., I, 11 in.   MAN-1

Railway supply industry yearbook. 1st ed.; 1952–. New York, Simmons-Board-man. I, 11.4 in.   MAN-2

MAPS

Centennial map of the United States of America (railroads and highways). Rand, McNally and Co. [Chicago, 1955]. M (C), 30.6 x 48.5 in.   MAP-1

List of maps showing railway lines. 1948–. AAR, Washington. 9 in.   MAP-2

Railroad map of the United States. Prepared, 1935. Rev. to Apr. 1957. Ed. 5–AMS. Army Map Service, Washington, 1957. M (C), 53 x 78 in. on 4 sheets, 31 x 42 in. (Series 8204).   MAP-3

Rand McNally's pioneer atlas of the American West; containing facsimile reproductions of maps and indexes from the 1876 first edition of Rand, McNally & Co.'s Business atlas of the great Mississippi Valley and Pacific slope, togehter with contemporary railroad maps and travel literature. Historical text by Dale L. Morgan. Chicago, 1969, c 1956. 80 p., I, M, 14.5 in.   MAP-4

Rand McNally handy railroad atlas of the United States. Chicago. M, 12.6 in.
                                                                                                                MAP-5

Railroad map of the United States. Prepared . . . 1935. Rev. 1951 from data furnished by Military Railway Service Division, Interstate Commerce Commission. 4th ed.–Army Map Service. [Washington] 1952. M, 53 x 78 in. on 4 sheets (8204).   MAP-6

Preliminary inventory of the cartographic records of the Office of the Secretary of the Interior (Record group 48). Compiled by Laura E. Kelsay. U. S. National Archives, Washington, 1955. 11 p. (pf.–5 p.), 10.6 in. (No. 55-13, prel. inv., 81).
                                                                                                                MAP-7

United States. Railroads printed in brown. Compiled under the direction of A. F. Hassan. Ed. of 1932, reprinted 1950. U. S. Geological Survey. [Washington, 1950.] M (C), 49 x 78 in. on 2 sheets 51 x 49 in.   MAP-8

U. S. railroads, classified according to capacity and relative importance. Edward L. Ullman. New York, Simmons-Boardman Pub. Corp., c 1950. M (C), 29 x 47 in.

MAP-9

See also individual companies and city and state locations of interest.

MARYLAND

Geographia Map Co.'s highway and railroad map of Maryland and Delaware; with population based on latest census. Alexander Gross. New York, Geographia Map Co. [1956]. M (C), 21.6 x 34.2 in.   MAR-1

MASSACHUSETTS

Mass transportation in Massachusetts; final report on a mass transportation demonstration project. Prepared under the direction of Joseph F. Maloney. Based on materials developed by the Mass Transportation Commission staff and [others. Boston] 1964. 144 p. (pf.–6 p.), I, M (C), 11 in.   MAS-1

Recommended highway and transit plan. Mass. Bu. of Trans. Planning & Development. [Boston] 1968. 115 p. (pf.–8 p.), M (PC), 11 in.   MAS-2

Report on transit facilities utilizing Old Colony Line, Ashmont to South Braintree. Mass. Mass Transportation Commission. Boston, Wright & Potter Print. Co., 1960. 25 p., I, 9 in. (House 2600).   MAS-3

Report relative to State tax and other relief for commuter railroads. Massachusetts Legis. Res. Bu. [Boston] 1961. 99 p., 9 in. (Senate Doc. No. 535).   MAS-4

Report to the Old Colony Area Transportation Commission on plans for improved suburban transit. De Leuw, Cather & Company. April 1959. Brookline, Mass. [1959]. I, M (PF), PL (PF), 11 in.   MAS-5

MERGERS, CONSOLIDATIONS, ETC.

The move toward railroad mergers, a great national problem. Leon H. Keyserling. [Washington] Railway Labor Executives' Association, 1962. 102 p., I, 9 in.

ME-1

The politics of railroad coordination. Earl Latham. Cambridge, Harvard Univ. Press, 1959. 338 p. (pf.–10 p.),   ME-2

Obstacles to railroad unification. Roy J. Sampson. Eugene, Bu. of Bus. Res., Univ. of Oregon, 1960. 40 l., 11 in.   ME-3

Railroad consolidation under the Transportation Act of 1920. William N. Leonard. New York, AMS Press, 1946.   ME-4

Railroad consolidations and the public interest, a preliminary examination; staff study. ICC Bu. of Trans. Econ. & Stat. Washington, 1962. 79 p. (pf.–2 p.), 6 p., 10.6 in.   ME-5

Railroad mergers and abandonments. Michael Conant. Berkeley, University of California Press, 1964. 212 p. (pf.–13 p.), 9.8 in.   ME-6

Rail merger legislation. Hearings; on S. Res. 258 on S. 3097, to amend section 7 of the Clayton act to give full force and effect to the operation of the provisions of that section applicable to certain railroad consolidations and mergers until December 31, 1963. Senate, Judiciary. 87C-2S. Washington, GPO, 1962. 2 pts. (1644)p.), I, M (PF), 9.4 in.   ME-7

Railroad mergers and the economy of New England, by James R. Nelson. Boston, New England Economic Research Foundation, 1966. 236 p., 19 l., 11 in.   ME-8

Selected impacts of railroad mergers. [By Ely M. Brandes, Robert C. Brown, and Paul S. Jones. Washington] U. S. Dept. of Commerce; for sale by GPO, 1965. 203 p. (pf.—8 p.), I, M (F), 11 in.   ME-9

The railroads. David M. Potter, ed. Rev. by E. David Cronon and Howard R. Lamar. New York, Holt [1960]. 66 p., 9.4 in.   ME-10

Western railroad mergers; a staff study by the Office of the Assistant Secretary for Policy Development and the Federal Railroad Administration. Dept. of Transportation. Ass't. Sec. for Policy Development. Washington, U. S. Dept. of Transportation, 1969. 50 p. (pf.—3 p.), I (PC), 10.2 in.   ME-11

The fall of a railroad empire [NH]. Staples.   sCO-194
Merger [L&N, NC&St.L]. U. S. House.   sCO-165

MEXICO

Ferrocarril de Chihuahua al Pacifico. New rails to old towns; the regional story of the Ferrocarriles Chihuahua al Pacifico by Joseph Wampler. Berkeley, Calif., 1969. 162 p. (pf.—11 p.), I, M, 9 in.   MEX-1

Straddling the Isthmus of Tehuantepec by Edward B. Glick. Gainesville, Univ. of Florida Press, 1959. 48 p., 9 in.   MEX-2

Mexican narrow gauge, by Gerald M. Best. Berkeley, Calif., Howell-North Books [1968]. 180 p., I, M, P, 11.4 x 9 in.   MEX-3

Rails, mines, and progress: seven American promoters in Mexico, 1867-1911. David M. Pletcher. Ithaca, N. Y., published for the American Historical Association [by] Cornell University Press [1958]. 321 p., I, 9.4 in.   MEX-4

The railways of Mexico, a study in nationalization, by John H. McNeely. [El Paso, Texas Western College Press] 1964. 56 p., I, M, P, 9 in.   MEX-5

The United States Railway Mission in Mexico [a summary report] by Fred E. Linden. Washington, Institute of Inter-American Transportation [1947]. 119 p., I, M, 10.6 in.   MEX-6

MICHIGAN

When the railroad was king; the nineteenth-century road era in Michigan, by Frank N. Elliott. Lansing, Michigan Historical Commission, 1966. 68 p., I, Fac, 8.7 in.
MI-1

MIDWEST

The Lake Superior iron ore railroads, by Patrick C. Dorin. [1st ed.] Seattle, Superior Pub. Co. [1969]. 144 p., I, 11 in.   MID-1

Sketch map covering that part of the United States located in central and western trunk line territories. Prepared by the Port of New York Authority, Port Development Dept., Traffic Management Staff. [New York] c 1954. M (C), 34 x 37 in.   MID-2

MILITARY RAILWAYS

Military railway service (Motion picture). U. S. Dept. of the Army, 1948. Released for public educational use through U. S. Office of Education, 1950. 30 min., sd., b&w, 16 mm.; another issue. 35 mm.   MIL-1

Operation, inspection, and maintenance of steam locomotives and locomotive cranes. U. S. Army [Washington] 1957. 358 p., I, 9.4 in.   MIL-2

Question and answer text on railway operating rules. U. S. Army Trans. School, Fort Eustis, 1953. 105 p., 10.6 in.   MIL-3

Standard plans, roadway, track, and structures. U. S. Army [Washington] 1944 [i. e. 1946]. 202 I. (chiefly D, PL, T), 10.2 x 16.5 in.   MIL-4

MINE RAILROADS

The coal viewer and engine builder's practical companion. John Curr. With a new introd. by Charles Lee. 2d ed. New York, A. M. Kelley, 1970. 96 p., I, 10.2 in.   MIN-1

Laying panel track at the Morenci open pit. Walter C. Lawson. [In Mining Technology, York Pa., 1937-48. 9 in., vol. 11, No. 4, July, 1947. 13 p., I.]   MIN-2

The Gilpin tram route. Ferrell.   sCO-126

MINNESOTA

Rails to the North Star, by Richard S. Prosser. Minneapolis, Dillon Press [1966]. 283 p., 11.4 in.   MINN-1

MISSISSIPPI

Balance of trade in recent Mississippi rail freight traffic. James E. Noblin. Jackson, Mississippi Industrial and Technological Research Commission, 1961. 39 l. (chiefly maps), 8.7 x 11 in. (No. 8).   MIS-1

MISSOURI

Missouri: railroad junction map, April 1, 1953. Missouri, Div. of Resources and Development. [Jefferson City, 1953.] M (C), 27.5 x 31.5 in.   MIS-2

MODELS . . . . see Section 2

MONORAILS

Monorails. Herman S. D. Botzow. New York, Simmons-Boardman Pub. Corp., 1960. 104 p., I, 11 in.   MO-1

Proposal for a demonstration model of a controlled high-speed Superail transit system for mass transportation, Washington, D. C., to Dulles International Airport. D. C. Transit System, Inc. In collaboration with S. H. Bingham. [Washington] c 1962. 83 l. (pf.—6), M (F), D, T, 11.8 in.   MO-2

Seattle monorail demonstration study, by Daniel E. Alexander [and others]. A study conducted under the sponsorship of the Univ. of Washington Civil Eng. Department for the Federal Housing and Home Finance Agency, Contract No. MTD-2, project No. WASH MTD-1. [Seattle] Transportation Research Group, Univ. of Washington, 1962. I, 11 in.   MO-3

Seattle monorail; a mass transportation demonstration study. Washington (State) Univ. Dept. of Civil Engineering. Washington, D. C., Housing and Home Finance Agency, Off. of Trans., 1962. 108 p., I, M, D, 10.6 in.   MO-4

MONTANA

Official map of Montana. McGill-Warner Co. [Helena] Board of Railroad Commissioners, c 1951. M (C), 31 x 51 in.   MON-1

Montana freight rates. Hearing . . . Helena, Mont., July 8, 1958. Senate, Int. & For. Comm. 85C-2S. Washington, GPO, 1958. 156 p. (pf.—4 p.), 9.4 in.   MON-2

Montana highway-rail grade crossing study; primary and secondary systems. Montana, State Highway Comm. Prepared in cooperation with U. S. Dept. of Trans., Fed. Hwy. Comm., Bu. of Public Roads. [Helena, Mont., 1969.] 11 in.   MON-3

MOTION PICTURES (inc. Film Strips)

Engines, rails, and roads (Filmstrip). Popular Science Pub. Co., Audio-Visual Division, in cooperation with World Book Encyclopedia, 1949. 55 frames, 35 mm (b & w), (No. 2).   MP-0

Railways in the cinema. Shepperton, Allan, 1969. 168 p., 64 plates, I, P, 9.4 in. By John Huntley.   MP-00

Davenport, Iowa; Blackhawk Films. Motion pictures from MP-1 through MP-61 are Blackhawk releases.

Eastern Railroads

Double headers on the Baltimore & Ohio.	MP-1
Circus train to Milwaukee.	MP-2
Railroading in the East. .	MP-3
Five Midwestern R.Rs. [steam].	MP-4
Focus on steam [mid Am.].	MP-5
Iron horse centennial. 1927.	MP-6
Days of steam [L&N].	MP-7
Return of the General.	MP-8
Hudsons of the New York Central.	MP-9

Mikados of the New York Central.	MP-10
On the Norfolk & Western.	MP-11
Mimories of steam at Horseshoe Curve.	MP-12
On the Pennsylvania.	MP-13
Pennsy's electrified speedway.	MP-14
Pennsylvania steam locomotives.	MP-15
September days of steam railroading.	MP-16
Some early stream liners.	MP-17
Steam on the Reading.	MP-18
Steam trains out of Dearborn.	MP-19
Ten-wheeler to duplex.	MP-20
Tracks of the iron horse.	MP-21
Wheels a'rolling.	MP-22
When steam was king.	MP-23

Western Railroads

Bustling narrow gauge.	MP-24
California Zepher.	MP-25
Climb to Cumbres.	MP-26
Memories of steam [Rio Grande].	MP-27
Narrow gauge to Silverton.	MP-28
Logging R.Rs. of the West.	MP-29
Rio Grande Southern.	MP-30
Santa Fe steam [Cajon].	MP-31
Super Chief.	MP-32
S. P.'s cab-forward mallets.	MP-33
Coast Daylight [steam].	MP-34
Donner Pass [S.P.].	MP-35
Steam kings of the rails.	MP-36
"Big Boy" and his brothers.	MP-37
Challengers and Big Boys [U.P.].	MP-38
At Sherman Hill [U.P.].	MP-39
Pacing U. P. steam [Neb.].	MP-40
Western Pacific fast freight.	MP-41
Western trains of long ago.	MP-42
Winter railroading in the Sierras.	MP-43
Winter railroading [S.P. Overland route].	MP-44

Other Railroads

White Pass & Yukon.	MP-45
Cedar Rapids & Iowa City [elec.].	MP-46
From horse car to subway [N.Y.C.].	MP-47
Illinois Terminal interurbans [elec.].	MP-48
Trolley lines and elevateds [N.Y.C.].	MP-49
Waterloo, Cedar Falls & Northern [elec.].	MP-50

Stories

Between Orton Jt. and Fallonville (1913).	MP-51
The block signal (1920).	MP-52
The ghost of the canyon (1920).	MP-53
The great train robbery (1903).	MP-54
The grit of the girl telegrapher (1912).	MP-55

In danger's path (1915).   MP-56
In the switch tower (1915).   MP-57
The leap from the water tower (1915).   MP-58
The Lonedale operator (1911).   MP-59
A romance of the rails (1912).   MP-60
The wild engine (1919).   MP-61

MOTOR CARS

Regulation of track motorcars. Hearings on S. 1425, a bill to amend the Interstate
Commerce Act so as to provide for the protection of railroad employees by regulating the use of track motorcars, July 23,1959, and September 9, 1959. Senate,
Int. & For. Commerce (Surface Trans.). 86C-1S. Washington, GPO, 1960. 172 p.
(pf.–3 p.), I, 9.4 in.   MR-1

MOUNTAIN RAILROADS

Intermountain railroads, standard and narrow gauge. Merrill D. Beal. Caldwell,
Idaho, Caxton Printers, 1962. 252 p., I, 8.7 in.   MT-1

Colorado Midland. Calky.   sCO-80
Rebel of the Rockies. Athearn.   sCO-93
Rails that climb [D&SL]. Bollinger.   sCO-102
The Rio Grande Pictorial. Sundance.   sCO-98
The story [PW&S]. Langsdale.   sCO-223

MUSEUMS

Ride down memory lane; the story of the Branford Trolley Museum. [Editing
committee: John R. Stevens, Richard H. Fletcher, and John Stern. 5th ed. Short
Beach, Conn., c 1965.] 58 p., I, M, 9 in.   MU-1

The story of the Steamtown and Edaville; describes the efforts of F. Nelson Blount
to preserve steam power. By Ron Ziel. Mt. Arlington, N. J., Camelback Publishing.
52 p., I (85, 22C).   MU-2

NARROW GAUGE . . . . **see Section 2**

NEBRASKA

National Railway Historical Society. Cornhusker Chapter. Publication. No. 1–.
Crete, Neb. [1970–]. I, 11.4 in.   NB-1

NEVADA

Opinions and orders. Public Service Commission. Carson City, State Print. Off.
9.4 in.   NE-1

NEW ENGLAND

Men, cities, and transportation; a study in New England history, 1820-1900.
Edward C. Chase. New York, Russell & Russell [1968, c 1948]. 2 v., I, F, M, P,
9.8 in.   NED-1

The New England railroads, by Martin L. Lindahl. Boston, New England Economic
Research Foundation, 1965. 169 p., 12 l., 11 in.   NED-2

From horse trails to steel rails. W. W. Wardwell. Published under the auspices of the
Worcester Historical Society, Worcester, Mass. Rockport, Me., Falmouth Pub.
House [1955]. 96 p., I, 11 in.   NED-3

Formation of New England R.R. systems. Baker.   sHT-36

R.R. mergers [N. E. economy]. Nelson.   sME-8

NEW HAMPSHIRE

Rand, McNally & Co.'s Indexed county and township pocket map and shippers'
guide of New Hampshire. Chicago. M (F, C), 6.7 in.   NH-1

NEW JERSEY

Benchmark survey; park'n ride station and service at New Brunswick, New Jersey,
on Pennsylvania Railroad. Submitted by Research Data Processing Corporation,
Traffic Research Corporation [and] R. L. M. Associates. [New York, Tri-State
Transportation Committee (Conn., N. J., N. Y.)] 1963. 78 l., forms, M (C), 11 in.
                                                                   NJ-1

The impending breakthrough in transportation. Dwight R. Palmer. Bu. of Info.,
New Jersey Hy. Dept., 1961. Trenton. 15 p., 8.7 in.   NJ-2

The New Jersey short line railroads; photo album. Howard E. Johnston. Deluxe ed.
[Plainfield, N. J., 1959.] 20 p. (chiefly illus.), 9 in.   NJ-3

Eleventh report: Railroad taxation in New Jersey—the end of an era. New Jersey,
Comm. on State Tax Policy. [Trenton] 1965. 89 p., 9.8 in.   NJ-4

Southern New Jersey mass transportation survey. Parson, Brinckerhoff, Quade
& Douglas. [Report to; Delaware River Port Authority of Pennsylvania and New
Jersey. New York] 1956. 70 p. (pf.—7 p.), M, D, T, 11 x 18 in.   NJ-5

Report on Assembly bill No. 692 (1059) [proposes meeting transportation problems by obtaining certain revenues of the New Jersey Turnpike Authority] to
Honorable Walter H. Jones, Senator, Bergen County. N. J. Com. on Transit problems. [Trenton] 1959. [41] l., 11 in.   NJ-6

Review [P.C. condition]. U. S. Senate.   sCO-198
Penn-Central investigation. N. J.   sCO-214

NEW MEXICO

New Mexico's railroads; an historical survey, by David F. Myrick. [Golden, Colorado Railroad Museum] 1970. 197 p., I, Fac, M, P, 9.4 in.   NM-1

Horny Toad man. Lenore Dils. [1st ed. El Paso, Tex.] Boots and Saddle Press
[1966]. 190 p., I, F, M, P, 9.4 in.   NM-2

New Mexico [and S.F.]. Gurley.   sCO-17

NEW YORK (state)

Grape belt trolleys, by Kenneth C. Springirth. Erie, Pa., 1970. 140 p., I, M, 11.4 in.
NY-1

Main line to oblivion; the disintegration of New York railroads in the twentieth century [by] Robert B. Carson. Port Washington, N. Y., Kennikat Press [1971]. 273 p. (pf.—9 p.), M, 9 in.
NY-2

Minisink Valley express; a history of the Port Jervis, Monticello & New York Railroad and its predecessors, by Gerald M. Best. Artwork by E. S. Hammack and Frederic Shaw. [Rev. ed.] San Marino, Calif., Golden West Books [1967]. 96 p., 8.7 in.
NY-3

Rip Van Winkle railroads; Canajoharie & Catskill R. R., Catskill Mountain Ry., Otis Elevating Ry., Catskill & Tannersville Ry., by William F. Helmer. Berkeley, Calif., Howell-North Books [1970]. 146 p., I (PC), Fac, M, P, 11.4 in.
NY-4

The Royal Blue line. William R. Gordon. [Rochester, N. Y., 1952.] 24 p., I, 11 in.
NY-5

Trolley lines of the Empire State, city and suburban. F. E. Reifschneider. [Orlando, Fla., 1950.] 55 p., I, 8.7 in.
NY-6

Railroads of New York; a study of government aid, 1826-1875. Harry H. Pierce. Cambridge, Harvard University Press, 1953. 208 p. (pf.—13 p.), I, 10 M, 9.8 in.
NY-7

Railroads of New York; a picture story of railroading in and around New York City. George W. O'Conner. [1st ed.] New York, Simmons-Boardman Pub. Corp. [1949]. 144 p., I, M (2F), 8.3 x 11 in.
NY-8

Analysis of the obligation and ability of the Port of New York Authority to help in improving New Jersey-New York rail commutation. Herman T. Stichman. [New York, 1959.] 14 p., 11 in.
NY-9

Long Island journey-to-work report—1963. N. Y. (St.) Off. of Trans. Albany, 1963. 36 p., M, D, T (3F), 11 in.
NY-10

A map of the railroads in New York State. 1953 rev. N. Y. Dept. of Commerce. Albany [1953]. M (C), 18.5 x 25.2 in.
NY-11

Report of investigation of the financial condition of the railroads operating in the State of New York, pursuant to concurrent resolution of March 25, 1958. N. Y. Public Service Comm. Albany, 1959. 146 p., I, 11 in.
NY-12

Proposed legislation [L.I. R.R.].   sCO-160
Farmers, merchants and railroads. Benson.   sLAW-10

NEW YORK CITY

Fifty years of rapid transit, 1864-1917. James B. Walker. New York, Arno Press, 1970. 291 p. (pf.—3 p.), I, P, 9 in.
NY(C)-1

Labor relation in the New York rapid transit systems, 1904-1944. James Joseph McGinley. New York, King's Crown Press, 1949. 635 p. (pf.—23 p.), 9.4 in.

NY(C)-2

Work staggering for traffic relief; an analysis of Manhattan's central business district [by] Lawrence B. Cohen. New York City Project. New York, Praeger [1968]. 646 p. (pf.—19 p.), I, M, 9.4 in.

NY(C)-3

Journey to work: Manhattan central business district. New York—New Jersey Transportation Agency. [New York, 1964.] 36 p., I, M (C), 9-12.2 in.

NY(C)-4

Report including analysis of operations of the New York City transit system for five years, ended June 30, 1945. N. Y. (city) Bd. of Transportation. [New York, 1945.] 171 p. (pf.—4 p.), D, T, 10.2 in.

NY(C)-5

The revision of the rapid transit fare structure of the city of New York. William S. Vickrey. [New York] 1952. 156 p. (pf.—12 p.), I, 8.7 in.

NY(C)-6

NEW YORK METROPOLITAN AREA

Commuter transportation. A study of passenger transportation in the New Jersey—New York—Connecticut metropolitan region with particular reference to railroad commutation. Report prepared for the Senate, Int. & For. Comm. pursuant to S. Res. 244 and S. Res. 328 of the 86th Congress. Washington, GPO, 1961. 81 p. (pf.—10 p.), M (9), 10.6 in.

NY(M)-1

Study of consolidated railroad marine and lighterage for New York harbor. Tri-State Transportation Com. (Conn., N. J. & N. Y.). [New York, 1964.] 55 p., I (PC), M (PC), 11 x 17 in.

NY(M)-2

Journey-to-work transportation analysis: Westchester, Putnam, and Rockland Counties. N. Y. (St.) Off. of Trans. [Albany] 1964. 40 p., I, M, 11 in.

NY(M)-3

Metropolitan rapid transit financing; legal, administrative, and financial studies. A report to the Metropolitan Rapid Transit Survey of New York and New Jersey sponsored by the Port of New York Authority and the Metropolitan Rapid Transit Commission of New York and New Jersey. [New York] 1957. 137 p., I, 11 in.

NY(M)-4

Metropolitan transportation politics and the New York region, by Jameson W. Doig. New York, Columbia University Press, 1966. 327 p. (pf.—6 p.), M, 9.4 in.

NY(M)-5

Railroads, Tri-State metropolitan region and environs, New Jersey—New York—Connecticut. Regional Plan Association. New York, c 1965. M (C), 39.7 x 41.5 in.

NY(M)-6

Railroad suburban equipment study. Tri-State Transportation Committee (Conn., N. J. and N. Y.). New York, 1963—. M (PC), D, T, 11 in.

NY(M)-7

Report. New York—New Jersey Transportation Agency. [New York] 1964. 21 p., 9 in.

NY(M)-8

Trans-Hudson rapid transit; a report to the project director of the Metropolitan Rapid Transit Survey. De Leuw, Cather & Co. [Chicago] 1957. 164 p., I, 11 in.
NY(M)-9

Transportation in the New York metropolitan region during the next twenty-five years. Austin J. Tobin. [New York] Regional Plan Association, 1954. 33 p., 11 in.
NY(M)-10

PORT OF NEW YORK AUTHORITY

A selected bibliography of the Port of New York Authority, 1921-1956. New York [1956]. 66 p., 9 in.
NY(P)-1

Port of New York Authority. Hearings, House, Judiciary. 86C-2S. Washington, GPO, 1961. 2 pts., 2,065 p. (pf.—9 p.), I, M, P, 9.4 in.
NY(P)-2

Return of subpenas, Port of New York Authority inquiry. Inquiry before Subcommittee No. 5. June 29, 1960. House, Judiciary. 86C. Washington, GPO, 1960. 75 p. (pf.—3 p.), 9.4 in. (No. 20).
NY(P)-3

NORTH CAROLINA

Crossties through Carolina; the story of North Carolina's early day railroads. Compiled and edited by John Gilbert. With text by Grady Jefferys. [1st ed.] Raleigh, N. C., Helios Press [1969]. 88 p., I, F, M, P, 8.7 x 11.4 in.
NOC-1

Hall of History railroad, written and illustrated by Ann Beal. N. C. Dept. of Archives and History. Raleigh, 1960. 8 p., I, 9 in.
NOC-2

Map of North Carolina railroads. N. C. Utilities Commission. Raleigh, 1954. M (C), 12.2 x 28.4 in.
NOC-3

NORTH DAKOTA

North Dakota. McGill-Warner Co. [Bismarck] Public Service Commission, State of North Dakota [1950] c 1949. M (C), 14.5 x 23 in.
NOD-1

NORTH WEST

This was railroading. [1st ed.] George B. Abdill. Seattle, Superior Pub. Co. [1958]. 192 p., I, 11 in.
NW-1

OHIO

Grade crossings in Ohio. Ohio Legis. Service Commission. Columbus, 1957. 24 l., I, 11.4 in. (No. 23).
O-1

Geographia Map Co.'s highway and railroad map of Ohio. Alexander Gross. New York, Geographia Map Co. [1956]. M (C), 26 x 26 in.
O-2

Ohio trolleys. Kenneth S. P. Morse. Baltimore, printed by the Sutherland Press [1960]. 67 p., I, M, 11 in.
O-3

Railroad reading rooms and libraries in Ohio, 1865-1900. Joan Frances Richie. [Kent, Ohio] 1964. 86 l. (pf.—8 p.), M, 11 in.
O-4

OKLAHOMA

The national, regional, and metropolitan relationships of railroad transport and the Tulsa expressway projects. Walter C. Sadler. [Tulsa, Okla., Pacific Planning & Research, 1958.] unpaged, I, 11 in.   OK-1

Railroad map of Oklahoma, prepared under the direction of Corporation Commission of Oklahoma. Compiled by Railroad Engineering Dept. of Corporation Commission. [Oklahoma City] 1956, c 1936. M (C), 16.3 x 32.3 in.   OK-2

OPERATIONS

G-R-S centralized traffic control: type K2, class M, coded system. General Railway Signal Company, Rochester, N. Y., 1955. 166 p., I, 9 in.   OP-1

Determination of the maximal steady State flow of traffic through a railroad network. Alexander W. Boldyreff. Santa Monica, Calif., Rand Corp., 1955. 36 1., D, 11.4 in. (RM-1532).   OP-2

Freight car distribution and car handling in the United States. Eugene W. Coughlin. [Washington] Association of American Railroads, Car Service Division [1956]. 338 p., I, 9.4 in.   OP-3

Integral train systems, by John G. Kneiling. [Milwaukee, Kalmbach Pub. Co., 1969.] various pagings, I, 9.4 in.   OP-4

Let's operate a railroad; being a textbook on operational aspects of railroading and of the men who perform the fascinating job. With a measure of railroadiana inserted. L. E. Roxbury. Warwick, Va., High-Iron Publishers [1957]. 352 p., I, 9 in.
OP-5

Railway line clearances and car dimensions [including weight limitations of railroads in the United States, Canada, Mexico and Cuba]. New York, Railway Equipment and Publication Co. I, 11 in., annual.   OP-6

Railway operating rules. U. S. Army. [Washington] 1964. 167 p., I, 7.5 in.
OP-7

Soviet transport experience: its lessons for other countries. Holland Hunter. Washington, Brookings Institution, Transport Research Program [1968]. 194 p. (pf.– 13 p.), I, 9.4 in.   OP-8

Standard time in America; why and how it came about and the part taken by the railroads and William Frederick Allen. John S. Allen. New York, 1951. 20 p., I, 9 in.   OP-9

The effects of weather upon railroad operation, maintenance, and construction. William W. Hay. Ann Arbor, University Microfilms [1956]. Publication No. 18,148.   OP-10

OREGON

Laws of the State of Oregon administered by Public Utilities Commissioner. Salem, G. H. Flagg, Public Utilities Commissioner, 1950. 262 p., I, 9 in.   OR-1

The O&C lands. Basler.   sLA-1
O&C counties. U. of Oregon.   sLA-2
Ore. and Calif. [grants]. Senate.   sLA-3

PACIFIC

Pacific railways and nationalism in the Canadian-American Northwest, 1845-1873.
Leonard Irwin. New York, Greenwood Press, 1968 [c 1939]. 246 p. (pf.—12 p.),
24 p.   PAC-1

PANAMA

Rails across Panama; the story of the building of the Panama Railroad, 1849-1855
[by] Joseph L. Schott. Indianapolis, Bobbs-Merrill [1967]. 224 p., I, 8.7 in.
                                                                            PAN-1

Message from the President of the United States transmitting the annual report of
the board of directors of the Panama Railroad Company. Washington, GPO. 9.4 in.
                                                                            PAN-2

PASSENGERS

The railroad passenger deficit problem; report of the Special Committee on Cooperation with the ICC in the Study of the Railroad Passenger Deficit Problem. Nat-
tional Assoc. of R.R. and Utilities Commissioners. Washington, GPO. 9.4 in.
                                                                            PAS-1

Railroad passenger service costs and financial results. Stanley Berge. Evanston, Ill.,
Northwestern University School of Commerce [1956]. 80 p., I, 11 in.   PAS-2

Segregation in interstate railway coach travel; a field research project of the Race
Relations Dept., American Missionary Association, Board of Home Missions, Con-
gregational Christian Churches, Fisk University, Nashville, Tennessee. By Herman H.
Long. [Nashville, 1952.] 91 l., D, 11 in.   PAS-3

1966 thru 1972 steam passenger service directory. Empire State Railroad Museum.
Middletown, N. Y., Empire State R.R. Mus., 1972. Also; 1966—80 p.; 67-96 p.;
68—104 p.; 69, 70, 71—128 p.; 72—136 p. 8.5 in.   PAS-4

High-speed ground transportation; extension. Hearings on H. R. 16024 . . . June
12, 13, 1968. House, Int. & For. Comm. (Trans. & Aero.). 90C-2S. Washington,
GPO, 1968. 88 p. (pf.—3 p.), I, 9 in.   PAS-5

Passenger train discontinuance: 30-day notice. Hearing on S. 2711 . . . February
20, 1968. House, Int. & For. Comm. 90C-2S. Washington, GPO, 1968. 64 p. (pf.—
3 p.), 9.4 in.   PAS-6

Passenger train abandonment. Hearings, April 25,26, May 8, 1967. House, Int. &
For. Comm. (Trans. & Aero.). 90C-1S. Washington, GPO, 1967. 132 p. (pf.—3 p.),
9.4 in.   PAS-7

Railroad passenger train service. Hearings, July 8 and 9, 1968. House, Int. & For.
Comm. (Trans. & Aero.). 90C-1S. Washington, GPO, 1968. 198 p. (pf.—4 p.),
9.4 in.   PAS-8

The crisis in passenger train service. Hearings, Senate, Comm. Com. 90C-1S. Washington, GPO, 1965. 340 p. (pf.—5 p.), 9.4 in. PAS-9

Passenger train discontinuances. Hearing, August 3, 1966. Senate, Comm. Com. (Surface Trans.). 89C-2S. Washington, GPO, 1966. 65 p. (pf.—3 p.), 9.4 in. PAS-10

Passenger train service. Hearings, 1967-68. Senate, Comm. Com. (Surface Trans.). 90C-1S. Washington, GPO, 2 v., 352 p. (pf.—4 p.), I, 9.4 in. PAS-11

Study of essential railroad passenger service. Hearings on S. 3861 . . . July 24, 25, and 29, 1968. Senate, Comm. Com. (Surface Trans.). 90C-2S. Washington, GPO, 1968. 155 p. (pf.—4 p.), M (F), 9.4 in. PAS-12

Passenger train service . . . report (to accompany H. R. 17849). House, Int. & For. Comm. 91C-2S. [Washington] 1970. 9 in. (No. 1580). PAS-13

Passenger train discontinuances. Hearing, August 3, 1966. Senate, Commerce (Surface Trans.). 89C-2S. Washington, GPO, 1966. 65 p. (pf.—3 p.), 9.4 in. PAS-14

Passenger train service. Hearings, Ninety-first Congress, first session. House, Int. & For. Comm. (Trans. & Aero.). Washington, GPO, c 1970. 543 p. (pf.—8 p.), I, M, 9.4 in. PAS-15

Passenger train service legislation. Hearings . . . September 23, 24, and 25, 1969. Senate, Commerce Com. (Surface Trans.). 91C-1S. Washington, GPO, 1969 [i. e. 1970]. 316 p. (pf.—4 p.), 9.4 in. PAS-16

Rail passenger service act of 1970; report, together with individual views and minority views, to accompany S. 3706. Senate, Commerce Com. 91C-2S. Washington, GPO, 1970. 326 p., 9.4 in. PAS-17

Passenger train service. Supplemental hearings, Ninety-first Congress, second session, on H. R. 17849 . . . [and] S. 3706 . . . June 2, 3, and 4, 1970. House, Int. & For. Comm. (Trans. & Aero.). 91C-2S. Washington, GPO, 1970. 187 p. (pf.— 4 p.), 9.4 in. PAS-18

Failing railroads. Hearings, Ninety-first Congress, second session, on S. 4011. S. 4014, and S. 4016. Senate, Commerce. Washington, GPO, 1970 [i. e. 1971]—71. 2 v., 624 p. (pf.—4 p.), I, M, 9.4 in. PAS-19

Diner in the dinner. Hollister. sDI-1
Offical lists [ticket agents, etc.]. Nat. Ry. Pub. Co. sGU-4
Federal interest [pass. service]. Saunders & Co. sGO-4
Administration-Metroliner & Turbo-Train. Fed. R.R. Adm. sGO-1
Surface Transportation [scope ICC]. Senate. sICC-23
Train discontinuance. Senate. sICC-24
See also: Companies—Pullman Co.

PENNSYLVANIA

The railroads of Pennsylvania [by] Roger B. Saylor. [University Park, Bu. of Bus. Res., College of Bus. Admin., Pennsylvania State Univ., 1964.] 332 p. (pf.—4 p.), I, M, 11 in. (Industrial res. report No. 4). PE-1

A history of Perry County railroads, by Roy F. Chandler. New Bloomfield, Pa., 1970. 128 p., I, Fac, M, P, 11.4 in.   PE-2

Recommendations for a system of intercity rail passenger service in Pennsylvania as a part of the basic national rail transportation system. Pa. Dept. of Transportation. [Harrisburg] 1970. 1 v., 11 in.   PE-3

Trains of the Pennsylvania Dutch country: Pennsylvania, Reading, Western Maryland, Strasburg, Stewartstown, Maryland & Pennsylvania, Wanamaker Kempton & Southern, and others. By John D. Denney, Jr. [Columbia, Pa.] 1966. 60 p., I, M, 11 in.   PE-4

Trolleys of Berks County, Pennsylvania. Harry Foesig. Forty Fort, Pa., H. E. Cox, 1970. 124 p., I, M (IF), 11 in.   PE-5

Trolleys of lower Delaware Valley, Pennsylvania, by Paul Schieck and Harold E. Cox. Forty Fort, Pa., printed and sold by H. E. Cox [1970]. 85 p., I, M (PC), 11 in.   PE-6

Trolleys of the Pennsylvania Dutch country: Harrisburg, Hershey, Lebanon, Reading, Lancaster, York, Hanover and Gettysburg, by John D. Denney, Jr. [Columbia, Pa.] 1970. 56 p. (pf.—4 p.), I, Fac, M, 11 in.   PE-7

Susquehanna trolleys. Gene D. Gordon. [Sunbury, Pa., 1951.] [40] p., I, M, 8.3 in.   PE-8

Pennsylvania R.R., Penn-Central—see Companies
Facts and arguments [Pa. R.Rs.]. Arno Press.   sCOMP-4

PERIODICALS
(Note: not all of these listed are currently published)

All-time index to Trains Magazine, Railroad Magazine, Model Railroader and Railroad Model Craftsman; covers all issues of these four magazines through December 1969. New York, Wayner Publications, 1970. 186 p., 8½ x 11 in.   PER-1

Modern cities via transportation. v. 1—. May 1966—. [Pittsburgh] Eutter Publications. I, 13 in., bimonthly.   PER-2

The Railfan. [Toledo, National Railroad Association.] I, 11 in., annual.   PER-3

The Railroad yardmaster. Periodical. [Chicago.] I, P, 11 in., bimonthly.   PER-4

Railway progress. [Washington, etc.] I, P, 11.4 in., monthly.   PER-5

Safe railroader. June 1948—. [Chicago, National Safety Council.] I (PC), 6.3 in., bimonthly, irregular.   PER-6

Trainman news. Periodical. Cleveland [etc.]. I, 17.2 in., weekly.   PER-7

Transportation. V. 1—. Jan. 1946—. [Warehouse Point, Conn.] National Railway Historical Society, Connecticut Valley Chapter. I, M, 11.4 in., irregular.   PER-8

The Western traction quarterly. v. 1—. Spring 1964—. [Hollywood, Calif.] Pacific Bookwork. I, 11 in.   PER-9

Canadian Pacific staff bulletin. C.P.R.   sCAN-36
Electric Railroader. Elec. R.R. Assoc.   sEL-4
Interurbans Magazine.   sEL-5
Keeping Track. C.N.R.   sCAN-33

PHILADELPHIA

Early electric cars of Philadelphia, 1885-1911, by Harold E. Cox. Forty Fort, Pa.
[1969]. 135 p., I, 11 in.   PH-1

A history and analysis of labor-management relations in the Philadelphia transit
industry. Thomas Roberts. Ann Arbor, Mich., University Microfilms [1959].
                                                                     PH-2

Property atlas of the Main Line, Penna. From office records, private plans, and
actual surveys. Franklin Survey Co., Philadelphia, 1961. v., M (F), 24.8 in. PH-3

Surface cars of Philadelphia, 1911-1965, by Harold E. Cox. [Forty Fort, Pa.,
1965.] 95 p., I, 11 in.   PH-4

SEPACT III final report: Operation Reading; final report to the U. S. Department
of Transportation (DOT) on Mass Transportation Demonstration Project. S. E.
Pennsylvania Transportation Auth. [Philadelphia] 1971. 104 p., I, 11.4 in.
                                                                     PH-5

Southern New Jersey rapid transit system. Haddonfield-Kirkwood line; report.
Delaware Valley Port Authority. [Camden, N. J.] 1961. 67 p., M (F, C), D,
11.4 in.   PH-6

Southern New Jersey [mass transit]. Parsons [etc.].   sNJ-5

PICTORIAL

Focus: the railroad in transition [by] Robert S. Carper. South Brunswick [N. J.]
A. S. Barnes [1968]. 260 p., I (PC), M, 12.6 in.   PI-1

Golden rails, by Wm. W. Kratville. [Omaha, Neb., Kratville Publications, c 1965.]
314 p., I, M, P, 11.4 in.   PI-2

Great railroad photographs, U. S. A., by Lucius Beebe and Charles Clegg. Berkeley,
Calif., Howell-North Books, 1964. 243 p., I (PC), P, 12.6 in.   PI-3

Hear the train blow; a pictorial epic of America in the railroad age [by] Lucius
Beebe and Charles Clegg. With 10 original drawings by E. S. Hammack and 860
illus. New York, Grosset & Dunlap [1958, c 1952]. 407 p., I, P, 11.4 in.   PI-4

Night train. Comp. by Donald Duke. San Marino, Calif., Pacific Railway Journal,
1961. 127 p., I, 11.4 in.   PI-5

Pacific slope railroads, from 1854 to 1900. George B. Abdill. [1st ed.] Seattle,
Superior Pub. Co. [c 1959]. 182 p., I, 11 in.   PI-6

The railroad scene [by] William D. Middleton. San Marino, Calif., Golden West
Books [1969]. 144 p., I, 11.4 in.   PI-7

Railroads in the woods, by John T. Labbe and Vernon Goe. Berkeley, Calif., Howell-North, 1961. 269 p., I, 11.4 in. PI-8

Rails across the midlands [by] Richard J. Cook. San Marino, Calif., Golden West Books [1964]. 144 p., I, 11.4 in. PI-9

Rails through Dixie [by] John Krause with H. Reid. San Marino, Calif., Golden West Books [1965]. 176 p., I, 11.4 in. PI-10

Rails west. George B. Abdill. [1st ed.] Seattle, Superior Pub. Co. [1960]. 191 p., I, 11 in. PI-11

Steam, steel & limiteds. William W. Kratville. George Barth [and] Arthur D. Dubin, associate editors. [Omaha, Barnhart Press, c 1962.] 413 p., I, 11.4 in. PI-12

The trains we rode [by] Lucius Beebe and Charles Clegg. Berkeley, Calif., Howell-North Books, 1965-66. 2 v., I (PC), 11.4 in. PI-13

Western trains, by Richard Steinheimer and Donald Sims. Contributing photographers: James L. Ehernberger [and others. San Marino, Calif., distributed by Golden West Books, 1965.] 71 p., I, 8.7 x 9.8 in. PI-14

When beauty rode the rails; an album of railroad yesterdays [by] Lucius Beebe and Charles Clegg. [1st ed.] Garden City, N. Y., Doubleday [1962]. 222 p., I, 11.4 in. PI-15

PIGGYBACK

Piggyback [Pac. N.W.]. Bowser. sFT-9

PITTSBURGH

The economic position of railroad commuter service in the Pittsburgh district— its history, present and future. William. T. Schusler. Ann Arbor, Mich., University Microfilms [1959]. PIT-1

Transfer values of private metropolitian transit systems, a study of Pittsburgh railways, by Frank J. Wright. Pittsburgh, Duquesne Univ. Press [1964]. 36 p., 9 in. PIT-2

PLANNING

Electronics in business, a case study in planning: Port of New York Authority. A research report prepared for Controllership Foundation, Inc., by Herbert F. Klingman [research director]. New York, 1956. 121 p., I, 9 in. PL-1

A guide to sources of information pertinent to planning a transportation system for the Washington metropolitan area. Prepared for the Northwest Committee for Transportation Planning. 2d ed. David S. Sanders. Washington, Northwest Committee for Transportation Planning, 1961. 38 p. (pf.—3 p.), 11 in. PL-2

Transcontinental railway strategy, 1869-1893; a study of businessmen. Julius Grodinsky. Philadelphia, Univ. of Pennsylvania Press [1962]. 443 p. (pf.—21 p.), M, T, 9.8 in. PL-3

Transport investment and economic development; planning and investment for developing nations. Gary Fromm, ed. Washington, Brooking Institution, 1965. 314 p.   PL-4

Transportation demand. Lawson.   sFT-14

POETRY

Great poems from Railroad Magazine; a collection of rhymes, songs and ballads of railroading from past issues of Railroad Magazine, with cartoons by Joe Easley. New York, Wayner Publications, 1968. 129 p., 8.5 x 11 in.   PO-1

POLICE

The railroad police. Henry S. Dewhurst. Springfield, Ill., C. C. Thomas [1955]. 211 p., I, 9.4 in.   POL-1

Railway Association of Special Agents and Police of the United States and Canada. Proceedings of the annual convention. I, 5.9 in.   POL-2

Railway Association of Special Agents and Police of the United States and Canada. Official directory. 5.9 in.   POL-3

POLICY

Future of rail transport [U.S.]. Lemly.	sFUT-3
Kansas City and the R.Rs. Gluab.	sK-2
Metropolitian transportation policy [N.Y.]. Doig.	sNY(M)-5
Politics of R.R. consolidation. Latham.	sME-2
Policy formation in R.R. finance. O'Neil.	sF-16
Railroad consolidation [Trans. Act-1920]. Leonard.	sME-4
Transport and national goals. Haefele.	sGO-10
Western R.R. mergers. U. S. Dept. of Trans.	sME-11

PORTERS

Memories of a retired Pullman porter. Robert Emanuel Turner. [1st ed.] New York, Exposition Press [1954]. 191 p., I, 8.3 in.   POR-1

PROBLEMS

The dillemma of freight transport regulation; an overview. Ann F. Friedlaender. Washington, Brookings Institution, 1969. 216 p.   PR-1

To hell in a day coach; an exasperated look at American railroads. [1st ed.] Peter Lyon. Philadelphia, Lippincott, 1968 [c 1967]. 324 p. (pf.–7 p.), 8.7 in.   PR-2

The metropolitan transportation problem. Wilfred Owens. Washington, Brookings Institute, 1966. 266 p.   PR-3

The railroad question; a historical and practical treatise on railroads, and remedies for their abuses. William Larrabee. 3d ed. Freeport, N. Y., Books for Libraries Press [1971]. 488 p., Fac, P, 9 in.   PR-4

Problems of the railroads; Senate, Int. & For. Comm. (Surface Trans.). Washington, GPO, 1958. 27 p. (pf.–2 p.), 9.4 in.   PR-5

Railroad problems. Hearings on railroad problems with particular reference to abandonment of service, construction reserve, and competive and intrastate rates. House, Int. & For. Comm. 85C-2S. Washington, GPO, 1958. 490 p. (pf.–6 p.), D, T, 9.4 in.   PR-6

Problems of the railroads. Hearings . . . Senate, Int. & For. Comm (Surface Trans.). 85C-2S. Washington, GPO, 1958. 4 pts (2355 p., pf.–4 p.), I, M (PF), 9.4 in.
PR-7

Problems of the railroads. Boston College.   sCOMM-8

PRODUCTIVITY

Productivity, supervision, and morale among railroad workers, by Daniel Katz [and others]. Ann Arbor, Survey Research Center, Institute for Social Research, Univ. of Michigan [1951]. 61 p., 9 in. (No. 5).   PRO-1

Restriction of output by the railroad labor unions. Normal J. Wood. Ann Arbor, University Microfilms [1954]. Publication No. 10,278.   PRO-2

PUBLIC OPINION

National survey of public opinion for Association of American Railroads. Opinion Research Corp., Princeton. 11.8 in.   PU-1

PULLMAN (S)

George M. Pullman, 1831-1897. Harding.   sBIO-15
Mr. Pullman's elegant [cars]. Beebe.   sCO-226
Pullman [cars]. Wayner.   sCO-228
Descriptive list [cars]. Davies.   sCO-229
Pullman Co. [manual]. Old Line.   sCO-230
See also Companies.

RAILROADING

Inside railroading. 1st–ed. AAR, Washington, 1954–. I, 6.3 x 9 in.   R-1

Railroading around the world. S. Kip Farrington. New York, Coward-McCann [1955]. 230 p., I, 11.4 in.   R-2

Railroading the modern way. S. Kip Farrington. New York, Coward-McCann [1951]. 395 p. (pf.–17 p.), I, 8.7 in.   R-3

Profiles of American railroading. General Electric Company. 1st ed. [Schenectady, N. Y., 1965.] 48 p., I, P, 9.4 x 13 in.   R-4

RAILROADS

The American railroads [by] John Francis Rando and Robert Francis Rando. Delaware City, J. F. R. Pub. House [1970]. 63 p. (pf.–2 p.), I, 8.7 in.   RA-1

The American railroads. John C. Weaver. [Prepared with the cooperation of the American Geographical Society.] Garden City, N. Y., N. Doubleday [1958]. 64 p., I, 8.3 in.   RA-2

American railroads, their growth and development. AAR, Washington, 1951. 32 p., I, M (C), 9 in.   RA-3

American railroad journal. 1966—. San Marino, Calif., Golden West Books. I, 11 in., annual.   RA-4

The American railway industry. [New rev. ed.] C. J. Corliss. Cambridge, Mass., Bellman Pub. Co. [1957]. 32 p., I, 9 in.   RA-5

The American railway industry. C. J. Corliss. Cambridge, Mass., Bellman Pub. Co. [1955]. 26 p., I, 9 in.   RA-6

Brotherhood of Railroad Trainmen. Report. [n. p.] 9 in. annual.   RA-7

A chronology of American railroads, including mileage by states and by years. 1945—. AAR, Washington. 8.7-10.3 in.   RA-8

Far wheels; a railroad safari. Charles S. Small. London, Cleaver-Hume Press; New York, Simmons Boardman Pub. Corp. [1959]. 153 p., I, 9.4 in.   RA-9

Great railway journeys of the world, by K. Westcott Jones. Brattleboro, Vt., Stephen Greene Press, 1965. 192 p., I, 8.7 in.   RA-10

The handbook of American railroads. Robert G. Lewis. [2d ed.] New York, Simmons-Boardman Pub. Corp. [1956]. 251 p. (pf.—12 p.), I, M, 8.7 in.; also, 1st ed., 1951, 242 p.   RA-11

The illustrated true book of American railroads. Robert N. Webb. New York, Grosset & Dunlap [1957]. 154 p., I, 11.4 in.   RA-12

Railroad industry overview—1971. Hearings, Senate, Commerce. 92C-1S. Washington, GPO, 1971. 634 p. (pf.—4 p.), 9.4 in.   RA-13

The life and decline of the American railroad [by] John F. Stover. New York, Oxford University Press, 1970. 324 p. (pf.—11 p.), I, M, 8.7 in.   RA-14

More unusual railways. John R. Day. New York, Macmillan [c 1960]. 214 p., I, 9 in.   RA-15

Organization and operation of railroads in the continental United States; pamphlet. U. S. Army Transportation School, Fort Eustis, 1953. 78 p. (pf.—2 p.), I, M, 10.6 in.   RA-16

The railroads, the Nation's first big business; sources and readings. Compiled and edited by Alfred D. Chandler, Jr. New York, Harcourt, Brace & World [1965]. 213 p. (pf.—9 p.), M, 9 in.   RA-17

Railways in the years of pre-eminence, 1905-1919, by O. S. Nock. Illustrated by Clifford and Wendy Meadway. [1st American ed. New York] Macmillan [1971]. 194 p., I (C), 7.9 in.   RA-18

Railways the world over. Geoffery F. Allen. New York, Philosophical Library [1957]. 128 p., I, 11.4 in.   RA-19

Railroad album. The story of American railroads in words and pictures. John O'Connell. [Chicago] Popular Mechanics Press [1953, c 1954]. 156 p., I, 9 in.
RA-20

The railroads of America. Merle Armitage. With more than 400 photos. [Boston] Duell, Sloan and Pearce-Little, Brown [1952]. 319 p., I, 10.2 in.   RA-21

Railroads in the U. S. A.; report by a group of European experts. Technical Assistance Mission No. 14. Org. for European Economic Cooperation, Paris, 1952. 445 p., I, 9.4 in.   RA-22

Railroads in the U. S. A.; general study. Technical Assistance Mission No. 14. Report by a group of European experts. Org. for European Economic Cooperation, Paris, 1951. 64 p., 9.4 in.   RA-23

Railways, an Encyclopaedia Britannica article . . . [Washington, AAR, 1951.] 39 p., 11 in.   RA-24

Yearbook of railroad facts. 1965—. Washington, Bu. of Railway Economics, Assoiation of American Railroads. I, 5.9 in.   RA-25

Commuter railroads. Dorin.   sCOMM-1

RAILWAY POST OFFICE

Catalogue of Great Britain railway letter stamps, 1957-1970. David Potter. London, Railway Philatelic Group, 1969. [1] 20 p., I, 8.7 in.   RAP-1

The mainliner program or the minipiggi train as a mail carrier, by F. S. Macomber. [Chicago, A. T. Kearney, 1968.] 68 p., I, M, 8.7 x 11 in.   RAP-2

Mail by rail; the story of the Postal Transportation Service [by] Bryant Alden Long with William Jefferson Dennis. New York, Simmons-Boardman Pub. Corp. [1951]. 414 p. (pf.—12 p.), I, P, 9 in.   RAP-3

Potential savings available in manpower costs of railway post offices; report to Congress [on the] Post Office Department by the Comptroller General. General Accounting Office [Washington] 1967. 3 l., 26 p., 10.6 in.   RAP-4

Report of the national president. National Postal Transport Association. [n. p.] 9 in.   RAP-5

Review of determinations of railway post office requirements, contracting practices, and other activities relating to transportation of mail by railroad companies: Post Office Department; report to Congress by the Comptroller General. [Washington] GAO, 1963. 53 p., 10.6 in.   RAP-6

Curtailment of certain railway post offices. Hearing before an ad hoc subcommittee, June 18, 1965. Senate, P. O. & Civil Ser. 89C-1S. Washington, GPO, 1965. 96 p. (pf.—3 p.), M, 9.4 in.   RAP-7

Repeal of the "round-trip" provisions of the Railway mail pay act of 1916; reports of the comprehensive study by the General Accounting Office, Post Office Department, General Services Administration, and correspondence with Interstate Commerce Commission. Senate, Post Off. & Civ. Service. Washington, GPO, 1950. 131 p. (pf.—3 p.), 8 in.   RAP-8

RAPID TRANSIT—see TRANSIT

RATES

Cost standards and rate discrimination. Ford K. Edwards. Presented before the Fifth Institute of Industrial Transportation and Traffic Management, American Univ., Washington, D. C. [Washington, Bituminous Coal Institute, 1953.] 17, 6 l., 11.4 in.   RAT-1

Directory of class rail freight rates by the publisher of Leonard's guide. New York, G. R. Leonard.   RAT-2

Essays on "traditional differentials" in railway rate-making; should they and can they by maintained under rivalry from contract and private transportaion? New York, Simmons-Boardman Pub. Corp. [c 1956]. 36 p., 12.2 in.   RAT-3

Techniques of transport pricing; explores theories of pricing, especially for low-income countries (vol. 1), applies techniques to problems in Columbia (vol. 2). John R. Meyer, ed. Washington, Brookings Institution, 1971. Vol 1, 343 p.: Vol. 2, 228 p.   RAT-4

The development of the transcontinental freight rate structure. Clarence H. Gillett. Chicago [University of Chicago Library, Dept. of Photographic Reproduction] 1955. Microfilm 4452 HE.   RAT-5

The economics of loyalty-incentive rates in the railroad industry of the United States. Robert F. Lundy. [Pullman] Washington State Univ. Press, 1963. 144 p., 9.4 in.   RAT-6

Factors affecting freight rates on agricultural commodities: the railroad passenger deficit [prepared principally by Donald C. Leavens and Robert G. Rhodes]. U. S. Production & Marketing Adm. Washington, 1951. 79 p. (pf.—4 l.), 11 in.   RAT-7

Chief factors underlying general changes in rail freight rates, with special reference to farm products, 1910-51 [by Ezeckiel Limmer, transportation economist]. Bu. of Agric. Econ. Washington, 1951. 58 p., I, 10.2 in.   RAT-8

Revenue-cost relationships in railroad pricing: a study of 30 selected freight commodity classes. William H. Dodge. Ann Arbor, University Microfilms [1958].
                                                                          RAT-9

Value of service in rate-making. ICC—Bu. TE&S. [Washington] 1959. 365 p. (pf.—7 p.), T, 10.6 in. (No. 5912).   RAT-10

General rail and rail-water freight rate changes made since October, 1914. ICC, Bu. of Traf. [Washington] 1948—. 10.6 in.   RAT-11

The interpretation of freight tariffs. Edward A. Starr. Fort Worth, Tex., Transportation Press [1961]. 189 p., I, 9.4 in.   RAT-12

Railroad freight rate indexes for farm products, 1957-63 [by Helen V. Smith. Washington] U. S. Dept. of Agriculture, Marketing Economics Division, Economic Research Service [1965]. 2, 21 [1], M, 10.2 in. (No.—358).   RAT-13

Railroad freight tariffs, by Charles S. Baxter assisted by Gilmer B. Randolph. Serial 6354A. [Ed. 1] Scranton, International Correspondence Schools, c 1960–. 7.5 in.
RAT-14

Reasonable freight rates: tests, standards, and practices explained and clarified. Glenn L. Shinn. Washington, Traffic Service Corp. [1952]. 195 p., 9.4 in. RAT-15

Rules of railroad freight classification. Gilmer B. Randolph. Serial 6353-1. [Ed. 2] Scranton, International Correspondence Schools, c 1962. 75 p., I, 7.5 in.; also Ed. 1, 1959, 73 p.   RAT-16

Interagency rate adjustments, rail and motor. Alexis P. Bukovsky. ICC, Bu. of Trans. Econ. & Stat. Washington, 1956. 270 p. (pf.–3 p.), D, T, 10.6 in. (Statement 567).   RAT-17

Indexes of average comparative intrastate freight rates, railroad carload traffic, 1950. ICC, Bu. of Trans. Econ. & Stat. Washington, 1952. 7 p., 10.6 in. (No. 5237).   RAT-18

Indexes of average freight rates on railroad carload traffic. 1947-50–. ICC, Bu. of Trans. Econ. & Stat. Washington. T, 10.6 in.((No. 5156, 535).   RAT-19

Making of railroad freight rates. [Prepared especially for home study] by G. Lloyd Wilson. Serial 5406-3. [Ed. 3] Scranton, International Correspondence Schools [1965]. 36 p., I, 7.5 in.   RAT-20

Methods used in computing rail freight-rate indexes for farm products. [By Robert B. Reese, agricultural economist.] U. S. Bu. of Agric. Econ. Washington, 1953. 45 p., 10.6 in.   RAT-21

Port differential rates, history of their inception and development since 1857. George H. Weiss. [Chicago] Journal of Commerce Pub. Co. [1956] c 1936. 64 l., 11.8 in.   RAT-22

Practice and procedure before rate-making associations, by G. E. Lowe. [2d ed., completely rev. and reset. Washington] Traffic Service Corp., 1965. 62 p. (pf.– 8 p.), M, 9 in.; also, 3rd ed., 1967.   RAT-23

Rail-water rate adjustments. Alexis P. Bukovsky. ICC, Bu. of Trans. Econ. & Stat. Washington, 1954. 195 p. (pf.–3 p.), M, T, 10.6 in. (Statement 5427).   RAT-24

Rail and water routes and rates, prepared especially for home study by C. E. Johnson. [Ed. 3] Scranton, International Correspondence Schools [1965]. 64, 3 p., F, 7.5 in.; also, 2 ed, 1959, 56 p.   RAT-25

The regulation of rail-motor rate competition. E. W. Williams. New York, Harper [1958]. 247 p., 8.7 in.   RAT-26

War materials reparation cases. No. 29572. United States of America v. Ahnapee & Western Railway Company et. al. ICC, Washington, GPO, 1955. 157 p., 9.4 in.
RAT-27

Comparison of average rates charged on intraterritorial carload freight. Harold B. Horton. ICC, Washington, 1950. 61 p. (pf.–2 p.), 10.6 in. (No. 5036).   RAT-28

Railroad rates on Alaska bound freight. Hearing on S. 1723, a bill to establish equitable railroad freight rates. Senate, Commerce Com. (Surface Trans.). 87C-2S. April 17, 1962. Washington, GPO, 1962. 46 p. (pf.–3 p.), 9.4 in.   RAT-29

A survey of the theory and regulatory aspects of freight rate discrimination with special reference to Montana. Henry K. Shearer. Missoula, Bu. of Bus. and Econ. Re., Montana State Univ., 1959. 88 p. (pf.–7 p.), D, T, 9 in.   RAT-30

Freight rates in truck [i. e. trunk] line, New England and central territories, by Gilmer B. Randolph and John Douglas Clark. Serial 6357. [Ed. 1] Scranton, International Correspondence Schools, 1964. 60, 2 p., P, 9 in.   RAT-31

Railroad shipments and rates into the Pacific Northwest [by] Roy J. Sampson. Eugene, Ore., Bu. of Bus. Res., 1963. 46 p. (pf.–8 p.), I, M, 9 in.; also, 1961, 64 p.   RAT-32

Southwestern Freight Bureau territory rates, by Gilmer B. Randolph and Carl M. Guelzo. Serial 6361. [Ed. 1] Scranton, International Correspondence Schools, c 1960. 53 p., I, 7.5 in.   RAT-33

Freight rates in Western Trunk Line territory. Gilmer B. Randolph. Serial 6362. [Ed. 1] Scranton, International Correspondence Schools, c 1960. 64 p., I, 7.5 in.   RAT-34

Amendment to the ICC Act. Senate.   sICC-14
Bituminous coal rates. Campbell.   sEC-1
Railroad monopoly and rate regulation. McFall.   sCOMP-8

REGULATION

Tedrow's regulation of transportation. Tedrow.   sICC-10

REORGANIZATION

Railroad reorganization. Stuart Daggett. New York, A. M. Kelley, 1967. 404 p. (pf.–10 p.), 8.7 in.   RE-1

RESEARCH

Railroad materials and facilities research; a symposium presented at the fourth Pacific area national meeting, AST&M, Los Angeles, Calif., October 5, 1962. [Sponsored by the West Coast Technical Program Comm.] Philadelphia, AST&M [1964, c 1962]. 62 p. (pf.–5 p.), I, D, 9 in. (No. 354).   RES-1

Use of Cybernetics on the Railways; Second International Symposium, Montreal, October 1-6, 1967. Proceedings edited by the International Union of Railways and Canadian National Railways. [Montreal, 1967.] 276 p., I, PL (PC), P, 9.8 in.   RES-2

Report. AAR, Chicago. I, 11 in., annual.   RES-3

RETIREMENT

Railroad retirement and unemployment insurance act, as amended. U. S., GPO. Washington, GPO. 9.4 in.   RET-1

Questions and answers on the Railroad retirement act. Chicago [etc.] R.R. Ret. Bd. 5.9-7.1 in. RET-2

Actuarial valuation of the assets and liabilities under the Railroad retirement acts. R.R. Retirement Bd., Chicago. 10.6 in. RET-3

Field operating manual. R.R. Retirement Bd. [Chicago, 1955–.] pts. (loose-leaf), 11.8 in. RET-4

Legal opinions; rulings in the administration of the Railroad retirement act and the Railroad unemployment insurance act, 1961. Railroad Retirement Board. [Washington, GPO, 1964.] iii, 110 p., 9.4 in.; also, 1960, 119 p. RET-5

Problem areas in implementing amendatory legislation affecting railroad retirement annuties; report to Congress [on the] Railroad Retirement Board by Comptroller · General. General Accounting Office. [Washington, 1968.] 33 p., 10.6 in. RET-6

RRB-SSA financial interchange; summary and documentation. 1st–determination; June 30, 1952–R.R. Retirement Bd. [Washington]. 10.6 in., annual. RET-7

Railroad retirement reporter, including unemployment insurance. Commerce Clearing House. Chicago, c 1956–. 10.2 in. RET-8

The railroad retirement and unemployment insurance systems, prepared for the 1959-60 informational conferences. R.R. Ret. Bd. [Washington] .1959. 196 p. (pf.–14 p.), D, T, 9 in. RET-9

Twenty-five years of railroad social insurance, 1935-1960. R.R. Ret. Bd. [Chicago, 1960.] [28] p., I, 5.9 x 8.3 in. RET-10

Government Reports

Railroad retirement annuity increase–1971. Hearing on S. 1304, 1473, and H. R. 6444 . . . May 13, 1971. Senate, Labor & Pub. Welfare (R.R. Ret.). 92C-1S. Washington, GPO, 1971. 108 p. (pf.–4 p.), 9.4 in. RET-11

Railroad retirement benefit increase–1971. Hearing . . . March 30, 1971. House, Int. & For. Comm. (Trans. & Aero.). 92C-1S. Washington, GPO, 1971. 91 p. (pf.–3 p.), 9.4 in. RET-12

Railroad retirement amendments of 1970. Hearing on H. R. 15733 . . . April 16, 1970. Senate, Labor & Pub. Welfare (R.R. Ret.). 91C-2S. Washington, GPO, 1970. 78 p. (pf.–4 p.), 9.4 in. RET-13

Railroad retirement 15 percent benefit increase. Hearings on H. R. 15733, February 24 and 25, 1970. House, Int. & For. Comm. (Trans. & Aero.). 91C-2S. Washington, GPO, 1970. 60 p. (pf.–3 p.), 9.4 in. RET-14

Amending the Railroad retirement act of 1937 and the Railroad retirement tax act; report, together with supplemental and minority views, to accompany H. R. 13300. Senate, Labor & Pub. Welfare. 91C-2S. [Washington, GPO, 1970.] 21 p., 9.4 in. RET-15

Railroad retirement supplemental annuities, 1969. Hearings on H. R. 13300 . . . [and] S. 988 . . . October 7 and 30, 1969. Senate, Labor & Pub. Welfare (R.R. Ret.). 91C-1S. Washington, GPO, 1969. 259 p. (pf.–4 p.), 9.4 in. RET-16

Railroad retirement supplemental annuities, 1969. Hearing, July 10, 1969. House, Int. & For. Comm. 91C-1S. Washington, GPO, 1969. 78 p. (pf.–4 p.), 9.4 in.

RET-17

Railroad retirement act and Railroad unemployment insurance act amendments of 1968. Hearings on S. 2839. January 24, 1968. Senate, Labor & Pub. Welfare (R.R. Ret.). 90C-2S. Washington, GPO, 1968. 66 p. (pf.–3 p.), 9.4 in.

RET-18

Amending the Railroad retirement act of 1937, and the Railroad unemployment insurance act. Hearing, January 16, 1968. House, Int. & For. Comm. 90C-1S. Washington, GPO, 1968. 39 p. (pf.–3 p.), 9.4 in.

RET-19

Widows' pensions under railroad retirement. Hearing on S. 2838 . . . May 1, 1968. Senate, Labor & Pub. Welfare (R.R. Ret.). 90C-2S. Washington, GPO, 1968. 42 p. (pf.–3 p.), I, 9.4 in.

RET-20

Railroad retirement benefits. Hearing on S. 3777, September 27, 1966. Senate, Labor & Pub. Welfare (R.R. Ret.). 89C-2S. Washington, GPO, 1966. 42 p. (pf.– 3 p.), 9.4 in.

RET-21

Technical amendments to railroad retirement, tax, and unemployment insurance acts, and providing benefits for students. Hearing . . . April 21, 1966. House, Int. & For. Comm. (Comm. & Fin.). 89C-2S. Washington, GPO, 1966. 53 p. (pf.–3 p.), 9.4 in.

RET-22

Railroad retirement act amendments: spouse benefits, wage base, tax rates. Hearing on H. R. 10874 . . . September 8, 1965. House, Int. & For. Comm. 89C-1S. Washington, GPO, 1965. 52 p. (pf.–3 p.), 9.4 in.

RET-23

RIGHT-OF-WAY

Progress report of joint investigation of the stability of roadbeds and embankments. Univ. of Illinois, Eng. Exp. Station. [Urbana] 1946–. I, D, 9 in.

RI-1

Standard plans. U. S. Army.

sMIL-4

ROBBERIES

Great train robberies of the West. Eugene B. Block. New York, Coward-McCann [1959]. 317 p., 8.7 in.

RO-1

ROCHESTER

Rochester Transit work stoppage. Final report to the Industrial Commissioner, State of New York. N. Y. Industrial Comm. [Albany, 1952.] 83 p. (pf.–6 p.), I, 11 in.

ROC-1

RULES

Economics of New York State full-crew laws. Jules Backman. [New York] N. Y. State Assoc. of Railroads, 1964. 52 p., 10.6 in.

RU-1

Manpower utilization in the railroad industry: an analysis of working rules and practices. Morris A. Horowitz. Boston, Bu. of Bus. and Econ. Res., Northeastern Univ., 1960. 68 p. (pf.–8 p.), D, T, 9 in.

RU-2

Railroad work rules dispute. Hearings on the administration of Public law 88-108. Senate, Comm. Com. 89C-1S. Washington, GPO, 1966. 1,002 p. (pf.–5 p.), I, M, 9.4 in.　　　　　　　　　　　　　　　　　　　　　　　　　　　RU-3

Railroad work rules dispute. Hearings on H. J. Res. 565, a joint resolution to provide for the settlement of the labor dispute between certain carriers by railroad and certain of their employees. Senate, Commerce Comm. 88C-1S. Washington, GPO, 1963. 1,026 p., I, 9.4 in.　　　　　　　　　　　　　　　RU-4

Railroad work rules dispute. Hearings on S. J. Res. 102, joint resolution to provide for settlement of the labor dispute between certain carriers by railroad and certain of their employees. Senate, Commerce Comm. 88C-1S. Washington, GPO, 1963. 740 p. (pf.–6 p.), T, 9.4 in.　　　　　　　　　　　　　　　　RU-5

SAFETY

Annual green book; report on the railroad employees' national safety award class I railroads. National Safety Council, Chicago. I, 11 in.　　　　　　　S-1

Federal standards for railroad safety. Hearings on H. R. 16980. House, Int. & For. Comm. 90C-2S. Washington, GPO, 1968. 427 p. (pf.–5 p.), I, 9 in.　　　S-2

Highway-railway grade crossing safety program; report. Joint action group on Grade Crossing Safety. Washington, U. S. Dept. of Transportation, 1969. 40 p. (pf.–2 p.), I, 10.6 in.　　　　　　　　　　　　　　　　　　　　　　S-3

Factors influencing safety at highway-rail grade crossings [by] David W. Schoppert and Dan W. Hoyt. [Washington] Highway Research Board, National Research Council, 1968. 113 p., I, 11 in. (Report 50).　　　　　　　　　　　S-4

Interstate Commerce Commission operations (railroad safety); twenty-fifth report by the Committee on Government Operations. House, 89C-2S. Washington, GPO, 1966. 22 p. (pf.–5 p.), 9.4 in. (No. 1452).　　　　　　　　　　　　S-5

Interstate Commerce Commission operations (railroad safety). Hearing before a subcommittee, House, Gov't. Ops. Com. 88C-2S. September 15, 1964. Washington, GPO, 1965. 251 p. (pf.–4 p.), I, M, 9.4 in.　　　　　　　　　　　S-6

Safety regulation of railroad track motorcars. Hearing on S. 1729, a bill to amend the Interstate Commerce Act so as to provide for the protection of railroad employees by regulating the use of track motorcars. Senate, Comm. Com. (Surface Trans.). 89C-2S. May 26, 1958. Washington, GPO, 1958. 119 p. (pf.–3 p.), I, 9.4 in.　　　　　　　　　　　　　　　　　　　　　　　　　　S-7

Railroad safety. Hearings on S. 539, a bill to authorize the ICC to make mandatory the installation of certain railroad communication systems; and S. 1401, a bill to authorize the ICC to require carriers engaged in interstate commerce by railroad to install power brakes, April 14 and 15, 1953. Senate, Int. & For. Comm. 83C-1S. Washington, GPO, 1953. 2 pts., 188 p. (pf.–4 p.), I, 9.4 in.　　　　S-8

Report. Submitted to the Secretary of Transportation, June 30, 1969. U. S. Task Force on R.R. Safety. Washington, 1969. 15 p., 10.6 in.　　　　　　S-9

Report, submitted by the Legislative Research Council, relative to ski lift and tramway safety. Massachusetts Legis. Res. Council. [Boston] 1963. 74 p., 9 in. (Senate No. 623).　　　　　　　　　　　　　　　　　　　　　　　　　　S-10

Standards of the National Board of Fire Underwriters for fire protection and prevention in transit operations as recommended by the National Fire Protection Association. New York, 1952. 30 p., 7.5 in. (No. 83). S-11

Surface transportation (safety legislation). Hearings on bills to provide for greater safety in surface transportation. House, Int. & For. Comm. 85C-1S. Washington, GPO, 1957. 241 p. (pf.—5 p.), I, 9.4 in. S-12

United States safety appliances for all classes of cars and locomotives. [Rev. to Jan. 1, 1950.] 16th ed. Richmond, Gibson, Pribble; Garrett & Massie, printers and sales agents, 1950. 124 p., I, 4 x 7.5 in. S-13

Introduction of [loco safety truck]. White. sLG-7
A study [Minn. crossings]. St. Martin. sCR-3

SAINT LOUIS

Saint Louis cable railways. Katz. sC-11

SAN FRANCISCO

BART at mid-point; San Francisco's bold new rapid-transit project, by Harre W. Demoro. [Los Angeles, Interurbans, 1968.] 117 p. (31), I, M, PL, P, 11 in.
SA-1

San Francisco's golden era; a picture story of San Francisco before the fire, by Lucius Beebe and Charles Clegg. Berkeley, Calif., Howell-North, 1960. 255 p., I, 11.4 in. SA-2

Urban transportation in the San Francisco Bay area. Richard M. Zettel. Berkeley, Calif., Inst. of Gov't. Studies, Univ. of California, 1963. 51 p. (pf.--3 p.), M (C), 9.4 in. SA-3

Feasibility report on use of Richmond-San Rafael Bridge for rapid transit. Calif., Div. of Bay-Toll Crossings. [Sacramento] 1965. 37 l., I, PL, 11 in. SA-4

The composite report: Bay area rapid transit. May, 1962. Reports describing the engineering, financial and economic phases of a rapid transit plan for Alameda, Contra Costa and San Francisco Counties by Parsons Brinckerhoff-Tudor-Bechtel [and others. New York, 1962.] 88 p., I (PC), M (PC), 9 x 13 in. SA-5

Regional rapid transit; a report to the San Francisco Bay Area Rapid Transit Commission, 1953-1955. Parsons, Brinckerhoff, Quade & Douglas. New York [1956]. 106 p. (pf.—8 p.), I, M (PC), 17.6 x 22.8 in. SA-6

Report on organizational and financial aspects of a proposed rapid transit system for the San Francisco Bay area [by J. Knight Allen and Morgan Sibbett]. Stanford Research Institute, San Francisco, Bay Area Rapid Transit Commission [1956]. 75 p. (pf.—10 p.), M, T, 11 in. SA-7

Report. Interim Committee on San Francisco Bay Area Metropolitian Rapid Transit Problems. California Senate. [Sacramento] 1953. I, 11 in. SA-8

Preliminary report. San Francisco Bay Area Rapid Transit Commission. [San Francisco, 1953.] 54 p., M (F—PC), D, 11 in. SA-9

The big heart. Van.	sC-4
San Francisco grip. Perine.	sC-12
Cable cars of S. F. Palmer.	sC-7
System [cable Rys.]. Pac. Cable Ry.	sC-13

SANITATION

Environmental pollution; discharge of raw human wastes from railroad trains. Thirty-second report, House, Gov't. Ops. 91C-2S. Washington, GPO, 1970. 30 p. (pf.—5 p.), 9.4 in. (91-1581). **SAN-1**

Handbook on sanitation of dining cars in operation; standards of sanitation for operation and maintenance of food and drink service facilities on railroad passenger cars. 1959 revision. U. S. Public Health Service, Washington [1959]. 11 p., I, 9.4 in. (No. 83); also, 1951, 14 p. **SAN-2**

Handbook on sanitation of railroad servicing areas; design and operation of sanitation facilities for servicing railroad passenger cars. Public Health Service [Washington, 1951]. 28 p. (pf.—6 p.), I, 9.4 in. (No. 66). **SAN-3**

Handbook on sanitation of railroad passenger cars. Washington, Public Health Service. G.P.O. I, 9.4 in. **SAN-4**

Certain health problems. Report to the Governor and the General Assembly [on means of protecting the public from wastes discharged from common carriers of passengers]. Advisory Legislative Council. Richmond, Commonwealth of Virginia Division of Purchase and Print., 1951. 8 p., 10.6 in. (Doc. 4). **SAN-5**

SEATTLE

| He built Seattle [Burke]. Nesbit. | sBIO-1 |
| Street R.R. in Seattle. Blanchard. | sSTR-9 |

SERVICE

Essays on inherent advantages of railway service. [Editor: James G. Lyne.] New York, Simmons-Boardman [1954]. 44 p. (pf.—9 p.), D, 12.2 in. **SE-1**

Emergency rail services legislation. Hearings, House, Int. & For. Comm. 91C-2S. Washington, GPO, 1970. 2 v. (1,212 p.), 9.4 in. **SE-2**

Review of the Emergency rail services act of 1970. Hearings . . . March 9, 10, and 11, 1971. House, Int. & For. Comm. 92C-1S. Washington, GPO, 1971. 120 p. (pf.—4 p.), 9 in. **SE-3**

Special R.R. freight services. Wilson. **sFT-12**

SHOPS

Survey of railway car repair shops, prepared and compiled by the Research Dept., Simmons-Boardman Publishing Corp., New York, c 1954. 27 p., 11 in. **SH-1**

SHORT LINES

American Short Line Railroad Association; weekly information bulletin. Washington. 11.4 in. **SHO-1**

Buffalo & Susquehanna. Paul Pietrak. Arcade, N. Y., The Baggage Car, 1972. 138
p., 11 in.   SHO-2

Coudersport & Port Allegany—New York & Pennsylvania. Paul Pietrak. These two
short line railroads served the lumber and tannery industry in Potter County, Pennsylvania, for many years. Arcade, N. Y., The Baggage Car. 180 p., I, stories, roster,
PL.   SHO-3

Mixed train daily; a book of short-line railroads, by Lucius Beebe. With photos. by
C. M. Clegg, Jr., and the author, and six original oil paintings by Howard Fogg.
[4th ed.] Berkeley, Calif., Howell-North, 1961 [c 1947]. 367 p. (pf.—13 p.), I
(6C), M, 11.4 in.   SHO-4

Railroads down the valleys; some short lines of the Oregon country. Randall V.
Mills. Palo Alto, Calif., Pacific Books [1960]. 151 p. (pf.—9 p.), I, M, 9.8 in.
                                                                              SHO-5

Wellsville, Addison & Galeton—Sole Leather Line. Edward A. Lewis. The history of
the railroad is told briefly, followed by many photos depicting the railroads operations. Arcade, N. Y., The Baggage Car. 40 p., 11 in.   SHO-6

Arcade & Attica. Lewis.   sCO-11
Crystal River pictorial. McCoy.   sCOL-7
Ghost R.Rs. of Indiana. Sulzer.   sIA-2
Nevada Northern. Allen.   sCO-185
Over the hills to Woodstock. Mead.   sCO-310
Pines across the mountain [McCloud R.]. Hanft.   sCO-166
Road to Paradise [S]. Moedinger.   sCO-266-7
A short haul [N.R.R.]. Henwood.   sCO-181
Short line to paradise [Y.V.]. Johnston.   sCO-311
Sierra Ry. Deane.   sCO-250
The Skunk R.R. Crump.   sCO-46
36 miles of trouble [W.R.]. Morse.   sCO-306

SIGNALS

Elements of railway signaling. General Railway Signal Co. Rochester, N. Y., 1954.
I, 7.5 in. (HB50).   SI-1

G-R-S automatic train control, intermittent inductive auto-manual system: operation, maintenance, adjustment. General Railway Signal Co. Rochester, N. Y.,
1954. I, 9 in. (HB6, 3d ed.).   SI-2

G-R-S model 9 switch machine: operation, installation, maintenance. General Railway Signal Co. Rochester, N. Y., 1949. 52 p., I, D, 7.1 in. (HB32).   SI-3

Model 10 electric switch lock: operation, installation, maintenance. General Railway Signal Co. Rochester, N. Y., 1953. 61 p., I, 7.1 in. (HB31).   SI-4

Railway operating and signaling techniques in Europe, Japan and the United
States of America; report. Expert Working Group [Asia & Far East]. [New York]
United Nations, 1954. 109 p. (pf.—4 p.), I, M, 11 in.   SI-5

Rules, standards, and instructions for installation, inspection, maintenance and
repair of automatic block signal systems, etc. Effective Oct. 1, 1950. ICC, Bu. of
Safety. Washington, GPO, 1950. 48 p., 6.7 in.   SI-6

GRS carrier control. GRS Co.   sCO-124
GRS-CTC. GRS Co.   sOP-1
R.R. safety. Senate.   sS-8

SNOW REMOVAL

Snowplow: clearing mountain rails, by Gerald M. Best. Berkeley, Calif., Howell-North Books, 1966. 119 p., I, M, 11.4 in.   SN-1

SOCIAL IMPACT

The great railroad conspiracy; the social history of a railroad war. Charles Hirschfeld. [East Lansing] Michigan State College Press, 1953. 128 p. (pf.–6 p.), M, 9 in.   SO-1

A social-economic study. Millican.   sL-4

SOUTH

Civil War railroads. George B. Abdill. [1st ed.] Seattle, Superior Pub. Co. [1961]. 192 p., I, 8.7 x 11 in.   SOU-1

The railroads of the South, 1865-1900; a study in finance and control. John F. Stover. Chapel Hill, Univ. of North Carolina Press [1955]. 310 p. (pf.–18 p.), M, 9.4 in.   SOU-2

Extra south, by H. Reid. [Susquehanna, Pa., Starrucca Valley Publications, 1964.] 143 p., I, P, 11.4 in.   SOU-3

SOUTH DAKOTA

Railroads of the Black Hills. Mildred Fielder. [1st ed.] Seattle, Superior Pub. Co. [1964]. 175 [1], p., I, 11 in.   SOU(D)-1

A review of considerations involved in freight rates and their application to South Dakota; staff memorandum. Legislative Research Council. Pierre, 1968. 55 p., M, 11 in.   SOU(D)-2

South Dakota interstate rail shipments: a comparison with Nebraska and North Dakota. C. S. Van Doren. Vermillion, Bus. Res. Bu. Sch. of Bus., State Univ. of South Dakota [1959]. 61 p., I, 9 in.   SOU(D)-3

Transportation rates, products transported and trade barriers important to South Dakota, 1949. L. A. Poth. Vermillion, Bus. Res. Bu., Univ. of South Dakota, 1950. 110 p., M, D, 9 in.   SOU(D)-4

SOUTHWEST

Then came the railroads; the century from steam to Diesel in the Southwest. Ira G. Clark. [1st ed.] Norman, University of Oklahoma Press [1958]. 336 p. (pf.–15 p.), I, P, M, 9.4 in.   SOU(W)-1

Railroads to the Rio. James Allhands. Salado, Tex., Anson Jones Press, 1960. 213 p., I, 9.8 in.   SOU(W)-2

Uriah Lott. Allhands.   sBIO-10
The Morleys. Cleaveland.   sBIO-12

SPOKANE

Indland Empire. Fahey.   sBIO-2

STATIONS (see also Terminals)

Down at the depot; American railroad stations from 1831 to 1920 [by] Edwin P.
Alexander. [1st ed.] New York, C. N. Potter; distributed by Crown Publishers
[1970]. 320 p., I, PL, 12.6 in.   ST-1

Famous railroad stations of the world, by Adele Gutman Nathan with W. C. Baker.
Illustrated by Graham Bernbach. New York, Random House [1953]. 100 p., I,
10.2 in.   ST-2

Nebraska C. B. & Q. depots, by William F. Rapp. Crete, Neb., J-B Pub. Co. [1970].
46 p., I, PL, 11 in.   ST-3

New Haven station improvement costs. Tone.   sCO-195
Reestablishing the link [commuter]. Sloan.   sCOMM

STATISTICS

Statistical analysis of the New York-Washington, D. C., rail passenger service, 1970.
U. S. Off. High-Speed Ground Trans. [Washington] 1971. 34 p., I, 10.6 in.
                                                                     STA-1

Railway statistical manual; a collection of information and reference material
relating to the source, preparation, and use of railroad statistics. AAR, Acct. Div.
Washington, 1953. 1 v. (various pagings), 9.4 in.   STA-2

Ratios of empty to loaded freight car-miles by type of car and performance factors: class I line-haul railroads, 1968. [Prepared by the Section of Cost Finding.]
ICC, Bu. Accts. Washington, 1969. 31 p., forms, 10.6 in. (No.-6-69). STA-3

Selected financial and operating statistics from annual reports of freight forwarders.
1st-12th; 1942-53. ICC, Bu. Tran. Econ. & Stat., Washington. 12 v., 8.3 x 12.6 in.,
annual.   STA-4

Man-hours expended per car, railroad freight cars. 1939/48–. Bu. of Labor Stat.
[Washington, GPO.] D, 9.8 in.   STA-5

Intercity passenger miles. 1949–. ICC, Bu. of Trans. Econ. & Stat. Washington. T,
10.6 in.   STA-6

Preliminary abstract of railway statistics (steam railways, Railway Express Agency,
Inc., and the Pullman Company), 1910/11-1953. ICC, Bu. of Trans. Econ. Washington, GPO. 44 v. in 15, T, 11 x 6, 12.6 x 17.3 in., annual.   STA-7

Railroad transportation, a statistical record. 1911-1949–. Bu. of Ry. Economics,
Washington. T, 8.7 x 11 in.   STA-8

Railway operating statistics; rules, instructions, interpretations and definitions used in connection with the reporting of railway operating statistics. ICC, Bu. of Trans. Econ. & Stat. Washington, 1953. 28 p., 10.6 in. (No. 5315). STA-9

Waybill statistics, their history and uses. ICC, Bu. of Trans. Econ. & Stat. Washington, 1954. 50 p., D, 9.8 in. (No. 543). STA-10

Percent of empty to loaded freight car-miles by class of equipment and performance factors for way, through, and all trains combined. 1950–. ICC–Bu. A. Washington. 10.6 in. STA-11

STEAM-General

The age of steam; a classic album of American railroading by Lucius Beebe & Charles Clegg. New York, Rinehart [1957]. 304 p., I, 11.4 in. STE-1

Over the rails by steam; a railroad scrapbook, by Clinton F. Thurlow. [Weeks Mills, Me., 1965.] 104 p., I, M, 9 in. STE-2

See also: Companies, History, Locomotives, Pictorial.

STORIES

The Big book of train stories. Pictures by Leonard Weisgard. New York, Grosset & Dunlap, c 1955. I, 13 in. STO-1

City of little bread: the St. Louis General Strike of 1877; the history of an American strike. David T. Burbank. St. Louis, c 1957. 7 cards, 3 x 3 in. STO-2

Clear the track, true stories of railroading; illustrated by Charles Geer. [1st ed.] Louis Wolfe. Philadelphia, Lippincott [1952]. 181 p., I, 8.3 in. STO-3

Fiddletown & Copperopolis; the life and times of an uncommon carrier. Carl Fallberg. Foreword by Lucius Beebe. Reseda, Calif., Hungerford Press, 1960. unpaged (chiefly illus.), 9.8 in.; also 1968. STO-4

Great railroad stories of the world. Samuel Moskowitz. Introd. by Freeman H. Hubbarb. New York, McBride Co. [1954]. 331 p., 8.7 in. STO-5

Headlights and markers; an anthology of railroad stories, edited by Frank P. Donovan, Jr., and Robert Selph Henry. San Marino, Calif., Golden West Books [1968]. 396 p., I, 9 in. STO-6

Open throttle; stories of railroads and railroad men, selected by Phyllis R. Fenner. Illustrated by Charles Geer. New York, Morrow, 1966. 222 p., I, 8.7 in. STO-7

Railroad avenue; great stories and legends of American railroading, by Freeman Hubbard. [Rev. ed. San Marino, Calif., Golden West Books, 1964.] 444 p., I, M, P, 9 in. STO-8

Spirit of the rails, by Burton N. Brin and Richard S. Prosser. With scratchboard illus. by Marshall Thomas. Colton, Calif., West Colton Press, 1960. 60 p., I, 9 in. STO-9

Stories of the railway, by George A. Hibbard [and others]. Freeport, N. Y., Books for Libraries Press [1970]. 195 p., I, 8.3 in. STO-10

Tales of the rails; illustrated by Bernard Safran. Veronica S. Hutchinson. [1st ed.] Cleveland, World Pub. Co. [1952]. 329 p., I, 8.7 in.   STO-11

Trains rolling; stories on railroads at home and abroad, with 237 illus. Harry A. McBride. New York, Macmillan 1953. 269 p., I, 9.4 in.   STO-12

Vintage steam; stories. By Frank Roberts. Edited by Gordon Troup. Christchurch, Caxton, 1967. 179 p., I, P, D, 10.2 in.   STO-13

Workin' on the railroad; reminiscences from the age of steam. Edited with commentary. Compiled by Richard Reinhardt. Palo Alto, Calif., American West Pub. Co. [1970]. 318 p., I, 9.8 in.   STO-14

Little engines and big men. Lathrop.   sCOL-9
The railroad caboose. Knape.   sCAR-10

STREET RAILROADS . . . . see Section 2

STRIKES

Annals of the great strikes in the United States; a reliable history and graphic description of the causes and thrilling events of the labor strikes and riots of 1877. Joseph A. Dacus. New York, B. Franklin [1969]. 480 p. (pf.—6 p.), I, 7.5 in.
                    STRI-1

1877: year of violence. [1st ed.] Robert V. Bruce. Indianapolis, Bobbs-Merrill [1959]. 384 p., 8.7 in.   STRI-2

Reign of the rabble; the St. Louis general strike of 1877, by David T. Burbank. New York, A. M. Kelley, 1966. 208 p., Fac, 8.7 in.   STRI-3

SUBWAYS

Famous subways and tunnels of the world, by Edward and Muriel White. Illustrated by Robin King. New York, Random House [1953]. 97 p., I, 10.2 in.
                    SUB-1

Interbrough Rapid Transit. IRT.   sCO-146

SURVEYING

New tracks in North America; a journal of travel and adventure whilst engaged in the survey for a southern railroad to the Pacific Ocean during 1867-8. William A. Bell. With contributions by W. J. Palmer [and others]. Albuquerque, N. M., Horn and Wallace [1965]. 564 p. (pf.—69 p.), I, M (F), 9.4 in.   SUR-1

Route location and design [by] Thomas F. Hickerson. 5th ed. New York, McGraw-Hill [1967]. 634 p. (pf.—16 p.), I, 7.1 in.   SUR-2

Route surveying and design [by] Carl F. Meyer. 4th ed. Scranton, Pa., International Textbook Co. [1969]. COL: 636 p. (pf.—9 p.), I, 7.1 in.; also 3 ed., 1962, 1 ed., 1949.   SUR-3

TAX

Income tax exemption for employees' contributions to railroad retirement fund. Hearing on H. R. 10578 and H. R. 11764, bills to amend the Railroad retirement act. House, Ways & Means. 84C-2S. July 3, 1956. Washington, GPO, 1956. 72 p. (pf.–3 p.), T, 9.4 in.   T-1

Obsolescence in railroad ad valorem tax assessments, by Lionel W. Thatcher and Richard C. Dubielzig. Madison, Univ. of Wisconsin, Grad. Sch. of Bus., Bu. of Bus. Res. and Service, 1967. 39 p., 9 in. (v. 8, No. 2).   T-2

Regulated property; fundamental valuation principles affecting governmental responsibility toward railroads and other public utilities. Robert K. Stuart. Hillsborough, Calif., 1958. 177 p., I, 9.4 in.   T-3

Regulations 114 (26 Code of Federal regulations, part 411) relating to the employers' tax, employees' tax, and employee representatives' tax under the Railroad retirement tax act, for tax-return periods beginning after December 31, 1948. IRS, Washington, GPO, 1949. 79 p. (pf.–9 p.), 9.4 in.   T-4

Study of the tax amortization program; railroad freight cars. Hearings, House, Govt. Ops. 84C-1S. Washington, GPO, 1955. 292 p. (pf.–5 p.), D, T, 9.4 in.
                                                                                 T-5

A survey of the theory and technique of railroad taxation in the United States. Albert C. Dambrun. [Ann Arbor] University Microfilms [1952]. (Publication No. 2934).   T-6

Taxes levied and chargeable to railway tax accruals in the states of Arizona, Arkansas, Colorado, Idaho, Illinois, Iowa, Kansas, Missouri, Montana, Nebraska, Nevada, New Mexico, North Dakota, Oklahoma, Oregon, South Dakota, Texas, Utah, Washington and Wyoming. Assoc. of Western Rys. [n. p.] 8.3-11 in.   T-7

Valuation of railroads for ad valorem tax purposes. John A. Gronouski. Ann Arbor, University Microfilms [1955]. (Publication No. 14,701.)   T-8

Federal valuation [R.Rs.]. Moore.   sF-19
11th report. N. J. Tax Policy Comm.   sNJ-4

TECHNOLOGY

Adhesion between rails and wheels of railway motive power. George M. Cabble. Ann Arbor, Mich., University Microfilms [1958]. Microfilm AC-1, No. 58-5396.
                                                                                 TE-1

An economic investigation of solid journal bearing operation in freight service on two large class I railways [by] Roy M. Wright [and others]. Urbana, Univ. of Illinois [1953]. 110 p., D, 9 in. (No. 406).   TE-2

Technological change and the future of the railways; selected papers from a three-day conference conducted by the Transportation Center at Northwestern University, Evanston, Illinois. Editors: Robert S. Nelson [and] Edward M. Johnson. [Evanston, Transportation Center, c 1961.] 239 p. (pf.–8 p.), 9 in.   TE-3

Technological change and labor in the railroad industry; a comparative study. Fred Cottrell. Lexington, Mass., Heath Lexington Books [1970]. 159 p. (pf.—10 p.), 9.4 in.   TE-4

TELEGRAPHERS

The telegraphers, their craft and their unions. Vidkunn Ulriksson. Washington, Public Affairs Press [1953]. 218 p., 9 in.   TEL-1

TENNESSEE

Studies on certain tax problems: railroad and utility assessments, privileges, State. Tenn. General Assembly, Legislative Council Com. [Nashville] 1966. 11 in.
                                                                                      TEN-1

Report. Tennesse, Public Service Commission. [Nashville.] 9 in.   TEN-2

TERMINALS

Passenger terminals and trains. John A. Droege. With a special introd. by George W. Hilton. 1st ed. New York, McGraw-Hill, 1916. Milwaukee, Kalmbach Pub. Co., 1969. 410 p. (pf.—7 p.), I, M, PL (PF), 9.4 in.   TER-1

The railroad station; an architectural history. Carroll L. V. Meeks. New Haven, Yale University Press, 1956. 203 p. (pf.—26 p.), I, PL, 11 in.   TER-2

Railroad stations of Pennsylvania; an architectural excursion, metropolitan terminals, by James D. Van Trump. [Pittsburgh, M. H. Wilmoth, 1964.] 48 p., I, P, 9 in.   TER-3

Railroad terminal strategy. Railway Systems and Management Association. Chicago [1967]. 96 [7] p., I, M, P, 11 in.   TER-4

The great Richmond terminal: a study in businessmen and business strategy. Maury Klein. Charlottesville, published for the Eleutherian Mills-Hagley Foundation [by] University Press of Virginia [1970]. 323 p. (pf.—13 p.), M, 9.4 in.
                                                                                      TER-5

The comparative efficiency of various arrangements of railroad tracks at stores in wholesale produce markets [by A. B. Lowstuter, A. J. Kelsey, and Joseph F. Herrick, Jr.]. Washington, GPO, 1951. 39 p. (pf.—2 p.), I, 10.6 in. (No. 55).   TER-6

The station agent's blue book, a practical reference book for those actively engaged in station work; an everyday guide for the station employee, a comprehensive text book for the student of railway station duties. Otto B. Kirkpatrick. [Chicago] Order of Railroad Telegraphers [1958]. 571 p., I, 11 in.   TER-7

Formula [terminal costs]. ICC.   sCOS-2
Map-Chicago terminal district. Ill. Ft. Assoc.   sCH-9
South Side Consolidated passenger terminal. Chic. Plan Assoc.   sCH-10

TEXAS

Early economic policies of the Government of Texas. Lee Van Zant. [El Paso, Texas Western Press] 1966. 48 p., I, 9 in.   TEX-1

Texas railroad map, 1953. Ira D. Dodge. Dallas, Texas Railroad Maps, c 1953. M
(C), 31 x 33.1 in.   TEX-2

TIES

Concrete cross ties, compiled by K. J. Polden. Adelaide, State Library of South
Australia, 1967. 8 p., 10.2 in.   TI-1

Crosstie industry facts for the Tennessee Valley counties, by William H. Ogden
[staff forester II]. Norris, Tennessee Valley Authority, Division of Forestry Relations, 1949. 21 p., M (C), T, 11 in.   TI-2

Practical covers for protecting crossties during air seasoning, by J. B. Huffman and
Don M. Post. Gainesville, 1962. 7 p., I, 11 in. (Univ. of Florida, Sch. of Forestry.
No. 8).   TI-3

TRACK

Actual track capacity of a railroad division. M. K. K. Mostafa. Urbana, 1951. 3 p.,
9 in.   TK-1

Improved methods of track construction and maintenance; interim report by the
executive secretary. U. N. Economic Comm. for Asia and Far East. [Bangkok]
1953. 177 p., I, 11 in.   TK-2

Progress reports of investigation of railroad rails and joint bars. [1945] –. Univ.
of Illinois Eng. Experiment Station [Urbana]. I, 9 in., annual.   TK-3

Railroad trackage. U. S. Bu. of Yards & Docks, Washington, 1952. [Washington,
U. S. Dept. of Commerce, Office of Technical Services, n. d.] 24 p. (pf.–10 p.),
D, T, 10.6 in.   TK-4

USS trackwork. 1st ed. United States Steel Corp. [Pittsburgh, 1955–]. 1 v. (loose-
leaf), I, 8.7 x 11 in.   TK-5

TRAFFIC

Basic study in traffic management. A. A. Polakoff. Baltimore, Kenmore Press
[1954, c 1952]. 346 p., I, 10.6 in.   TRF-1

The capacity and capital requirements of the railroad industry. ICC, Bu. of Trans.
Econ. & Stat. Washington, 1952. 109 p. (pf.–3 p.), 10.6 in. (No. 5227).   TRF-2

Effects of traffic capacity and locomotive performance on the design of railroads.
M. Chang. Urbana, 1949. 6 p., 9 in.   TRF-3

Fundamentals of freight traffic. George L. Wilson. Washington, Traffic Service
Corp. [1950-52]. 4 v., I, 9.4 in.   TRF-4

Your future in traffic management [by] Robert E. Heine. [1st ed.] New York, R.
Rosen Press [1967]. 158 p., I, 8.7 in.   TRF-5

Import traffic of Chicago and its hinterland. Edwin H. Draine. Chicago, 1963.
138 p. (pf.–11 p.), I, M, D, T, 9 in. Univ. of Chicago.   TRF-6

New loose-leaf atlas of traffic maps. LaSalle Extension Univ. [Chicago] c 1950.
104 p., 55 M (PC), 9.8 x 13.4 in.   TRF-7

Oregon rail and water commodity-flow trends, by Roy J. Sampson. [Eugene] Bu.
of Bus. and Econ. Res., Univ. of Oregon, 1965. 107 p. (pf.—11 p.), I, 9 in. TRF-8

Pattern of distribution of fruits and vegetables shipped by railroad, 1939 and
1947, and transportation charges, 1947 [by George T. Reeves and Helen V.
Smith]. U. S. Bu. of Agric. Econ. Washington, 1950. 55 p., 10.6 in.   TRF-9

Ratios of empty to loaded freight car-miles by type of car and performance factors
for way, through, and all trains combined: class I line-haul railroads, calendar year
1968. [Prepared by the Section of Cost Finding] ICC, Bu. Acct's. Washington,
1969. 31 p., forms, 10.6 in.   TRF-10

Transportation of grain in the Southwestern States by rail and truck, 1960-62 [by
Helen V. Smith. Washington] U. S. Dept. of Agriculture, Economic Research Service [1966]. 26 p. (pf.—4 p.), 10.2 in.   TRF-11

Transportation and traffic management, by William J. Knorst. 10th ed. Chicago,
College of Advanced Traffic, 1966—. I, 9.4 in.; also, 9 ed.-1964, 7 ed.-59, 6 ed.-57,
5 ed.-55, 3 ed.-1950-55.   TRF-12

Determination [max. flow-R.R. network]. Boldyreff.   sOP-2
Balance of trade [Mississippi]. Noblin.   sMIS-1

TRAINS

Great trains of all time. Freeman H. Hubbard. Illustrated by Herb Mott.
New York, Grosset & Dunlap [1962]. 156 p., I, 11.4 in.   TRN-1

The lore of the train; concentrates on the train and its components, cars, locomotives, etc., illustrated by drawings, reproductions, paintings. By C. Hamilton Ellis.
New York, Grosset & Dunlap, 1971. 320 p., I (C), 11.6 in.   TRN-2

Mary takes a trip by train (Filmstrip). Long Filmslide Service. Released by Society
for Vidual Education and Long Filmslide Service, 1949. 31 frames, 35mm (b & w)
(3).   TRN-3

Names and nicknames of freight trains operated on the railroads of the United
States and Canada. AAR 1946— Washington. 9 in.   TRN-4

Railway passenger lists of overland trains to San Francisco and the West, by Louis
J. Rasmussen. Colma, Calif., San Francisco Historic Records [1966—]. 9.4 in.
                                                                             TRN-5

The real book about trains; illustrated by David Millard. Davis Cole, pseud. Garden
City, N. Y., Garden City Books, by arrangement with F. Watts [New York, 1951].
183 p., I, 8.3 in.   TRN-6

Road movement of trains. L. E. Roxbury. Serial 6445A [—B. Ed. 1]. Scranton,
International Correspondence Schools, c 1959. 2 v., I, 7.5 in.   TRN-7

Some classic trains, by Arthur D. Dubin. [Milwaukee, Kalmbach Pub. Co., 1964.]
434 p., I (PC), F, M (F), 11.8 in.   TRN-8

Trains, by John Day. Illustrated by David A. Warner and Nigel W. Hearn. New York, Grosset & Dunlap [1970]. 159 p., I (C), 8.7 in.　　　　　　TRN-9

Trains album of photographs. [Milwaukee, Kalmbach Pub. Co., 1943-50.] 19 v., I, 10.2 x 14.2 in.　　　　　　TRN-10

Trains and how to draw them. Amy Hogeboom. New York, Vanguard Press [1953]. 39 p., I, 9 in.　　　　　　TRN-11

Whistle in the night (Motion picture). RKO-Pathe. Released by McGraw-Hill Book Co., 1947. 17 min., sound, b & w, 16mm.　　　　　　TRN-12

With a cinder in my eye; a layman's memories and sketches of American trains. Kenneth W. Downing. Moline, Ill., 1951. 43 p., I, 7.5 x 10.6 in.　　　　　　TRN-13

The wonder book of trains. Norman V. Carlisle. New and rev. ed. Philadelphia, Winston [1957]. 313 p., I, 9.8 in.　　　　　　TRN-14

Yonder comes the train. Lance Phillips. New York, A. S. Barnes [1965]. 395 p., I, F, M, P, 13.8 in.　　　　　　TRN-15

TRANSIT . . . . **see Section 2**

TRANSPORTATION

The demand for transportation: regional and commodity studies in the United States, by Eugene D. Perle. Chicago [Dept. of Geography, University of Chicago] 1964. 130 p. (pf.−20 p.), M, 9 in. (No. 95).　　　　　　TT-1

Fundamentals of transportation, by Charles F. Walden and Charles J. Fagg. New York, Traffic Pub. Co. [1952]. 314 p., I, 8.3 in.　　　　　　TT-2

Transportation and logistics education in graduate schools of business administration [by] Paul W. Cherington [and] Lewis M. Schneider. Boston, Harvard University, Graduate School of Business Administration, 1967. 165 p. (pf.−10 p.), 8.3 in.
　　　　　　TT-3

Transportation to the Seaboard: the "Communication Revolution" and American Foreign Policy, 1860-1900. Howard B. Schonberg. Westport, Conn., Greenwood Publishers, 1971. 265 p.　　　　　　TT-4

Transportation act of 1958; report on S. 3778, together with individual views. Senate, Int. & For. Comm. 85C-2S. Washington, GPO, 1958. 37 p. (pf.−2 p.), 9.4 in. (No. 1647).　　　　　　TT-5

Amendments to the Transportation act of 1958 (train discontinuance). Hearings on S. 1331, a bill to strengthen and improve the national transportation system; S. 1450, a bill relative to the discontinuance or change of the operation of certain trains or ferries. Senate, Int. & For. Comm. (Surface Trans.). 86C-1S. Washington, GPO, 1959. 493 p. (pf.−6 p.), I, M (F), 9.4 in.　　　　　　TT-6

TRI-STATE (Conn.-N. J.-N. Y.) TRANSPORTATION COMMITTEE

Journey-to-work in the Tri-State region; a summary of census travel data by counties. Tri-State Transportation Committee. [New York] 1964. 52 p., I, M, 8.7 x 11.4 in.   TTC-1

Prospectus for Tri-State Transportation Committee. [New York] 1962. 51 p., M, (C), D, 11 in.   TTC-2

Rail freight of the Tri-State region [by] I. Stuart Bick and Robert Teas Wood. Tri-State Trans. Comm. [New York] 1967—. I, M (PC), 11 in.   TTG-3

TUNNELS

Famous subways and tunnels of the world; by Edward and Muriel White. Illustrated by Robin King. New York, Random House [1953]. 97 p., I, 10.3 in.
                                                                                  TU-1

Historic Alpine Tunnel. Don Helmers. Denver, Sage Books [1963]. 200 p., I, P, M, D, F, PL, 11.4 in.   TU-2

Using precast reinforced-concrete sets in the Pioneer Tunnel of Great Northern Railway's Cascade Tunnel, King County, Wash. Edward W. Parsons. [Washington] U. S. Dept. of the Interior, Bureau of Mines, 1958. 10 p., I, 10.6 in. (7858).
                                                                                  TU-3

UNITED STATES GOVERNMENT

Army operation of the rail transportation systems, pursuant to Executive orders Nos. 10141 and 10155; report prepared by Office, Under Secretary of the Army. Dept. of Army. Washington, 1952. 10.2 in.   US-1

Follow-up examination on certain aspects of United States assistance to the Central Treaty Organization for a rail link between Turkey and Iran, Agency for International Development, Department of State; report to Congress by the Comptroller General. General Accounting Office [Washington] 1965. 2 l., 22 p., 10.6 in.   US-2

Unnecessary costs incurred for commercial protective service used for shipments of classified material, U. S. Army; report to Congress by the Comptroller General. General Accounting Office [Washington] 1965. 2 l., 20 p., 10.6 in.   US-3

UNITED TRANSPORTATION UNION

United Transportation Union. UTU transportation news. v. 1—. Jan. 4, 1969—. [Cleveland.] v., I, P, 16.5 in.   UT-1

VIRGINIA

Virginia railroads in the Civil War. Angus J. Johnston. Chapel Hill, published for the Virginia Historical Society by the Univ. of North Carolina Press, 1961. 336 p. (pf.—14 p.), I, M, T, 9.4 in.; also, Ann Arbor, Mich., University Microfilms [1959]. (No. 59-4811).   VA-1

Constitutional provisions, statutes, and public regulations governing railroads and other common carriers in the State of Virginia, rev. to July 1, 1966. Charlottesville, Michie Co., 1966. 119 p., 9 in.; also, 1950, 107 p. VA-2

Constitutional provisions, statutes, and public regulations governing railroads and other common carriers in the State of Virginia. Revised to July 1, 1950. Charlottesville, Michie Co., 1950. 107 p., 9 in. VA-3

The economic situation of passenger railroad traffic in Virginia. Report to the Governor and the General Assembly of Virginai. Advisory Legislative Council. Richmond, Commonwealth of Virginia Dept. of Purchases and Supply, 1961. 21 p., 10.2 in. (Doc. No. 14). VA-4

Geographia Map Co.'s highway and railroad map of Virginia and West Virginia; with population based on latest census. Alexander Gross. New York, Geographia Map Co. [1956]. M (C), 26 x 40 in. VA-5

Interim report of the Virginia representatives of the Joint Commission to Study Passenger Carrier Facilities and Services in the Washington Metropolitan Area. Richmond, Commonwealth of Virginia Division of Purchase and Print., 1955 [i. e. 1956]. 32 p., T, 10.2 in. (House, No. 26). VA-6

Taxes extended on car line companies [year next preceding December 31, 1951]. Virginia, State Corporation Commission [Richmond]. 11.8 x 17.7 in., annual.
VA-7

Certain health problems. sSAN-6

WAGES

Railroad wages and labor relations, 1900-1952; an historical survey and summary of results, by Harry E. Jones, chairman, Executive Committee. Eastern Railway, Bu. of Info. [New York] 1953. 375 p. (pf.—8 p.), D, T, 9.4 in. W-1

WAR

The Northern railroads in the Civil War, 1861-1865. Thomas Webber. Westport, Conn., Greenwood Press [1970, c 1952]. 318 p. (pf.—12 p.), 9 in. WA-1

Department of Defense experience under section 22 of the Interstate Commerce Act. Ass't. Sec. (Supply & Logistics). [Washington] Dept. of Defense, 1955. 16 p., D, Form, 10.2 in. WA-2

Rail transport and the winning of wars, by General James A. Van Fleet. Washington, Association of American Railroads, 1956. 71 p. (pf.—8 p.), I, 9 in. WA-2

Railway and transit equipment, 1940-45. 1st draft. April, 1946. Grant McColley. [Washington] Defense Production Administration, 1951. 17 p. (pf.—3 p.), T, 10.6 in. WA-4

Steel rails to victory. Ron Ziel. New York, Hawthorn Books [1970]. 288 p., I, M, P, 11 in. WA-5

Victory rode the rails; the strategic place of the railroads in the Civil War. Maps by George R. Turner. [1st ed.] Indianapolis, Bobbs-Merrill [1953]. 419 p., I, P, M, 9.8 in. By George Edgar Turner. WA-6

Andrews raiders. Feuerlicht.   sCO-55
Civil War railroads. Abdill.   sSOU-1
In pursuit [General]. Pittenger.   sCO-86
War material [cases]. ICC.   sRAT-27

WASHINGTON (ST)

Washington and northern Idaho. McGill-Warner Co. [St. Paul] Northern Pacific
Railway [1951]. M (C), 22.8 x 37 in.   WAS-1

Statistics of railroad companies. Washington Public Service Commission. Olympia.
13.9 in.   WAS-2

WASHINGTON (DC)

Union Station train accident, Washington, D.C. Hearings. Jan. 21 and 22, 1953.
Senate, Comm. on Int. & For. Comm. 83C-1S. Washington, GPO, 1953. 130 p.
(pf.–3 p.), 9.4 in.   WDC-1

WASHINGTON (DC) TRANSIT

General

Washington Metropolitan area transit regulation compact. A communication from
the President (Lyndon B. Johnson) of the United States, transmitting a draft of
proposed legislation to grant the consent of Congress to amend the Washington
Metropolitan area transit regulation compact . . . Washington, GPO, 1966. 30 p.,
9.4 in. (89C-2S, House No. 452).   WDT-1

Capital Transit guide map, Washington, D. C.; street car and bus lines. Rev. to
Nov. 9, 1950. Charles R. Wittmann. [Washington] Capital Transit Co., c 1950.
M (C), 19.6 x 25.5 in.; also, Rev. 1951.   WDT-2

General development plan for the National Capital region. Prepared for the mass
transportation survey as directed by the National Capital Planning Commission and
the National Capital Regional Planning Council. Adams, Howard & Greeley [firm].
[Washington, 1959.] 34 p. (pf.–6 p.), M, 11 in.   WDT-3

A guide to sources of information pertinent to planning a transportation system for
the Washington metropolitan area. David S. Clark. Prepared for the Northwest
Committee for Transportation Planning. 2d ed. Washington, Northwest Committee
for Transportation Planning, 1961. 38 p. (pf.–3 p.), 11 in.   WDT-4

A mass transport integral. Metropolitan Planning Associates [Washington, Citizens
Transit Improvement Association, 1961–]. I, M, 11 in.   WDT-5

Mass transportation survey, National Capital region: civil engineering report, for
the National Capital Planning Commission [and the] National Capital Regional
Planning Council. De Leuw, Cather & Co. Chicago, 1959. 98 p. (pf.–8 p.), I, M
(C), PL, 11.8 x 19 in.   WDT-6

Metro: adopted Regional rapid rail transit plan and program, March 1, 1968. Rev.
Feb. 7, 1969. Washington Metropolitan Area Transit Study. [Washington, 1969.]
44 p., I, Fac, M (IFC), 11 in.; also 1968, 30 p.   WDT-7

Metropolitan area pilot transportation study. Study implementing Senate resolution 250 concerning highway facilities and other modes of commuter service to and from the Washington, D. C. area . . . and, the feasibility of solid waste disposal using rail haul techniques. Day and Zimmerman, Inc., Washington, GPO, 1968.　　WDT-8

NCTA technical report; a study of bus rapid transit operations of the National Capital region. Prepared by NCTA staff, with supplementary studies by Operations Research Incorporated, Kaiser Engineers, Wilbur Smith & Associates. National Capital Transportation Agency. [Washington] 1963. 1 v. (various pagings), M (PC), D, PL, T, 10.6 in.　　WDT-9

Organization for transportation in the national capital region, selected documents. Congress, Jt. Com. Wash. Metro. Problems. Washington, GPO, 1960. 111 p. (pf.– 5 p.), 9.4 in.　　WDT-10

Preliminary financial and organizational report regarding metropolitan transportation. Institute of Public Adm., Joint Committee on Washington metropolitan problems. Washington, GPO, 1957. 25 p. (pf.–8 p.), D, T, 9.4 in.　　WDT-11

Report on the City Council approval of the mass transportation and major thoroughfare plans for the District of Columbia. [Washington, 1969.] 101 p., M (F, PC), 10.6 in.　　WDT-12

Traffic, revenue and operating costs; adopted regional system 1968, revised February 1969. Prepared for the Washington Metropolitan Area Transit Authority by W. C. Gilman & Co., Inc. and Alan M. Voorhees & Associates, Inc. McLean, Va., 1969. 106 p. (pf.–16 p.), I, M, 11.4 x 18.5 in.　　WDT-13

Transportation plan, National Capital region; the mass transportation survey report [by] National Capital Planning Commission [and] National Capital Regional Planning Council. [Washington, GPO, 1959.] 85 p., I, M, D (PC), T, 11.8 x 19 in.
　　WDT-14

Activities. U. S. National Park Service. National Capital Region. [Washington, GPO.] I, 5.1 x 7.5 in.　　WDT-15

Report. U. S. National Capital Transportation Agency. 1st–. 1965–. Washington. 10.6 in., annual.　　WDT-16

Report. Washington Metropolitan Area Transit Commission. 1st–. 1961–. [Washington.] I, P, 9.4 in., annual.　　WDT-17

Technical report. Washington Metropolitan Area Transit Authority. [Washington] 1967. 5 v., I, M, 11 in.　　WDT-18

Transportation planning in certain urban areas. Hearings on section 134 of title 23, United States code . . . House, Public Works (roads). 88C-1S. Washington, GPO, 1963. 305 p. (pf.–4 p.), I, M, 9.4 in.　　WDT-19

Financing subway system for National Capital region. Joint hearings on S. 2185 and H. R. 11193 . . . June 10 and 11, 1969. Senate, Dist. of Columbia. 91C-1S. Washington, GPO, 1969. 176 p. (pf.–5 p.), I, M, 9.4 in.　　WDT-20

Public assistance or public ownership of D. C. Transit. Hearing on S. 1813 [and] S. 1814, April 29, 1969. Senate, Dist. of Columbia. Washington, GPO, 1969. 312 p. (pf.–4 p.), 9.4 in.　　WDT-21

Amend the National Capital transportation act of 1965. Hearings on S. 2094 and H. R. 11395 . . . November 14 and 15, 1967. Senate, Dist. of Columbia. 90C-1S. Washington, GPO, 1967 [i. e. 1968]. 84 p. (pf.–4 p.), M (PF), 9.4 in.   WDT-22

Amend the National Capital transportation act of 1965. Hearings on H. R. 11395. House, Dist. of Columbia (4). 90C-1S. July 26 and August 23, 1967. 69 p. (pf.–3 p.), M, 9.4 in.   WDT-23

Washington Metropolitan Area Transit Authority compact. Hearing on S. 3488 . . . August 22, 1966. Senate, Judiciary. 89C-2S. Washington, GPO, 1966. 118 p. (pf.–4 p.), 9.4 in.   WDT-24

Rapid rail transit for the Nation's Capital. Hearings, House, Dist. of Columbia. 89C-1S. Washington, GPO, 1965. 316 p. (pf.–8 p.), I, M, 9.4 in.   WDT-25

Rail rapid transit for the National Capital region. Hearings, July 20, 21, and 23, 1965. Senate, Dist. of Columbia. 89C-1S. Washington, GPO, 1965. 287 p. (pf.–7 p.), **I, M,** 9.4 in.   WDT-26

Rail rapid transit for the National Capital region. Senate, Dist. of Columbia. 89C-1S. [Washington, GPO, 1965.] 55 p., I, M, 9.4 in. (No. 637).   WDT-27

Transit development program for the National Capital region; report to accompany H. R. 8929. House, Dist. of Columbia. 88C-1S. [Washington, GPO, 1963.] 59 p., M (F), T, 9.4 in. (No. 1005).   WDT-28

Transit program for the National Capital region. Hearings on H. R. 6633 and H. R. 7240 [i. e. 7249] to authorize a transit development program. House, Dist. of Columbia.(6). 89C-1S. Washington, GPO, 1963. 462 p. (pf.–7 p.), I, M, 9.4 in.   WDT-29

Transportation in the National Capital region: finance and organization; a report to the President for transmittal to Congress. National Capital Development Agency. [Washington, GPO, 1962.] 92 p. (pf.–21 p.), I, M, D, 9.4 in.   WDT-30

National Capital transit development program. Authorize median strips, transit stations, parking lots. Hearing on S. 2397. Senate, Dist. of Columbia. 87C-1S. Washington, GPO, 1961. 34 p. (pf.–3 p.), M, T, 9.4 in.   WDT-31

National Capital transportation act of 1960. Hearings pursuant to S. Con. Res. 101 on S. 3193 and H. R. 11135. May 5 and 6, 1960. Joint Com. on Washington Metro. Problems. 86C-2S. Washington, GPO, 1960. 299 p. (pf.–3 p.), I, M, 9.4 in.   WDT-32

Transportation plan for the National Capital region. Hearings, Congress, Jt. Com. Wash. Metro. Problems. 86C-1S. Washington, GPO, 1960. 1,070 p. (pf.–5 p.), I, PL, 9.4 in.   WDT-33

National Capital Transportation Authority; preliminary draft for discussion purposes. Staff report prepared for the Joint Committee on Washington Metropolitan Problems. Columbia Univ., Legis. Res. Fund. Washington, GPO, 1959. 31 p. (pf.–5 p.), 9.4 in.   WDT-34

Washington Metropolitan Area transportation problems. Hearings on transportation problems in Maryland, Virginia, and the Washington Metropolitan Area. May 22, 23, and June 10, 1958. U. S. Congress, Joint Com. on Wash. Metro Problems. 89C-2S. Washington, GPO, 1958. 382 p. (pf.—4 p.), I, M, 9.4 in.   WDT-35

Washington (D. C.) Metropolitan Transit Authority. Hearings on H. R. 8901 and H. R. 8947, bills to provide for sound transportation system or systems to serve the District of Columbia; to create a public body corporate with powers to carry out the provisions of this act. House, Int. & For. Comm. 84C-2S. Washington, GPO, 1956. 530 p. (pf.—5 p.), I, M, 9.4 in.   WDT-36

Public transportation serving the District of Columbia; report . . . pursuant to S. Res. 192. Senate, Dist. of Columbia. 83C-2S. Washington, GPO, 1954. 76 p., M, T, 9.4 in. (No. 1274).   WDT-37

Washington metropolitan area transit problem. Hearings on H. R. 1555, a bill to provide for an investigation and study by the Interstate Commerce Commission of the adequacy and convenience of passenger carrier facilities and services . . . in the District of Columbia; and H. R. 3771 and S. 922, bills to provide for a commission to regulate the public transportation within the metropolitan area of Washington, District of Columbia . . . House, Int. & For. Comm. 83C-1S. Washington, GPO, 1953. 176 p. (pf.—4 p.), 9.4 in.   WDT-38

Washington Metropolitan Area transit problem. Hearings on S. 1868 . . . and S. J. Res. 135 . . . May 21 and 22, 1952. Senate, Int. & For. Comm. 82C-2S. Washington, GPO, 1952. 71 p. (pf.—4 p.), 9.4 in.   WDT-39

Washington Metropolitan area transit regulation compact. Report to accompany H. J. Res. 402. Senate, Judiciary. [Washington, GPO, 1960.] 56 p., 9.4 in.   WDT-40

District of Columbia, Maryland, and Virginia mass transit compact. Hearings on H. J. Res. 402, compact related to the regulation of mass transit in the Washington, D. C., metropolitan area. Senate, Judiciary. 86C-2S. Washington, GPO, 1960. 131 p. (pf.—3 p.), 9.4 in.   WDT-41

District of Columbia, Maryland, and Virginia mass transit compact. Hearings, compact related to the mass transit, Washington metro. area. August 25, 1959. House, Judiciary. Washington, GPO, 1959. 2 pts., 288 p. (pf.—4 p.), T, 9.4 in.   WDT-42

WEST

Backwoods railroads of the West; a portfolio. Richard Steinheimer. [Milwaukee, Kalmbach Pub. Co., c 1963.] 177 p., I, 9.8 x 13 in.   WE-1

End of track, by James H. Kyner as told to Hawthorne Daniel. With an introd. by James C. Olson. [Lincoln] Univ. of Nebraska Press, 1960 [c 1937]. 280 p., 8.3 in.   WE-2

Railroads of Nevada and eastern California. David F. Myrick. Berkeley, Calif., Howell-North Books, 1962-63. 2 v., 933 p. (pf.—15 p.), I (IC), P, M (IF), F, 11.4 in.   WE-3

The story of the western railroads, from 1852 through the reign of the giants. Robert E. Riegel. Lincoln, University of Nebraska Press [1964, c 1926]. 345 p. (pf.—15 p.), 9.3 in.   WE-4

They built the West; an epic of rails and cities. Glenn C. Quiett. New York, Cooper Square Publishers, 1965 [c 1934]. 569 p. (pf.—20 p.), I, M, P, 9.4 in.   WE-5

The track going back; text by Everett L. DeGolyer, Jr. Fort Worth [Tex.] Amon Carter Museum [1969]. [7] p., 103 plates, F, P, 8.3 in.   WE-6

The transportation frontier: trans-Mississippi West, 1865-1890. Oscar O. Winther. New York, Holt, Rinehart and Winston [1964]. 224 p. (pf.—14 p.), I, M (PC), F, 9.4 in.   WE-7

Great train [robberies]. Block.   sRO-1

WEST VIRGINIA

The market structure of West Virginia industry; a study of rail freight shipments, 1948-1952. Jere W. Clark. Morgantown, Bu. of Bus. Res., College of Commerce, West Virginia Univ. [1955]. 37 p. (pf.—5 p.), D, T, 11 in.   WEV-1

WISCONSIN

The myth of a progressive reform; railroad regulation in Wisconsin, 1903-1910 [by] Stanley P. Caine. Madison, State Historical Society of Wisconsin, 1970. 226 p. (pf.—16 p.), P, 9 in.   WIS-1

Summaries of fatal motor vehicle traffic accidents involving R.R. trains in Wisconsin. [Madison.] I, 11 in., Highway Safety Promotion Div.   WIS-2

WRECKS

The case of Train No. 3. Arthur O. Ridgway. Denver, Rocky Mountain Railroad Club [c 1957]. 68 p., I, P, M (4F), 8.7 in.   WK-1

Tragedy at Eden. Dow Helmers. [Pueblo, Colo., 1971.] 149 p., I, M, P, 9.4 in.   WK-2

Train wreck! By Wesley S. Griswold. Illustrated with contemporary engravings and photographs. Brattleboro, Vt., S. Greene Press, 1969. 8, 150 p., I, 8.7 in.   WK-3

Train wrecks; a pictorial history of accidents on the main line, by Robert C. Reed. [1st ed.] Seattle, Superior Pub. Co. [1968]. 183 p., I, 11 in.   WK-4

The wreck of Old 97. Pat Fox. Danville, Va., Fox Publications [1969]. 100 p., I, F, M, P, 8.7 in.   WK-5

YARDS

Operation of railroad yards. L. E. Roxbury. Serial 6444. [Ed. 1] Scranton, International Correspondence Schools, c 1959. 110 p. (pf.—2 p.), I, 7.5 in.   Y-1

SECTION 3

SUBJECT ENTRIES – MAJOR CATEGORY

BIOGRAPHIES

"He built Seattle"; a biography of Judge Thomas Burke. Robert C. Nesbit. Seattle, Univ. of Washington Press, 1961. 455 p., I, 9.4 in.   BIO-1

Inland Empire; D.C. Corbin and Spokane. John Fahey. Seattle, Univ. of Washington Press [1965]. 270 p. (pf.−10 p.), I, M, P, 9.4 in.   BIO-2

John W. Garrett of the Baltimore & Ohio: a study in seaport and railroad competition, 1820-1874. William B. Catton. Ann Arbor, Mich., University Microfilms [1959].   BIO-3

Lincoln's railroad man: Herman Haupt [by] Francis A. Lord. Rutherford, N.J., Fairleigh Dickinson Univ. Press [1969]. 325 p., I, M, P, 8.7 in.   BIO-4

Henry Huntington and the Pacific Electric; a pictorial album. Spencer Crump. 1st ed., Los Angeles, Calif., Trans-Anglo Books [1970]. 112 p., I, Fac, M, P, 11.4 in.   BIO-5

Rails from the West; biography of Theodore D. Judah, about the transcontinental railway and pioneer West. Helen Hinckley. San Marino, Calif., Golden West Books. 208 p., I, 6 x 9 in.   BIO-6

Minor C. Keith, pioneer of the American tropics. John Keith Hatch. McLean, Va. [1962, c 1963]. 82 l. 82 l. (pf.−3 l.), 9 in.   BIO-7

Abraham Lincoln and the Illinois Central Railroad, main line of mid-America; its organization, financing, and subsequent simplification of debt and capital structure through May 1955. Edwin S.S. Sunderland. New York, 1955. 117 p., I, 9.4 in.   BIO-8

Abraham Lincoln and the Illinois Central Railroad, main line of Mid-America. Carlton J. Corliss. [Chicago, 1950.] 20 p., I, 8.7 in.   BIO-9

Uriah Lott. James L. Allhands. San Antonio, Naylor [c 1949]. 187 p. (pf.−12 p.), I, P, M (F), 8.7 in.   BIO-10

Railroads, land and iron; a phase in the career of Lewis Henry Morgan. Saul Benison. Ann Arbor, University Microfilms [1954], Publication 6575.   BIO-11

The Moreleys—young upstarts on the southwest frontier, by Norman Cleaveland, with George Fitzpatrick. [1st ed.] Albuquerque, N.M., C. Horn [1971]. 269 p. (pf.−11 p.), I, 9.4 in.   BIO-12

General Wm. Jackson Palmer, 1836-1909, and the D. & R.G.W. Railroad! Wilson McCarthy. New York, Newcomen Society in North America, 1954. 28 p., I, 9 in.   BIO-13

Henry Varnum Poor, business editor, analyst, and reformer. Alfred D. Chandler. Cambridge, Harvard Univ. Press, 1956. 362 p., P, M (F), F, 9.8 in.   BIO-14

George M. Pullman, 1831-1897, and the Pullman Company. Carroll Reade Harding. New York, Newcomen Society in North America, 1951. 44 p., I, 9 in.   BIO-15

Railroad leaders, 1845-1890; the business mind in action [by] Thomas C. Cochran.
New York, Russell & Russell, 1965 [i.e. 1966, c 1953]. 564 p. (pf.—9 p.), M,
9.8 in.   BIO-16

Railroad men; a book of photographs and collected stories. Simpson Kalisher.
With an introd. by Jonathan Williams. [New York, Clarke & Way, 1961.] 83 p.,
I, 9.8 in.   BIO-17

The robber barons; the great American capitalists, 1861-1901. Matthew Josephson.
New York, Harcourt, Brace & World [1969]. 474 p., 9.4 in.   BIO-18

The robber barons revisted. Edited with an introd. by Peter d'A. Jones. Boston,
Heath [1968]. 128 p. (pf.—14 p.), 9.4 in.   BIO-19

The life of George Stephenson, Railway engineer. Samuel Smiles. 5th ed., rev.
with additions. Ann Arbor, Mich., Plutarch Press, 1971. 557 p. (pf.—16 p.), P,
8.7 in.   BIO-20

Reference list of the writings by and about Charles Ely Rose Sherrington, 1923-
1962. Elizabeth O. Cullen. Washington, Association of American Railroads, Bureau
of Railway Economic Library, 1962. 32 p., 11.4 in.   BIO-21

Henry Villard and the Northern Pacific. Robert S. Macfarlane. New York, Newcomen Society in North America, 1954. 28 p., I, 8.7 in.   BIO-22

Henry Villard and the railways of the Northwest. James B. Hedges. New York,
Russell & Russell [1967, c 1930]. 224 p., M (2), 8.7 in.   BIO-23

Robert R. Young, the populist of Wall Street. Joseph Borkin. [1st ed.] New York,
Harper & Row [1969]. 236 p. (pf.—11 p.), I, F, P, 8.7 in.   BIO-24

Chief Engineers [I.C.].   sCO-142
Jay Cooke and Minnesota. Harnsberger, 1958.   sCO-133
The fall of a railroad empire [N.H.]. Staples.   sCO-197
Henry M. Flagler. Martin, 1956.   sCO-111
The giant's ladder [Moffat]. Boner.   sCO-91
Men of vision. DeButts, 1955.   sCO-256
My railroad saga. Tigrett, 1952.   sCO-133
Pioneering the Union Pacific. Ames.   sCO-274

CARS

General

The car-builder's dictionary (1906); features a representative selection of cars of the early 20th century. Master Car Builder's Assoc. Reprint. Kentfield, Calif., Newton K. Gregg, Pub., 1972. 900 p., I (6,344), 11½ in.   CAR-1

The car-builder's dictionary (1888); complete reference terminology as used on railway cars and parts up to 1888. Reprint. Kentfield, Calif., Newton K. Gregg, Publisher. 608 p., I (2000), 8 in.   CAR-2

The car-builder's dictionary (1879); first dictionary published by Railroad Gazette for Master Car Builders Assoc. Reprint. Kentfield, Calif., Newton K. Gregg, Publisher. 544 p., I, 5 x 8 in.   CAR-3

Car and locomotive cyclopedia of American practice. 1st ed.; 1966—. New York, Simmons-Boardman Pub. Corp. I, 11.8 in.   CAR-4

The Original 1879 Car-builder's Dictionary; illustrations, car plans, and advertisements; an illustrated vocabulary of terms which designate American railroad cars, their parts, and attachments. Compiled for the Master Car-Builders' Association by Matthias N. Forney, assisted by Leander Garey and Calvin A. Smith. New York, Simmons-Boardman Pub. Corp., 1949. 190—491 p. (pf.—14 p.), 84 p., I, 9.1 x 7.9 in.   CAR-5

100 years of railroad cars. Walter A. Lucas, ed. New York, Simmons-Boardman Pub. Corp. [1958]. 196 p., I, 11.8 in.   CAR-6

U. S. railroad freight car study, March 1952, to establish requirement and production goals and tax amortization goal for traffic levels forecast to July 1, 1954. Defense Trans. Adm. [Washington, 1952.] 14 l., 10.6 in.   CAR-7

An international exhibition of aluminium in railway rolling stock, organized by the Centre international de developpement de l'aluminium. Strasbourg, France, June 21 to 26, 1960. London, Aluminium Development Association, 1960. 87 p., I (PC), 11.8 in.   CAR-8

Report. Car Service Div., AAR, Washington. 10.6 in., annual.   CAR-9

Freight

The railroad caboose; its 100 year history, legend and lore, by William F. Knapke with Freeman Hubbard. San Marino, Calif., Golden West Books [1968]. 237 p., I, 9 in.   CAR-10

Mechanical refrigerator car equipment. Serial 6391. [Ed. 1] Glenn E. Rodgers. Scranton, International Correspondence Schools, c 1959. 102 p., I, 7.5 in. CAR-11

Freight cars rolling. Lawrence W. Sagle. New York, Simmons-Boardman Pub. Corp. [c 1960]. 105 p., I, 11.4 in.   CAR-12

Standard and special flatcars. Merrill G. Marshall. Serial 6611. [Ed. 1] Scranton, International Correspondence Schools, c 1962. 66 p., I, 7.5 in.   CAR-13

Steel gondola and hopper cars. Wesley Castles. Serial 6438. [Ed. 1] Scranton, International Correspondence Schools, c 1959. 74 p., I, 7.5 in.   CAR-14

Stock cars, refrigerators, and cabooses. Wesley Castles. Serial 6433. [Ed. 1] Scranton, International Correspondence Schools, c 1959. 71 p., I, 7.5 in.   CAR-15

Freight-car trucks. Serial 6422. Laurence C. Bowes. [Ed. 1] Scranton, International Correspondence Schools, c 1959. 130 p., I, 7.5 in.   CAR-16

User-furnished freight cars. Chicago, Railway Systems & Management Assoc. [1971]. 80 p., I, P, 11 in.   CAR-17

Milwaukee Road freight cars. Martin, 1972.   sCO-70

Passenger

Car names, numbers and consists; a complete record of all lightweight and stream-lined passenger cars ever operated in the U. S., with all car numbers, names, types, builders, assignments, etc., with over 240 floor plan diagrams of individual cars. New York, Wayner Publications, 1972. 249 p., 8½ x 11 in.   CAR-18

A five-year market forecast for commuter railroad cars. [Prepared by Robert I. Sewall.] U. S. Bus. & Defense Serv. Adm. Washington, GPO [1966]. 18 p. (pf.– 6 p.), I, 10.6 in.   CAR-19

Mansions on rails; the folklore of the private railway car. Lucius M. Beebe. Berke-ley, Calif., Howell-North, 1959. 382 p., I (PC), PL, 11 in.   CAR-20

The railroad passenger car; an illustrated history of the first hundred years, with accounts by contemporary passengers. August Mencken. Baltimore, Johns Hopkins Press [1957]. 209 p., I, 9.4 in.   CAR-21

"X," symbol of independence and progress. William M. Spencer. New York, New-comen Society in North America, 1956. 28 p., I, 9 in.   CAR-22

New York Central cars. Wayner, 1972.   sCO-189
Pennsy car plans. Wayner, 1970.   sCO-216
Mr. Pullman elegant [cars]. Beebe.   sCO-226
Pullman [private cars-1939]. Wayner.   sCO-228
Descriptive list [Pullmans]. Davies, 1970.   sCO-229
Santa Fe [pass trains-1937]. Wayner.   sCO-18

Rail cars: diesel, gas-electric, motor, etc.

Self-propelled Diesel cars and multiple-unit trains; a review of recent developments in the United States and overseas. Stanley Berge. Chicago, Northwestern Univ. School of Commerce [1952]. 80 p., I, 11 in.   CAR-23

Brill 250hp [B-E]. Old Line.   sCO-43
Edwards [model 10]. Old Line.   sCO-109
Edwards [model 20]. Old Line.   sCO-110
FWD railroad equipment. Old Line.   sCO-122
McKeen car scrapbook. Old Line.   sCO-167
Mack railcars. Old Line.   sCO-168

Shortage (rail car shortage)

Freight car supply. Hearing, May 13, 1969. Senate, Comm. Com. (Surface Trans.). 91C-1S. Washington, GPO, 1969. 131 p. (pf.–3 p.), 9.4 in.   CAR-24

National freight car shortage. Hearings, October 5, 6, and 7, 1965. House, Int. & For. Comm. 89C-1S. Washington, GPO, 1965. 283 p. (pf.–6 p.), I, M, 9.4 in.
                                                                        CAR-25

Freight car shortages; report to accompany S. 1098. Senate, Comm. Com. (Ft. Car Shortage). 89C-1S. [Washington, GPO, 1965.] 18 p., 9.4 in. (No. 386).   CAR-26

Freight car shortages. Hearings, Senate Senate Comm. Com. (Ft. Car Shortage). 89C-1S. Washington, GPO, 1965. 450 p. (pf.–9 p.), I, M, 9.4 in.   CAR-27

National freight car supply; report, together with minority views, to accompany S. 1063. Senate, Comm. Com. 88C-2S. [Washington, GPO, 1964.] 22 p., 9.4 in. (No. 1192).   CAR-28

Freight car shortage. Hearings on S. 1063, to amend sec. 1(14) (a) of the Interstate Commerce Act to insure the adequacy of the national railroad freight car supply, June 17 and 25, 1963. Senate, Comm. Com. 88C-1S. Washington, GPO, 1963. 143 p. (pf.–3 p.), D, T, 9.4 in.   CAR-29

Freight car shortage. Hearings on S. 886 and S. 1840, similiar [i e similar] bills to amend section 1 (14) (a) of the Interstate Commerce Act to insure the adequacy of the national railroad freight car supply, June 13 and 14, 1961. Senate Comm. Com. 87C-1S. Washington, GPO, 1962. 103 p. (pf.–3 p.), D, T, 9.4 in.   CAR-30

Freight car supply. Hearings on S. 1789 . . . S. 1811 . . . [and] S. 1812. Senate, Int. & For. Comm. (Ft. Car Shortage). 86C-1S. Washington, GPO, 1959. 210 p. (pf.–4 p.), T, 9.4 in.   CAR-31

Amending Interstate Commerce Act (to alleviate freight car shortage). Hearings on S. 2770, a bill to amend section 1 (15) of the Interstate Commerce Act, so as to aid in alleviating shortages of railroad freight cars during periods of emergency or threatened emergency, March 29, May 7 and 8, 1956. Senate, Int. & For. Comm. 84C-2S. Washington, GPO, 1956. 278 p. (pf.–7 p.), I, 9.4 in.   CAR-32

Freight car shortage. Hearings, July 27 and 28, 1955. Senate, Int. & For. Comm. 84C-1S. Washington, GPO, 1955. 136 p. (pf.–6 p.), M, T, 9.4 in.   CAR-33

Shortage of boxcars for transportation of grain. Hearing on methods to alleviate shortage of boxcars for movement of wet grain, February 21, 1951. Senate, Com. on Agric. & For. 82C-1S. Washington, GPO, 1951. 39 p. (pf.–3 p.), 9.4 in. CAR-34

Railroad car shortage. Hearing on H. Res. 813 and H. R. 9480, a bill to amend part I of the Interstate Commerce Act, so as to make provision for an adequate reserve supply of railroad freight cars to supplement the normal supply in time of tempo-rary shortage or national emergency, August 29, 1950. House, Int. & For. Comm. 81C-2S. Washington, GPO, 1950. 65 p. (pf.–3 p.), 9.4 in.   CAR-35

COMPANIES

Alaska Railroad

The Alaska Railroad, by Edwin M. Fitch. Foreword by E. L. Bartlett. New York, Praeger, 1967. 326 p. (pf.—10 p.), I, M (PF), P, 8.7 in.   CO-1

The Alaska Railroad, history and organization. Dept. of Int. [n. p., 1955]. 15 p., 3 l., 10.6 in.   CO-2

Alaska coal lands. Hearing related to Sec. of Int.'s alleged failure to build the Alaskan railroad spur. June 1, 1955, Senate Int. and Ins. (Terr. and Ins. Affairs), 84C, 1S. Washington, GPO, 1955. 195 p. (pf.—3 p.), T, 9.4 in.   CO-3

Improvements in the budget presentation of proposed major capital expenditures, the Alaska Railroad, Dept. of Interior; Report to Congress by the Comptroller-General. Washington, GPO, 1966. 2 l., 15 p., 10.6 in.   CO-4

Effects of the earthquake of March 27, 1964 on the Alaska Railroad, by David S. McCulloch and Manuel G. Bonilla. Washington, GPO, 1970. 161 p. (pf.—8 p.), I, M, PL, 11.4 in.   CO-5

Regulation of Alaska Railroad. Hearing on S. 2413, a bill to provide for economic regulation of the Alaska Railroad under the Interstate Commerce Act, June 25, 1962. Senate Commerce, 87C-2S. Washington, GPO, 1962. 46 p. (pf.—3 p.), 9.4 in.   CO-6

Albany & Susquehanna Railroad

High finance in the sixties. C. F. Adams, Jr., F. C. Hicks (and others).   CO-7

American Locomotive Company (Alco)

An acquaintance with Alco, by Robert P. Olmsted. [Maywood, Ill., 1968.] [80] p. (chiefly illus.), 11.4 in.   CO-8

Ann Arbor Railroad

Late history of the Ann Arbor car ferries No. 6 and 7 by Arthur C. and Lucy F. Frederickson. [Frankfort, Mich.] c 1951. 34 p., I, 8.6 in.   CO-9

The early history of the Ann Arbor car ferries, by Arthur C. and Lucy F. Frederickson. Frankfort, Mich., printed by the Detroit Pub. Co., c 1949. 40 p., I, 9 in.   CO-10

Arcade and Attica Railroad

Arcade and Attica Railroad; from the narrow gauge of the 1880's to today's steam excursions and diesel freight service. Arcade, N. Y., the Baggage Car. 100 p., I (90), M, T, 11 in. By Edward A. Lewis.   CO-11

Atchison, Topeka and Santa Fe Railway

Santa Fe: steel rails through California [by] Donald Duke and Stan Kistler. San Marino, Calif. [Golden West Books, 1963]. 104 p., I, M (PF, PC), Fac, 11.4 in.
                CO-12

Steel trails to Santa Fe. Lawrence L. Waters. University of Kansas Press, 1950. 500 p., I, P, M, 9.4 in.   CO-13

Santa Fe, the railroad that built an empire. James L. Marshall. New York, Random House [1945]. 465 p. (pf.—7, 16 p.), I, P, M, 8.7 in. CO-14

Iron horses of the Santa Fe Trail; a definitive history, in fact and photograph, of the motive power of one of America's great railroads, by E. D. Worley. [Dallas] Southwest Railroad Historical Society [c 1965]. 479, D128 p., I, 12.2 in. CO-15

Arid domain; the Santa Fe Railway and its western land grant. William S. Greever. Stanford [Calif.], Stanford University Press [1954]. 184 p. (pf.—10 p.), M, 10.6 in. CO-16

New Mexico and the Santa Fe Railway. Fred G. Gurley. New York, Newcomen Society in North America, 1950. 32 p., M, 9 in. CO-17

Santa Fe Passenger Train Consists of 1937—detailed consists, schedules, equipment lists, plus a few car photos and plans. New York, Wayner Publications. 44 p., 8½ x 11 in. CO-18

Valuation study of the Pottawatomie Reserve lands, sold by the United States of America to the Atchison, Topeka & Santa Fe Railroad Company, August 7, 1868. William D. Davis. Kansas City, Mo., Farm Management Associates, 1949, c 1950. 156 p. (i. e. 166), l., I, M, 11.4 in.
Supplement. Kansas City, Mo., Farm Management Associates, 1949-[50] c 1950. 2 v. in 4, D, 11.4 in. CO-19

Santa Fe steam [Cajon] Movie. sMP-31
Super Chief Movie. sMP-32

Atlanta and West Point Railroad

Atlanta and West Point Railroad Company. Steam locomotives and history, Georgia Railroad and West Point Route. Richard E. Prince. Green River, Wyo. [1962]. 114 p., I, M, D, 11.4 in. CO-20

Atlantic Coast Line Railroad

Atlantic Coast Line Railroad; steam locomotives, ships, and history, by Richard E. Prince. Green River, Wyo., 1966. 232 p., I, M, P, 11 in. CO-21

Atlantic Coast Line, fragments of its history during over a century. Champion McDowell Davis. New York, Newcomen Society in North America, 1950. 28 p., I, 9 in. CO-22

Atlantic and East Carolina Railroad

Atlantic and East Carolina Railroad. Camp Lejeune Railroad, N. C. Hearings on proposal of Navy Dept. to lease to Camp Lejeune Railroad Co., a subsidiary of Southern Ry., the Camp Lejeune R.R. Feb. 7, 1955. Senate Armed Ser. Com. (Real Est. & Mil. Const.), 84C, 1S, Washington, GPO, 1955. 61 p. (pf.—3 p.), 9.4 in. CO-23

Baldwin Locomotive Works

History of the Baldwin Locomotive Works; unabridged reproduction of the last company-sponsored promotional history. Baldwin Loco. Works. Milwaukee, Old Line Publishers. 212 p., I (177), 9 x 6 in. CO-24

The locomotives that Baldwin built, by Fred Westing. [1st ed.] Seattle, Superior Pub. Co. [1966]. 191 p., I, M, P, 11 in.   CO-25

Baldwin locomotives [and] Baldwin index, 1922-1948. Prepared by Thomas T. Taber, III [and] Paul T. Warner. November, 1948. [n. p., Railroadians of America, 1948.] 71 l., 11 in.   CO-26

Baldwin locomotive works, 1913 illustrated catalog. Reprint. Ocean, N. J., Speciality Press, Inc., 1972. 128 p., I, T, 9 x 6 in.   CO-27

Baldwin locomotive works, illustrated catalog, 1881. Reprint with foreword by Grahame Hardy. Berkeley, Howell-North. 155 p., I, 11 in.   CO-28

Baldwin records of recent construction. Reprints from old locomotive publications. San Marino, Calif., Golden West Books. 40 p., I, 9 x 6 in. (each): No. 56—Steam locomotives [AT & ST]; 72—Mallet locomotives; 78—Industrial and contractors; 79—Pacific type; 89—8 wheel.   CO-29

Baltimore and Ohio Railroad

The Baltimore and Ohio; the story of the railroad that grew up with the United States. Carroll Bateman. Baltimore, printed at the Baltimore & Ohio Railroad Print Plant, c 1951. 32 p., I, M (C), 11 in.   CO-30

A picture history of B & O motive power. Lawrence W. Sagle. [1st ed.] New York, Simmons-Boardman [1953, c 1952]. 82 p., I, 10.6 in.   CO-31

Report to RFC Administrator W. Stuart Symington re Reconstruction Finance Corporation's purchase of Baltimore & Ohio Railroad Company's 4% collateral trust bonds maturing January 1, 1965. Joseph J. Smith. [Washington, 1952.] 92 l. (pf.—2), 10.6 in.   CO-32

RFC loans to the Baltimore & Ohio Railroad; analysis of the loan of the Reconstruction Finance Corporation to the Baltimore & Ohio Railroad. Proposed report submitted to a subcommittee of the Banking and Currency Committee on July 25, 1947, and not adopted. Senate Banking & Currency. Washington, GPO, 1951. 74 p. (pf.—3 p.), 9.4 in.   CO-33

Maryland's influence upon land cessions to the United States; with minor papers on George Washington's interest in western lands, the Potomac Company, and a National University. Herbert B. Adams. Baltimore, N. Murray, Publication Agent. Johns Hopkins University, 1885. St. Clair Shores, Mich., Scholarly Press [1969]. 102 p., 9 in.   CO-34

John W. Garrett of the B & O. Catton, 1959.   sBIO-3
Double-headers [B & O]. Movie.   sSMP-1

Bangor and Aroostook Railroad

Bangor and Aroostook Railroad, and connections. National Survey Co., Chester, Vt. [1952]. M (C), 27 x 19.6 in.   CO-35

Bessemer and Lake Erie Railroad

The Bessemer and Lake Erie Railroad, 1869-1969, by Roy C. Beaver. San Marino, Calif., Golden West Books [1969]. 184 p., I, F, M (IF), P, 11.4 in.   CO-36

Boston & Albany Railroad

The State, the investor, and the railroad; the Boston & Albany, 1825-1867. Stephen Salsbury. Cambridge, Harvard Univ. Press, 1967.   CO-37

Boston and Maine Railroad

New shares for old; the Boston and Maine stock modification, by Robert L. Masson with the assistance of Carolyn Stubbs. Boston, Harvard University, Division of Research, Graduate School of Business Administration, 1958. 398 p., 8.7 in.   CO-38

A case study of balloting regulation; the Boston and Maine recapitalizes, 1948-1953. Robert L. Masson. Boston, Harvard University, Division of Research, Graduate School of Business Administration, 1956. 373 p. (pf.—16 p.), D, 8.7 in.
                                    CO-39

Bradford, Bordell & Kinzua Railroad

Bradford, Bordell & Kinzua; narrow gauge. Arcade, N. Y., the Baggage Car. 140 p., 11 in. By Tom Barber and Jim Woods.   CO-40

Bridgton & Saco River Railroad

Bridgton & Saco River Railroad; reprint—operating rule book. Arcade, N. Y., the Baggage Car. 20 p., T.   CO-41

Busted and still running; story of Maine's 2-ft. gauge Bridgton & Saco River (B & H) R.R. Edgar T. Mead, Jr. Brattleboro, Vt., Stephen Green Press, 58 p., I, M, T, 8.5 in.   CO-42

Brill Co.

Brill 250 h.p. gas-electric car; technical description. Milwaukee, Old Line Publishers. 24 p., I (16), P.   CO-43

City and interurban cars. J. G. Brill Co. San Marino, Calif., Golden West Books [1966]. 80 p. (chiefly illus.), 11 in.   CO-44

California Western Railroad

Redwoods, Iron Horses, and the Pacific; the story of the California Western "Skunk" Railroad. Spencer Crump. 2nd ed., revised, Los Angeles, Trans-Anglo Books, 1965. 168 p., I, M, P, 11.4 in.; also 1963, 159 p.   CO-45

The Skunk Railroad: Ft. Bragg to Willits. Spencer Crump. Los Angeles, Trans-Anglo Books, 1965. 64 p., I, M, P, 8.3 in.   CO-46

Canandaigua Street Railway

The story of the Canandaigua Street Railway Company, the Canandaigua Electric Light and Railway Company, Ontario Light and Traction Company, and the Rochester and Eastern Rapid Railway. William R. Gordon. Rochester, N. Y., 1953. 107 p., I, 9 in.   CO-47

Canadian National Railways

History of the Canadian National Railways; the absorbing and definitive history of America's largest railway system. George R. Stevens. Riverside, N. J., Macmillan Co. [1972]. 384 p., I, 9.2 in.   CO-48

Canadian National Railways. George R. Stevens. With a foreword by Donald Gordon, and an introd. by S. W. Fairweather. Toronto, Clarke, Irwin, 1960-62. 2 v., I, 9.4 in.   CO-49

Canadian National steam power, by Anthony Clegg and Ray Corley. Montreal, Trains & Trolleys, c 1969. 128 p., illus., 9.4 x 12.2 in.   CO-50

Keeping Track [magazine].

Canadian Pacific Railway

Building the Canadian West; the land and colonization policies of the Canadian Pacific Railway. James B. Hedges. New York, Russell & Russell [1971]. 422 p. (pf.–7 p.), 9 in.   CO-51

The Pacific tourist. Adams & Bishop's illustrated transcontinental guide of travel, from the Atlantic to the Pacific Ocean. A complete traveler's guide of the Union and Central Pacific railroads. Frederick E. Shearer, editor. With special contribution by F. V. Hayden [and others]. Illus. by Thomas Moran [and others]. New York, Adams & Bishop, 1884. New York, Bounty Books [1970]. 373 p., I, P, 9.4 in.   CO-52

Canadian Pacific Spanner [magazine].

Carson and Colorado Railroad

Slim rails through the sand, by George Turner; the classic of the narrow gauge Carson and Colorado-Southern Pacific. Conora del Mar, Calif., Trans-Anglo Books. 110 p., I, 11 in.   CO-53

Cedar Rapids and Iowa City. Movie.   sMP-46

Central Pacific Railroad (see also Southern Pacific)

Life and times of the Central Pacific Railroad. [Edited by David F. Myrick.] San Francisco, printed by L. and A. Kennedy, 1969. 12 folders in case. I (C), Fac (PC), M, 10.2 in.   CO-54

Chattanooga Railroad

Andrews' Raiders. Roberta S. Feuerlicht. New York, Crowell-Collier Press, 1967. 116 p., I, D, 8.3 in.   CO-55

In pursuit of the General; a history of the Civil War R.R. raid. William Pittenger. San Marino, Calif., Golden West Books, 1965. 416 p., I, Fac, M, P, 9 in.   CO-56

Chesapeake and Ohio Railway

Chessie's road. Charles W. Turner. Richmond, Garrett & Massie, 1956. 286 p., I, 9.4 in.   CO-57

C & O Power; steam and diesel locomotives of the Chesapeake and Ohio Railway, by Philip Shuster, E. L. Huddleston and Alvin Staufer. Medina, Ohio, A. Staufer, 1965. 351 p., I (PC), M, 11.4 in.   CO-58

Robert R. Young. Borkin, 1969. s.

Chicago, Burlington and Quincy Railroad

The Burlington in Transition, by Bernard G. Corbin. Associate editor: Joseph C. Hardy. [Red Oak, Iowa, Corbin Publications, 1967.] 208 p., I (PC), F, M, P, 11.8 in.　　　　　　　CO-59

Burlington west; a colonization history of the Burlington Railroad, by Richard C. Overton. New York, Russell & Russell [1967, c 1941]. 583 p. (pf.—18 p.), I, F, M, P, 9 in.　　　　　　　CO-60

Guide to the Burlington archives in the Newberry Library, 1851-1901, compiled by Elisabeth Coleman Jackson and Carolyn Curtis. Chicago, Newberry Library, 1949. 374 p. (pf.—23 p.), 9.4 in.　　　　　　　CO-61

Trail of the Zephyrs; the Burlington Route in Northern Illinois, by Robert P. Olmsted. [n. p., c 1970.] 91 p., I, 11.4 in.　　　　　　　CO-62

Diesels west! The evolution of power on the Burlington. David P. Morgan. [Milwaukee, Kalmbach Pub. Co., 1963.] 164 p., I, P, M, D, 10.2 in.　　CO-63

Steam locomotives of the Burlington route, by Bernard Corbin [and] William Kerka. [1st ed. Red Oak, Iowa, 1960.] 304 p., I, P, M, D, 11.4 in.　　CO-64

Map of the West. CB&Q R.R. Co. Chicago [1949] c 1947. M (C), 43 x 60 in.　　　　　　　CO-65

The great Burlington Strike of 1888; a case study in labor relation. Donald LeCrone McMurry. Cambridge, Harvard Univ. Press, 1956. 377 p. (pf.—10 p.), M, 9.8 in.　　　　　　　CO-66

Nebraska CB&Q depots.　　　　　　　sST-3
California Zepher. Movie.　　　　　　　sMP-25

Chicago and Eastern Illinois Railroad

The economic history of the Chicago and Eastern Illinois Railroad. Richard Jack Teweles. Urbana, 1949. 4 p., 9 in.　　　　　　　CO-67

Chicago Great Western Railway

Six units to Sycamore; Chicago Great Western in Illinois, by Robert P. Olmsted. [Janesville, Wis., 1967.] [32] p. (chiefly illus.), 11.4 in.　　　　　　　CO-68

Chicago, Milwaukee, St. Paul and Pacific Railroad

Milwaukee Road West; a pictorial history of the Chicago, Milwaukee, St. Paul and Pacific. Charles R. and Dorothy M. Wood. Seattle, Superior Publishing Co., 1972. 192 p., I (300), T, 11 in.　　　　　　　CO-69

Milwaukee Road freight cars; drawings of company owned freight car roster (1937) plus steam era caboose roster. Charles F. Martin. Chicago, Normandie House Publishers, 1972. 94 p., loose leaf, 11 x 4 in.　　　　　　　CO-70

The Hiawatha story. Jim Scribbins [Milwaukee, Kalmbach Pub. Co., 1970.] 267 p., I, 9 x 11.4 in.　　　　　　　CO-71

Milwaukee Road locomotives; tracings of shop diagram blue prints of steam, electric, shay and narrow gauge locomotives. Charles F. Martin. Chicago, Normandie House Publishers, 1972. 110 p., D, PL, T, 11 x 4 in. CO-72

Chicago, North Shore & Milwaukee Railroad

North Shore; America's fastest interurban [by] William D. Middleton. San Marino, Calif., Golden West Books [1964]. 125 p., I, M (C), P, 11.4 in. CO-73

Scenes from the Shore Lines: North Shore Line, South Shore Line, by Robert P. Olmsted. [Janesville, Wis., 1964.] 1 v. (chiefly illus.), 11.4 in. CO-74

Chicago, South Shore and South Bend Railroad

South Shore; America's last interurban. William D. Middleton. San Marino, Calif., Golden West Books. 186 p., I, 11 in. CO-75

Chicago and North Western Railway

Chicago and North Western Railway steam power, 1848-1956, classes A−Z, by Charles T. Knudsen. Chicago, Knudsen Publications [1965]. 187 p. (pf.−20 p.), I, M, P, 11.4 in. CO-76

Chicago, Rock Island and Pacific Railroad

Iron road to empire; the history of 100 years of the progress and achievements of the Rock Island lines. William Edward Hayes. [New York, Simmons-Boardman, 1953.] 306 p., I, 9.4 in. CO-77

Cleveland, Cincinnati, Chicago and St. Louis Railway

Cleveland, Cincinnati, Chicago & St. Louis Ry. Co.; a pioneer carrier of Delaware County, Ohio. Ed. and compiled by Anna C. Smith Pabst. Delaware, Ohio, 1963. 81 p. [51] 31, I, Fac, M, P, 11 in. CO-78

Cleveland & Erie Railway

Erie to Conneault by trolley; history of the Cleveland & Erie Ry. Co., by Kenneth C. Springirth. Erie, Pa., 1968. 103 l., I, Fac, 11 in. CO-79

Colorado Midland Railway

Colorado Midland [Ry. Co.], Morris Calky, Denver, Rocky Mountain R.R. Club, 1965. 467 p. (pf.−15 p.), I, M, P, plate (4C), 11.4 in. CO-80

Colorado & Southern Railway

Gulf to Rockies; the heritage of the Fort Worth and Denver-Colorado at Southern Railways, 1861-1898, by Richard C. Overton. With pen sketches by Reginald Marsh. Westport, Conn., Greenwood Press [1970, c 1953]. 410 p. (pf.−13 p.), I, Fac, M, P, 9 in. CO-81

Colorado & Southern (Ry.), Northern Div., by James L. Ehernberger and Francis G. Gschwind. Callaway, Neb., E. & E. Pub., 1966. 64 p., I, M, 11.4 in. CO-82

Concord & Claremont Railroad

Through covered bridges to Concord, a recollection of the Concord & Claremont R.R. By Edgar T. Mead, Jr. Brattleboro, Vt., Stephen Greene Press. I, D, M, 8.5 in. CO-83

Delaware and Hudson Railway

Delaware & Hudson; an illustrated history of the important coal and bridge railroad from the time of the antecedent canal network. Jim Shaughnessy. Berkeley, Calif., Howell-North Books, 1967. 476 p. (pf.—12 p.), I (PC), Fac, M, P, 11.4 in.

CO-84

The gravity railroads of the Delaware & Hudson Canal Co. and the Pennsylvania Coal Co. Honesdale, Pa., Wayne County Historical Soc., c 1950. M (C), 15.8 x 21.2 in.

CO-85

The Delaware and Hudson Canal, a history. Edwin D. Le Roy. Honesdale, Pa., Wayne County Historical Historical Society, c 1950. 95 p., I, M, F, 9 in.   CO-86

Coal boats to tidewater; the story of the Delaware & Hudson Canal, by Manville B. Wakefield. Foreword by Carl Carmer. [South Fallsburg, N. Y., printed by Steingart Associates, 1965.] 206 p. (pf.—17 p.), I, F, M, P, 10.2 in.   CO-87

Delaware, Lackawanna and Western Railroad

The Lackawanna story; the first hundred years of the Delaware, Lackawanna and Western Railroad, by Robert J. Casey and W. A. S. Douglas. New York, McGraw-Hill [1951]. 223 p., I, P, M, 9.4 in.   CO-88

The Lackawanna, "the route of Phoebe Snow," 1851-1951; a centenary address, William White. New York, Newcomen Society in North America, 1951. 40 p., I, 9 in.   CO-89

Denver, Boulder & Western Railroad

The Switzerland trail of America; an illustrated history of the romantic narrow gauge lines running west from Boulder, Colorado: the Greeley, Salt Lake & Pacific, and the Colorado & Northwestern, later the Denver, Boulder & Western. Forest Crossen. [Limited ed. Boulder Colo., Pruett Press, 1962.] 417 p. (pf.—10 p.), I (PC), M (3F), 11.4 in.   CO-90

Denver, North West & Pacific Railroad

The giant's ladder: David H. Moffat and his railroad. Harold A. Boner. [Milwaukee, Kalmbach Pub. Co., 1962.] 224 p., I, 11.4 in.   CO-91

The Moffat Road [by] Edward T. Bollinger and Frederick Bauer. Denver, Sage Books [1962]. 359 p., I (PC), P, M, 11.4 in.   CO-92

Denver and Rio Grande Western Railroad

Rebel of the Rockies; a history of the Denver and Rio Grande Western Railroad. Robert G. Athearn. New Haven, Yale University Press, 1962. 395 p. (pf.—14 p.), I, M, Fac, 11 in.   CO-93

Rio Grande: mainline of the Rockies, by Lucius Beebe & Charles Clegg. Berkeley, Calif., Howell-North, 1962. 380 p., I (PC), M, 11.4 in.   CO-94

Kansas West. George L. Anderson. San Marino, Calif., Golden West Books [1963]. 268 p., I, P, M, 9 in.   CO-95

Steam in the Rockies; a steam locomotive roster of the Denver Rio Grande. Colorado R.R. Museum. Golden, Colo. [c 1963]. 82 p., I, 11 in.   CO-96

Logging along the Denver & Rio Grande: narrow gauge logging railroads of southwestern Colorado and northern New Mexico [by] Gordon S. Chappell. Golden, Colorado Railroad Museum [1971]. 190 p., I, 11.4 in.   CO-97

The Rio Grande pictorial; one-hundred years of railroading thru the Rockies. Denver, Sundance, Ltd, 1971. 216 p., I (47C, 51 tinted, 156 b&w), 11 x 8.5 in.   CO-98

Chili line, the narrow rail trail to Sante Fe; the story of the narrow gauge Denver and Rio Grande Western's Sante Fe Branch 1880-1941, by John A. Gjevre. [Espanola, N. M., printed by the Rio Grande Sun Press, 1969.] 82 p., I, 9.4 in.   CO-99

Narrow gauge to Silverton; D&RGW Silverton Branch. John B. Hungerford. San Marino, Calif., Golden West Books. 36 p., I, 8.5 in.   CO-100

Narrow gauge to Silverton; the story of an American heirloom [by] John B. Hungerford. Reseda, Calif., Hungerford Press, 1963. 36 p., I, M, 8.7 in.; also, 1956, 3ed.-1957, 5ed.-1959, 6ed.-1960,7 ed.-1960, 8ed.-1961.   CO-101

Gen. Wm. J. Palmer. McCathy.	sBIO-13
California Zepher. Movie.	sMP-25
Climb to Cumbres. Movie.	sMP-26
Memories of steam. Movie.	sMP-27
Narrow gauge to Silverton. Movie.	sMP-28

Denver & Salt Lake Railroad

Rails that climb; the story of the Moffat Road. Edward T. Bollinger. Drawings by Wilfred Stedman. [W. C. Jones Edition.] Santa Fe, Tydal Press [1950]. 402 p. (pf.—17 p.), I, P, M, 9.4 in.   CO-102

Denver, South Park & Pacific Railroad

Denver, South Park & Pacific; a history of the Denver, South Park & Pacific Railroad and allied narrow gauge lines of the Colorado & Southern Railway Company. Meredith C. Poor. [Denver, Rocky Mountain Railroad Club, 1949.] 498 p. (pf.—22 p.), I, P, M, 11.4 in.
Pictorial Supplement. [By] R. H. Kindig, E. J. Haley [and] M. C. Poor. [Limited ed. Denver, Rocky Mountain Railroad Club, 1959.] 467 p. (pf.—14 p.), I (PC), P, M, 11.4 in.   CO-103

Dickson Manufacturing Co.

Locomotives of the Dickson Manufacturing Co; history and locomotive roster and a reprint of the 1885 catalog. Gerald M. Best. San Marino, Calif., Golden West Books. 176 p., I, 7 x 10 in.   CO-104

Duluth, Missabe and Iron Range Railway

The Missabe Road; the story of the Duluth, Missabe and Iron Range Railway. Frank A. King. San Marino, Calif., Golden West Books, 1972. 224 p., I (350, 4C), 11 in.   CO-105

Duluth, South Shore and Atlantic Railway

Duluth, South Shore and Atlantic (Ry. Co.). Railway and Loco. Historical Society. Boston, 1964 (Bulletin 111). CO-106

East Broad Top Railroad

A ramble into the past on the East Broad Top Railroad, Rockhill Furnace, Pennsylvania. Frank Kyper. Official EBT souvenir booklet. [Rockhill Furnace, Pa., East Broad Top Railroad and Coal Co., 1971.] 62 p., I, 9 in. CO-107

A quick review of the East Broad Top. Editor: Joseph A. Mannix. 1st ed. [Rockhill Furnace, Pa.] c 1960. 38 p., I, 6.3 x 9.4 in. CO-108

Edwards Railway Motor Car Co.

Edwards Railway Motor Car Co., 1928 Model 10 catalog; popular line of 31' light duty passenger cars. Milwaukee, Old Line Publishers. 30 p., I, 8.5 in. CO-109

Edwards Railway Motor Car Co., 1926 Model 20 brochure; describes 43' heavy duty cars. Milwaukee, Old Line Publishers. 20 p., I, 8.5 in. CO-110

Erie Railroad

Stories and history of the Erie Railroad; Rochester Div.; steam and diesels, 1854-1964; electric from 1907-1934; 110 years of Erie service in the Genessee Valley. William R. Gordon. Rochester, N. Y., 1965. 144 p., I, Fac, P, 11 in. CO-111

Chapters of Erie, by Charles Francis Adams, Jr. and Henry Adams. Ithaca, N. Y., Great Seal Books [1956]. 193 p., 7.5 in. CO-112

Erie power; steam and diesel locomotives of the Erie Railroad from 1840 to 1970. Frederick Westing. Captions by F. Westing and A. Staufer, edited and published by Alvin F. Staufer. Medina, Ohio, c 1970. 447 p., I (PC), M, 11.4 in. CO-113

Erie-Lackawanna Railway

The Erie Lackawanna Railroad Company and suburban passenger service in New Jersey; report to Governor Richard J. Hughes. N. J. Dir. of R.R. Trans. [Trenton], 1965. 75 l. (pf.–6), I, 11 in. CO-114

Evans Products Co.

Evans rail car forecast, 1966-1970. Evans Products Company, Portland, Ore., 1966. 36 p. (pf.–3 p.), I (PC), 11 in. CO-115

Florida East Coast Railway

The Railroad that died at sea; the Florida East Coast's Key West Extension, Pat Parks. Brattleboro, Vt., S. Greene Press, 1968. 44 p., I, P, 8.7 in. CO-116

Henry M. Flagler, 1830-1913; Florida's East Coast is his monument! John Wellburn Martin. New York, Newcomen Society in North America, 1956. 24 p., I, 9 in.
CO-117

Building out to sea: the Key West extension of the Florida East Coast Railway; a talk before the Lexington Group, Mississippi Valley Historical Association, Lexington, Kentucky, May 7, 1953. C. J. Corliss [n. p., 1953 or 4.] 13 l., 11 in.
CO-118

Fonda, Johnstown and Gloversville Railroad

Steam and trolley days on the Fonda, Johnstown and Gloversville Railroad [by] David F. Nestle [and] William R. Gordon. [n. p.] Fonda, Johnstown & Gloversville R.R. Co. [1958]. I, 11 in.   CO-119

Trolleys down the Mohawk Valley. Schenectady Rys., Ballston Terminal R.R. Co., Fonda, Johnstown & Gloversville R.R., Cayadutta Ry. Co., Amsterdam St. Ry. Co. William R. Gordon. Rochester, N. Y., 1968. 208 p., I (C), M, P, 11 in. CO-120

Fort Worth and Denver Railway

Gulf to Rockies; the heritage of the Fort Worth and Denver-Colorado and Southern Railways, 1861-1898. Richard C. Overton. With pen sketches by Reginald Marsh. Austin, Univ. of Texas Press, 1953. 410 p. (pf.—13 p.), I, P, M, 9.4 in. CO-121

FWD Co.

FWD railroad equipment; covers 1920's line of self-propelled rail cars. Milwaukee, Old Line Publishers. 12 p., I (15), 11 in.   CO-122

General Motors Corp., Electro-Motive Div.

Our GM scrapbook. [Milwaukee, Wis., Kalmbach Pub. Co., 1971.] 148 p., I, 12.8 in.   CO-123

Engineer's operating manual (FP-7).   sLD-11

General Railway Signal Co.

G-R-S carrier control; description, operation and maintenance. General Railway Signal Co., Rochester, N. Y., 1949. 71 p., I, D (PF), 9 in. (34). CO-124

Georgia Railroad

Steam locomotives and history; Georgia Railroad and West Point Route. Richard E. Prince, Green River, Wyo. [1962]. 114 p., I, M, D, 11.4 in. CO-125

Gilpin Tram Route

The Gilpin gold tram, Colorado's unique narrow-gauge. Mallory H. Ferrell. Boulder, Colo., Pruett Pub. Co. [c 1970]. 112 p., I, Fac, M, PL, 11.4 in. CO-126

Glendale & Montrose

Glendale & Montrose [by] Jeffrey Moreau and James Walker, Jr. [Los Angeles], Pacific Bookworld [1966]. 65 p., I, 11 in.   CO-127

Grand View Beach Railroad

Manitou Beach trolley days, 1891-1925. William Reed Gordon. [Rochester, N. Y., 1957.] 112 p., I, 9 in.   CO-128

Great Northern Railway

Lines West; a pictorial history of the Great Northern Railway operations and motive power from 1887 to 1967, by Charles R. Wood. [1st ed.] Seattle, Superior Pub. Co. 190 p., I, F, M, PL, P, 11 in.   CO-129

An economic history of the Mesabi Division of the Great Northern Railway Company to 1915. Joseph W. Thompson. Ann Arbor, University Microfilms.   CO-130

Locomotives of the empire builder; history and roster of Great Northern steam
locomotives, Charles F. Martin. Chicago, Normandie House Publishers, 1972.
84 p., I (82 photos), T, 11 x 9 in.   CO-131

Gulf, Mobile and Ohio Railroad

The Gulf, Mobile and Ohio; a railroad that had to expand or expire. James H.
Lemly. Homewood, Ill, R.D. Irwin, 1953. 347 p. (pf.—8 p.), I, P (PC), M, 9.4 in.
                                                                       CO-132
My railroad saga. Issac B. Tigrett. New York, Newcomen Society in North
America, 1952. 24 p., 9 in.   CO-133

Hagerstown & Frederick Railway

Blue Ridge Trolley; the Hagerstown & Frederick Railway, the trolley nucleus of
Potomac Edison Co. Herbert H. Harwood. San Marino, Calif., Golden West Books.
144 p., I, 11 in.   CO-134

Hawaiian Railroad

Narrow gauge in a kingdom; the history of the Hawaiian Railroad Company, 1979-
1897. J. C. Conde. Felton, Calif., Glenwood Publishers. 96 p., I, doc, M, 11 in.
                                                                       CO-135

Hoosac Tunnel & Wilmington Railroad

Hoot, toot & whistle; illustrated history of the Hoosac Tunnel & Wilmington R.R.
Bernard R. Carman. Brattleboro, Vt., Stephen Green Press. 44 p., I, 8.5 in.
                                                                       CO-136

Illinois Central Railroad

Main line of Mid-America; the story of the Illinois Central. Carlton J. Corliss.
New York, Creative Age Press, 1950. 490 p. (pf.—18 p.), I, P, M (PC), 8.7 in.
                                                                       CO-137

The Illinois Central heritage, 1851-1951; a centenary address. Wayne A. Johnston.
New York, Newcomen Society in North America, 1951. 32 p., I, P, 9 in.   CO-138

Illinois Central Railroad Company, a centennial bibliography, 1851-1951, compiled by Helen R. Richardson, reference librarian. Bureau of Railway Economics,
Washington, 1950. 239 p. (pf.—13 p.), M, 9 in.   CO-139

Guide to the Illinois Central archives in the Newberry Library, 1851-1906, compiled by Carolyn Curtis Mohr. Chicago, Newberry Library, 1951. 210 p. (pf.—
16 p.), 9.8 in.   CO-140

The Illinois Central Railroad and its colonization work, by Paul W. Gates. New
York, Johnson Reprint Corp., 1968. 374 p. (pf.—7, 13 p.), I, M, 9 in.   CO-141

Chief engineers of the Illinois Central Railroad. I.C.R.R. [n. p., 1950.] 27 l., P, F,
10.6 in.   CO-142

Illinois Central Railroad, main line of Mid-America; the simplification of its debt
structure, 1938-1952. Edwin S. S. Sunderland. [New York.] Priv. print. [Pandick
Press] 1952. 23 p., I, 10.2 in.   CO-143

Abraham Lincoln [and I. C.] Sunderland, 1955. sBIO-8
Abraham Lincoln [and I. C.] Corliss, 1950. sBIO-9

Illinois Terminal Railroad

Illinois Terminal R.R. Co. The Lincoln Land Traction, compiled by James D. Johnson. 1st chapter by John P. Carroll. Wheaton, Ill., Traction Orange Co., 1965. 147 p., I, P, 11.4 in. CO-144

Illinois Terminal interurbans. Movie. MP-48

Ilwaco Railroad & Nav. Co.

The railroad that ran with the tide; 40 year history of Ilwaco Railroad & Nav. Co. R. J. Feagans. Berkeley, Howell-North. 148 p., I (181), 11 in. CO-145

Interurban Rapid Transit [N.Y.C.]

Interborough Rapid Transit; the New York subway; its construction and equipment. New York, Interborough Rapid Transit Co., 1904. New York, Arno Press, 1969. 150 p., I, M (C), PL, 12.6 in. CO-146

Kansas City, Mexico and Orient Railway

Destination Topolobampo; the Kansas City, Mexico & Orient Ry. by John L. Kerr with Frank Donovan. San Marino, Calif., Golden West Books, 1968. 270 p., I, M, P, 8.7 in. CO-147

Kansas Pacific Railway

Guide map of the best and shortest cattle trail to the Kansas Pacific Railway; with a concise and accurate description of the route, showing distances, streams, crossings, camping grounds, wood and water, supply stores, etc., from the Red River crossing to Ellis, Russell, Ellsworth, Brookville, Salina, Solomon, and Abilene. Kansas Pacific Ry. Co. [Kansas City, Mo., 1875.] Pecos, Tex., B. Leftwich, c 1958. 21 p., M (FC), 6.3 in. CO-148

Guide map of the best and shortest cattle trail to the Kansas Pacific Railway; with a concise and accurate description of the route, showing distances, streams, crossings, camping grounds, wood and water, supply stores, etc., from the Red River crossing to Ellis, Russell, Ellsworth, Brookville, Salina, Solomon and Abilene. Kansas Pacific Ry. Co. [Kansas City, Mo., 1874. Evanston, Ill., The Branding Iron Press, c 1956.] Fac: 21 p., I, M (F), 7.1 in. CO-149

Kendall & Eldred

Kendall & Eldred; narrow gauge. Arcade, N. Y., the Baggage Car. 40 p., 11 in. By Robert Stout. CO-150

Krauss-Maffei

Krauss-Maffei operational manual. Milwaukee, Old Line Publishers. 144 p., I, D, 7 in. CO-151

Lima Locomotive Works

Lima locomotives, 1911 catalog; reprint. San Marino, Calif., Golden West Books. 48 p., I, 11 in. CO-152

Long Island Railroad

Steel rails to the sunrise, by Ron Ziel and George H. Foster. 1st ed. New York, Duell, Sloan and Pearce, 1965. 320 p., I, Fac, M, P, 11 in.   CO-153

Early history of the Long Island Railroad, 1834-1900. Mildred H. Smith. Uniondale, L. I., Salisbury Printers, 1958. 63 p., I, 9.4 in.   CO-154

Change at Jamaica, westbound [and eastbound] ; a commuter's guide to survival, written, illustrated, and suffered by Warren Goodrich, Commuter. New York, Vanguard Press [1957]. 48 p., I, 9.4 in.

Long Island R.R. 1914 map; shows L.I.R.R. at its greatest extent. Mt. Arlington, N. J., Camelback Publishers. M, 52 x 20 in.   CO-155

Editorial comment which has appeared in daily newspapers, concerning the recently announced plan of the Long Island Transit Authority for rehabilitation of the Long Island Railroad, and a letter to the Times from Major General William H. Draper, Jr., former trustee of the railroad. Long Island Transit Authority, New York, 1954. [15] p., I, 11 in.   CO-156

Technical analysis of Plan for the prompt rehabilitation of the Long Island Railroad road. Sidney H. Bingham. [New York, Long Island Transit Authority, 1954.] 34 p., I, 11 in.   CO-157

Plan of reorganization proposed by Long Island Transit Authority, August 14, 1952. William W. Golub, counsel for the Authority. Long Island Transit Authority, [New York, 1952]. 37 p., 11 in.   CO-158

Plan for the Long Island Railroad. Long Island Transit Authority [New York] 1952. 15 p., 8.7 in.   CO-159

Proposed legislation recommended in report to Hon. Thomas E. Dewey; Long Island Transit Authority act; bill to amend the Bankruptcy act; bill to amend the Interstate Commerce act. N. Y. Long Island R.R. Commission [New York, 1951]. 41 p., 9 in.   CO-160

Louisville & Nashville Railroad (see also Chattanooga Railroad, NC&StL Railway)

History of the Louisville & Nashville Railroad; describes L&N since 1859. Maury Klein. Riverside, N. J., Macmillan Co. [1972]. 384 p., I, 9.2 in.   CO-161

L&N; its first 100 years. John E. Tilford. New York, Newcomen Society in North America, 1951. 32 p., I, M, 9 in.   CO-162

Louisville & Nashville steam locomotives, by Richard E. Prince. Rev. ed. Green River, Wyo., 1968. 228 p., I, M, 11.4 in.   CO-163

Louisville & Nashville steam locomotives. Richard E. Prince. Green River, Wyo. [1959]. 128 p., I, M, T, 11.4 in.   CO-164

Merger in a regulated industry; a case study of the proposed merger of the Louisville & Nashville and Nashville, Chattanooga, & St. Louis Railroads. A staff report to subcommittee No. 5. House-Judiciary Com. (No. 5). Washington, GPO, 1956. 61 p. (pf.—3 p.), M (C-F), T, 9 in.   CO-165

Steam days [L&N]. Movie.   sMP-7
Return of the General [L&N]. Movie.   sMP-8

McCloud River Railroad

Pine across the mountain; California's McCloud River Railroad. Robert M. Hanft.
San Marino, Calif., Golden West Books. 224 p., I (295), 11 in.   CO-166

McKeen Car Co.

McKeen Car scrapbook; based on 1912 McKeen catolog which is reproduced.
Milwaukee, Old Line Publishers. 32 p., I, PL, T, D, 11 in.   CO-167

Mack Truck Co.

Mack railcars; models AB and AC. Milwaukee, Old Line Publishers. 18 p., I (17),
PL, 11 in.   CO-168

Milwaukee and Suburban Transport Co.

Map showing transportation system of the Transport Co. within the Milwaukee
metropolitian area. Milwaukee and Suburban Transport Company, Milwaukee,
c 1953. Map (C), 27 x 17.7 in.   CO-169

Minneapolis & St. Louis Railway

Mileposts on the prarie; the story of the Minneapolis & St. Louis Railway. Frank
Pierce Donovan. New York, Simmons-Boardman Pub. Co. [1950]. 310 p. (pf.–
9 p.), I, P, M, 8.7 in.   CO-170

Minnesota Transfer Railway

Gateway to the Northwest; the story of the Minnesota Transfer Railway. Frank
Pierce Donovan. [Minneapolis, 1954.] 32 p., I, 8.3 in.   CO-171

Monticello & Port Jervis Railway

Minisink Valley express; a history of the Port Jervis, Monticello & New York Railroad and its predecessors. Gerald M. Best. Art work by E. S. Hammock and
Frederic Shaw. Beverly Hills, Calif., 1956. 93 p., I, 9.4 in.   CO-172

Morristown & Erie Railroad

Morristown and Erie Railroad; people, paper and profits. Thomas T. Taber. [Rah-
way, N. J., Railroadians of Ameirca, 1967.] 67 p. (pf.–12 p.), I, M, P, 11.4 in.
                                                                        CO-173

Missouri-Kansas-Texas Railroad

The Katy Railroad and the last frontier. Vincent Victor Masterman. [1st ed.]
Norman, Univ. of Oklahoma Press [1952]. 312 p. (pf.–16 p.), I, P, M, 9.4 in.
                                                                        CO-174

"Katy," pioneer railroad of the Southwest, 1865. Donald Vincent Fraser. New
York, Newcomen Society in North America, 1953. 28 p., I, 9 in.   CO-175

Missouri & North Arkansas Railroad

The North Arkansas line; the story of the Missouri & North Arkansas Railroad, by James R. Fair, Jr. Berkeley, Calif., Howell North Books, 1969. 304 p. (pf.—10 p.), I, M, P, 9.4 in.   Co-176

Missouri Pacific Railroad

Missouri Pacific lines news reel. St. Louis, Missouri Pacific News Bureau. I, 11.4 in. monthly.   CO-177

Mt. Tamalpais and Muir Woods Railroad

The crookedest railroad in the world; a history of the Mt. Tamalpais and Muir Woods Railroad of California, by Theodore G. Wurm and Alvin C. Graves. [2d rev. ed.] Berkeley, Calif., Howell-North, 1960. 123 p., I, 9.4 in.   CO-178

Mt. Washington Railway

Railway to the moon, by Glen M. Kidder. [Littleton, N. H., Courier Print Co., 1969.] 184 p., I, P, 9.4 in.   CO-179

Mount Washington Railway Co.; the world first log railway. Mount Washington, N. H. [by] Ellen C. Teague. New York, Newcomen Society in North America, 1970. 28 p., I, 9 in.   CO-180

Narragansett Pier Railroad

A short haul to the bay; history of the Narragansett Pier R.R. [Rhode Island]. By James N. Henwood. Brattleboro, Vt., Stephen Greene Press. 48 p., I, M, D, 8.5 in.   CO-181

Nashville, Chattanooga and St. Louis Railway

The Nashville, Chattanooga and St. Louis Railway: history and steam locomotives, by Richard E. Prince. Green River, Wyo [1967]. 196 p., I, M, P, 11.4 in.   CO-182

Wages, earnings, and employment, Nashville, Chattanooga & St. Louis Railway, 1866-1896. Rendigs Fels. [Nashville, 1953.] 72 p., D (PC), 8.7 in. (Vanderbilt Univ. Inst. of Rec. & Training in Social Sciences, No. 10.)   CO-183

Nevada County Narrow Gauge Railroad

Nevada County Narrow Gauge, by Gerald M. Best. Berkeley, Calif., Howell-North Books, 1965. 214 p. (pf.—8 p.), I, Fac, M, P, 11.4 in.   CO-184

Nevada Northern Railway

Nevada Northern; sage brush short line, by Gary G. Allen. Los Angeles, Trans-Anglo Books [1964]. 49 p., I, M (C), 8.3 in.   CO-185

New York, Chicago and St. Louis Railway [Nickel Plate Route]

The Berkshire era; a pictorial review of the Nickel Plate Road, 1934-1958. Edited by John A. Rehor and Philip T. Horning. [Rocky River, Ohio, 1967.] 160 p., (chiefly illus.), 11.4 in.   CO-186

The Nickel Plate Road; a short history of the New York, Chicago & St. Louis R.R. Lynne L. White. New York, Newcomen Society in North America, 1954. 28 p., I, 9 in.　　　　　　　　　　　　　　　　　　　　　　　　　　　　CO-187

Nickel Plate Road [N.Y.C. & St. L.]. Magazine. Cleveland. I (PC), P 10.2 in.
　　　　　　　　　　　　　　　　　　　　　　　　　　　　　　　　CO-188

New York Central Railroad

New York Central cars (published 1972) a picture-album of New York Central passenger and freight cars, wooden and steel. New York, Wayner Publications, 1972. 8½ x 11 in., 64 p.　　　　　　　　　　　　　　　　　　　CO-189

Steam power of the New York Central system. Alvin F. Staufer. [n. p.] c 1961-[1967]. 2 v., I, 11.4 in. [Medina, Ohio.]　　　　　　　　　　　　CO-190

Steam and electric locomotives of the New York Central Lines: numbering and classification. Compiled by William D. Edson and Edward L. May. [Irvington-on-Hudson, New York, 1966.] 136 p., I, D, 11 in.　　　　　　　　　　CO-191

20th Century, the greatest train in the world. Lucius Beebe. Berkeley, Calif., Howell-North, 1962. 180 p., I, 11.4 in.　　　　　　　　　　　　　CO-192

The run of the Twentieth Century, reprint of 1930 book on operation of Twentieth Century Limited train. New York, Wayner Publications. 111 p., I, 6 x 9 in.　　　　　　　　　　　　　　　　　　　　　　　　　　CO-193

Robert R. Young. Borkin 1959　　　　　　　　　　　　　　　　sBIO-24
Hudsons of the N.Y.C. Movie　　　　　　　　　　　　　　　　　sMP-9
Mikados of the N.Y.C. Movie　　　　　　　　　　　　　　　　　sMP-10

New York, New Haven & Hartford Railroad

The fall of a railroad empire; Brandeis and the New Haven merger battle, by Henry Lee Staples and Alpheus Thomas Mason. Syracuse, N. Y., Syracuse Univ. Press, 1947. 209 p. (pf.−10 p.), I, P, 8.3 in.　　　　　　　　　　　　CO-194

New Haven railroad station and line improvements; preliminary plans and cost estimates, September, 1966. Prepared by John C. Tone, under the direction of Harold Wanaselja. [New York, Tri-State Transportation Commission,] 1968. 115 p. (pf.−6 p.), I, 11 in.　　　　　　　　　　　　　　　　　　　CO-195

Two trains to remember: the New England Limited, the Air Line Limited, by Lucius Beebe. [Virginia City, Nev.,] 1965 (privately published). 54 p., I (PC), 9.4 in.　　　　　　　　　　　　　　　　　　　　　　　　　　CO-196

A financial study and analysis of the transportation costs and revenues of the New York, New Haven and Hartford Railroad. A report to the State of New York Office of Transportation [by] Ford K. Edwards of Edwards and Peabody. [n. p.] 1962. 17 [15] p., T, 11 in.　　　　　　　　　　　　　　　　　　　　CO-197

The New Haven Railroad; its rise and fall, by John L. Weller. New York, Hastings House, 1969. 248 p. (pf.−7 p.), I, M, P, 9.4 in.　　　　　　　CO-198

Passenger trains and terminals. Droege.　　　　　　　　　　　sTER-1

New York, Ontario & Western Railway

O & W; the long life and slow death of the New York, Ontario & Western Railway. William F. Helmer. Berkeley, Calif., Howell-North, 1959. 211 p., I, 9.4 in.   CO-199

Norfolk & Western Railway

From mine to market; the history of coal transportation in the Norfolk and Western Railway. Joseph T. Lambie. New York, New York Univ. Press. 1954. 380 p. (pf.—18 p.), I, P, M, 9.8 in.   CO-200

North Pacific Coast Railway

Narrow gauge to the redwoods; the story of the North Pacific Coast Railroad and San Francisco Bay ferries, by A. Bray Dickinson with Roy Graves [and others]. Los Angeles, Trans-Anglo Books [1967]. 168 p., I, Fac, M, P, 11.4 in.   CO-201

Northern Indiana Railway

The Northern Indiana Railway. George K. Bradley. [Chicago, Electric Railway Historical Society, 1953.] 51 p. (inc. cover), I, M, 7.5 in. (No. 6).   CO-202

Northern Ohio Traction Co.

Northern Ohio Traction revisited, by James M. Blower. With photos from the collection of McKinley Crowley, Leonard Seigel, and many others as noted, and incorporating the research of Robert S. Korach. Akron, Ohio [1968]. 181 p., I, M, P, 11 in.   CO-203

The NOT&L story, by James M. Blower and Robert S. Korach. Also including: Stark Electric, Mahoning Valley Line, Inter-City Rapid Transit, Salem [and] Twin City Traction. Chicago, Central Electric Railfans' Association [1966]. 268 p., I (PC), M (C), 11.4 in. (CERA bulletin 109).   CO-204

Northern Pacific Railroad

The Northern Pacific Railroad: its route, resources, progress, and business; the new Northwest and its great thoroughfare. [Philadelphia,] J. Cooke [1871]. 46 p., M, 9 in.   CO-205

Jay Cooke and Minnesota; the formative years of the Northern Pacific Railroad, 1868-1873. John L. Harnsberger. Ann Arbor, University Microfilm [1958].   CO-206

Henry Villard [and N.P.] Macfarlane. 1954   sBIO-22
Henry Villard [and Rys. of N. West] Hedges. 1930.   sBIO-23

Northwestern Pacific Railroad

The Northwestern Pacific Railroad, Redwood Empire route [by] Fred A. Stindt and Guy L. Dunscomb. [1st ed. Redwood City, Calif., 1964.] 272 p., I, Fac, M, 11.4 in.   CO-207

Pacific Coast Co.

Ships and narrow gauge rails; the story of the Pacific Coast Company, by Gerald M. Best. Berkeley, Calif., Howell-North, 1964. 153 p., I, M, 11.4 in.   CO-208

Pacific Electric

Ride the big red cars; how trolleys helped build Southern California. Spencer Crump. Costa Mesa, Calif., Trans-Anglo Books, 1970. 256 p., I (PC), M, P, 11.4 in.; also, 2ed.-1965, 240 p.; 1ed.-1962, 200 p.   CO-208A

Pacific Electric; pictorial history of world's greatest interurban system. Donald Duke. San Marino, Calif., Golden West Books. 64 p., I, 11 in.   CO-209

Pacific Electric's big red cars; a pictorial account of the decline of the world's largest interurban electric railway system. Raphael Long. Universal City, Calif., T. C. Phillips [c 1966]. 1 v. (unpaged), I, M, 11 in.   CO-210

Henry Huntington [and the PE] Crump, 1970.   sBIO-5

Pacific Great Eastern Railway

Pacific Great Eastern Railway, also proposed extensions and optential resources of central interior and northern British Columbia, 1949. Ry. Dept., Victoria, 1949. 61 p., I, M (5), 10.6 in.   CO-211

Penn-Central

The wreck of the Penn Central, by Joseph R. Daughen and Peter Binzen. [1st ed.] Boston, Little, Brown, 1971. 365 p. (pf.—16 p.), I, 8.7 in.   CO-212

Review of the Penn Central condition, Hearings, July 27, 1971. Senate Commerce (Surface Trans). Washington, GPO, 1971. 465 p. (pf.—3 p.), M (F), 9.4 in. CO-213

Penn Central investigation report. [N. J. Dept. of Trans., Trenton, 1969.] 20, 50 p. (pf.—4 p.), I, 8.7 x 13.4 in.   CO-214

Pennsylvania Railroad

Pennsylvania Railroad: the early days. Terrence Brooks. [Los Angeles, Trans-Anglo Books, 1964.] 49 p., I, M, P, 8.3 in.   CO-215

Pennsy car plans; a book of small diagram drawings and floor plans of typical Pennsylvania Railroad passenger, freight and work-car equipment. New York, Wayner Publications, 1970. 99 p., I, 7 x 10 in.   CO-216

Pennsylvania Railroad K-4s; picture study of the locomotive including drawings and roster. San Marino, Calif., Golden West Books. 40 p., I, 9 x 6 in.   CO-217

Locomotives of the Pennsylvania Railroad, 1834-1924. Paul T. Warner. Chicago, O. Davies [1959]. 79 p., I, 11 in.   CO-218

Pennsy power; steam and electric locomotives of the Pennsylvania Railroad, 1900-1957, by Alvin F. Staufer. Text writing by Bert Pennypacker. Research by Martin Flattley. Carrollton, Ohio, printed by the Standard Print & Pub. Co. [1962-68]. 2 v., I (PC), 11.4 in.; also, 1962, 315 p.   CO-219

Pennsy, A to T; [PRR steam picture history] by Paul and Daphne Carleton. [Fairview, N. J., 1959.] 94 p., I, 9.8 in.   CO-220

Railroad stations of Pennsylvania. Van Trump, 1964.   sTER-3
Memories of steam [PRR]. Movie.   sMP-12

On the [PRR]. Movie.   sMP-13
Pennsy's electrics. Movie.   sMP-14
Pennsylvania steam. Movie.   sMP-15

Philadelphia Transportation Co.

Street map of Philadelphia and vicinity, showing streetcar, bus and subway-
elevated lines, January, 1953. 13th ed., Philadelphia Transportation Company.
[Philadelphia, 1953.] Map 31.5 x 23 in. (C),   CO-221

Manitou & Pike's Peak Railway

The Pike's Peak Cog Road; story of the Manitou & Pike's Peak Railway. Morris
W. Abbott. San Marino, Calif., Golden West Books, 1972. 176 p., I (230), M, T,
11 in.   CO-222

Pittsburg, Westmoreland & Somerset Railroad

The story of a mountain railroad. Franklin Johnston Langsdale. Somerset, Pa.,
printed by Somerset Daily American, c 1951. 33 p., I, 9 in.   CO-223

Pino Grande

Pino Grande; logging railroads and cables of Michigan-California Lumber Co. R. S.
Polkinghorn. Berkeley, Howell-North. 146 p., I (200), M, 11 in.   CO-224

H. K. Porter Co., Inc.

A new and dynamic concept for growth; H. K. Porter Company, Inc. Thomas
Mellon Evans. New York, Newcomen Society in North America, 1955. 24 p., I,
9 in.   CO-225

Pullman Co.

Mr. Pullman's elegant palace car, the railway carriage that established a new dimen-
sion of luxury and entered the nation lexicon as a symbol of splendor. Lucius M.
Beebe. Garden City, N. Y., Doubleday, 1961. 574 p., I, P, 11.4 in.   CO-226

The Pullman scrapbook; material on Pullman operations and history from company's "Pullman News" magazine. New York, Wayner Publication, 1971. 100 p.,
8½ x 11 in.   CO-227

Pullman private car service of 1939 (reprinted 1971); a booklet for renters of
Pullman private cars (description, carplans). New York, Wayner Publications,
1971. 18 p., 8½ x 11 in.   CO-228

Descriptive list of cars of the Pullman Company, March, 1961, with supplements
to June 15, 1967. [Douglas C. Wornom, editor. Chicago, Ill., O. Davies, 1970.]
97 p., 11.4 in.   CO-227

Pullman Company offical commissary instruction book and procedure manual;
covers all phases of service and rules. Milwaukee, Old Line Publishers. 208 p., I,
(127).   CO-230

System of accounts for the Pullman Company, issue of 1950. ICC [Washington,
1950]. 40 p. (pf.–4 p.), 10.2 in.   CO-231

The Pullman boycott of 1894; the problem of Federal intervention. Colston E.
Warne. Boston, Heath [1955]. 112 p., I, 9.4 in.   CO-231

Pullman; an experiment in industrial order and community planning, 1880-1930.
Stanley Buder. New York, Oxford Univ. Press, 1967. 263 p. (pf.–12 p.), I, P, M, M, 8.7 in. CO-232

George M. Pullman. Harding, 1951. sBIO-15

REA Express

Study of REA Express (staff study). [Prepared by] Staff Liaison Group V-C, Research Collaboration [of the] Civil Aeronautics Board, Federal Maritime Commission and ICC. Washington, GPO, 1965. 46 p. (pf.–3 p.), 9 in. CO-233

Reading Railroad

The Reading's heritage, 1833-1958; 125th anniversary of a pioneer railroad. Joseph Anton Fisher. New York, Newcomen Society in North America, 1958. 32 p., I, 9 in. CO-234

Reading steam pictorial; [a cavalcade of modern power from 1938 to the end of steam]. Fairview, N. J., P. & D. Carleton, 1964. 129 p., I, M, 11 in. CO-235

Locomotives of the Reading, 1836-1923; with photo supplement and roster of steam locomotives, 1924-1950, by Bert Pennypacker. Paul T. Warner. Chicago, O. Davies [1963]. 28 p., I, 11 in. CO-236

Steam on the Reading. Movie. sMP-18

Rio Grande Southern Railroad

The Rio Grande Southern story. Josie Moore Crum. Durango, Colo., Railroad-iana, 1957. 533 p. (pf.–14 p.), I, P, M, F, 10.6 in. CO-237

Rio Grande Southern. Movie. sMP-30

Rutland Railroad

The Rutland Road; story of a railroad that influenced the history and economy of New England. Jim Shaughnessy. Berkeley, Howell-North. 365 p., I (468), 11 in.
CO-238

Sacramento Northern Railway

Cars of Sacramento Northern [Ry.]. [Editor; Ira L. Swett. Los Angeles, I. L. Swett, 1963.] 112 p., I, D, 11 in. CO-239

St. John's Railroad

The St. John's Railroad, 1858 to 1895; a commemorative history of a pioneer railroad. Greville Bathe. [Centenial ed.] St. Augustine, 1958. 70 p., I, 11.4 in.
CO-240

St. Joseph Valley Railroad

The St. Joseph Valley Railway, by Joseph A. Galloway and James J. Buckley. [Chicago, Electric Railway Historical Society, c 1955.] 43 p., I, 11 in. (No. 16).
CO-241

St. Louis-San Francisco Railway

Frisco folks; stories and pictures of the great steam days of the Frisco Road (St. Louis—San Francisco Railway Company). William E. Bain. Denver, Sage Books [1961]. 272 p., I, 9 in. CO-242

Sandley

The Sandley story. Denis Rooksby. With foreword by Frederic Shaw. [1st ed.] San Francisco, Hesperian House [1960]. 72 p., I, 9 in. CO-243

Seaboard Air Line Railroad

Seaboard Air Line Railway; steam boats, locomotives and history, by Richard E. Prince. Green River, Wyo., c 1969. 268 p., I, M, P, 11 in. CO-244

Building a railroad, 1832-1952; the Seaboard Air Line, its beginnings and its contributions. John Walter Smith. New York, Newcomen Society in North America, 1952. 32 p., I, 9 in. CO-245

Seashore Electric Railway [and S.S. Trolley Mus.]

Historic cars of the Seashore Trolley Museum, Kennebunkport, Maine. [5th ed. Edited by O. R. Cummings. New Eng. Elec. Ry. Hist. Society, Kennebunkport, Me., 1967.] 66 p., I, 9 in.; also, 4ed.-1962. CO-246

Historic cars of the Seashore Electric Railway. New England Electric Ry. Historical Soc. [2nd ed. Newton Highlands, Mass., 1955.] 29 p., I, 9 in.; also, 1954, 27 p. CO-247

Seattle and Rainier Valley Railroad

Trolley days in Seattle, the story of the Seattle and Rainier Valley Railroad, by Leslie Blanchard. [Los Angeles, Trans-Anglo Books, 1965.] 49 p., I, 8.3 in.
CO-248

John Stephenson Co.

Electric railway cars and trucks, 1905. By John Stephenson Co. Reprint. Felton, Calif., Glenwood Publishers, 1972. 92 p., I, 11 x 8.2 in. CO-249

Sierra Railroad

Sierra railway. Dorothy (Newell) Deane, Berkeley, Calif., Howell-North, 1960. 181 p., I, 9.4 in. CO-250

Sierra Mts. [San Joaquin & Eastern Railroad]

The railroad that lighted Southern California, by Hank Johnston; story of Henry Huntington's High Sierra, San Joaquin & Eastern. Corona del Mar, Calif., Trans-Anglo Books. 128 p., I, 11 in. CO-251

Silverton Railroad; Silverton, Gladstone & Northerly Railroad; Silverton Northern Railroad

Three little lines; the Silverton R.R. the Silverton, Gladstone & Northerly R.R., and the Silverton Northern R.R. Josie Moore Crum. Durango, Colo., Durango Herald-News, 1960. 71 p. (pf.—7 p.), I, M (F), 9 in. CO-252

South Pacific Coast Railroad

South Pacific Coast; 50 years of narrow gauge in California redwoods. Bruce A. MacGregor. Berkeley, Howell-North. 278 p., I (425), D, M, 11 in.　　　CO-253

South Side Elevated Railroad

Chicago elevated railroads consolidation of operations, 1913. Owen Davies, editor. South Side Elevated Railroad Company. Chicago, O. Davies [1967]. 57 p., I, 10.6 in.　　　CO-254

Southern Railway

Southern steam specials; the story of the steamers and the men who keep them running. By Ron Ziel and Mike Eagleson. Mt. Arlington, N. J., Camelback Publishing, 1972. I (C), 8.5 in.　　　CO-255

Men of vision "who served the South!" Harry A. DeButts. New York, Newcomen Society in North America, 1955. 24 p., I, 9 in.　　　CO-256

Steam locomotives and boats, Southern Railway system, by Richard E. Prince. Green River, Wyo. [1965]. 204 p., I, M, 11.4 in.　　　CO-257

Locomotive 4501, Morgan, 1968.　　　sLS-20

Southern Pacific

Central Pacific & Southern Pacific Railroads; centennial story of a great transcontinental. Lucius Beebe. Berkeley, Howell-North. 640 p., I (900), 11 in. CO-258

Chapters on the history of the Southern Pacific. Stuart Daggett. New York, A. M. Kelley, 1966. 470 p. (pf.–6 p.), I, M, P, 817 in.　　　CO-259

Survey of a route on the 32nd parallel for the Texas Western Railroad, 1854: the A. B. Gray report, and including the reminiscences of Peter R. Brady, who accompanied the expedition. Andrew B. Gray. Edited and with introd. and notes by L. R..Bailey. Los Angeles, Westernlore Press, 1963. 249 p. (pf.–19 p.), I, P, M, Fac, 8.3 in.　　　CO-260

Southern Pacific daylight, by Richard K. Wright. [Thousand Oaks, Calif., Wright Enterprises, 1970.] I, M, P, 11.4 in.　　　CO-261

A century of Southern Pacific steam locomotives, 1862-1962. Guy L. Dunscomb. [Modesto, Calif., 1963.] 480 p., I (PC), M, 11 in.　　　CO-262

Southern Pacific steam locomotives; a pictorial anthology of western railroading. [2nd ed.] Donald Duke. San Marino, Calif., Pacific Railway Journal [1962]. 88 p., I, 11.4 in.　　　CO-263

Cab-in-front; the half-century of an unconventional locomotive. John B. Hungerford. Reseda, Calif., Hungerford Press [1959]. 35 p., I, 8.7 in.　　　CO-264

Locomotives of the Southern Pacific Company, by Gerald M. Best and David L. Joslyn. Boston, Railway & Locomotive Historical Society, 1956. 172 p., I, 9 in. (No. 4).　　　CO-265

The slim princess; the story of the Southern Pacific narrow gauge. John B. Hungerford. 4th ed. Reseda, Calif., Hungerford Press, 1961. 32 p., I, 8.7 in.; also 3d ed.-1959; and 1956.   CO-265A

Life and times of the Central Pacific. Myrick.   sCO-54
Building [first transcontinental]. Nathan, 1962.   sHT-6
First transcontinental R.R.: UP, SP. Galloway, 1950.   sHT-11
Golden spike; Am. Geographical Soc., 1969.   sHT-12
Golden spike.   sHT-13
Great iron trail. Howard, 1962.   sHT-14
Iron horse to Promontory Best, 1969.   sHT-21
Moguls and iron men. McCague, 1964.   sHT-22
Rails across the continent. Messner, 1965.   sHT-28
A work of giants. Griswold, 1962.   sHT-33
Rails from the West [T. D. Judah], Hinckley.   sBIO-6
Tracks of the iron horse. Movie.   sMP-21
S.P.'s cab-forward. Movie.   sMP-33
Coast daylight [steam]. Movie.   sMP-34
Donner Pass [SP]. Movie.   sMP-35
Winter railroading-Overland Route. Movie.   sMP-36

Strasburg Railroad

The road to Paradise; the story of the Strasburg Railroad [by] William M. Moedinger. Rev. ed. [n. p., 1966]. 27 p., I (C), M, 9 in.

CO-266
The road to Paradise; the story of the Strasburg Railroad. William M. Moedinger. With 52 natural color photos. [Lancester, Pa. J. E. Hess, 1962.] Unpaged, I, 9 in.
CO-267

Sumpter Valley Railway

Rails, sage brush, and pine; a garland of railroad and logging days in Oregon's Sumpter Valley. Mallory H. Ferrell. San Marino, Calif., Golden West Books [1967]. 128 p., I, 11.4 in.   CO-268

Tennessee Coal, Iron and Railroad Company

Biography of a business. United States Steel Corp., Tennessee Coal and Iron Div. [n. p. 1960]. 72 p., I, 8.3 in.   CO-269

Texas & Pacific Railway

The Franco-Texan Land Company, by Virginia H. Taylor. Austin, Univ. of Texas Press, 1969. 331 p. (pf.—14 p.), I, Fac, M, P, 9.4 in.   CO-270

Toledo, Port Clinton and Lakeside Railway

The Toledo, Port Clinton and Lakeside Railway, by George N. Hilton. [Chicago] Electric Railway Historical Society [1964]. 59 p., I, F, M, 11 in. (Bulletin 42).
CO-271

Uintah Railway

Uintah Railway; the Gilsonite Route, by Henry E. Bender, Jr. Berkeley, Calif., Howell-North Books [1970]. 239 p., I, M, P, 11.4 in.   CO-272

Ulster & Delaware Railroad

The Ulster & Delaware; railroad through the Catskills. Gerald M. Best. San Marino, Calif., Golden West Books, 1972. 208 p., I (320), M, T, 11 in.   CO-273

Union Pacific Railroad

Pioneering the Union Pacific; a reappraisal of the builders of the railroad. Charles E. Ames. New York, Appleton-Century-Crofts [1969]. 591 p. (pf.—17 p.), I, Fac, M, P, 9.4 in.   CO-274

Union Pacific; the building of the first transcontinental railroad. Garry Hogg. New York, Walker, 1969, c 1967. 166 p., I, M, 8.3 in.   CO-275

Westward to Promontory; building the Union Pacific across the plains and mountains; a pictorial documentary, with text by Barry B. Combs. Palo Alto, Calif., American West Pub. Co. [1969]. 77 p., I, 11.4 in.   CO-276

The Union Pacific: hell on wheels, by John Carson [Best]. [Santa Fe, N. M., Press of the Territorian, 1968.] 36 p., I, 23 cm.   CO-277

Union Pacific: the building of the first transcontinental railroad. Garry Hogg. London, Hutchinson, 1967. 166 p. (pf.—9 p.), 12 plates, 8.1 in.   CO-278

How we built the Union Pacific Railway, and other railway papers and addresses, by Grenville M. Dodge. Denver, Sage Books [1965]. 171 p., I, P, 23 cm.   CO-279

How we built the Union Pacific Railway. Grenville M. Dodge. Ann Arbor [Mich.], University Microfilms [1966]. 40 p., plates, P, 9.4 in.   CO-280

History of the Union Pacific; a financial and economic survey, by Nelson Trottman. New York, A. M. Kelley, 1966. 412 p. (pf.—6 p.), I, M, 8.7 in.   CO-281

The Union Pacific Railroad; a case in premature enterprise. Robert W. Fogel. Baltimore, Johns Hopkins Press, 1960. 129 p., 9.4 in. (ser. 78, No. 2).   CO-282

Epic of the overland. With a sketch of the life of the author by Herbert Wynford Hill. San Francisco, A. M. Robertson, 1924. Robert L. Fulton. [Los Angeles, N. A. Kovach, 1954.] 109 p. (pf.—8 p.), plates, P, M (F), 7.9 in.   CO-283

A history of the Kansas Central Railway, 1871-1935. Harold Crimmons. Emporia, Graduate Division of the Kansas State Teachers College, 1954. 34 p., I, 9 in.
          CO-284

Union Pacific railroad, a brief history. Union Pacific R. R. [Omaha, The Omaha Printing Company, 1946]. 30 p., I,(M), 8.3 in.   CO-285

Union Pacific in Colorado, 1867-1967 [by] R. A. LeMassena. [Denver, printed by Hotchkiss and Nelson, 1967.] 40 p., I, F, M, 9 in.   CO-286

The Overland Limited. Lucius Beebe. Berkeley, Calif., Howell-North Books, 1963. 157 p., I (PC), P, M, F, 11.4 in.   CO-287

Smoke down the canyons; Union Pacific, Idaho Division [by] Ehernberger and Gschwind. [Callaway, Neb., E. & G. Publications, 1966.] 64 p., I, M, 11.4 in.
          CO-288

Smoke above the plains: Union Pacific, Kansas Division [by] Ehernberger and Gschwind. [Callaway, Neb., E. & G. Publication, 1965.] 64 p., I, M, 11.4 in.
CO-289

Smoke across the prairie: Union Pacific, Nebraska Division [by] Ehernberger and Gschwind. [Golden, Colo., Intermountain Chapter, National Railway Historical Society, c 1964.] 61 p., I, M, 11.4 in.   CO-290

Smoke along the Columbia: Union Pacific, Oregon Division [by] Ehernberger and Gschwind. [Callaway, Neb., E. G. Publications, 1968.] 64 p., I, M, 11.4 in.
CO-291

Smoke over the divide: Union Pacific, Wyoming Division [by] Ehernberger and Gschwind. [Callaway, Neb., E. & G. Publications, 1965.] 64 p., I, M, 11.4 in.
CO-292

Union Pacific locomotives [by] W. W. Kratville [and] Harold E. Ranks. [Omaha] Barnhart Press, 1960–. I, 8.7 x 11 in.   CO-293

Motive power of the Union Pacific, by William Kratville and Harold E. Ranks. [Omaha, Barnhart Press, 1958.] 253 [73] p., I, P, 11.4 in.   CO-294

Building [first transcontinental]. Nathan, 1962.	sHT-6
First transcontinental RR: UP, SP. Galloway, 1950.	sHT-11
Golden spike. Am. Geographical Soc., 1969.	sHT-12
Golden spike.	sHT-13
Great iron trail. Howard, 1962.	sHT-14
Iron horse to Promontory. Best, 1969.	sHT-21
Moguls and iron men. McCague, 1964.	sHT-22
Rails across the continent. Messner, 1965.	sHT-28
A work of giants. Griswold, 1962.	sHT-33
Tracks of the iron horse. Movie.	sMP-21
Big Boy and his brothers. Movie.	sMP-37
Challengers and Big Boys. Movie.	sMP-38
At Sherman Hill. Movie.	sMP-39
Pacing U.P. steam. Movie.	sMP-41

Virginia Central Railroad

The story of the Virginia Central Railroad, 1850-1860. Elizabeth D. Coleman. Ann Arbor, University Microfilms [1957].   CO-295

Virginia & Truckee Railroad

Virginia & Truckee, a story of Virginia City and Comstock times, by Lucius Beebe and Charles Clegg. Decorations by E. S. Hammack. Maps and lettering by Frederic Shaw. Berkeley, Calif., Howell-North, 1963. 67 p., I, 9 in.   CO-296

Virginia & Truckee; a story of Virginia City and Comstock times, by Lucius Beebe and Charles Clegg. Decorations by E. S. Hammack. Maps and lettering by Frederic Shaw. [5th ed.] Stanford, Stanford University Press [1955]. 67 p., I, 9.4 in.
CO-297

Steamcars to the Comstock; the Virginia & Truckee Railroad, the Carson & Colorado Railroad: their story in picture and prose by Lucius Beebe and Charles Clegg. Berkeley, Calif., Howell-North, 1957. 74 p., I, 11.4 in.   CO-298

Virginian Railway

The Virginian Railway. H. Reid. [Milwaukee, Kalmbach Pub. Co., 1961.] 208 p., I, 11.8 in.   CO-299

Washington, Baltimore & Annapolis Railroad

Annapolis Short Line; the big red cars. John E. Merriken. Springfield, Va., 1965. 9 p.; 2 p., I, M (C), 11 in. Capital Traction Quarterly, vol. 1, No. 3.   CO-300

A pictorial history of the Washington, Baltimore & Annapolis Electric Railroad. Charles M. Wagner. Washington, Washington Electric Railway Historical Society [1951]. 7 p., I, M, 11 in.   CO-301

Waterloo, Cedar Falls & Northern. Movie.   sMP-50

Western Maryland Railway

The Western Maryland Railway story; a chronicle of the first century, 1852-1952. Harold A. Williams. Contemporary photography by A. Aubrey Bodine. Baltimore, 1952. 134 p., I, 10.2 in.   CO-302

Western Pacific Railroad

Western Pacific; the railroad that was built too late. Spencer Crump. [Los Angeles, Trans-Anglo Books, 1963.] 48 p., I (PC), P, M (PF), 8.3 in.   CO-303

Western Pacific—its first forty years! A brief history, 1910-1950. Frederic Bennett Whitman. New York, Newcomen Society in North America, 1950. 32 p., I (part mounted), 9 in.   CO-304

Western Pacific fast freight. Movie.   sMP-41
California Zepher. Movie.   sMP-25

Western Railroad of Massachusetts (see B&A RR)

State [investor & railroad]. Salsbury, 1967.   sCO-37

Western Railway of Alabama

Steam locomotives and history, Georgia Railroad and West Point Route. Richard E. Prince. Green River, Wyo. [1962]. 114 p., I, M, D, 11.4 in.   CO-305

West River Railroad

36 miles of trouble; the story of the West River R. R. Victor L. Morse. Brattleboro, Vt., Book Cellar, 1959. 40 p., I, 8.7 in.   CO-306

West Side Lumber Co.

Last of the 3-foot loggers; California's famed West Side Lumber Co. Allan Krieg. San Marino, Calif., Golden West Books. 96 p., I, 11 in.   CO-307

White Pass and Yukon

On the "White Pass" payroll, by S. H. Graves. New York, Paladin Press, 1970.
258 p., I, P, 11 in.   CO-308

Gold rush narrow gauge; the story of the White Pass and Yukon Route. [1st ed.]
Cy. Martin. Los Angeles, Trans-Anglo Books, 1969. 96 p., I, 11.4 in.   CO-309

Woodstock Railway

Over the hills to Woodstock; saga of the Woodstock Railway. Edgar Mead, Jr.
Brattleboro, Vt., Stephen Green Press. 43 p., I, M, 8.5 in.   CO-310

Yosemite Valley Railway

Short Line to Paradise, by Hank Johnston. Format; story of the Yosemite Valley
Railroad. Corona del Mar, Calif., Trans-Anglo Books. 96 p., I, 6.7 in.   CO-311

ELECTRIC RAILROADS

Articulated cars of North America [by] E. Harper Charlton. London, Light Railway Transport League [1966]. 26 p., I, T, D, 8.7 in.   EL-1

Destination valley, edited by J. Richardson. 2d ed. Canberra City, A. C. T., Traction Publications; distributor in U. S. A., O. Davies, Chicago, 1964. 51 p., I, 8.7 in.   EL-2

Earl Clark's directory of world electric lines. [Cincinnati.] 11 in.   EL-3

Electric railroads. New York, Electric Railroaders' Association. I, 11.4 in., irregular, periodical.   EL-4

Electric traction systems and equipment, by D. W. Hinde and M. Hinde. [1st ed.] Oxford, New York Pergamon Press [1968]. 149 p. (pf.—8 p.), I, 9.8 in.   EL-5

Interurbans magazine. Los Angeles. I, M, PL, P, 11 in.   EL-6

Interurbans to the loop; North Shore line, South Shore line, by Robert P. Olmsted. [Janesville, Wis., 1969.] 1 v. (chiefly illus.), 11.4 in.   EL-7

Selected financial and operating statistics from annual reports of electric railways, 1917-53. ICC, Bu. Tran. Econ. & Stat., Washington. T, 11 in., annual.   EL-8

The time of the trolley, by William D. Middleton. [Milwaukee, Kalmbach Pub. Co., 1967.] 436 p., I, P, 11.4 in.   EL-9

City and interurban cars. Brill.	sCO-44
Steam and trolley days [FJ&G]. Nestle.	sCO-119
Illinois Terminal R.R. Johnson.	sCO-144
North Shore. Middleton.	sCO-73
The Northern Indiana Rys. Bradley.	sCO-202
North Ohio Traction revised. Blower.	sCO-203
The NOT&L story. Blower, 1966.	sCO-204
Ride the big red cars. Crump.	sCO-208
Pacific Electric. Duke.	sCO-209
Pacific Electric [cars]. Long.	sCO-210
Cars of the Sacramento Northern. Swett.	sCO-239
Scenes [Shore Lines]. Olmstead.	sCO-74
South Shore. Middleton.	sCO-75
Erie to Conneault [trolley]. Springirth.	sCO-79
Historic cars [Seashore Elec. Ry.].	sCO-247-8
Annapolis Short Line [WB&A]. Merrikan.	sCO-300
A pictorial history [WB&A]. Wagner.	sCO-301
Steam and electric locos. [N.Y.C.]. Edson.	sCO-191
Pennsy power. Staufer.	sCO-219

HISTORY

All aboard! A history of railroads in Michigan. Willis F. Dunbar. Grand Rapids, Mich., W. B. Eerdmans Pub. Co. [1969]. 308 p., I, Fac, M, 9.4 in.   HT-1

The American railroad network, 1861-1890 [by] George Rogers Taylor [and] Irene D. Neu. Cambridge, Harvard University Press, 1956. 113 p. (pf.—8 p.), M (3F), 9.4 in.   HT-2

American railroads. John F. Stover. [Chicago] University of Chicago Press [1961]. 302 p., I, 8.3 in.   HT-3

The American railroads. John C. Weaver. [Prepared with the cooperation of the American Geographical Society.] Garden City, N. Y., N. Doubleday [1963]. 63 p., I, 9 in.   HT-4

Ante bellum studies in slavery, politics and the railroads. Robert R. Russel. Kalamazoo, Sch. of Grad. Studies, Western Michigan Univ., 1960. 98 p., 9 in. (see 5, No. 1).   HT-5

The building of the first transcontinental railroad; illustrated by Edw. A. Wilson. Adele Nathan. New York, Random House [1950]. 180 p. (pf.—10 p.), I, 8.7 in.
          HT-6

Canal or railroad? Imitation and innovation in the response to the Erie Canal in Philadelphia, Baltimore, and Boston. Julius Rubin. Philadelphia, American Philosophical Society, 1961. 106 p., M, D, 11.8 in. (v. 51, pt. 7).   HT-7

City-makers, by Remi Nadeau; the dramatic story of how Southern California grew in 1860's when Los Angeles struggled for rail connections. Conora del Mar, Calif., Trans-Anglo Books. 168 p., I, 11 in.   HT-8

A congressional history of railways in the United States, by Lewis H. Haney. New York, A. M. Kelley, 1968. 2 v. in 1, M, 9 in.   HT-9

A description of the canals and railroads of the United States, comprehending notices of all the works of internal improvements throughout the several States, by Henry S. Tanner. New York, A. M. Kelley, 1970. 272 p. (pf.—7 p.), I, M, 8.7 in.
          HT-10

The first transcontinental railroad: Central Pacific, Union Pacific. John D. Galloway. New York, Simmons-Boardman [1950]. 319 p. (pf.—10 p.), I, P, M, 9.4 in.
          HT-11

The golden spike; a centennial remembrance [by] E. Roland Harriman [and others]. American Geographical Society of New York. New York, 1969. 118 p., I, M, P, 9 in.   HT-12

Golden spike, by Robert M. Utley and Francis A. Ketterson, Jr. [Washington] U. S. National Park Service [1969]. 58 p., I, M, P, 9.4 in. (No. 40).   HT-13

The great iron trail; the story of the first transcontinental railroad. Robert W. Howard. New York, Putnam [1962]. 376 p., I, 8.7 in.   HT-14

Highlights of American railroad history. Illus. by Lary Gaynor. AAR. Washington [1955]. 27 p., I, 10.6 in.   HT-15

Historical sketches of early railroading days. Compilation. William A. Schultz. Jonesboro, Ark., Sammons Print. Co., c 1961. I, 11 in.   HT-17

A history of American railroads [by] John F. Stover. Chicago, Rand McNally [1967]. 64 p., I, M, 9 in.   HT-17

History of the Grange movement; or, the farmer's war against monopolies, being a full and authentic account of the struggles of the American farmers against the extortions of the railroad companies. James D. McCabe. With a history of the rise and progress of the Order of Patrons of Husbandry, to which is added sketches of the leading Grangers, by Edward Winslow Martin. New York, B. Franklin [1967]. 539 p., 9 in.; also: New York, A. M. Kelley, 1969.   HT-18

History of the railroads and canals of the United States of America. Henry V. Poor. New York, A. M. Kelley, 1970. 632 p., M (2), 9 in.   HT-19

A history of transportation of the eastern Cotton Belt to 1860. Ulrich B. Phillips. New York, Octagon Books, 1968 [c 1908]. 405 p. (pf.−17 p.), M (IFC), 8.3 in.
HT-20

Iron horses to Promontory [by] Gerald M. Best. Golden spike ed. [San Marino, Calif.] Golden West Books [1969]. 207 p., I, F, M, P, 11.4 in.   HT-21

Moguls and iron men; the story of the first transcontinental railroad. [1st ed.] James McCague. New York, Harper & Row [1964]. 392 p. (pf.−8 p.), I, M, P, 9.8 in.   HT-22

Bulletin. National Railway Historical Society. [Westmont, N. J., etc.] I, 9 in., quarterly.   HT-23

New Orleans and the railroads; the struggle for commercial empire, 1830-1860 [by] Merl E. Reed. [Baton Rouge] Louisiana State Univ. Press for Louisiana Historical Association, 1966. 172 p., M, 9 in.   HT-24

Pioneer railroads. Hank Bowman. Greenwich Conn., Fawcett Publications, c 1954. 143 p., I, 9.4 in.   HT-25

The railroads of the Confederacy. Robert C. Black. Chapel Hill, University of North Carolina Press [1952]. 360 p. (pf.−14 p.), I, P, M (IF), F, 9.8 in.   HT-26

Railroads of the hour. S. Kip. Farrington. New York, Coward-McCann [1958]. 333 p., I, 8.7 in.   HT-27

Rails across the continent; the story of the first transcontinental railroad. Enid Johnson. New York, J. Messner [1965]. 190 p., I, Fac, P, 9.7 in.   HT-28

A short history of American railways, covering ten decades. Slason Thompson. Freeport, N. Y., Books for Libraries Press [1971]. 473 p., I, M, P, 9 in.   HT-29

Steel trails and iron horses; a pageant of American railroading. Lamont Buchanon. New York, Putnam [1955]. 159 p., I, 9.8 in.   HT-30

Strikers, communists, tramps and detectives. Alan Pinkerton. New York, Arno Press, 1969. 411 p., I, P, 9 in.   HT-31

Transportation: early railroad period, 1840-1881. Edited by Rolla Milton Tryon, James Alton James [and] Carl Russel Fish. Indianapolis, G. F. Cram Co. [1954]. M, 35 x 50 in.   HT-32

A work of giants; building the first transcontinental railroad. [1st ed.] Wesley S. Griswold. New York, McGraw-Hill [1962]. 367 p., I, 9.4 in.   HT-33

A history of travel in America; showing the method of travel and transportation form the crude methods of the canoe and the dog-sled to the highly organized railway systems of the present. Seymour Dunbar. Indianapolis, 1915. Reprint: Westport, Conn., Greenwood Press. 4 v., I, plates, M, Fac.   HT-34

Great Lakes car ferries. George W. Hilton. Berkeley, Calif., Howell-North, 1962.
                                                                        HT-35

The formation of the New England railroad systems; a study of railroad combination in the nineteenth century. George Pierce Baker. Cambridge, 1937. Reprint: Westport, Conn., Greenwood Press. 283 p. (pf.–31 p.), M, D.   HT-36

Pittsburg, Shawmut & Northern. Paul Pietrak. When the 198 mile long P. S. & N. was abandoned in 1947, it was the longest railroad to have ever been abandoned. The complete history includes locomotive rosters, track plans and many photos. 178 p., I, PL, 11 in.   HT-37

Information entries—History

Note; see also sections on: biographies, companies, electric railways, locomotives, narrow gauge, short lines, street railways, and individual cities and states for histories on specific subjects of interest.

Lincoln's railroad man [Haupt]. Lord.	sBIO-4
To the west. Hinckley.	sBIO-6
Life of George Stephenson. Smiles.	sBIO-20
R.R. leaders. Cochran.	sBIO-16
Robber barrons. Josephson.	sBIO-18
Archaeology of the cable car. Hanscom.	sC-3
Cable car carnival. Beebe.	sC-5
Cable cars in America. Hilton.	sC-6
Cable cars of San Francisco. Palmer.	sC-7
San Francisco grip. Perine.	sC-12
Bonanza railroads. Kneiss.	sCA-1
History of transcontinental [Canada]. Glazebrook.	sCAN-17
Intercity electric Rys. [Can.]. Due.	sCAN-19
National dream. Benton.	sCAN-24
Oil lamps and iron ponies. Shaw.	sCAN-22
Railway interrelations [U.S. & Can.]. Wilgus.	sCAN-23
Orginal 1879 car-builders dictionary. Forney.	sCAR-5
100 years of R.R. cars. Lucas.	sCAR-6
Railroad caboose. Knape.	sCAR-10
Mansions on rails. Beebe.	sCAR-20

Railroad passenger cars. Mencken.	sCAR-21
Cavalcade of R.Rs. [Colo.]. Everett.	sCOL-3
Colorado mountain R.Rs. Le Massewa.	sCOL-4
Little engines and big men. Lathrop.	sCOL-9
Railroads and the Rockies. Ormes.	sCOL-10
Burlington strike. Salmons.	sC-5
Chapters of the Erie. Adams.	sCO-112
History-Baldwin Locomotive Works. Old Line.	sCO-24
Locomotives [Dickson Mfg. Co.]. Best.	sCO-104
A productive monolopy. Taylor.	sCOMP-1
Railway conductors. Robbins.	sCON-1
Boston capitalists and western R.Rs. Johnson.	sF-1
British investments [Am. R.Rs.]. Adler.	sF-2
Story of Florida R.Rs. Pettengill.	sFLA-2
Enterprise denied. Martin.	sCO-3
Government promotion [canals & R.Rs.]. Goodrich.	sGO-5
Granger movement. Buck.	sGO-6
Indiana's abandoned R.Rs. Sulzer.	sIA-3
Kansas City and the R.Rs. Gluab.	sK-2
Ghost R.Rs. of Kentucky. Sulzer.	sKE-1
Railroads, land and politics. Decker.	sLA-7
Locomotive engineer. Richardson.	sLAW-3
Railroads and the Granger laws. Miller.	sLAW-5
Merchants, railroads and politics. Benson.	sLAW-10
Railroads and regulation. Kolkoe.	sLAW-12
American locomotives. White.	sLG-2
Development [loco. engine]. Sinclair.	sLG-5
Locomotives and cars since 1900. Lucas.	sLG-8
Pictorical history [electric locos.]. Haut.	sLE-2
Early Am. steam locomotives. Kinert.	sLS-8
Norris locomotives. Dewhurst.	sLS-23
Pacific Coast Shay. Ranger.	sLS-24
Pioneer locomotives [N. Am.]. Brown.	sLS-27
Steam locomotive in N. Am. Bruce.	sLS-31
Move toward railroad mergers. Keyserling.	sME-1
Politics and R.R. mergers. Latham.	sME-2
Railroad consolidation [Trans. Act-1920]. Leonard.	sME-4
Railroad merger and abandonment. Conant.	sME-6
Railroad mergers and [N. Eng. economy]. Nelson.	sME-8
Lake Superior iron ore R.Rs. Dorin.	sMID-1
Little Rys. [world]. Shaw.	sN-1
Narrow gauge nostalgia. Turner.	sN-2
Narrow gauge in the Rockies. Beebe.	sN-3
Narrow gauge Rys. [Am.]. Fleming.	sN-4
Men, cities and transportation [N. Eng.]. Chase.	sNED-1
Main line to oblivion. Carson.	sNY-2
Railroads of New York. Pierce.	sNY-7
Fifty years of rapid transit. Walker.	sNY(C)-1
Standard time in America. Allen.	sOP-9
Pacific R.Rs. and nationalism. Irwin.	sPAC-1
Rails across Panama. Schott.	sPAN-1
Railroads of Pennsylvania. Saylor.	sPE-1
Steam, steel & limiteds. Kratville.	sPI-12
When beauty rode the rails. Beebe.	sPI-13
American railroads. Rando.	sRA-1

American railroads. Weaver.	sRA-2
Life and decline [Am. R.Rs.]. Stover.	sRA-11
Railroads—nation's first big business. Chandler.	sRA-17
Railroads of America. Armitage.	sRA-21
Mail by rail. Long.	sRAP-3
25 years of R.R. social insurance. R.R. Ret. Bd.	sRET-10
Great train robberies. Block.	sRO-1
San Francisco's golden era. Beebe.	sSA-2
Mixed train daily. Beebe.	sSHO-4
Railroads down the valley. Mills.	sSHO-5
Civil War railroads. Abdill.	sSOU-1
Railroads [south]. Stover.	sSOU-2
Railroads [Black Hills]. Fielder.	sSOU(D)-1
Then came the railroads. Clark.	sSOU(W)-1
Down at the depot. Alexander.	sST-1
Age of steam. Beebe.	sSTE-1
Electric interurban Rys. Hilton.	sSTR-3
Interurban era. Middleton.	sSTR-6
Trolley car treasury. Rowsome.	sSTR-11
Annals [strikes]. Dacus.	sSTRI-1
Railroad stations. Meeks.	sTER-2
Great trains of all time. Hubbard.	sTRN-1
Lore of the train. Ellis.	sTRN-2
Railway passenger [trains to S.F.]. Rasmussen.	sTRN-5
Some classic trains. Dubin.	sTRN-8
Virginia R.Rs. [Civil War]. Johnston.	sVA-1
Northern R.Rs. [Civil War]. Webber.	sWA-1
Victory rode the rails. Turner.	sWA-6
Railroads [Nev. & N. Calif.]. Myrick.	sWE-1
Story of western R.Rs. Riegel.	sWE-4
They built the west. Quiett.	sWE-5
Track going back. DeGolyer.	sWE-6
Transportation frontier. Winther.	sWE-7

JUVENILE LITERATURE

General

The how and why wonder book of railroads. Robert Scharff. Illustrated by
George Zaffo. New York, Wonder Books [1964]. 48 p., I (PC), 11 in.   JLG-1

Monorails, by Derek G. T. Harvey. With illus. by Leigh Hunt. New York,
Putnam [1965]. 95 p., I, 7.5 x 9.4 in.   JLG-2

My little library. Dotty Andes. [Illustrated by Blake Hampton. Riverside, N. J.,
Rutledge Books, 1963.] 3 v., I (C), 5.1 in.   JLG-3

Quiz, Jr., railroad questions and answers. AAR, [Washington, 1950—]. I,
10.2 x 3.6 in.   JLG-4

Railroads. [Prepared with the cooperation of the American Geographical
Society.] Garden City, N. Y., N. Doubleday [1968]. 64 p., I (PC), M, P,
8.3 in.   JLG-5

Railroads, today and yesterday, written and illustrated by Walter Buehr. New
York, Putnam [1958, c 1957]. 72 p., I, 9 in.   JLG-6

Your world: let's visit the railroad [by] Billy N. Pope [and] Ramona Ware
Emmons. [Dallas, Taylor Pub. Co., 1968.] 32 p., I (C), 11 in.   JLG-7

History

End o' steel; men and rails across a wilderness, Glen Dines. Illustrated by Dick
Moore. New York, Macmillan, 1963. 47 p., I (C), P, M (2), Fac., 8.3 x 10.6 in.
JLH-1

The golden age of railroads. Stewart H. Holbrook. Illustrated by Ernest Richardson. New York, Random House [1960]. 182 p., I, 8.7 in.   JLH-2

The golden spike; the story of America's first transcontinental railroad. Harold
Littledale. Illustrated by Tony Kokinos. [New York, Parents' Magazine Press,
1963.] Unpaged. I, 11.4 in.   JLH-3

Let's go to build the first transcontinental railroad. Bernard Rosenfield.
Illustrated by Albert Micale. New York, Putnam [1963]. 48 p., I, 8.7 in.   JLH-4

1898—Race to the golden spike. Paul I. Wellman. Illustrated by Lorence
Bjorklund. Boston, Houghton Mifflin, 1961. 184 p., I, 8.7 in.   JLH-5

We were there at the driving of the golden spike. David Shepard. Historical
consultant: Josef Berger. Illustrated by William K. Plummer. New York, Grosset
& Dunlap [1960]. 179 p., I, 8.7 in.   JLH-6

When the rails ran west. James McCague. Illustrated by Victor Mays. Champaign,
Ill., Garrard Pub. Co. [1967]. 95 p., I (PC), 9.4 in.   JLH-7

Locomotives

The big book of real locomotives. George J. Zaffo. New York, Grosset & Dunlap, c 1951. Unpaged. I, 13.4 in. JLL-1

Diesel-electric 4030, written and illustrated by Henry Billings. New York, Viking Press, 1950. 69 p., I, 11 in. JLL-2

Iron horse to diesel. Paul Snow. Illustrated by Robert Pious. Racine, Wis., Whitman Pub. Co. [1961]. 91 p., I, 9.4 in. JLL-3

Iron horses and the men who rode them. Edith S. McCall. Illus. by Carol Rogers. New York, Grosset & Dunlap [1961, c 1960]. 125 p., I, 8.7 in. JLL-4

The iron horse; story in pictures of American railways steam locomotives, for boys and girls of all ages. Oran Kelley. [n. p.] 1958. I, 8.3 in. JLL-5

Locomotives in our lives; railroad experiences of three brothers for more than sixty years, 1890-1951. Albert S. Pennoyer. New York, Hastings House [1954]. 238 p., I, 11.4 in. JLL-6

Railroads in the days of steam, by the editors of American heritage. Narrative by Albert L. McCready, in consultation with Lawrence W. Sagle. New York, American Heritage Pub. Co.; book trade distribution by Golden Press [1960]. 153 p., I (PC), P, M, 10.6 in. JLL-7

Operations

The freight yard. Dorothy V. Stever. Illustrated by Robert Bartram. Los Angeles, Melmont [1958]. 31 p., I, 8.7 in. JLO-1

The fun and work of railroading, by Nicholas V. Murphy. Philadelphia, Dorrance [1968]. 94 p., I, 8.7 in. JLO-2

Let's go to a freight yard. Bernard Rosenfield. Illustrated by Don Shepler. New York, Putnam [1958]. 47 p., I, 8.3 in. JLO-3

Railroads at work, a picture book of the American railroads in action. 4th ed. AAR, Washington, 1950. 63 p., I, M, 7.9 in. JLO-4

Richard learns about railroading. Michael Braude. Illus. by Howard E. Lindberg. Minneapolis, T. S. Denison [1969]. 31 p., I (PC), 11.4 in. JLO-5

Railroad Men

About the engineer of a train. Joe S. Johnson. Illustrated by Harry Garo. Chicago, Melmont Publishers [1959]. 30 p., I, 9.4 in. JLR-1

I want to be a train engineer. Carla Greene. Illus. by Victor Havel. [Chicago] Childrens Press [1956]. I, 9.8 in. JLR-2

Long Eye and the iron horse; a biography of Grenville Dodge and the Union Pacific Railroad, by Dorothy Wood. New York, Criterion Books [1966]. 208 p., I, M, P, 8.7 in.   JLR-3

Perhaps I'll be a railroad man. Pictures and story by Ray Bethers. New York, Aladdin Books [1951]. 46 p., I, 8.7 in.   JLR-4

True adventures of railroaders; [David P. Morgan]; illustrated by W. A. Akin, Jr. [1st ed.] Boston, Little Brown [1954]. 209 p., I, 7.9 in.   JLR-5

Trains

All aboard! The railroad trains that built America. Mary Elting. [Rev. ed.] New York, Four Winds Press [1970, c 1969]. 127 p., I, Fac., M, P, 10.2 in.   JLT-1

At the railroad station, by Alma Kehoe Reck and Helen Hall Fichter. Illustrated by Harry Garo. Los Angeles, Melmont Publishers [1958]. 35 p., I, 8.7 in.   JLT-2

The big book of real streamliners, by George J. Zaffo. Text by Scott Stewart. New York, Grosset & Dunlap, c 1953. Unpaged. I, 13.4 in.   JLT-3

The big book of real trains. Text by Elizabeth Cameron. Illustrated by George J. Zaffo. New York, Grosset & Dunlap, 1963. [41] p., I (PC), 11.4 in.   JLT-4

The first book of trains. Russell Hamilton. Pictures by Jeanne Bendick. New York, Watts, c 1956. 69 p., I, 9 in.   JLT-5

The first book of trains, by Campbell Tatham [pseud.]. Mary Elting. Pictures by Jeanne Bendick. New York, F. Watts [1948]. [44] p., I (PC), 9 in.   JLT-6

Freight train; illustrated by George Pollard. Edwin C. Reichert. Chicago, Rand McNally, c 1956. Unpaged. I, 8.7 in.   JLT-7

The golden book of trains. Jane Watson. Pictures by Robert Sherman. New York, Simon and Schuster [1953]. 88 p., I, 11 in.   JLT-8

Great trains of the world; illustrated by Jack Coggins. Wyatt Blassingame. New York, Random House [1953]. Unpaged. I, 11.4 in.   JLT-9

How they travelled in Engine whistles, part 2 (Filmstrip). Society for Visual Education and Row, Peterson, 1950. 49 frames, 35 mm, (b&w).   JLT-10

Let's look at trains [by] Ernest F. Carter. Illustrated by Kenneth E. Carter. Chicago, A. Whitman [1968, c 1964]. 63 p., I (PC), 8.7 in.   JLT-11

Railroad transportation: Passenger (Filmstrip). Society for Visual Education, 1947. 75 frames, b&w, 35mm (7).   JLT-12

Read aloud train stories. Wonder Books, Inc. Illustrated by Art Seiden. New York [1957]. 160 p., I, 8.3 in.   JLT-13

The real book about trains, by Davis Cole. Mary Elting. Illustrated by David Millard. Garden City, N. Y., Garden City Books, by arrangement with F. Watts [New York, 1951]. 183 p., I, 8.3 in.   JLT-14

The story of trains. Mortimer Simmons. New York, Putnam [1964, c1963].
77 p., I (C), M, 12.6 in.   JLT-15

Tooooot! A train whistle counting book. Betty Lou La Well. Illustrated by Paul
Julian. Los Angeles, Melmont [1958]. 19 p., I, 7.9 x 9.4 in.   JLT-16

Train and engine books for children. [1st– ed.] AAR, Washington, 1946–
I, 9 in.   JLT-17

Trains. Electronic age ed. Robert S. Henry. New York, Bobbs-Merrill [1957].
152 p., I, 12.6 in.   JLT-18

Trains. Twentieth anniversary ed. Robert S. Henry. Indianapolis, Bobbs-
Merrill [1954]. 136 p., I, 12.6 in.   JLT-19

Trains, written and illustrated by Richard Scarry. New York, Golden Press
[1967]. Unpaged. I (C), 9.4 x 4 in.   JLT-20

Trains; illustrated by Chuck Smith. Helen J. Fletcher. New York, S. Gabriel
Sons, c 1955. I, 12.6 in.   JLT-21

Trains at work. Mary Elting. Illustrated by David Lyle Millard. [Rev. ed.]
Irvington-on-Hudson, N. Y., Harvey House [1962]. 90 p., I, 8.7 in.   JLT-22

Trains at work; illustrated by David Lyle Millard. Mary Elting. Garden City,
N. Y., Garden City Books [1953]. 90 p., I, 8.7 in.   JLT-23

Trains work like this. David St. J. Thomas. With 43 illus. by H. Jones. London,
Phoenix House; New York, Rov [1962, c 1961]. 54 p., I, 10.2 in.   JLT-24

Your freight trains; things to know about freight yard operations. Written and
illustrated by George J. Zaffo. Garden City, N. Y., Garden City Books, c 1958.
56 p., I, 12.6 in.   JLT-25

LOCOMOTIVES

General

American locomotive engineering illustrated and companion text; orginally published in serial form in 1871, intended to provide technical assistance to railroad men. Gustavus Weissenborn. Felton, Calif., Glenwood Publishers. 104 p., text 225 p., I, 12.2 in.   LG-1

American locomotives; an engineering history, 1830-1880, by John H. White, Jr. Baltimore, Johns Hopkins Press [1968]. 504 p. (pf.—23 p.), I, P, 9.4 x 10.2 in.   LG-2

Complete index to steam, electric, diesel and traction rosters of railroads, rapid transit and street car lines from Alaska to the Yucatan and beyond, as appearing in North American railfan magazines over the past thirty years. F. H. Worsfeld. [n. p.] 1964. 24 p., 11 in.   LG-3

Demise of the iron horse, by George S. Rainey. [Berne, Ind., Economy Printing Concern, 1969.] 431 p., P, 7.9 in.   LG-4

Development of the locomotive engine; a history of the growth of the locomotive from its most elementary form, showing the gradual steps made toward the developed engine, with biographical sketches of the eminent engineers and inventors who nursed it on its way to the perfected form today. Angus Sinclair. Annotated ed. prepared by John H. White, Jr. Cambridge, M. I. T. Press [1970, c 1907]. 708 p. (pf.—9 p.), I, 9.4 in.   LG-5

Famous locomotives of the world. Sketches by the author. C. Hamilton Ellis. London, F. Muller [1957; stamped: distributed by Sportshelf, New Rochelle, N. Y.] 143 p., I, 7.5 in.   LG-5A

International locomotives; from the collection of railroad paintings by the late H. M. Le Fleming, half of British locomotives, others U. S., Germany, etc. Text by H. E. Durrant. New York, Arco Publishing, 1972. 192 p., I (92C), T, 11.5 x 8.5 in.   LG-6

Introduction of the locomotive safety truck. John H. White. Washington, Smithsonian Institution, 1961. 113-113 p., I, D, 11 in. (paper 24).   LG-7

Locomotives and cars since 1900. Walter L. Lucas. New York, Simmons-Boardman Pub. Corp. [1959]. [8] 119 p. (chiefly I, D), 11.4 in.   LG-8

Pocket guide to American locomotives. Walter A. Lucas. New York, Simmons-Boardman Pub. Corp. [1953]. 290 p., I, 8.7 in.   LG-9

Popular picture and plan book of railroad cars and locomotives. New York, Simmons-Boardman Pub. Corp. [1951]. 288 p., I, 11.8 in. By W. A. Lucas. LG-10

The Locomotive engineer. [Cleveland.] I, P, 16.9 in., biweekly.   LG-11

U. S. railroad locomotive study, April 1952, to establish requirement and production goals and tax amortization goal for traffic levels forecast to July 1, 1954, and for full mobilization to July 1, 1956. U. S. Def. Trans. Adm. [Washington, 1952]. 29 l., 10.6 in.   LG-12

Railway motive power. Henry C. Webster. With a foreword by Harold Rudgard. London, New York, Hutchinson's Scientific and Technical Publications, 1952. 310 p., I, 8.7 in.   LG-13

Study of railroad motive power. [Prepared by John T. Warren and Alexis P. Bukovsky.] Washington, 1950. 208 p. (pf.–12 p.), 10.6 in. (No. 5025).   LG-14

2750: legend of a locomotive. Henry C. Webster. Illustrated by R. Barnard Way. London, New York, T. Nelson [1953]. 209 p. (pf.–12 p.), I, plates (C), 7.9 in.
                                                                            LG-15

An acquaintance with Alco. Olmsted, 1968.   sCO-8
Iron horses [S.F.]. Worley, 1965.   sCO-15
Locomotives [Baldwin]. Westing, 1966.   sCO-25
Picture history [B&O]. Sagle, 1952.   sCO-31
C&O power. Staufer, 1965.   sCO-58
Milwaukee Road locos. Martin, 1972.   sCO-72
Erie power. Westing, 1956.   sCO-113
Motive power of [U.P.]. Kratville.   sCO-294

Diesel and Diesel-Electric

American Society of Mechanical Engineers. Diesel and Gas Engine Power Division. Proceedings. Chicago. 11 in.   LD-1

ASTM manual for rating diesel fuels by the cetane method. Philadelphia, American Society of Testing Materials, 1959. 130 p., I, 9.4 in.   LD-2

Automatic and fluid transmissions. John G. Giles. London, Odhams Press [1961; label: Hollywood-by-the-Sea, Fla., Transatlantic Arts]. 328 p., I, 9 in.   LD-3

Diesel locomotives: mechanical and electrical fundamentals. Rev. by the staff of the American Technical Society [1954]. 344 p., I, 8.7 in. By John Draney. LD-4

Diesel locomotives; report of a visit to the U. S. A. in 1950. London, New York, published for the Diesel Locomotive Industry Productivity Team by the AngloAmerican Council of Productivity, 1950. 51 p., I, P, M, 10.2 in.   LD-5

Diesel railway traction. London. I, 11.8 in., monthly.   LD-6

Diesel spotter's guide, by Jerry A. Pinkepank. Milwaukee, Kalmbach Pub. Co. [1967]. 1 v. (chiefly illus.), 5.5 x 8.3 in.   LD-7

The diesel electric locomotive dictionary for the locomotive fireman and engineer. Paul E. Craig. [Lyons, Ill., 1950.] 192 p., I, 6.3 in.; also, 1951.   LD-8

Diesel-electric locomotive handbook; a basic reference book for enginemen, maintenance man and other railroad personnel engaged in operating and maintaining diesel-electric locomotives. George F. McGowan. New York, Simmons-Boardman Pub. Corp. [1951]. 2 v., I, 8.3 in.   LD-9

Diesel-electrics: how to keep 'em rolling. New York, Simmons-Boardman Pub. Corp. [1954]. 139 p., I, 11 in.   LD-10

Engineer's operating manual for EMD F-7 and FP-7; authentic reproduction of engineer's bible. Milwaukee, Old Line Publishers. 158 p., I (75), T (f), 7 in.

LD-11

Loco 1, the diesel. Compiled by the staff of Railroad Model Craftsman. [Editor, Harold H. Carstens.] Ramsey, N. J., Model Craftsman Pub. Corp., c 1966. 142 p., I, PL, 8.3 x 11.4 in.

LD-12

Operation and maintenance of diesel-electric locomotives. [Washington] Departments of the Army and the Air Force, 1965. 287 p., I, 10.2 in.

LD-13

Outloading of diesel locomotives (Motion picture). U. S. Dept. of the Army, 1952. Released for public educational use through U. S. Office of Education, 1952. 13 min., sd., b&w, 16mm.

LD-14

Symposium of diesel locomotive engine maintenance, including spectrographic analysis, filtering cooling water treatment [and] railroad the electron microscope. Alco Products, Inc. May 11 and 12, 1953, Schenectady, N. Y. New York [1953]. 146 p. (pf.—12 p.), I, P, 9 in.

LD-15

Diesels west! [CB&Q]. Morgan, 1963.   sCO-63
Our GM scrapbook. Kalmbach, 1971.   sCO-123
Krauss-Maffei operational manual. Old Line.   sCO-151

Electric

NEMA standards publication: mining and industrial electric locomotives. National Electrical Mfgs. Assoc. [New York] c 1956. 48 p., 11.4 in. (MI-1-1956).   LE-1

The pictorial history of electric locomotives [by] F. J. G. Haut. [1st Am. ed.] South Brunswick, N. J., A. S. Barnes [1970, c 1969]. 147 p., I (PC), PL (4F), 11.4 in.

LE-2

Steam and electric [locos.-N.Y.C.]. Edson.   sCO-191
Pennsy power. Staufer.   sCO-219

Mine

Diesel power for underground haulage, by J. H. East, Jr. and E. R. Maize. Mining Technology, York, Pa., 1937-48. 9 in.

LM-1

Mine transportation, pumping and power transmission. Pierce Management, Inc., Scranton, Pa. [c 1952]. 98 p., I, 11 in.

LM-2

NEMA standard publication: mining and industrial locomotives. National Electrical Manufacturers Associates [New York c 1956. 48 p., I, 11.4 in. (MI-1-1956).

LM-3

Steam

American locomotives; a pictorial record of steam power, 1900-1950. Edwin P. Alexander. [1st ed.] New York, Norton [1950]. 254 p., I, D, 11.4 in.   LS-1

American locomotives, 1871-1881; a collection of locomotive drawings and plans with descriptions, specifications and details, originally published in 1883 under the title Recent locomotives, by Railroad Gazette Publishing Co., New York, and augmented with new material from various sources. Railway Age. Edited by Grahame Hardy and Paul Darrell. Decorations by E. S. Hammack. [1st ed.] Oakland, Calif., G. Hardy, 1950. 1 v. (chiefly illus.), 16.1 in.   LS-2

The American steam locomotive, by F. M. Swengel. [Davenport, Iowa, Midwest Rail Publications, 1967-.] I, 11.8 in.   LS-3

Apex of the Atlantics. Frederick Westing. [Milwaukee, Kalmbach Pub. Co., 1963.] 167 p., I, 9.8 in.   LS-4

Articulated locomotives. Lionel Wiener. New York, R. R. Smith, Milwaukee, Kalmbach Pub. Co., 1970. 628 p. (pf.—15 p.), I, PL, 9 in.   LS-5

A century of locomotive building by Robert Stephenson & Co. 1823-1923, by J. G. H. Warren. New York, A. M. Kelley, 1970. 461 p. (pf.—13 p.), I, Fac, P, 10.2 in.   LS-6

Climax—an unusual steam locomotive, by Thomas T. Taber, III, and Walter Casler. [1st ed. Rahway, N. J., Railroadians of America, 1960.] 97 p., I (PC), P, 11.4 in.; also, "second binding," 4 p. addenda as of Jan., 1961.   LS-7

Early American steam locomotives; 1st seven decades, 1830-1900. Reed C. Kinert. Text and drawings by Reed Kinert. [1st ed.] Seattle, Superior Pub. Co. [1962]. 158 p., I, 8.7 x 11 in.   LS-8

Eastern steam pictorial; the anthracite roads. Bert Pennypacker. [River Vale, N. J., P & D Carleton, 1966.] 381 p., I, 11.4 in.   LS-9

The Fairlie locomotive [by] Rowland A. S. Abbot. Newton Abbot, David & Charles, 1970. 103 p., I, P, 9.8 in.   LS-10

Farewell to steam. David Plowden. Toronto, Burns and MacEachern; Brattleboro, Vt., Stephen Greene Press [c 1966]. 154 p. (pf.—6 p.), I, 11.4 in.   LS-11

The first quarter-century of steam locomotives in North America; remaining relics and operable replicas, with a calalog of locomotive models in the U. S. National Museum. Smith H. Oliver. Washington, Smithsonian Institution, 1956. 112 p., I, 9.4 in. (210).   LS-12

First steam west of the Big Muddy, by Byron E. Guise. 1st ed. Marysville, Kan. [Marysville Pub. Co., 1970.] 51 p., I, Fac, M, P, 11 in.   LS-13

4-8-4 Pictorial (published 1972); a picture-album of 4-8-4 wheel arangement steam locomotives of over 30 railroads. New York, Wayner Publications, 1972. 8½ x 11 in., 64 p.   LS-14

4-8-0 tender locomotives; discusses origin and development around the world. By D. Rock Carling. New York, Drake Publishers. 112 p., I, D, 10 in.   LS-15

The Garratt locomotive [by] A. E. Durrant. New York, A. M. Kelley [1969]. 144 p., I, PL, 10.2 in.   LS-16

The Georgian locomotive, some elegant steam locomotive power in the South and Southwest, 1918-1945, an episode in American taste. Homer S. Bryant. Barre, Mass., Barre Gazette, 1962. 89 p., I, 11 in.   LS-17

The iron horse [by] Henry B. Comstock. Illus. by the author. New York, Crowell [1971]. 228 p., I, 11.4 in.   LS-18

The last of steam; a billowing pictorial pageant of the waning years of steam railroading in the United States. Joe G. Collias. Berkeley, Calif., Howell-North, 1960. 269 p., I, 11.4 in.   LS-19

Locomotive 4501, by David P. Morgan. [Milwaukee, Wis., Kalmbach Pub. Co., 1968.] 127 p., I, M, PL, 9 in.   LS-20

A long look at steam, by Robert P. Olmsted. [Janesville, Wis., 1965.] [96] p., I (chiefly), 11.4 in.   LS-21

1925 Shay locomotive catalog; exact reproduction of Shay line of 1925. Milwaukee, Old Line Publishers. 30 p., I, D, T, 11 in.   LS-22

The Norris locomotives. Paul C. Dewhurst. Boston, Railway & Locomotive Historical Society, 1950. 80 p., I, 9. in. (No. 79).   LS-23

Pacific coast Shay, strong man of the woods, by Dan Ranger, Jr. [San Marino, Calif., Golden West Books, 1964.] 103 p., I, Fac, M, P, 11.4 in.   LS-24

A pictorial catalog of steam locomotive types and wheel arrangements [by W. Alva Long. Easton, Md., printed by the Easton Pub. Co., 1971.] 1 v. (chiefly illus.), 11.4 in.   LS-25

The "Pioneer": light passenger locomotive of 1851 [by] John H. White. Washington, Smithsonian Institution; GPO, 1964. 243-267 p., I, M, 11 in. (Mus. of Hist. & Tech., No. 42).   LS-26

Pioneer locomotives of North America. Robert R. Brown. [Boston] Railway & Locomotive Historical Socity, 1959. 91 p., I, 9 in. (No. 101).   LS-27

Reorganization plan No. 3 of 1965: locomotive inspection. Hearing before a subcommittee of the Committee on Government Operations, House of Representives, Eighty-ninth Congress, first session. July 7, 1965. House, Gov't. Ops., Washington, GPO, 1965. 72 p. (pf.—4 p.), I, 9.4 in.   LS-28

Rules for construction of boilers of locomotives; section III, ASME boiler construction code. 1949 ed. Report of subcommittee of Boiler Code Committee on boilers of locomotives. New York [1950]. 63 p., I, 7.9 in.   LS-29[

Steam in the sixties, by Ron Ziel and George H. Foster. [1st ed.] New York, Meredith Press [1967]. 208 p., I (PC), Fac, 11 in.   LS-30

The steam locomotive in America: its development in the twentieth century. [1st ed.] Alfred W. Bruce. New York, Norton [1952]. 443 p., I, 9.4 in.   LS-31

The steam locomotives in 1838; reprint of engravings and text covering "Stephenson's Patent Locomotive Engine." By Thomas Tredgold. Felton, Calif., Glenwood Publishers. 32 p., I, engravings, 12 in.   LS-32

Steam, wide and narrow. Ed Wojtas. [n. p.] c 1959. 64 p. (chiefly illus.), 8.3 in.
LS-33

Steam's finest hour. David P. Morgan. Milwaukee, Kalmbach Pub. Co., c 1959.
126 p., I, 11.4 x 16.5 in.   LS-34

Super power steam locomotives, by Richard J. Cook. San Marino, Calif., Golden
West Books [1966]. 144 p., I, P, 11.4 in.   LS-35

The twilight of steam locomotives. Ron Ziel. New York, Grosset & Dunlap [1970].
208 p., I (PC), 11 in.; also, 1963.   LS-36

U. S. steam locomotive directory, compiled and edited by Victor Koenigsberg. 1st
ed. [Sheffield, Iowa, 1967–.] 1 v. (loose-leaf), 11.8 in.   LS-37

World steam in action. Harold Edmonson. With 130 photos by Victor Hand. London, I. Allan [1970]. 160 p., I (PC), M, 12.2 in.   LS-38

Steam locos [and history, G&WP R.R.s]. Prince.	sCO-20
Atlantic Coast Line R.R. Prince, 1966.	sCO-21
History [Baldwin Loco Works]. Old Line.	sCO-24
Baldwin [locos & index]. Warner, 1948.	sCO-26
Baldwin [1913 catalog]. Speciality.	sCO-27
Baldwin [1881 catalog]. Howell-North.	sCO-28
Baldwin [construction records]. Golden West.	sCO-29
Canadian National [steam]. Clegg, 1969.	sCO-50
Steam locos [CB&Q]. Corbin, 1960.	sCO-64
Chicago and North Western [steam]. Knudsen, 1965.	sCO-76
Steam in the Rockies [D&RGW]. Colo. R.R. Mus.	sCO-96
Locomotives [Dickson Mfg. Co.]. Best.	sCO-104
Locomotives of the Empire Builder [GN]. Martin.	sCO-131
Lina locomotives, 1911 catalog. Golden West.	sCO-152
Steel rails to the sunrise [LI]. Ziel.	sCO-153
Early history [LI]. Smith, 1958.	sCO-154
Louisville & Nashville [steam]. Prince, 1968.	sCO-163
Louisville & Nashville [steam]. Prince, 1959.	sCO-164
The Nashville, Chattanooga & St. Louis. Prince.	sCO-184
The Berkshire era. [NYC & St. L.] Rehor.	sCO-186
Steam power [of NYC]. Staufer, 1967.	sCO-190
Steam and electric [locos-NYC]. Edson.	sCO-191
Pennsylvania R.R. K-4s. Golden West.	sCO-217
Locomotives [of PRR]. Warner, 1959.	sCO-218
Pennsy power. Staufer.	sCO-219
Pennsy, A to T. Carleton, 1959.	sCO-220
Reading steam pictorial. Carleton.	sCO-235
Locomotives of the Reading. Warner.	sCO-236
Southern steam specials. Ziel.	sCO-255
Steam locomotives [and boats–SR]. Prince.	sCO-257

A century [of S.P. steam]. Dunscomb.   sCO-262
Southern Pacific steam [locos]. Duke.   sCO-263
Cab-in-front. [S.P.] Hungerford.   sCO-264
Locomotives [of S.P.]. Best, 1956.   sCO-265
Smoke down the canyons. Ehernberger.   sCO-288
Smoke above the plains. Ehernberger.   sCO-289
Smoke across the prarie. Ehernberger.   sCO-290
Smoke along the Columbia. Ehernberger.   sCO-291
Smoke over the divide. Ehernberger.   sCO-292
Steam locomtoives and history [W. Ry. of Ala.]. Prince.   sCO-305

MODELS

General

Advanced model railroading. [1st ed.] Louis H. Hertz. New York, Simmons-
Boardman Pub. Corp., [c 1955]. 340 p., I, 9.8 in.   MOG-1

The complete book of model railroading. David Sutton. Englewood Cliffs,
N. J., Prentice-Hall [1964]. 311 p. (pref.—8 p.), I, F, P, 11.4 in.   MOG-2

The complete book of model railroading. [1st ed.] Louis Hertz. New York,
Simmons-Boardman Pub. Corp. [1951]. 335 p., I, 9.4 in.   MOG-3

Frank Ellison on model railroads. [Greenwich, Conn., Fawcett Publications,
1954.] 144 p., I, 9.4 in.; also New York, Arco Pub., 1954, 10.2 in.   MOG-4

HO primer: model railroading for all. Linn H. Westcott. Milwaukee, Kalmbach
Pub. Co., c 1962. 79 p., I, 11.4 in.   MOG-5

The model railroad book. Warren F. Morgan. Greenwich, Conn., Fawcett
Publications, c 1953. 144 p., I, 9.4 in.: also, New York, Arco Pub. Co., c 1953,
10.2 in.   MOG-6

Model railroading; written and illustrated by Harry Zarchy. [1st ed.] New York,
Knopf [1955]. 172 p., I, 8.7 in.   MOG-7

New roads to adventure in model railroading. [1st ed.] Louis Hertz. New York,
Simmons-Boardman Pub. Corp. [1952]. 340 p., I, 9.4 in.   MOG-8

Scale model railroading. Leslie T. White. New York, T. Nelson [1964]. 192 p.,
I, 10.2 in.   MOG-9

The world of model trains [by] Guy R. Williams. New York, Putnam [1970].
256 p., I (PC), P (PC), 10.2 in.   MOG-10

764 helpful hints for model railroaders, from Kinks column of Model Railroader
magazine. Edited by Bob Warren and Model Railroader staff. Milwaukee,
Kalmbach Pub. Co. [1965]. 64 p., I (PC), 11.4 in.   MOG-11

Cars

Freight car lettering plan book for model railroaders; 600 authentic freight
car plans, representing 208 different railroads and private owners. [2nd ed.]
Minot, N. D., Champion Decal Company [1965]. 80 p. (chiefly illus.), 11 in.
11 in.   MOD-1

Construction

The HO railroad that grows. Linn H. Westcott. Milwaukee, Kalmbach Pub. Co.,
c 1958. 63 p., I, 11.4 in.   MOC-1

How to build and operate a model railroad. Marshall McClintock. [New York,
Dell Pub. Co., 1955.] 192 p., I, 6.7 in.   MOC-2

How to build model railroads and equipment. Barton K. Davis. New York, Crown
Publishers [1956]. 191 p., I, 11.4 in.   MOC-3

How to improve your model railroad. Drawings and diagrs. by the author.
Raymond F. Yates, New York, Harper [1953]. 98 p., I, 8.7 in.   MOC-4

How to wire your model railroad. Linn H. Westcott. Milwaukee, Kalmbach
Pub. Co., c 1950. 60 p., I (PC), P, 11.4 in.   MOC-5

Making your model railroad. Louis Hertz. Illustrated by Ava Morgan. New
York, Crowell [1954]. 216 p., I, 7.5 in.   MOC-6

Model railroading. [Experts show you how to build and operate a pike. Trend
Books, Inc., Los Angeles, 1956]. 127 p., I, 9.8 in.   MOC-7

Scenery for model railroads. Bill McClanahan. With chapters by Linn H.
Westcott. Wash drawings by Gil Reid. Rev. ed. Milwaukee, Kalmbach Pub. Co.,
1967. 103 p., I (PC), 11.4 in.   MOC-8

Scenery for model railroads. Bill McClanahan. Wash drawings by Gil Reid.
Milwaukee, Kalmbach Pub. Co., c 1958. 79 p., I, D, 11.4 in.   MOC-9

Small railroads you can build, by Linn H. Westcott [and others]. Milwaukee,
Kalmbach Pub. Co., c 1954. 32 p., I, 11.4 in.   MOC-10

Encyclopaedias

Blue book of hobbies; catalog and cyclopedia of model railroads. New York,
Polk's Model Craft Hobbies. I, 8.7 in.   MOE-1

Model railroader cyclopedia. Edited by Linn H. Westcott. [Milwaukee, Kalmbach
Pub. Co., 1960—] I, D, 11.4 x 14.6 in.   MOE-2

The Model railroader cyclopedia; railroad equipment prototype plans. [1st] —
6th ed. Milwaukee [etc.] Kalmbach Pub. Co. [etc.] 1936-49. Gr., I, D, 10.6
in.   MOE-3

The model railway encyclopaedia. [1st American ed.] E. F. Carter. London,
Burke Pub. Co.; New York, Anglobooks [1951]. 496 p., I, D, J, 9 in.   MOE-4

Handbooks

Complete guide book to model railroading. David Sutton. [Los Angeles, Trend
Books, 1960.] 128 p., I, 9.8 in.   MOH-1

Electrical handbook for model railroaders. Paul Mallery. New York, Simmons-
Boardman Pub. Corp. [1955]. 260 p., I, 9.4 in.   MOH-2

Handbook for model railroaders. William K. Walters. Milwaukee, Kalmbach Pub.
Co., 1949. 218 p., I, 9.4 in.   MOH-3

Model railroad handbook. A. C. Kalmbach. [Greenwich, Conn., Fawcett Publications, 1951.] 144 p., I, 9.4 in. (No. 133).   MOH-4

National Model Railroad Association. Directory. 1965/66– Canton, Ohio.
7.5 x 8.7 in.   MOH-5

Practical guide to model railroading, edited by Linn H. Westcott and Richard
H. Wagner. Milwaukee, Kalmbach Pub. Co., c 1952. 60 p., I, 11.4 in.   MOH-6

Operation

Operating manual for model railroaders, by Boomer Pete [pseud.]. Albert C.
Kalmbach. Milwaukee, Kalmbach Pub. Co. [1954, c 1944]. 153 p., I, 9 in. MOO-1

Structures

Bridges & buildings for model railroads, edited by Willard V. Anderson and Model
Railroader staff. [Milwaukee, Kalmbach Pub. Co., 1965.] 96 p., I (PC), 11.4 in.
                                                                                       MOS-1

Bridge and trestle handbook for model railroaders. Paul Mallery. New York,
Simmons-Boardman Pub. Corp., 1958. 146 p., I, 9.4 in.   MOS-2

East-to-build model railroad structures. Edited by Willard V. Anderson. Milwaukee, Kalmbach Pub. Co., c 1958. 95 p., I, D, P, 11.4 in.   MOS-3

Toys and Tinplate

Collecting model trains. Louis H. Hertz. New York, Simmons-Boardman Pub.
Corp. [c 1956]. 352 p., I, 9.8 in.   MOT-1

The boys' book of model railroading; illustrated with drawings by the author
and photos. Raymond F. Yates. New York, Harper [1951]. 172 p., I, 8.7 in.
                                                                                       MOT-2

The boys' book of model railways. Ernest F. Carter. New York, Roy Publishers [1959, c 1958]. 144 p., I, 10.2 in.   MOT-3

Iron ponies (Motion picture), Lionel Corp. Released by Institute of Visual
Training, 1951. 10 min., sound, b&w, 16 mm.   MOT-4

Model railroading; prepared by the editorial staff of Lionel Corporation.
[4th big new ed.] New York, Bantam Books [1955]. 384 p., I, 7.1 in.; also 3rd
ed., 1953;2nd ed., 1957.   MOT-5

Model railroading. Lionel Corp. New York, Bantam Books [1950]. 256 p.,
I, 6.7 in. (A-2).   MOT-6

Track and Layout

Model railroad track and layout. A. C. Kalmbach. 5th ed. Milwaukee, Kalmbach
Pub. Co., 1951. 106 p., I, M, 10.2 in.   MTL-1

Track design for scale model railroading; scale layout designs for every railroad
modeler. By Hal Carstens and Bill Schopp. Ramsey, N. J., Penn Publications,
c 1960. 66 p., I, D, 11 in.   MTL-2

Track planning for realistic operation. John H. Armstrong. 1st ed. Milwaukee, Kalmbach Pub. Co., 1963. 103 p., I, 11.4 in.   MTL-3

Prize model railroad layouts. A. C. Kalmbach. [Greenwich, Conn., Fawcett Publications, 1952.] 144 p., I, 9.4 in. (n-169).   MTL-4

New ideas in railroad modeling, by Jim Mourning and Bob Rolofson; latest pike layouts for all gauges, how to create and operate your models. [Los Angeles, 1957.] 128 p., I, 9.4 in.   MTL-5

N scale model railroad track plans, by the Model railroader staff. Edited by Russ Larson. Milwaukee, Kalmbach Pub. Co., 1969. 43 p., I, 11.4 in.   MTL-6

The 7-foot model train book; make your own train. Locomotive, tender and eight cars; all parts die-stamped, no cutting required. Authentic scale models ready to assemble. Wallis Rigby. New York, Grosset & Dunlap, c 1950. 10 l., I (PC), 11 x 14.2 in.   MTL-7

Train collectors quarterly. v. 1— . Jan. 1955— . [Pittsburgh, Train Collectors Association.] I, 11.4 in.   MTL-8

The trains of Lionel's standard gauge era; history of Lionel standard gauge, toy trains of yesteryear. [By Harold H. Carstens. Ramsey, N. J., Model Craftsman Pub. Corp., 1964.] 35 p.,(incl. cover), I, 11 in.   MTL-9

NARROW GAUGE

Little railways of the world. Frederic J. Shaw. Drawings by the author. [1st ed.] Berkeley, Calif., Howell-North, 1958. 261 p. (pf.—9 p.), I, P, M, 9.8 in.   N-1

Narrow gauge nostalgia, by George Turner. [Harbor City, Calif., J-H Publications, 1965.] 159 p., I, F, M, 11.4 in.   N-2

Narrow gauge in the Rockies, by Lucius Beebe and Charles Clegg. Berkeley, Calif., Howell-North, 1958. 224 p., I (PC), M, D, F, 11.4 in.   N-3

Narrow gauge railways in America; edited by Grahame Hardy and Paul Darrell; foreword by Lucius Beebe. Including a list of narrow gauge railways in America, 1871 to 1949, compiled by Brian Thompson. Howard Fleming. Decorations by E. S. Hammack. Oakland, Calif., G. H. Hardy, 1949. 101, 39 p., I, 9 in.   N-4

Steam on the Sierra; the narrow gauge in Spain and Portugal [by] Peter Allen and Robert Wheeler. London, Cleaver-Hume Press [1960]. 203 p., I, 10.2 in.   N-5

The Weeks Mills "Y" of the two-footer, by Clinton F. Thurlow. [Weeks Mills, Me.] 1964. 63 p., I, F, M, P, 8.7 in.   N-6

The W W & F two-footer, hail and farewell, by Clinton F. Thurlow. Weeks Mills, Me. [1964]. 110 p., I, F, M, P, 8.7 in.   N-7

Bradford, Bordell & Kinzua.	sCO-40
Bridgton & Saco River.	sCO-41
Busted and still running. Mead.	sCO-42
Slim rails [Carson & Colo.]. Turner.	sCO-53
The Switzerland trail. Crossen.	sCO-90
Chili line [D&RGW]. Gjevre.	sCO-99
Narrow gauge to Silverton. Hungerford.	sCO-100
Denver, South Park & Pacific. Poor.	sCO-103
A ramble [E.B.T.]. Kyper.	sCO-107
A quick review [E.B.T.]. Mannix.	sCO-108
Intermountain R.Rs. Beal.	sMT-1
Kendall & Eldred.	sCO-108
Last of the three foot loggers. Krieg.	sCO-307
Maine two footers. Moody.	sM-1
Mexican narrow gauge. Best.	sMEX-1
Narrow gauge in a kingdom. Conde.	sCO-135
Narrow gauge to the redwoods [N.P.C.]. Dickinson.	sCO-201
Nevada County narrow gauge. Best.	sCO-184
The Rio Grande Southern story. Crum.	sCO-237
The Sandley story. Rooksby.	sCO-243
Ships and narrow gauge rails. Best.	sCO-208
Steam, wide and narrow. Wojtas.	sLS-33
Three little lines [S, SG&N, SN]. Crum.	sCO-252
On the "White Pass" payroll. Graves.	sCO-308
Gold rush narrow gauge [WP&Y]. Martin.	sCO-309

STREET RAILROADS

The American transportation token catalog of United States fare tokens, arranged alphabetically by the stamping on the tokens. Clyde A. Logsdon. Omaha, c 1953—. 1 v. (loose-leaf), 8.7 in. STR-1

The Birney car, by Harold E. Cox. [Forty Fort, Pa., 1966.] 118 p., I, 11 in. STR-2

The electric interurban railways in America [by] George W. Hilton and John F. Due. Stanford, Calif., Stanford University Press, 1960. 463 p. (pf.–9 p.), I, M, 9.4 in. STR-3

Fares, please! A popular history of trolleys, horse-cars, street-cars, buses, elevateds, and subways. John A. Miller. New York, Dover Publications [1960]. 204 p., I, 8.3 in. STR-4

Fort Wayne's trolleys, 1870-1963; horse cars, street cars, interurbans, trolley coaches, motor buses. George K. Bradley. Chicago, O. Davies [1963]. 176 p., I, M (F,C), D, 10.6 in. STR-5

The interurban era. William D. Middleton. [Milwaukee] Kalmbach [1961]. 432 p., I, 11.8 in. STR-6

PCC cars of North America. Harold E. Cox. [Philadelphia, sold by J. W. Boorse, Jr., 1963.] 71 p., I, 11.4 in. STR-7

Public transportation in Detroit; illustrated by William T. Woodward; edited by Joe L. Norris. Harry Dahlheimer. Detroit, Wayne University Press [1951]. 20 p., I, 8.7 in. STR-8

The street railway era in Seattle; a chronicle of six decades, by Leslie Blanchard. Forty Fort, Pa., H. E. Cox [1968]. 151 p., I, Fac, M (4F), 11 in. STR-9

Street cars and interurbans of yesterday; a collection of car illustrations and drawings, selected and arr. by Owen Davies. From the Electric railway dictionary, compiled under the direction of the American Electric Railway Association, by Rodney Hitt. Orginally published in 1911 by McGraw Pub. Co. Chicago, O. Davies, 1960. 166 p., I, 12.2 in. STR-10

Trolley car treasury; a century of American streetcars, horsecars, cable cars, interurbans, and trolleys. Frank Rowsome. Technical editor, Stephen D. Maguire. New
York, McGraw-Hill [1956]. 200 p., I, P, M, 11 in.   STR-11

Traction planbook and photo album. [Edited by Harold H. Carstens. Ramsey,
N. J., 1964.] 66 p., I, 11 in.   STR-12

Ride down memory lane [Branford Mus.]. Stevens.	sMO-1
The great third rail [Chicago]. CERA.	sCH-8
Cincinnati street cars. Wagner.	sCI-1
History of Cleveland street cars. Morse.	sCLE-1
Mile high trolleys [Denver]. Jones.	sD-1
Electric Ry. cars. Stephenson Co.	sCO-249
Glendale & Montrose. Moreau.	sCO-127
Rip Van Winkle R.Rs. Helmer.	sNY-4
The Royal Blue Line. Gordon.	sNY-5
Grape belt trolleys. Springirth.	sNY-1
Trolley lines [empire state]. Reifschneider.	sNY-6
Articulated cars [N.Y.]. Charlton.	sEL-1
Ohio trolleys. Morse.	sO-3
St. Louis cable railways. Katz.	sC-11
Trolley days in Seattle. Blanchard.	sCO-248
Time of the trolley. Middleton.	sEL-9

TRANSIT

General

Crowded streets; a symposium on public transportation. Urban Land Institute. Washington, 1955. 77 p., I, M, 11 in. (26).   TSG-1

Facts about modern transit. Transit Improvement Assoc. New York, c 1950. 39 p., I, 9 in.   TSG-2

Free transit [by] Thomas A. Domencich [and] Gerald Kraft. Lexington, Mass., Heath Lexington Books [1970]. 104 p. (pf.—7 p.), 9.4 in.   TSG-3

Federal aid for urban transportation. Compiled by Marian T. Hankerd. [Washington, Automotive Safety Foundation] 1969. 94 p. (pf.—2 p.), 11 in.   TSG-4

Intergovernmental responsibilities for mass transportation facilities and services in metropolitan areas; a commission report. U. S. Advisory Comm. on Intergovernmental Relations. [Washington] 1961. 54 p. (pf.—5 p.), 10.6 in.   TSG-5

Metropolitan transportation. Staff report prepared [by Arthur Lazarus, consultant] on investigation of status and prospects for the mass transportation survey. U. S. Congress, Joint Com. of Wash. Metro. Problems. Washington, GPO, 1958. 34 p. (pf.—3 p.), 9.4 in.   TSG-6

The Negro in the urban transit industry, by Philip W. Jeffress. Philadelphia, Wharton School of Finance and Commerce, Univ. of Pennsylvania; distributed by Univ. of Pennsylvania Press [c 1970]. 106 p. (pf.—10 p.), 9 in.   TSG-7

Principles of urban transportation. Frank H. Mossman, ed. [Cleveland] Press of Western Reserve University [c 1951]. 236 p., I, 11 in.   TSG-8

Report, submitted by the Legislative Research Council, relative to the use of zone fares in major American cities. Mass. Legislative Res. Bu. [Boston] 1961. 35 p., 9 in. (No. 520).   TSG-9

Some social aspects of mass transit in selected American cities. Joel Smith. East Lansing, Mich., Michigan St. Univ., 1959. 26 p. (pf.—6 p.), 9 in.   TSG-10

Measurement [unionization on wages]. Lurie.   sL-27
Seattle monorail study. Alexander.   sMO-3
Seattle monorail study. Wash. St. Univ.   sMO-4
Washington [D.C.] metro transit. Pres. L. B. Johnson.   sWDT-1

Engineering

Dynamics of vehicle-structure interaction; rapid transit structures. Prepared for Parsons, Brinckerhoff, Tudor, Bechtel, engineers for the Bay Area Rapid Transit District, San Francisco, Calif., by Bechtel Corp., in cooperation with C. F. Scheffey, consulting engineer. [San Francisco, 1964.] 1 v. (various pagings), I, 11.4 in.   TSE-1

Implementation requirements for four advanced urban transportation systems; final report. Transportation System Technology (firm). Los Angeles, North American Rockwell Corp., 1968. 211 p. (pf.—8 p.), 11.4 in.   TSE-2

Interdisciplinary research topics in urban engineering; a report. Washington, American Society for Engineering Education, 1969. 312 p. (pf.—8 p.), I, 11 in.   TSE-3

The technology of urban transportation, by Donald S. Berry [and others. Evanston, Ill.,] Northwestern University Press [c 1963]. 145 p. (pf.—14 p.), M, D, T, 9 in.
TSE-4

Mass transit survey. De Leuw, etc.   sWDT-6

Planning

The Accessible City; shows how transportation can be applied in ways to reduce congestion and improve service. Wilfred Owens. Washington, Brookings Institution, 1972. 150 p.   TSP-1

A reference guide to metropolitan transportation; an annotated bibliography. Northwestern Univ. Transportation Center. [Evanston, 1964.] 42 p., 8.7 in.
TSP-2

Transit modernization and street traffic control; a program of municipal responsibility and administration [by] John Bauer and Peter Costello. Chicago, Public Administration Service, 1950. 271 p. (pf.—13 p.), 9.4 in.   TSP-3

Transportation and urban land. Lowdon Wingo. [Washington] Resources for the Future [1961]. 132 p. (pf.—8 p.), M, D, 9 in.   TSP-4

Urban transit development in twenty major cities. Automotive Safety Foundation. Washington, 1968. 72 p., I, M (C), 11 x 14.2 in.   TSP-5

General plan—Nat. Capital region. Adams, etc.   sWDT-3
Guide [planning sources]. Clark.   sWDT-4
A mass transit integral. Metro. Pl. Assoc.   sWDT-5
Updating [opportunity model]. Curry.   sCH-6
Transportation planning. U. S. House.   sWDT-19

Rapid

Passenger transport annual. New York, American Transit Association. I, 13.8 in.
TSR-1

Rapid transit systems in six metropolitan areas; staff report prepared for the Joint Committee on Washington Metropolitan Problems, Congress of the United States. Gunther M. Gottfeld. Washington, GPO, 1959. 39 p. (pf.—5 p.), 9.4 in.   TSR-2

Urban (and Mass) Transit

Mass transportation survey, National Capital region: traffic engineering study, 1958. Wilbur Smith & Assoc. [New Haven, 1959.] 125 p., M (C), D, T, 12 x 19 in.
TSU-1

Transport inputs at urban residential sites; a study in the transportation geography of urban areas. Duane F. Marble. Ann Arbor, Mich., University Microfilms [1959]. Microfilm AC-1, No. 59-3335.   TSU-2

Urban rail transit: its economics and technology [by] A. Scheffer Lang [and] Richard M. Soberman. Cambridge, published for the Joint Center for Urban Studies of the Massachusetts Institue of Technology and Harvard University by the M. I. T. Press, Massachusetts Institute of Technology [1964]. 139 p. (pf.—12 p.), I, D, 9.4 in.   TSU-3

Urban transportation dilemma; Stephen Paranka. Atlanta, Georgia State College of Business Administration, 1961. 42 l., 11 in. (No. 21).   TSU-4

The urban transportation problem. John R. Meyer, J. K. Kain, M. Wohl. Cambridge, Harvard Univ. Press, 1965. 427 p. (pf.—19 p.), I, T.   TSU-5

Mass transportation—1970. Hearings on S. 676 and S. 3499 . . . April 8 and 9, 1970. Senate (Housing & Urban Affairs). 91C-2S. Washington, GPO, 1970. 60 p. (pf.—3 p.), I, M (F), 9.4 in.   TSU-6

Urban mass transportation assistance act of 1970. Report to accompany H. R. 18185. House, Banking & Currency. 91C-2S. Washington, GPO, 1970. 24 p., 9.4 in. (No. 91-1264).   TSU-7

Urban mass transportation. Hearings, House, Banking & Currency (Housing). 91C-2S. Washington, GPO, 1970. 732 p. (pf.—9 p.), I, M, 9.4 in.   TSU-8

Mass transportation 1969., Hearings, Ninety-first Congress, first session . . . Senate, (Housing & Urban Affairs). Washington, GPO, 1969. 631 p. (pf.—9 p.), I, M, 9.4 in.   TSU-9

Urban mass transportation assistance act of 1969; report to accompany S. 3154, together with individual views. House, Banking & Currency. 91C-2S. Washington, GPO, 1969. 42 p. (pf.—3 p.), 9.4 in. (91-632).   TSU-10

Urban mass transportation act of 1963, Report to accompany S. 6 together with individual views. Senate, Banking & Curr. Washington, GPO, 1963. 58 p. (pf.—3 p.), 9.4 in. (No. 82).   TSU-11

Section-by-section summary of the provisions of S. 6, the Urban mass transportation act pf 1963, as passed by the Senate on April 4, 1963 . . . Senate, Banking & Curr. Washington, GPO, 1963. 7 p. (pf.—2 p.), 9.4 in.   TSU-12

Urban mass transportation act of 1963; report to accompany H. R. 3881. House, Banking & Curr. [Washington, GPO, 1963.] 30 p., 9.4 in. (No. 204).   TSU-13

Urban mass transportation act of 1963; report (bill S. 6). Senate, Commerce. 88C-1S. Washington, GPO, 1963. 9.4 in.((No. 83).   TSU-14

Urban mass transportation, 1963. Hearins on S. 807, S. 6, and S. 917, bills concerning proposed means of providing adequate facilities and service in urban transportation. Senate, Commerce (Sur. Trans.). 88C-1S. Washington, GPO, 1963. 308 p. (pf.—5 p.), form, T, 9.4 in.   TSU-15

Urban mass transportation act of 1963. Hearings on H. R. 3881, a bill to authorize additional assistance for the development of comprehensive and coordinated mass transportation systems. House, Banking & Curr. 88C-1S. Washington, GPO, 1963. 708 p. (pf.—7 p.), I, M, 9.4 in.   TSU-16

Urban mass transportation, 1963. Hearings on S. 6 and S. 917, bills to authorize additional assistance for the development of mass transportation systems. Senate, Banking & Curr. 88C-1S. Washington, GPO, 1963. 484 p. (pf.—8 p.), form, T, 9.4 in.   TSU-17

Urban mass transportation act of 1962. Hearings on H. R. 11158, a bill to authorize additional assistance for the development of comprehensive and coordinated mass transportation systems. House, Banking & Curr. 87C-2S. Washington, GPO, 1962. 896 p. (pf.—8 p.), I, M, 9.4 in.   TSU-18

Section-by-section summary of the Urban mass transportation act of 1962 (as agreed to by committee). H. R. 11158, a bill to authorize additional assistance for the development of comprehensive and coordinated mass transportation systems. House, Banking & Curr. 87C-2S. Washington, GPO, 1962. 4 p., 9.4 in.   TSU-19

The Urban mass transportation act of 1962. H. R. 11158, a bill to provide additional assistance for the development of comprehensive and coordinated mass transportation systems. House, Banking & Curr. 87C-2S. Washington, GPO, 1962. 40 p. (pf.—5 p.), 9.4 in.   TSU-20

Urban mass transportation, 1962. Hearings on S. 3615, a bill to authorize additional assistance for the development of comprehensive and coordinated mass transporportation systems. Senate, Commerce. 87C-2S. Washington, GPO, 1962. 163 p. (pf.—3 p.), 9.4 in.   TSU-21

Urban mass transportation act of 1962. Report to accompany S. 3615. Senate, Banking & Curr. 87C-2S. Washington, GPO, 1962. 35 p. (pf.—3 p.), T, 9.4 in.
                                                                                                   TSU-22

Urban mass transportation, 1962. Hearings on bills to authorize (additional assistance for the development of mass transportation systems) . . . Senate, Banking & Curr. 87C-2S. Washington, GPO, 1962. 533 p. (pf.—8 p.), I, M, 9.4 in.   TSU-23

Urban mass transportation, 1961. Hearings, June 27 and 28, 1961. House, Banking & Curr. 87C-1S. Washington, GPO, 1961. 194 p. (pf.—4 p.), M, T, 9.4 in.   TSU-24

Urban mass transportation, 1961. Hearings on S. 345, a bill to authorize the administrator of HHFA to assis State and local governments in planning and providing for necessary community facilities to preserve and improve essential mass transportation services in urban and metropolitan areas. March 20, 21, and 22, 1961. Senate, Banking & Curr. 87C-1S. 449 p. (pf.—5 p.), I, M, 9.4 in.   TSU-25

Metropolitan mass transportation. Hearings on metropolitan mass transportation legislation. June 29 and 30, 1960. House, Banking & Curr. 86C-2S. Washington, GPO, 1960. 94 p. (pf.—4 p.), D, 9.4 in.   TSU-26

Metropolitan mass transportation. Hearings . . . June 29 and 30, 1960. House, Banking & Curr. 86C-2S. Washington, GPO, 1960. 92 p. (pf.—4 p.), 9.4 in. TSU-27

Mass transportation act of 1960. Senate, Banking & Curr. 86C-2S. Report to accompany S. 3278. Washington, GPO, 1960. 23 p. (pf.—3 p.), 9.4 in.   TSU-28

Canadian transit.	sCAN-5-6
Chicago transit.	sCH-3-6
Colorado transit.	sCOL-1
Detroit transit.	sDE-1
Florida transit.	sFLA-3
Massachusetts transit.	sMAS-1
New York transit.	sCOMM-5-6, NY(C)-1,3,5, NY(M)-9
San Francisco transit.	sSA-1-9
Seattle transit.	sMO-3-4
Washington transit.	sWDT-1-42

SECTION 4

AUTHOR INDEX

AUTHOR INDEX

Author	Short Title	Location
Abbott, Morris W.	The Pike's Peak Cog Road	CO-222
Abbot, Rowland A. S.	The Fairlie locomotive	LS-10
Abdill, George B.	Civil War RRs	SOU-1
	A locomotive engineer's album	LO-2
	Pacific slope railroads	PI-6
	Rails west	PI-11
	This was railroading	NW-1
Adams, Charles Francis, Jr.	Chapters of Erie	CO-112
	High finance in the sixties	CO-7
Adams, Henry	Chapters of Erie	CO-112
Adams, Herbert B.	Maryland's influence [land cessions]	CO-34
Adams, Howard & Greeley (firm)	General development plan [National Capital]	WDT-3
Adams, Kramer	Logging railroads of the west	LOG-2
Adler, Dorothy, R.	British investment [Am. Rys.]	F-2
Alaska	Alaska-Ry-highway crossings	CR-1
Alco Products, Inc.	Symposium [diesel maintenance]	LD-15
Alexander, Daniel E.	Seattle monorail demonstration study	MO-3
Alexander, Edwin P.	American locomotives	LS-1
	Down at the depot	ST-1
Allhands, James	Railroads to the Rio	SOU(W)-2
	Uriah Lott	BIO-10
Allen, Gary G.	Nevada Northern	CO-185
Allen, Geoffrey F.	Railways the world over	RA-19
Allen, J. Knight	Report [financial aspects S.F. transit]	SA-7
Allen, John S.	Standard time	OP-9
Allen, Peter	Steam on the Sierra	N-5
Ambelang, Paul L.	Selected special freight statistics	FT-12
American Geographical Society	Railroads	JLG-5
American Law Institute	ALI-ABA course of study	LAW-1
American Map Co.	Clear type map [Ala.]	AL-1
	Clear type map [Ark.]	ARK-1
	Clear type map [Calif.]	CA-2
	Clear type map [La.]	LA-1
American Railway Engineering Association		ENG-1
American Short Line Assoc.		SHO-1
American Society for Engineering Education	Interdisciplinary research	TSE-3
American Society of Mechanical Engineers		LD-1
	Rail transportation proceedings	CONG-3
	Rules for construction [boilers]	LS-29
American Society for Testing and Materials	ASTM manual	LD-2
	Symposiums [materials 9 and 0 oils]	CONG-4
	Railroad materials and facilities research	RES-1
American Transit Assoc.	Passenger transport annual	TSR-1
Ames, Charles E.	Pioneering the Union Pacific	CO-274

Andersen, A.	Interstate Comm. Comm. jurisdiction [fin. statem.]	ICC-6
Anderson, Edward A.	PCC cars of Boston	BO-2
Anderson, Eugene	ICC practice and procedure	ICC-4
	Manual of practice	ICC-7
Anderson, George L.	Kansas West	CO-95
Anderson, Willard V.	Bridges & buildings [models]	MOS-1
	Easy to build [model structures]	MOS-3
Andes, Dotty	My little library	JLG-3
Andrews, W. Earle	Detroit expressway & transit	DE-1
Anglo-Am. Council on Productivity	Diesel locomotives [productivity]	LE-5
Arco RR series [employment]		EMP-1
Armitage, Merle	The railroads of America	RA-21
Armstrong, John H.	Track planning	MTL-3
Arno Press	Facts and arguments, railways	COMP-4
Arnold, Ian	Locomotive, trolley, and car bldrs.	BU-1
Association of ICC Practitioners	Abstracts of Supreme Court decisions [ICC]	ICC-1
	Selected reading [principal laws]	ICC-2
Association of American Railroads	Agenda	ACT-1
	American railroads	RH-3
	American railroads	DEV-1
	The Assoc. of Am. RRs	AS-2
	Bibliography	BI-2, 3
	A chronological list [Fla. RRs]	RA-8
	A chronology [Am. RRs]	CI-1
	Conducting transportation	ACT-2
	Inside railroading	R-1
	List of maps	MAP-2
	Names and nicknames [freight trains]	TRN-4
	Quiz, Jr.	JLG-4
	Railroads at work	JLO-4
	Railway statistical manual	STA-2
	Railways	RA-24
	Report	CAR-9
	Report	COM-2
	Report	RES-3
	Train and engine books for children	JLT-17
	Working in the shops	ACT-13
	Working on the tracks	ACT-14
	Yearbook of railroad facts 1965–	RA-25
Association of Western Railways	Taxes levied and chargeable	T-7
Athearn, Robert G.	Rebel of the Rockies	CO-93
Atwood, Roland C.	Atwood's catalog [tokens]	GO-1
Automotive Safety	Urban transit development	TSP-5

B

Backman, Jules	Economics [NY full crew laws]	RU-1
Baggage Car (Pub.)	Bridgton & Saco River	CO-41
Bain, William E.	Frisco folks	CO-242
Baker, George Pierce	The formation [New England RR systems]	HT-36

Banks, (RL) & Assoc.	Separable suburban costs [New York]	COS-5
Barber, Tom	Bradford, Bordell & Kinzua	CO-40
Barringer, John W.	Super-railroads	FUT-4
Barth, George	Steam, steel & limiteds	PI-12
Basler, Christian O.	The O & C lands	LA-1
Bateman, Carroll	The Baltimore & Ohio	CO-30
Bathe, Greville	The St. John's Railroad	CO-240
Bauer, Frederick	The Moffat Road	CO-92
Bauer, John	Transit modernization and street traffic	TSP-3
Baxter, Charles S.	Railroad freight tariffs	AT-14
Beal, Ann	Hall of History railroad	NOC-2
Beal, Merrill D.	Intermountain RRs	MT-1
Beatty, Jerome	Show me the way	ANE-2
Beaver, Roy C.	The Bessemer and Lake Erie	CO-36
Beckmann, Martin	Studies [economics of transportation]	EC-8
Beebe, Lucius Morris	The age of steam	STE-1
	Cable car carnival	C-5
	Central Pacific & Southern Pacific	CO-258
	Great railroad photographs	PI-3
	Hear the train blow	PI-4
	Mansions on rails	CAR-20
	Mixed train daily	SHO-4
	Narrow gauge in the Rockies	N-3
	The Overland Limited	CO-287
	Mr. Pullman's elegant palace car	CO-226
	Rio Grande	CO-94
	San Francisco's golden era	SA-2
	Steamcars to the Comstock	CO-298
	The trains we rode	PI-13
	20th Century	CO-192
	Two trains to remember	CO-196
	Virginia & Truckee	CO-296
	When beauty rode the rails	PI-15
Beggs, Alexander K.	The railway [grade crossing problem]	CR-2
Bell, William A.	New tracks in North America	SUR-1
Bender, Henry E., Jr.	Uintah Railway	CO-272
Bennett, Henry Arnold	The commission and common law	ICC-3
Benson, Lee	Merchants, farmers & railroads	LAW-10
Berge, Stanley	Railroad passenger [costs]	PAS-2
	Self-propelled [cars and M.U.s]	CAR-23
Berger, Robert E.	Holding [company ownership of RR securities]	F-9
Berry, Donald S.	The technology of urban transportation	TSE-4
Berton, Pierre	The national dream	CAN-21
Best, Gerald M.	Iron horses to Promontory	HT-21
	Locomotives [Dickson Mfg. Co.]	CO-104
	Locomotives of the Southern Pacific	CO-265
	Mexican Narrow gauge	MEX-3
	Minisink Valley express	NY-3, CO-172
	Nevada County Narrow Gauge	CO-184
	Ships and narrow gauge rails	CO-208
	Snowplow	SN-1
	The Ulster & Delaware	CO-273
Best, John C.	The Union Pacific	CO-277
Bethers, Ray	Perhaps I'll be a railroad man	JLR-4

Beuhr, Walter	Railroads, today and yesterday	UG-6
Bick, I. Stuart	Rail freight [Tri-State region]	TTG-3
Billings, Henry	Diesel-electric 4030	JLL-2
Bingham, S. H.	Proposal [Superail transit]	MO-2
Bingham, Sidney H.	Technical analysis [rehabilitation of LIRR]	CO-157
Binzen, Peter	The wreck [Penn-Central]	CO-212
Bishop, David W.	Railroad decisions [ICC]	LAW-6
Black, Robert C.	The railroads of the Confederacy	HT-26
Blanchard, Leslie	The street railway era in Seattle	STR-9
	Trolley days in Seattle	CO-248
Blackhawk Films [movies]		MPI-61
Blanton, Burt C.	400,000 miles by rail	EXP-1
Blatteau, John W.	Reestablishing the link	COMM-9
Black, Eugene B.	Great train robberies of the West	RO-1
Blower, James M.	Northern Ohio Traction revisited	CO-203
	The NOT&L story	CO-204
Boldyreff, Alexander W.	Determination [maximum flow−RRs]	OP-2
Bollinger, Edward T.	The Moffat Road	CO-92
Boner, Harold A.	The giant's ladder	CO-91
Bonilla, Manuel G.	Effect [earthquake−Alaska RR]	CO-5
Bonright, James C.	Railroad capitalization	F-4
Boorse, J. W., Jr.	Rapid transit in Canada	CAN-4
Borkin, Joseph	Robert R. Young	BIO-24
Boston College	Problems of the railorads	COMM-8
Botzow, Herman S. P.	Monorails	MO-1
Bouser, William	Piggyback transportation [Northwest]	FT-9
Bowes, Laurence C.	Freight-car trucks	CAR-16
Bowman, Hank	Pioneer railroads	HT-25
Bradley, George K.	Fort Wayne's trolleys, 1870-1963	STR-5
	The Northern Indiana Railway	CO-202
Brandes, Ely M.	Selected impacts [mergers]	ME-9
Braude, Michael	Richard learns about railroading	JLO-5
Brill Co.	City and interurban cars	CO-44
Brin, Burton N.	Spirit of the rails	STO-9
British Columbia		CAN-25
	Pacific Great Eastern Railway	CO-211
	Submissions [on transportation]	CAN-28
Brooks, Terrence	Pennsylvania Railroad	CO-215
Brotherhood RR Trainmen	[N.T.]	RA-7
	Federal laws [governing employees]	LAW-9
	The pros and cons [compulsory arbitration]	L-8
Brotherhood of Ry & Steamship Clerks	Contributory health plans	EMP-11
Brown, Robert C.	Selected impacts [mergers]	ME-9
Brown, Robert R.	The last broad gauge	CAN-20
	Pioneer locomotives	LS-27
Brown, Robert T.	Transport and economic integration [S. Am.]	EC-9
Bruce, Alfred W.	The steam locomotive in America	LS-31
Bruce, Robert V.	1877: year of violence	STRI-2
Bryant, E. T.	Railways: a readers guide	BI-9
Bryant, Homer S.	The Georgian locomotive	LS-17
Buchanon, Lamont	Steel rails and iron horses	HT-30

162

Buck, Solom J.	The Granger movement	GO-6
Buck, Thomas	Skokie Swift	CH-4
Buckley, James J.	The St. Joseph Valley Railway	CO-241
Buder, Stanley	Pullman	CO-232
Bukovsky, Alexis P.	Interagency rate adj.	RAT-17
	Rail-water rate adjustments	RAT-24
	Studies of railroad motive power	LG-14
Bunce, William H.	Freight train	FT-6
Bunnell, Edward H.	Railroad accounting and statistics	ACT-5
Bureau of Railway Economics	Associations [RR officers]	AS-4
	Railroad land grants	LH-6
	Railroad transportation	STA-8
Burbank, David T.	City of little bread	STO-2
	Reign of the rabble	STRI-3
Butlin, Noel G.	Finding list [Canadian Ry companies]	CAN-30

C

Cabble, George Merrsfield	Adhesion between rails and wheels	TE-1
Cadfryn-Roberts, John	Coaches and trains	ART-1
Caine, Stanley P.	The myth of a progressive reform	WIS-1
Calky, Morris	Colorado Midland	CO-80
	Rails around Gold Hill	COL-11
California	Feasibility [Richmond Bridge for rapid transit]	SA-4
	General grade crossing survey	CA-3
	Report of accidents	CA-6
Camelback Publishers	Long Island RR 1914 map	CO-155
Cameron, Elizabeth	The big book [trains]	JLT-4
Campbell, Thomas C.	The bituminous coal [rates]	EC-1
Canada	Concordance [Ry. Act]	CAN-10
	Equalization [rates]	CAN-40
	Manitoba's submissions [rates]	CAN-29
	Preliminary inventory [Dept. of Transport]	CAN-12
	Railway freight traffic	CAN-42
	Railway operating statistics	CAN-11
	Railway revenue freight loadings	CAN-43
	Report [employment of firemen]	CAN-8
	Steam railway employees [compensation]	CAN-7
	Waybill analysis	CAN-44
Canadian National Rys.	Magazine	CAN-33
Canadian Pacific	Magazine	CAN-36
Capital Transit	Map	WDT-2
Cardi, Frank	Report [Railroad Insurance Rating Bureau]	I(N)-1
Carleton, Paul and Daphne	Pennsy, A to T	CO-220
	Reading steam pictorial	CO-235
Carling, D. Rock	4-8-0 tender locomotives	LS-15
Carlisle, Norman V.	The wonder book of trains	TRN-14
Carman, Bernard R.	Hoot, toot & whistle	CO-136
Carper, Robert S.	Focus	PI-1
Carson, Clarence B.	Throttling the railroads	GO-9
Carson, Robert B.	Mail line to oblivion	NY-2

Carstens, Harold H.	Loco 1, the diesel	LD-12
	Track design [model]	MTL-2
	Traction planbook and photo album	STR-12
	The trains of Lionel's standard gauge era	MTL-9
Carter, Ernest Frank	The Boy's book [model Rys.]	MOT-3
	Let's look at trains	JLT-11
	The model railway encyclopaedia	MOE-4
Cascio, J. P.	RPM	GU-5
Casey, Robert J.	The Lackawanna story	CO-88
Casler, Walter	Climax	LS-7
Castles, Wesley	Steel gondola and hopper cars	CAR-14
	Stock cars, refrigerators and cabooses	CAR-15
Catton, William B.	John W. Garrett	BIO-3
Central Electric Railfans		
Assoc.	The great third rail	CH-8
Chamberlin, Walter J.	Railroad financial modifications	F-8
Champion Decal Co.	Freight car lettering	MOD-1
Chandler, Allison	Trolley through the countryside	K-1
Chandler, Alfred D.	Henry Varnum Poor	BIO-14
	The railroads [first big business]	RA-17
Chandler, Roy F.	A history of Perry County railroads	PE-2
Chang, Meng-te	Effects [RR design]	TRF-3
Chappell, Gordon S.	Logging along the Denver & Rio Grande	CO-97
Charles River Associates	Competition [rail & truck]	COMP-1
Charlton, E. Harper	Articulated cars	EI-1
Chase, Edward C.	Men, cities, and transportation	NED-1
Cherington, Paul W.	Transportation and logistics education	TT-3
Chicago Area Transit Study	The Skokie Swift	CH-5
Chicago Plan Commission	South Side [terminal for Chicago]	CH-10
Chicago Transit Authority	Chicago's mass [trans.]	CH-2
Chicago, Burlington & Quincy	Map of the West	CO-65
Choda, Kelly	Thirty pound rails	COL-14
Cincinnati Planning Commission	Public transit	CI-2
Civil Service Publishing Corp.	Employment guides	EMP-18
Clark, David S.	A guide [to planning a transportation system]	WDT-4
Clark, Earl	Earl Clark's directory (electric RRs)	EL-3
Clark, Ira G.	Then came the railroads	SOU(W)-1
Clark, John Douglas	Freight rates [New England and central]	RAT-31
Clarke, Bradley H.	Rapid transit Boston	BO-4
	The trackless trolleys of Boston	BO-8
Clark, Jere W.	The market structure [West Va.]	WEV-1
Cleaveland, Norman	The Moreleys	BIO-12
Clegg, Aldheim Anthony	Canadian National steam power	CO-50
Clegg, Charles	The age of steam	STE-1
	Cable car carnival	C-5
	Great railroad photographs	PI-3
	Hear the train blow	PI-4
	Narrow gauge in the Rockies	N-3
	Rio Grande	CO-94
	San Francisco's golden era	SA-2
	Steam cars to the Comstock	CO-298
	The trains we rode	PI-13
	Virginia & Truckee	CO-296
	When beauty rode the rails	PI-15

Cochran, Thomas C.	Railroad leaders, 1845-1890	BIO-16
Coggins, Jack	Great trains of the world	JLT-9
Cohen, Lawrence	Work staggering for traffic relief	NY(C)-3
Cohen, William M.	Lettering guide [Colorado narrow gauge]	COL-8
Cole, Arthur H.	A tentative check-list [Euro. lit.]	BI-4
Cole, Davis	The real book about trains	TRN-6
Coleman, Elizabeth	The story of the Virginia Central	CO-295
Collias, Joe G.	The last of steam	LS-19
Collman, Russ	The Crystal River Pictorial	COL-7
Colorado	Urban mass transportation	COL-1
Colorado Railroad Museum	Colorado rail annual	COL-5
	Steam in the Rockies	CO-96
Columbia Univ.	National Capital Transportation Authority	WDT-34
Combs, Barry B.	Westward to Promontory	CO-276
Commerce Clearing House	Railroad retirement reporter	RET-8
	Trade cases	ICC-11
Commodity Research Bureau	Railroad employees' benefits	EMP-4
Comstock, Henry B.	The iron horse	LS-18
Conant, Michael	Railroad mergers and abandonments	ME-6
Conde, J. C.	Narrow gauge in a kingdom	CO-135
Cook, Richard J.	Rails across the midlands	PI-9
	Super power steam locomotives	LS-35
Cooke, J.	The Northern Pacific Railroad	CO-205
Coombs, Charles I.	Wheels, wings, and water	FT-15
Corbin, Bernard C.	The Burlington in transition	CO-59
	Steam locomotives [Burlington]	CO-64
Corley, Ray	Canadian National steam power	CO-50
Corliss, Carlton J.	Abraham Lincoln and [Illinois Central]	BIO-9
	The American Ry. industry	RA-5, 6
	Development [RR transportation]	DEV-3
	The human side of railroading	EMP-2
	Main Line of Mid-America	CO-137
	Railway developments in Maine	M-2
Cornish, R. P.	A list of postage stamps	CAT-1
Costello, Peter	Transit modernization and street traffic	TSP-3
Cotterell, S.	Bibliography [1893]	BI-1
Cottrell, Fred	Technological change and labor	TE-4
Coghlin, Eugene W.	Freight car distribution	OP-3
Count, Gloria	Employment outlook [RRs]	EMP-12
Cover, Virgil D.	Rates of return	F-16
Cox, Harold E.	The Birney car	STR-2
	Early electric cars [Phila.]	PH-1
	PCC cars of North America	STR-7
	Surface cars of Boston	BO-7
	Surface cars of Philadelphia	PH-4
	Trolleys of lower Delaware Valley	PE-6
Craig, Paul Eastman	The diesel-electric [dictionary]	LD-8
Crimmons, Harold	A history [Kansas Central]	CO-284
Crossen, Forrest	The Switzerland trail of America	CO-90
Crum, Josie Moore	The Rio Grande Southern story	CO-237
	Three little lines	CO-252, COL-13

Crump, Spencer	Henry Huntington [Pacific Electric]	BIO-5
	Redwoods, Iron Horses, and the Pacific	CO-45
	Ride the big red cars	CO-208A
	The Skunk Railroad	CO-46
	Western Pacific	CO-303
Cullen, Elizabeth	Reference list [writings, Charles Sherrington]	BIO-21
	Suggestions for books	BI-11
Cummins, O. R.	Historic cars [Seashore Museum]	CO-246
Curr, John	The coal viewer	MIN-1
Currie, Archibald W.	The Grand Trunk Railway of Canada	CAN-37
Curtis, Carolyn	Guide to Burlinton archives [Newberry Library]	CO-61
Curry, James P.	Updating the opportunity [trans. planning]	CH-6

D

Dacus, Joseph A.	Annals [great strikes]	STRI-1
Daggett, Stuart	Chapters of history [SP]	CO-259
	Principles of inland transportation	LAW-11
	Railroad reorganization	RE-1
Dahlheimer, Harry	Public transportation in Detroit	STR-8
Dahm, Margaret	Experience [disability insurance laws]	L-37
Dambrun, Albert C.	A survey [taxation]	T-6
Daniel, Mann, Johnson & Mendenhall	Baltimore [rapid transit]	BA-2
Darrell, Paul	Narrow gauge railways in America	N-4
Dauehen, Joseph R.	The wreck [Penn Central]	CO-212
Davies, Owen	Chicago [elevateds consolidation]	CO-254
	Street cars and interurbans of yesterday	STR-10
Davis, Barton K.	How to build [model]	MOC-3
Davis, Champion McDowell	Atlantic Coast Line	CO-22
Day, John R.	More unusual railways	RA-15
	Trains	TRN-9
Day and Zimmerman, Inc.	Metropolitan area pilot [study]	WDT-8
Dean, F. E.	Famous cableways of the world	C-9
Deane, Dorothy (N)	Sierra railway	CO-250
DeCamp, Roderick Kyle	The Chicago Transit Auth.	CH-1
Deem, Warren H.	Problem Boston's Transit	BO-3
DeButts, Harry A.	Men of vision	CO-256
de Glazebrook, G. P.	A history [transportation in Canada]	CAN-17
DeGloyer, Everett L.	The track going back	WE-6
Delaware Valley Port Authority	Southern New Jersey Port Authority [transit]	PH-6
DeLeuw, Cather & Co.	Mass transportation survey [Planning Comm.]	WDT-6
	Report [Old Colony Area]	MAS-5
	Trans-Hudson rapid transit	NY(M)-9
Demoro, Harre W.	BART at mid point	SA-1
Denney, John D.	Trains [Pennsylvania Dutch country]	PE-4
Denney, John D., Jr.	Trolleys of the Pennsylvnaia Dutch country	PE-7
Dennis, William Jefferson	Mail by rail	RAP-3
Denniston, Frederick W.	Regulation of railroads	LAW-13
Desker, Leslie E.	Railroads, lands and politics	LA-7

Dewhurst, Henry S.	The railroad police	POL-1
Dewhurst, Paul C.	The Norris locomotives	LS-23
Dickinson, A. Bray	Narrow gauge to the redwoods	CO-201
Diesel railway traction	Magazine	LD-6
Dils, Lenore	Horny Toad man	NM-2
Dines, Glen	End o' steel	JLH-1
Disney, Charles P.	Modern railroad structures	ENG-3
District of Columbia	Report [District of Columbia]	WDT-12
Dodge, Grenville M.	How we built [Union Pacific]	CO-279, 280
Dodge, Ira D.	Texas railroad map	TEX-2
Dodge, William H.	Revenue-cost relationships	RAT-9
Doig, Jamison W.	Metropolitan transportation politics [N.Y.]	NY(M)-5
Domencich, Thomas A.	Free transit	TSG-5
Donovan, Frank Pierce	Gateway to the Northwest	CO-171
	Headlights and markers	STO-6
	Mileposts on the prairie	CO-170
Dorin, Patrick C.	Commuter RRs	COMM-1
	The Lake Superior iron ore RRs	MID-1
Douglas, W. A. S.	The Lackawanna story	CO-88
Downing, Kenneth W.	With a cinder in my eye	TRN-12
Draine, Edwin H.	Import traffic [Chicago]	TRF-6
Draney, John	Diesel locomotives	LD-4
Drennan, Carl Mac	Chalk talk [brakes]	BR-1
Drew, F. P.	Structural fatigue	BRI-4
Droege, John H.	Passenger terminals and trains	TER-1
Dubin, Arthur D.	Some classic trains	TRN-8
	Steam, steel & limiteds	PI-12
Dudielzig, Richard C.	Obsolescence [tax assessments]	T-2
Due, John F.	The intercity electric railway [Canada]	CAN-19
Duke, Donald	Night train	PI-5
	Pacific Electric	CO-209
	Santa Fe	CO-12
	Southern Pacific steam locomotives	CO-263
Dunbar, Seymour	A history of travel	HT-34
Dunbar, Willis Frederick	All aboard [Michigan]	HT-1
Dunscomb, Hugh	A century [SP steam]	CO-262
Durrant, A. E.	The Garratt locomotive	LS-16

E

Eagleson, Mike	Southern steam specials	CO-255
East, J. H., Jr.	Diesel power [mines]	LM-1
Edmonson, Harold	Journey to Amtrack	AM-2
	World steam in acation	LS-38
Edson, William D.	Steam and electric locomotives [N.Y. Central]	CO-191
Edwards, Ford K.	A financial study	CO-197
Edwards, Ford Kingsbury	Cost standards [& rates]	RAT-1
Ehernberger, James L.	Colorado & Southern	CO-82
	Smoke across the prairie	CO-290
	Smoke above the plains	CO-289
	Smoke along the Columbia	CO-291
	Smoke down the canyons	CO-288
	Smoke over the divide	CO-292

Electric Railway Historical Society	Saint Louis cable railways	C-11
Elliott, Frank N.	When the railroad was king	MI-1
Ellis, C. Hamilton	Famous locomotives of the world	LG-5A
	The lore of the train	TRN-2
Ellison, Frank	Frank Ellison on model RRs	MOG-4
Elting, Mary	All aboard	JLT-1
	The real book about trains	JLT-14
	Trains at work	JLT-22
Emmons, Ramona Ware	Your world	JLG-7
Empire State RR Museum	1966 thru 1972 steam passenger service directory	PAS-4
Evans Products Co.	Evans [car forecast]	CO-115
Evans, Thomas M.	A new and dynamic concept for growth	CO-225
Everett, George O.	The cavalcade of RRs [Colo.]	COL-3

F

Fagg, Charles J.	Fundamentals of transportation	TT-2
Fahey, John	Inland Empire	BIO-2
Fair, James R., Jr.	The North Arkansas line	CO-176
Fallberg, Carl	Fiddletown & Copperopolis	STO-4
Farley, William T.	AAR	AS-1
Farm Management Assoc.	Valuation study [Pottawatomie lands]	CO-19
Farrington, S. Kip	Railroading around the world	R-2
	Railroading the modern way	R-3
	Railroads of the hour	HT-27
Farris, Martin T.	Domestic transportation	FT-4
Feagans, R. J.	The railroad that ran with the tide	CO-145
Feeney, Joseph D.	Manual of practice	ICC-7
Fels, Rendias	Wages, earnings and employment	CO-183
Feitz, Leland	Cripple Creek RRs	COL-6
Fenner, Phyllis R.	Open throttle	STO-7
Fenton, Edward A.	Specifications [bridges]	BRI-3
Ferrell, Mallery	The Gilpin gold tram	CO-126
	Rails, sage brush, and pine	CO-268
Feuerlicht, Roberta S.	Andrews raiders	CO-55
Fichter, Helen Hall	At the RR station	JLT-2
Fielder, Mildred ·	Railroads of the Black Hills	SOU(D)-1
Fish, Carl Russell	Transportation	HT-32
Fisher, Clement, Jr.	Oil lamps and iron ponies	CAN-22
Fisher, Joseph A.	The Reading's heritage	CO-234
Fishlow, Albert	American RRs [antebellum economy]	DEV-1
Fitch, Edwin M.	The Alaska Railroad	CO-1
Flagg, G. H.	Laws [Oregon]	OR-1
Flebbe, D. R.	Working on the railroad	EMP-10
Fletcher, Richard H.	Ride down memory lane	MU-1
Fogel, Robert W.	Railroads and American economic growth	EC-6
	The Union Pacific Railroad	CO-282
Forney, Matthias	The Original 1879 Car-builder's Dictionary	CAR-5
Foster, George H.	Steam in the sixties	LS-30
Fox, Pat	The wreck of Old 97	WK-5
Franklin Survey Co.	Property atlas [Main Line, Penna.]	PH-3
Fraser, Donald V.	"Katy"	CO-175

Frederickson, Arthur C. and Lucy F.	The early history [AA ferries]	CO-10
	Late history [Ann Arbor ferries]	CO-9
Friedlaender, Ann F.	The dilemma [regulation]	PR-1
Froom, Gary	Transport investment and [development]	PL-4
Fulton, Robert L.	Epic of the overland	CO-283

G

Galloway, John D.	The first transcontinental railroad	HT-11
Galloway, Joseph A.	The St. Joseph Valley Railway	CO-241
Gates, Paul W.	The Illinois Central RR [colonization]	CO-141
Gaynor, Lary	Highlights [railroad history]	HT-15
General Electric Co.	Profiles of American railroading	R-4
General Ry. Signal Co.	Elements of railway signaling	
	G-R-S carrier control	CO-124
	G-R-S centralized traffic control	OP-1
	G-R-S automatic train control	SI-2
	G-R-S model 9 switch machine	SI-3
Georgia Institute of Technology	Downtown Atlanta transit	AT-1
Gibson, Pribble & Co.	United States regulations [locomotives]	LAW-8
	United States safety appliances	S-13
Gilbert, John F.	Crossties through Carolina	NOC-1
Giles, John George	Automotive [transmissions]	LD-3
Gillett, Clarence H.	The development [transcontinental rates]	RAT-5
Gilman, W. C. & Co.	Traffic, revenue and operating costs	WDT-13
Gjevre, John A.	Chili line [D & RGW]	CO-99
Glaab, Charles N.	Kansas City and the RR	K-2
	Local RR promotion in Kansas City	K-3
Glick, Edward B.	Straddling the Isthmus of Tehuantepec	MEX-2
Gocek, Matilda A.	Library serv. for commuting students	COMM-4
Goe, Vernon	Railroads in the woods	PI-8
Goesig, Harry	Trolleys of Berks County	PE-5
Golden West Books	American railroad journal	RA-4
	Baldwin [construction]	CO-27
	Lima locomotives, 1911 catalog	CO-152
	Pennsylvania RR K-4s	CO-217
Goodfellow, Thomas M.	Your future in railroading	EMP-14
Goodrich, Carter	Government promotion [canals and railroads]	GO-5
Goodrich, Warren	Change at Jamaica	CO-154A
Gordon, Gene D.	Susquehanna trolleys	PE-8
Gordon, William Reed	Manitou Beach trolley days	CO-128
	The Royal Blue line	NY-5
	Steam and trolley days [F. J & G]	CO-119
	Stories and history [Erie]	CO-111
	The story [Canandaigua Street Ry]	CO-47
	Trolleys down the Mohawk Valley	CO-120
Gottfeld, Gunther M.	Rapid transit [six metropolitan areas]	TSR-2
Graves, S. H.	On the "White Pass" payroll	CO-308
Gray, A. B.	Survey [Texas Western Railroad]	CO-260
Greene, Carla	I want to be a train engineer	JLR-2
Greening, W. E.	It was never easy, 1908-1958	CAN-6

Greever, William S.	Arid domain	CO-16
Gregg, Newton K. (Pub)	The car-builder's dictionary (1906)	CAR-1
	The car-builder's dictionary (1888)	CAR-2
	The car-builder's dictionary (1879)	CAR-3
Grimble, U. G. & Associates	Description [guided transport]	CAN-2
Grinell, George M.	A discussion [RR bond analysis]	F-17
Griswold, Wesley S.	Train wreck	WK-3
	A work of giants	HT-33
Grodinsky, Julius	The Iowa pool	COMP-5
	Transcontinental railway strategy	PL-3
Gronouski, John A.	Valuation of railroads	T-8
Gross, Alexander	Geographia Map Co. [Illinois]	I-1
	Geographia Map Co. [Maryland and Delaware]	MAR-1
	Geographia Map Co. [Ohio]	O-2
	Geographia Map Co. [Virginia and West Virginia]	VA-5
Graves, Alvin C.	The crookedest railroad	CO-178
Gschwind, Francis G.	Colorado & Southern	CO-82
Guelzo, Carl M.	Southwestern [rates]	RAT-33
Guise, Byron E.	First steam west of the Big Muddy	LS-13
Gurley, Fred G.	New Mexico and the Santa Fe	CO-17

H

Haber, William	Maintenance of way employment	EMP-16
Haefele, Edwin T.	Transport and national goals	GO-10
Hamilton, Russell	The first book of trains	JLT-5
Haney, Lewis Henry	A congressional history [RRs]	HT-9
Hanft, Robert M.	Pine across the mountain	CO-166
Hankerd, Marian T.	Federal aid [urban transportation]	TSG-4
Hansbury, John E.	"Percent variable" study	COS-3
Hanscom, W. W.	Teh archaeology [cable car]	C-3
Harding, Carroll Reade	George M. Pullman, 1831-1897	BIO-15
Hardy, Graham	Narrow gauge railways in America	N-4
Harlan, George H.	Oil lamps and iron ponies	CAN-22
Harnsberger, John L.	Jay Cooke and Minnesota	CO-206
Harriman, E. Roland	The golden spike	HT-12
Harrison, C. William	Find a career	EMP-13
Harrison, Frederick G.	Cinders and timber	LOG-1
Harrison, Harlan A.	Investment in transportation	F-10
Harvey, Derek G. T.	Monorails	JLG-2
Harwood, Herbert H.	Blue Ridge Trolley	CO-134
Hatch, John K.	Minor C. Keith	CIO-7
Haut, F. J. G.	The pictorial history of electric locomotives	LE-2
Hay, William Walter	The effects [weather on operation]	OP-10
	Railroad engineering	NG-4
Hayes, William Edward	Iron road to empire	CO-77
Hedges, James Blaine	Building the Canadian west	CO-51
	The federal [land subsidy Canada]	CAN-9
	Henry Villard [Northwest]	BIO-23
Hedlund, Earl C.	The transportation econ. [soybean processing]	EC-10
Helmer, William F.	O & W	CO-199
	Rip Van Winkle railroads	NY-4

Helmers, Dow	Historic Alpine Tunnel	TU-2
	Tragedy at Eden	WK-2
Heine, Robert E.	Your future in traffic management	TRF-5
Hennick, Louis C.	Louisiana [street rys.]	LOU-2
Henry, Robert Selph	Headlights and markers	STO-6
	Trains	JLT-18, 19
Henwood, James N.	A short haul to the bay	CO-181
Herapath, John	Mathematical physics and selected papers	ENG-2
Herrick, Joseph F., Jr.	The comparative efficiency [trucks]	PER-6
Hertz, Lewis Heilbroner	Advanced model railroading	MOG-1
	Collecting model trains	MOT-1
	The complete book [model RR]	MOG-3
	Making your model railroad	MOC-6
	New roads to adventure in model railroading	MOG-8
Hibbard, George A.	Stories of the railway	STO-10
Hickerson, Thomas F.	Route location and design	SUR-2
Hillman, Jordan Jay	Competition and [price discrimination]	COMP-2
Hilton, George W.	The cable car in America	C-6
	The electric interurban rys. [Am.]	STR-3
	Great Lakes car ferries	HT-35
	The Toledo, Port Clinton and Lakeside	CO-271
Hinckley, Helen	Rails from the West	BIO-6
Hinde, Douglas W. and M.	Electric traction [eg.]	EL-5
Hirschfeld, Charles	The great railroad conspiracy	SO-1
Hochschild, Harold K.	Adirondack railroads	E-1
	Adirondack steamboats	E-2
Hogeboom, Amy	Trains and how to draw them	TRN-11
Hogg, Garry	Union Pacific	CO-275, 278
Holbrook, Stewart H.	The golden age of railroads	JLH-2
Hollenback, Frank R.	The Argentine Central	COL-2
Hollister, Will C.	Dinner in the diner	DI-1
Horning, Philip T.	The Berkshire era	CO-186
Horowitz, Morris A.	Manpower utilization	RU-2
Horton, Harold Burke	Comparison of average rates	RAT-28
Howard, Robert W.	The great iron trail	HT-14
Howell-North Books	Baldwin locomotive [catalog]	CO-28
Hoyt, Dan W.	Factors [safety-grade crossings]	S-4
Hubbard, Freeman H.	Great trains of all time	TRN-1
	Railroad avenue	STO-8
Huddleston, E. L.	C & O power	CO-58
Huffman, J. B.	Practical covers [crossties]	TI-3
Hull, Clifton E.	Shortline railroads of Arkansas	ARK-2
Hungerford, John B.	Cab-in-front	CO-264
	Hawaiian railroads	HA-1
	Narrow gauge to Silverton	CO-100, 101
	The slim princess	CO-265A
Hunt, Lewis	The Silverton train	COL-12
Hunt, Robert S.	Law and locomotives	LAW-7
Hunter, Holland	Soviet transport experience	OP-8
Huntley, John	Railways in the cinema	MP-00
Hutchinson, Veronica S.	Tales of the rails	STO-11

I

Illinois	Report [High Speed Rail Transit Commission]	HI-7
Illinois, University of	Progress reports [rails and joint bars]	TK-3
	Progress report [roadbeds and embankments]	RI-1
Illinois Central	Chief engineer's [IC]	CO-142
Illinois Freight Assoc.	Official map, Chicago Terminal District	CH-9
Institute of Contemporary Art	Design in transit	ART-2
Institute of Public Adm.	Preliminary [report metro. transportation]	WDT-11
	Report [N.Y. Central and New Haven commuter]	COMM-10
	Suburbs to Grand Central	COMM-12
An international exhibition [aluminum stock]		CAR-8
International Railway Publications	Canadian guide	CAN-1
International ropeway review		C-10
Interborough Rapid Transit		C-146
Interstate Commerce Commission (U.S.)	The capacity and capital requirements T [RRs]	F-3
	Consolidated cross index [ICC]	ICC-26
	Exercises [ICC 75th year]	ICC-25
	Explanation [cost finding]	ACT-3
	Formula [rail terminal costs]	COS-2
	General rail [rate changes]	RAT-11
	Indexes [rates]	RAT-18. 19
	Intercity passenger miles	STA-6
	Interpretations system of accounts	ACT-4
	The Interstate Comm. Act	ICC-28
	Interstate Comm. Comm. activities	ICC-29
	List [typical RR ocupations]	EMP-15
	Man-hours expended [freight cars]	STA-5
	Percent of empty to loaded freight car-miles	STA-11
	Preliminary abstract [railway statistics]	STA-7
	Rail carload cost scales	COS-4
	Railroad consolidations and the public interest	ME-5
	Railway operating statistics	STA-9
	Ratios [empty to loaded car-miles]	STA-3
	Recorded depreciation and amortization	F-5
	Rules governing [classification of employees]	EMP-8
	Rules governing [expenses]	ACT-8
	Rules, standards, and instructions [automatic block signal]	SI-6
	Selected elements of value	F-21
	Selected financial and operating statistics	EL-8
	Selected financial and operating statistics	STA-4
	Signature reproductions [commissioners]	ICC-30

	Some rules of evidence	ICC-27
	Statistical report	IO-2
	Summary [freight station costs]	COS-6
	Summary [freight station costs]	COS-7
	System of accounts [Pullman]	CO-231
	Uniform system of accounts	ACT-9
	Uniform system of accounts	ACT-10
	Uniform system of accounts	ACT-11
	Uniform system [accounts for persons furnishing cars	ACT-12
	Value of service	RAT-10
	War materials reparation cases	RAT-27
	Waybill statistics	STA-10
Interurbans Magazine		
Iowa	Iowa [assessments]	IO-1
Irwin, Leonard	Pacific railways and nationalism	PAC-1

J

Jackson, Elisabeth C.	Guide to Burlington archives [Newberry Library]	CO-61
James, James Alton	Transportation	HT-32
Jeffress, Philip W.	The Negro in the urban transit industry	TSG-7
Johnson, Arthur Menzies	Boston capitalists and western RRs	F-1
Johnson, C. E.	Rail and water routes	RAT-25
Johnson, Edward M.	Technological change and [future]	TE-3
Johnson Enid	Rails across the continent	HT-28
Johnson, James David	A century of Chicago street cars	CH-7
Johnson, Lorenzo M.	The war of the gauges	G-1
Johnson, Lyndon B. (Pres.)	Washington [transit compact]	WDT-1
Johnson, Marion M.	Preliminary inventory [Comm. of RR]	GO-8
Johnson, Siddle Joe	About the engineer	JLR-1
Johnston, Angus J.	Virginia railroads [Civil War]	VA-1
Johnston, Clarence Elmer	Canadian transportation [freight class]	CAN-39
Johnston, Hank	The railroad that lighted Southern California	CO-251
	Short Line to Paradise	CO-311
	They felled the redwoods	LOG-4
	Thunder in the mountains	LOG-3
Johnston, Howard E.	The New Jersey short line railroads	NJ-3
Johnston, James D.	Illinois Terminal RR Co.	CO-144
Johnston, Wayne A.	The Illinois Central heritage	CO-138
Jones, Harry E.	Railroad wages and labor relations	EMP-6
Jones, K. Westcott	Great railway journeys	RA-10
Jones, Paul S.	Selected impacts [mergers]	ME-9
Jones, Peter	The robber barons revisted	BIO-19
Jones, Walter H.	Report on N.J. Assembly bill No. 692	NJ-6
Jones, William C.	Mile-high trolleys	D-1
Josephson, Mathew	The robber barons	BIO-18
Joslyn, David L.	Locomotives of the Southern Pacific	CO-265
Josserand, Peter	Rights of trains	DIS-1, 2

K

Kain, J. K.	The urban transportation problem	TSU-5
Kaiser Engineers	Baltimore [rapid transit]	BA-2
Kalisher, Simpson	Railroad men	BIO-17

Kalmbach, Albert C.	Model railroad handbook	MOH-4
	Model railroad track and layout	MTL-1
	Operating manual for model railroaders	MOO-1
	Prize model railroad layouts	MTL-4
Kalmbach Pub. Co.	The Model railroader cyclopedia	MOE-3
	Our GM scrapbook	CO-123
	Trains album of photographs	TRN-10
Kamat, Ganpat J.	An analysis [loco dynamics]	DY-1
Kansas Pacific Ry.	Guide map [Kansas Pacific	CO-148, 149
Katz, Daniel	Productivity, supervision, and morale	PRO-1
Kaufman, Jacob Joseph	Collective bargaining	L-19
Keating, Edward	The story of "labor"	L-2
Kelley, A. M.	Bradshaw's railway annual	GU-2
Kelley, Oran	The iron horse	JLL-5
Kelley, William	Employment [& occupational patterns]	L-36
Kelsay, Laura E.	Preliminary inventory [cartographic records—Secretary of the Interior]	MAP-7
Kelsey, H.J.	The comparative efficiency [trucks]	TER-6
Kennedy, John F. (Pres.)	Railroad-labor dispute	L-3
Kerka, William	Steam locomotives [Burlington]	CO-64
Kerley, James W.	The failure [labor leadership]	L-7
Kerr, John L.	Destination Topolobampo	CO-147
Kerr, Kathel Austin	American railroad politics	GO-2
Ketterson, Francis A., Jr.	Golden spike	HT-13
Keyserling, Leon H.	The move toward railroad mergers	ME-1
Kidder, Glen M.	Railway to the moon	CO-179
Kinert, Reed Charles	Early American steam locomotives	LS-8
King, Frank A.	The Missabe Road	CO-105
Kirkpatrick, Otto B.	The station agent's blue book	TER-7
Klein, Maury	History [Louisville & Nashville]	CO-161
	The great Richmond Terminal	TER-5
Klingsman, Herbert F.	Electronics in business	PL-1
Knapke, William F.	The railroad caboose	CAR-10
Kneiss, Gilbert H.	Bonanza RRs	CA-1
	Redwood railways	CA-5
Kneiling, John G.	Integral train systems	OP-4
Knorst, William J.	Transportation and traffic management	TRF-12
Koenigsberg, Victor	U.S. steam locomotive directory	LS-37
Kolkoe, Gabriel	Railroads and regulation, 1877-1916	LAW-12
Kolsen, H. M.	The economics and control [road-rail comp.]	FT-5
Korach, Robert S.	The NOT&L story	CO-204
Kotler, Joseph Mark	Alphabetical index [tokens]	CAN-13
Kraft, Gerald	Free transit	TSG-3
Kratville, William W.	Golden rails	PI-2
	Motive power [Union Pacific]	CO-294
	Steam, steel and limiteds	PI-12
	Union Pacific locomotives	CO-293
Krause, John	Rails through Dixie	PI-10
Krieg, Allan	Last of the 3-foot loggers	CO-307
Kyner, James Henry	End of track	WE-2
Kyper, Frank	A ramble into the past [East Broad Top]	CO-107

L

Labbe, John T.	Railroads in the woods	PI-8
Ladd Publications	Railroad books checklist	BI-8
Lambie, Joseph T.	From mine to market	CO-200
Lang, A. Scheffar	Urban rail transit	TSU-3
Langsdale, Franklin Johnston	The story of a mountain railroad	CO-223
Lardner, D.	Railway economy	EC-7
Larrabee, William	The railroad question	PR-4
Larson, Russ	N scale [track plans]	MTL-6
LaSalle Extension Univ.	New loose-leaf atlas	TRE-7
Latham, Earl	The politics of railroad coordination	ME-2
Lathrop, Gilbert A.	Little engines and big men	COL-9
La Well, Betty Lou	Tooooot!	JLT-16
Larson, Raymond D.	Employment outlook [RRs]	EMP-12
Lawson, Richard	Transportation demand projection	FT-14
Lawson, Walter C.	Laying panel track [Morenci]	MIN-2
Lazarus, Arthur	Metropolitan transportation	TSG-6
Lazar, Joseph	Due process	L-20, 26
Leavens, Donald C.	Factors affecting freight rates	RAT-7
Legget, Robert F.	Modern railroad structures	ENG-3
Le Fleming, H. M.	International locomotives	LG-6
Le Massena, R. A.	Colorado Mountain railroads	COL-4
	Union Pacific in Colorado	CO-286
Lemly, James H.	The future of rail transport	FUT-3
	The Gulf, Mobile and Ohio	CO-132
Leonard, G. R.	Directory [rates]	RAT-2
Leonard, William N.	Railroad consolidation [Transportation Act of 1920]	ME-4
LeRoy, Edwin D.	The Delaware & Hudson Canal	CO-86
Lewis, Edward	Arcade & Attica	CO-11
	Wellsville, Addison & Galeton	SHO-6
Lewis, Robert G.	The handbook of American railroads	RA-11
Liddell, Ken	I'll take the train	CAN-3
Limmer, Ezeckiel	Chief factors [rates]	RAT-8
Lindahl, Martin L.	The New England railroads	NED-2
Linden, Fred E.	The United States Railway Mission in Mexico	MEX-6
Lionel Corp.	Iron ponies	MOT-4
	Model railroading	MOT-5
	Model railroading	MOT-6
Littledale, Harold	The golden spike	JLH-3
Locklin, D. Philip	Economics of transportation	EC-3
Logsdon, Clyde B.	The American [transportation token]	SJR-1
The Locomotive Engineer	Biweekly	LG-11
Long, Bryant B.	Mail by rail	RAP-3
Long Filmslide Service	Mary takes a trip	TRN-3
Long, Herman H.	Segregation in [railway travel]	PAS-3
Long Island RR Commission	Proposed legislation [L.I. Transit Auth.]	CO-160
Long Island Transit Auth.	Editorial comment [LIRR plan]	CO-156
	Plan for the Long Island Railroad	CO-159
	Plan of reorganization	CO-158
Long, Raphael	Pacific Electric's big red cars	CO-210
Long, W. Alva	A pictorial catalog [steam locomotives]	LS-25
Longini, Arthur	Industrial potentialities [Wabash RR]	IA-4

Lord, Francis A.	Lincoln's RR man [Haupt]	BIO-4
Lowe, G. F.	Practice and procedure [rate-making assoc.]	RAT-23
Lowstuter, A. B.	The comparative efficiency [trucks]	TER-6
Lucas, Walter A.	Locomotives and cars since 1900	LG-8
	100 years of railroad cars	CAR-6
	Pocket guide to American locomotives	LG-9
Lucas, W. A.	Popular picture and plan book	LG-10
Lundy, Robert F.	The economics [incentive rates]	RAT-6
Lurie, Melvin	The measurement [unionization on wages]	L-27
Lustig, John E.	Rights of railroad workers	L-21
Lyne, James G.	Essays [rys. advantages]	SE-1
Lyon, Peter	To hell in a day coach	PR-2

M

McBride, Harry A.	Trains rolling	STO-12
McCabe, James D.	History of the Grange movement	HI-18
McCague, James	Moguls and iron men	HT-22
McCague, James	When the rails ran west	JLH-7
McCall, Edith S.	Iron horses [men who rode]	JLL-4
McClanahan, Bill	Scenery for model railroads	MOC-8, 9
McClintock, Marshall	How to build [model]	MOC-2
McColley, Grant	Railway and transit equipment, 1940-45	WA-4
McConnell, John A.	Railroad freight classification	CL-1, 2
McCoy, Dell A.	The Crystal River Pictorial	COL-7
McCarthy, Wilson	General Wm. Jackson Palmer	BIO-13
McCready, Albert L.	Railroads in the days of steam	JLL-7
McGraw-Hill	Jane's world railways, 1970-71	H-1
McCulloch, David S.	Effect [earthquake—Alaska RR]	CO-5
McFall, Robert J.	Railway monopoly and rate regulation	COMP-8
McGill-Warner	Official map of Montana	MON-1
	North Dakota	NOD-1
	Washington and northern Idaho	WAS-1
McGinley, James J.	Labor relation [New York transit]	NY(C)-2
McGowan, George F.	Diesel-electric [handbook]	LD-9
McGuire, C. B.	Studies [economics of transportation]	EC-8
McKeever, Gene C.	Mile-high trolleys	D-1
McKillup, Norman	Western rail trail	CAN-24
McMurry, Donald Le Crone	The great Burlington Strike of 1888	CO-66
McNeely, John H.	The railways of Mexico	MEX-5
McPhee, Malcolm D.	Prospects [railfreight statistics as a mktg. tool]	MA-2
MacAvoy, Paul W.	The economic effects [regulation]	EC-2
	Regulation of transport innovation	ICC-8
Macfarlane, Robert S.	Henry Villard [Northern Pacific]	BIO-22
MacGregor, Bruce A.	South Pacific Coast	CO-253
MacMillan, Duncan H.	Freight rates in Canada	CAN-41
Macomber, F. S.	The mainliner program [mail carrier]	RAP-2
Maize, E. R.	Diesel power [mines]	LM-1
Mallery, Paul	Bridge and trestle handbook [models]	MOS-2
	Electrical handbooks [model RRs]	MOH-2
Maloney, Joseph F.	Mass transportation in Massachusetts	MAS-1
Manitoba	Argument	CAN-27

Mannix, Joseph A.	A quick review [East Broad Top]	CO-108
Marble, Duane F.	Transport input [urban sites]	TSU-2
Margret, Charles O.	Careers [RRs]	MA-1
Marlette, Jerry	Electric RRs [Indiana]	IA-1
Marsh, Michael	Strike control proposals	L-11
Marshall, Charles R.	Economic analysis [freight car mfg.]	MAN-1
Marshall, James L.	Santa Fe	CO-14
Marshall, Merrill G.	Standard and special flatcars	CAR-13
Martin, Albro	Enterprise denied	GO-3
Martin, Charles F.	Locomotives of the empire builder	CO-131
	Milwaukee Road freight cars	CO-70
	Milwaukee Road locomotives	CO-72
Martin, Cy	Gold rush narrow gauge	CO-309
Martin, John Wellborn	Henry M. Flagler, 1830-1913	CO-117
Massachusetts	Recommended [transit plan]	MAS-2
	Report [ski lift and tramway safety]	S-10
	Report [tax and relief commuter railroads]	MAS-4
	Report [utilizing Old Colony Line]	MAS-3
	Report [zone fares]	TSG-9
Mass. Bay Transit Authority	Report [commuter service]	BO-5
Masson, Robert L.	New shares for old	CO-38
	A case study [balloting]	CO-39
Mason, Alpheus Thomas	The fall of a railroad empire	CO-194
Masterman, Vincent V.	The Katy Railroad	CO-174
Maxlish, Bruce	The railroad and the space program	DEV-4
May, Edward L.	Steam and electric locomotives [N.Y.C.]	CO-191
Mead, Edgar T., Jr.	Busted and still running	CO-42
	Over the hills to Woodstock	CO-310
	Through covered bridges to Concord	CO-83
Meeks, Carroll V.	The railroad station	TER-2
Mencken, August	The railroad passenger car	CAR-21
Merriken, John E.	Annapolis Short Line	CO-300
Metropolitan Planning Assoc.	A mass transport integral	WDT-5
Metropolitan Trans. Auth.	Air view [Boston]	BO-1
Meyer, Carl F.	Route surveying and design	SUR-3
Meyer, John R.	The economics of competition	COMP-3
	Techniques of transport pricing	RAT-4
	The urban transportation problem	TSU-5
Michaud, William	Pioneer railways of central Ontario	CAN-35
Michie Co.	Constitutional provisions [Va.]	VA-2, 3
Middleton, William D.	The interurban era	STR-6
	North Shore	CO-73
	The railroad scene	PI-7
	South Shore	CO-75
	The time of the trolley	EL-9
Miller, George H.	The Granger law	LAW-4
	Railroads and the Granger laws	LAW-5
Miller, John A.	Fares, please [trolleys]	STR-4
Miller, Sidney	Rates or return	F-16
Millican, Richard D.	A socio-economic [workers families]	L-4
Mills, John M.	History [Niagara, St. Catharines & Toronto]	CAN-38
Mills, Randall V.	Railroads down the valleys	SHO-5

Milwaukee and Suburban Trans. Co.	Map	CO-169
Missouri	Missouri [map]	MIS-2
Missouri Pacific	Over the railroad air waves	COM-1
Mississippi Valley Hist. Assoc.	Building out to sea [FEC]	CO-118
Moedinger, William M.	The road to Paradise	CO-266, 267
Mohr, Carolyn C.	Guide to Illinois Central archives [Newberry Library]	CO-140
Montana	[grade crossing]	MON-3
Moody, Linwood W.	Maine two-footers	M-1
Moore, Bowman H.	The Federal valuation of railroads	F-19
Moreau, Jeffery	Glendale & Montrose	CO-127
Morgan, David P.	Canadian steam	CAN-14
	Diesels west	CO-63
	Locomotive 4501	LS-20
	Steam's finest hour	LS-34
	True adventures of railroaders	JLR-5
Morgan, Lewis H.	Railroads, land and iron	BIO-11
Morgan, Warren F.	The model railroad book	MOG-6
Morse, Kenneth S. F.	A history [Cleveland streetcars]	CLE-1
	Ohio trolleys	O-3
Morse, Victor L.	36 miles of trouble	CO-306
Moskowitz, Samuel	Great railroad stories	STO-5
Mossman, Frank H.	Principles of urban transportation	TSG-8
Mostafa, M. K. K.	Actual track capacity	TK-1
Mourning, Jim	New ideas in railroad modeling	MTL-5
Munse, W. H.	The lateral distribution of loading bridges	BRI-2
	Structural fatigue	BRI-4
Murphy, Nicholas V.	The fun and work of railroading	JLO-2
Myrick, David F.	Life and times [Central Pac.]	CO-54
	New Mexico's railroads	NM-1
	Railroads of Nevada and eastern California	WE-3

N

Nadeau, Remi	City makers	HT-8
Nathan, Adele Gutman	Famous railroad stations	ST-2
National Assoc. of RRs	The passenger deficit	PAS-1
National Capital [Trans. Ag.]	NCTA technical report	WDT-9
	Report [National Capital]	WDT-16
National Capital [Plan. Comm.]	Transportation plan [National Capital]	WDT-14
National Capital [Dev. Ag.]	Transportation [National Capital]	WDT-30
National Elec. Mfg. Assoc.	Standards	LE-1
National Fire Protection Assoc.	Standards	S-11
National Learning Corp.	Passbook	EMP-19
National Mediation Board	Fifteen year [Railway labor act]	L-31
	Transcript of proceeding [wage increase]	L-23
National Model RR Assoc.	Directory	MOH-5
National RR Adj. Bd.	Digest of Awards	L-18
National RR Assoc.	The Railfan	PER-3
National Ry. Pub. Co.	The Official list [ticket agents]	GU-4
National Ry. Hist. Soc.	Bulletin	HT-23
	[N.T.]	NB-1
	Transportation	PER-8

Nat. Safety Council	Annual green bookq	S-1
Nat. Survey Co.	Bangor and Aroostock	CO-35
National Transport Association	Report	RAP-5
Nelson, James R.	Railroad mergers [economy of New England]	ME-8
Nelson, Robert S.	Technological change and [future]	TE-3
Nesbit, Robert C.	He built Seattle	BIO-1
Nestle, David F.	Steam and trolley days [F, J&G]	CO-119
Nevada	Opinions and orders [Nevada]	NE-1
New, Irene D.	The American railroad network	HT-2
New Jersey	Eleventh report [RR Taxes—N.J.]	NJ-4
	The Erie-Lackawanna RR	CO-114
	The Japanese National Railway	HI-8
	Penn Central investigation report	CO-214
New York	Journey-to-work	NY(M)-3
	Long Island journey-to-work report	NY-10
	A map [New York]	NY-1
	Report [financial condition N.Y. railroads]	NY-12
New York (City)	Report [New York transit]	NY(C)-5
N.Y.-N.J. Trans. Ag.	Journey to work	NY(C)-4
	Report	NY(M)-8
New York Electric RR Assoc.	Electric railroads	EL-4
New York Industrial Comm.	Rochester Transit work stoppage	ROC-1
New York (Port Auth.)	A selected bibliography [Port of N.Y. Auth.]	NY(P)-1
	Metropolitan rapid transit financing	NY(M)-4
	Sketch map [central and western]	MID-2
New York Reg. Plan. Assoc.	Railroads, Tri-State	NY(M)-6
Nickle Plate Road		CO-188
Noble, Joseph H.	From cab to caboose	EN-1
Noblin, James B.	Balance of trade [Mississippi]	MIS-1
Nock, O. S.	Railways [years of pre-eminence, 1905-1919]	RA-18
North Carolina	Map [North Carolina]	NOC-3
Northwestern Univ.	A reference guide to metropolitan transportation	TSP-2

O

O'Connell, John	Railroad album	RA-20
O'Conner, George W.	Railroads of New York	NY-8
Ogden, William H.	Crosstie industry facts	TI-2
Ohio	Grade crossings in Ohio	O-1
Oklahoma	Railroad map [Oklahoma]	OK-2
Old Line Publishers	History [Baldwin Locomotive Works]	CO-24
	Brill 250 hp gas-electric	CO-43
	Edwards Ry. Motor Co. [model 10]	CO-109
	Engineer's operating manual [F-7]	LD-11
	FWD railroad equipment	CO-122
	Krauss-Maffei [manual]	CO-151
	McKeen Car scrapbook	CO-167
	Mack railcars	CO-168
	1925 Shay locomotive catalog	LS-22
	Pullman Company [instruction book]	CO-230

Oliver, Smith H.	The first quarter-century [steam locos]	LS-12
Olmsted, Robert P.	An acquaintance with Alco	CO-8
	Interurbans to the loop	EL-7
	A long look at steam	LS-21
	Scenes from the Shore Lines	CO-74
	Six units to Sycamore	CO-68
	Trail of the Zephyrs	CO-62
O'Neil, John T.	Policy formation in railroad finance	F-15
Opinion Research Corp.	National survey of public opinion	PU-1
Oregon, Univ. of	O & C counties	LA-2
Organization for European Econ Coop.	Railroads in the U.S.A.	RA-22
	Railroads in the U.S.A.	RA-23
Ormes, Robert M.	Railroads and the Rockies	COL-10
Ornati, Oscar A.	Transportation needs of the poor	COMM-13
Overton, Richard C.	Burlington West	CO-60
	Gulf to Rockies	CO-81, 121
Owens, Wilfred	The Accessible City	TSP-1
	The metropolitan transportation problem	PR-3

P

Pabst, Anna C. Smith	Cleveland, Cincinnati, Chicago & St. Louis	CO-78
Pacific Bookwork	The Western traction quarterly	PER-9
Pacific Cable Ry. Co.	The system of wire-cable railways	C-13
Palmer, Dwight R.	The impending breakthrough in trans.	NJ-2
Palmer, Phil	The cable cars [S.F.]	C-7
Palmer, Gen. William J.	The war of the gauges	G-1
Pan American Ry. Cong.	Charter	CONG-1
	Conference	CONG-2
Paranka, Stephen	Urban transportation dilemma	TSU-4
Parks, Pat	The railroad that died at sea	CO-116
Parmelee, Julius H.	Railroad trends	AN-2
Parsons, Edward W.	Using precast [concrete sets]	TU-3
Parson, Brinkerhoff, Quade & Douglas	Baltimore [mass trans.]	BA-1
	The composite report [BART]	SA-5
	Dynamics [transit structures]	TSE-1
	Mass transit study	FLA-3
	Regional rapid transit [S.F.]	SA-6
	Southern New Jersey [mass transportation]	NJ-5
Peck, Morton J.	The economics of transportation	COMP-3
Pennoyer, Albert S.	Locomotives in our lives	JLL-6
Pennypacker, Bert	Eastern steam pictorial	LS-9
	Locomotives of the Reading	CO-236
Pennsylvania	Recommendations [rail passenger service]	PE-3
	SEPACT III final report	PH-5
Perini, Jimo	San Francisco Grip	C-12
Perle, Eugene D.	The demand for transportation	TT-1
Pettingill, George W.	The story of Florida railroads	FLA-2
Philadelphia Trans. Co.	Street map [Philadelphia]	CO-221

Phillips, Irene	The railroad story of San Diego County	CA-4
Phillips, Lance	Yonder comes the train	TRN-15
Phillips, R. A. J.	Canada's Railways	CAN-15
Phillips, Ulrich B.	A history of transportation [eastern Cotton Belt]	HT-20
Pierce, Harry H.	Railroads of New York	NY-7
Pierce Management, Inc.	Mine transportation	LM-2
Pietrak, Paul	Buffalo & Susquehanna	SHO-2
	Coudersport & Port Allegheny	SHO-3
	Pittsburg, Shawmut & Northern	HT-37
Pinkepank, Jerry A.	Diesel spotter's guide	LD-7
Pinkerton, Alan	Strikers, communists, tramps and detectives	HT-31
Pittenger, William	In pursuit of the General	CO-86
Pletcher, David M.	Rails, mines, and progress	MEX-4
Plowden, David	Farewell to steam	LS-11
Polakoff, A. A.	Basic study [traffic]	TRF-1
Polden, K. J.	Concrete crossties	TI-1
Polkinghorn, R. S.	Pino Grande	CO-224
Polk's Hobbies	Blue book [hobbies]	MOE-1
Poole, Ernest	Costs	COS-1
Poor, Henry V.	History [railroads and canals]	HT-19
Poor, Meredith	Denver, South Park & Pacific	CO-103
Pope, Billy N.	Your world	JLG-7
Popular Science	Engines, rails and roads	MP-0
Post, Don M.	Practical covers [cross-ties]	TI-3
Poth, L. A.	Transportation rates [South Dakota]	SOU(D)-4
Potter, David M.	The railroads	ME-10
Potter, David	Catalogue [British stamps]	RAP-1
President (U.S.)	Message from the President [Panama Railroad]	PAN-2
President's Cabinet Comm.	Summary presentation	AS-3
Presidental RR Commission	Report	L-28
Prince, Richard E.	Atlanta and West Point	CO-20
	Atlantic Coast Line	CO-21
	Louisville & Nashville steam	CO-163, 164
	Nashville, Chattanooga and St. Louis	CO-182
	Seaboard Air Line Railway	CO-244
	Steam locomotives and boats [Southern]	CO-257
	Steam locomotives and history [Georgia & W.P.]	CO-125, 305
Prosser, Richard S.	Rails to the North Star	MINN-1
	Spirit of the rails	STO-9

Q

Quiett, Glenn C.	They built the West	WE-5

R

Rand, McNally	Centennial Map	MAP-1
	Handy railroad atlas	MAO-5
	[New Hampshire]	NH-1
	Pioneer atlas [West]	MAP-4
Rando, John F. and Robert F.	The American railroads	RA-1

Randolph, Gilmer B.	Freight cars in Canada	CAN-41
	Freight rates [New England and central]	RAT-3
	Freight rates [Western]	RAT-34
	Railroad freight classification	CL-1
	Rules [freight classification]	RAT-16
	Southwestern [rates]	RAT-33
Rainey, George S.	Demise [iron horse]	LG-4
Railroad Gazette	American locomotives	LS-2
The Railroad yardmaster		PER-4
Railway Assoc.	Railway Association [Special Agents and Police]	POL-2, 3
Railway Equipment & Pub. Co.	Railway [clearances and car dimensions]	OP-6
Railway & Locomotive Hist. Soc.	Duluth, South Shore & Atlantic	CO-106
Railway Progress	Periodical	PER-5
Railway Systems & Management Association	Costs and decision making	FT-3
	The developing transportation revelation	FUT-1
	The dynamics [trade]	DY-2
	The financial community [RR treasurer]	F-7
	Proceedings	MA-3
	Railroad terminal strategy	TER-4
	Simulation of railroad operations	MA-4
	User-furnished freight cars	CAR-17
Ramsey, Bruce	PCE railway to the north	CAN-34
Ranger, Dan	Pacific coast Shay	LS-24
Ranks, Harold E.	Motive power [Union Pacific]	CO-294
	Union Pacific locomotives	CO-293
Rapp, William F.	Nebraska CB & Q depots	ST-3
Rasmussen, Louis J.	Railway passenger lists of overland trains	TRN-5
Reck, Alma Kehoe	At the RR station	JLT-2
Redit, W. H.	Protection [shipments of fruits and vegetables]	FT-10
Reed, Merl F.	Louisiana's transportation revolution	LOU-3
	New Orleans and the railroads	HT-24
Reed, Robert C.	Train wrecks	WK-4
Reese, Robert B.	Methods [rate indexes]	RAT-21
Reeves, George T.	Pattern of distribution [fruits and vegetables]	TRF-9
Rehor, John A.	The Berkshire era	CO-186
Reichert, Edwin C.	Freight train	JLT-7
Reid, H.	Extra south	SOU-3
	The Virginian Railway	CO-199
Reifschneider, F. E.	Trolley lines of the Empire State	NY-6
Reinhardt, Richard	Workin' on the railroad	STO-14
Research Data Processing Corp.	Benchmark survey [park and ride]	NJ-1
	Origin-destination survey	COMM-5
Rhodes, Robert G.	Factors affecting freight rates	RAT-7
Rice, Herbert W.	Index of the Valuation reports	F-20
Richardson, Helen R.	Illinois Central Railroad Co.	CO-139
	Nationalization of railways	BI-5
	Railroads in defense and war	BI-10
Richardson, J.	Destination Valley	EL-2

Richardson, Reed C.	The locomotive engineer	LAW-3
Richie, Joan F.	Railroad reading rooms [Ohio]	O-4
Ridgway, Arthur O.	The case of train 3	WK-1
Riegel, Robert E.	The story of the western railroads	WE-4
Rigby, Wallis	The 7-foot model train book	MTL-7
RKO	Whistle in the night	TRN-12
R.L.M. Associates	Benchmark Survey [park and ride]	NJ-1
	Origin-distenation survey	COMM-5
Robb, Dean A.	Rights of railroad workers	L-21
Robbins, Edwin C.	Railway conductors	CON-1
Roberts, Frank	Vintage steam	STO-13
Roberts, Thomas	A history and analysis [labor-management relations]	PH-2
Rodgers, Glenn E.	Mechanical refrigerator car equipment	CAR-11
Rolofson, Bob	New ideas in model railroading	MTL-5
Rooksby, Denis	The Sandley story	CO-243
Rosenfield, Bernard	Let's go [build the first transcontinental]	JLH-4
	Let's go to a freight yard	JLO-3
Rowsome, Frank	Trolley car treasury	STR-11
Roxbury, L. E.	Let's operate a railroad	OP-5
	Opération of railroad yeards	Y-1
	Road movement of trains	TRN-7
Russel, Robert R.	Ante bellum studies	HT-5

S

Sadler, Walter C.	The national, regional, and metropolitan relationships [Tulsa expressway]	OK-1
Safe Railroader		PER-6
Sagle, Lawrence W.	A picture history of B&O motive power	CO-31
	Freight cars rolling	CAR-12
St. Martin, John T.	A study [grade crossing collisions]	CR-3
Salmons, Charles H.	The Burlington strike	L-5
Sampson, Roy J.	Domestic transportation	FT-4
	Obstacles to railroad unification	ME-3
	Oregon rail and water [trends]	TRF-8
	Railroad shipments [Northwest]	RAT-32
Salsbury, Stephen	The State [investor, and railroad]	CO-37
Sanders, W. W.	The lateral distribution of loading bridges	BRI-2
San Francisco	Preliminary report [BART]	SA-9
	Report [San Francisco Bay]	SA-8
Sato, Natalie G.	Methods [trip destinations]	CH-3
Saunders, Stuart T.	The American railroads	AD-1
Saunders, W. B. & Co.	The Federal interest [passenger service]	GO-4
Saylor, Roger B.	The railroads of Pennsylvania	PE-1
Scarry, Richard	Trains	JLT-20
Scharfman, I. L.	The Interstate Comm. Comm.	ICC-5
Schieck, Paul	Trolleys of lower Delaware Valley	PE-6
Schneider, Lewis M.	Transportation and logistics education	TT-3
Schneigert, Z.	Aerial tramways and funicular Rys	C-1
Schonberg, Howard B.	Transportation to the Seaboard	TT-4
Schopp, Bill	Track design [model]	MTL-2

Schoppert, David W.	Factors influencing safety grade crossings	S-4
Schott, Joseph L.	Rails across Panama	PAN-1
Schrader, Herman J.	The effect [brake shoe action]	BR-2
Schraff, Robert	The how and why wonder book	JLG-1
Schultz, William A.	Historical sketches	HT-17
Schurman, Bernard	The history [railway emergency boards]	EM-1
Schusler, William T.	The economic position [Pittsburgh commuting]	PIT-1
Scott, Roy V.	The methods of [RRs promoting development]	EC-4
Scribbins, Jim	The Hiawatha story	CO-71
Seiden, Art	Read aloud train stories	JLT-13
Sewall, Robert I.	A five-year forecast [commuter cars]	CAR-19
Shaughnessy, Jim	Delaware & Hudson	CO-85
	The Rutland Road	CO-238
Shaw, Frederic J.	Little railways of the world	N-1
	Oil lamps and iron ponies	CAN-22
Shearer, Frederick E.	The Pacific tourist	CO-52
Shaw, Robert B.	Down brakes	HC-1
Shearer, Henry K.	A survey [rate descrimination]	RAT-30
Shepard, David	We were there [golden spike]	JLH-6
Sheppard, Harvey	Dictionary of Ry slang	GO-3
Shinn, Glenn L.	Reasonable freight rates	RAT-15
Shott, John G.	The railroad monopoly	COMP-9
Shuster, Philip	C&O Power	CO-58
Sibbett, Morgan	Report [financial aspects S.F. transit]	SA-7
Sidebottom, Omar M.	The effect [brake shoe action]	BR-2
Simmons, Mortimer	The story of trains	JLT-15
Simmons-Boardman Pub. Corp.	Car and locomotive cyclopedia	CAR-4
	Diesel-electrics [repairs]	LD-10
	Essays [rates differentials]	RAT-3
	Railway supply industry yearbook	MAN-2
	Survey [car shops]	SH-1
Sims, Donald	Western trains	PI-14
Sinclair, Angus	Development of the locomotive engine	LG-5
Sites, James N.	Quest for crisis	AN-1
Sloan, Anthony R.	Reestablishing the link	COMM-9
Sloss, James	Regulation of transport innovation	ICC-8
Small, Charles S.	Far wheels	RA-9
Smiles, Samuel	The life of George Stephenson	BIO-20
Smith, Chuck	Trains	JLT-21
Smith, Helen V.	Pattern of distribution [fruits and vegetables]	TRF-9
	Railroad freight rate indexes [farm]	RAT-13
	Transportation of grain [Southwestern]	TRF-11
Smith, Joel	Some social aspects [mass transit]	TSG-10
Smith, John Walter	Building a RR [SAL]	CO-245
Smith, Joseph J.	Report to RFC [Baltimore & Ohio]	CO-32
Smith, Mildred H.	Early history [LI RR]	CO-154
Snow, Paul	Iron horse to diesel	JLL-3
Smith Wilbur & Assoc.	Mass transportation survey	TSU-1
Soberman, Richard M.	Urban rail transit	TSU-3
Society for Visual Education	How they travelled [whistles]	JLT-10
	Railroad transportation	FT-11, JLT-1

South Dakota	A review [freight rates South Dakota]	SOU(D)-2
Specialty Press	Baldwin locomotive [catalog]	CO-27
	Rail Book Bibliography	BI-7
Spencer, William	"X," symbol [progress]	CAR-22
Springirth, Kenneth C.	Erie to Conneault by trolley	CO-79
	Grape belt trolleys	NY-1
Stagner, Ross	Working on the railroad	EMP-10
Stallmeyer, J. E.	Structural fatigue	BRI-4
Staples, Henry Lee	The fall of a railroad empire	CO-194
Starr, Edward A.	The interpretation [tariffs]	RAT-12
Staufer, Alvin F.	C&O power	CO-58
	Pennsy power	CO-219
	Steam power [N.Y.C.]	CO-190
Stead, William	Chicago today	L-6
Stedman, Wilfred	Rails that climb	CO-102
Stein, Leon	The Pullman strike	L-9
Steinheimer, Richard	Backwoods railraods	WE-1
	Western trains	PI-14
Stenason, John	The economics of transportation	COMP-3
Stephenson, John C.	Electric Ry [cars 7 trucks]	CO-249
Stern, John	Ride down memory lane	MU-1
Stevens, George R.	Canadian National Rys.	CO-49
	History [Canadian National]	CO-48
Stevens, John R.	Ride down memory lane	MU-1
Stever, Dorothy V.	The freight yard	JLO-1
Stewart, Scott	The big book [streamliners]	JLT-3
Stichman, Herman T.	Analysis [Port of N.Y. Auth. obligation]	NY-9
Stindt, Fred A.	The Northwestern Pacific Railroad	CO-207
Stinett, Caskie	Will not run February 22nd	ANE-1
Stout, Robert	Kendall & Eldred	CO-150
Stover, John F.	American railroads	HT-3
	A history of American railroads	HT-17
	The life and decline [RR]	RA-14
	The railroads of the South, 1865-1900	SOU-2
Street, Donald M.	Railroad equipment financing	F-6
Stuart, Robert K.	Regulated property	T-3
Stuckey, William A.	Public Service Commission laws of Indiana	IA-5
Sulzer, Elmer G.	Ghost railroads of Indiana	IA-2
	Indiana's abandoned RRs	IA-3
Sundance, Ltd.	The Rio Grande pictorial	CO-98
Sunderland, Edwin S. S.	Abraham Lincoln [Illinois Central]	BIO-8
	Illinois Central Railroad	CO-143
Supple, Barry E.	Boston capitalists and western RRs	F-1
Sutton, David	The complete book [model RR]	MOG-2
	Complete guide [model RR]	MOH-1
Swengel, F. M.	The American steam locomotive	LS-3
Swett, Ira L.	Cars of Sacramento Northern	CO-239

T

Taber, Thomas T., III	Baldwin locomotives	CO-26
	Climax	LS-7
	Morristown and Erie	CO-173
Tanner, Henry S.	A description [canals & RRs]	HT-10

Task Force RR Safety	Report	S-9
Tatham, Campbell	The first book of trains	JLT-6
Taylor, George Rogers	The American railroad network	HT-2
Taylor, Virginia H.	The Franco-Texan Land Company	CO-270
Taylor, William L.	A productive monopoly	COMP-7
Teague, Ellen C.	Mount Washington Railway	CO-180
Tedrow, Joseph H.	Tedrow's regulation of transportation	ICC-10
Tennessee	Report	TEN-2
	Studies [tax problems]	TEN-1
Teweles, Richard Jack	The economic history [C&EL]	CO-67
Thatcher, Lionel W.	Obsolescence [tax assessments]	T-2
Thomas, David St. J.	Trains work like this	JLT-24
Thompson, Joseph W.	An economic history [GN Div.]	CO-130
Thompson, Slason	A short history [railways]	HT-29
Thurlow, Clinton F.	Over the rails by steam	STE-2
	The Weeks Mills "Y"	N-6
	The WW&F Two-footer	N-7
Tice, Henry A.	Early RR days [N. Mex.]	EX-1
Tigrett, Issac B.	My railroad saga	CO-133
Tilford, John E.	L&N	CO-162
Tobin, Austin J.	Transportation [New York]	NY(M)-10
Tomlin, John W.	Adjustment of retired railroaders	L-1
Tone, John C.	New Haven [station and line improvements]	CO-195
Toronto	Growth and travel	CAN-5
Traffic Research Corp.	Benchmark survey [park and ride]	NJ-1
	Origin-destination survey	COMM-5
Train collectors quarterly		MTL-8
Trainman news		PER-7
Transit Improvement Assoc.	Facts about modern transit	TSG-2
Transportation Facts, Inc.	Let's look ahead	FUT-2
Transportation Sys. Tech. Corp.	Implementation requirements [urban trans.]	TSE-2
The Traveling Engineers' Association		H-2
Tredgold, Thomasq	The steam locomotives in 1838	LS-32
Trend Books, Inc.	Model railroading	MOC-7
Tri-State Transportation Committee	Consolidated bus-rail services [NY]	COMM-2
	Journey-to-work	TTC-1
	Park 'n ride rail service	COMM-7
	Prospectus	TTC-2
	Railroad suburban equipment	NY(M)-7
	Study [marine lighterage]	NY(M)-2
	Suburban service adjustment [N.Y.C.]	COMM-11
Trottman, Nelson	History [Union Pacific]	CO-281
Trout, J. M. & Edw.	The railways of Canada for 1870-1	CAN-31
Tryon, Rolla Milton	Transportation	HT-32
Turner, Charles W.	Chessie's road	CO-57
Turner, George	Narrow gauge nostalgia	N-2
Turner, George	Slim rails through the sand	CO-53
Turner, George E.	Victory rode the rails	WA-6
Turner, Robert Emanuel	Memories of [Pullman porter]	POR-1
Tyler, P.	Outlook for the railroads	EC-5

U

Ullman, Edward L.	U.S. railroads [capacity]	MAP-9
Ulmer, Melville J.	Trends and cycles [capital formation]	F-18
Ulriksson, Vidkunn	The telegraphers	TEL-1
Union Pacific	Union Pacific railroad	CO-285
United Nations	Improved methods [track constr.]	TK-2
	Railway operating and signaling techniques	SI-5

US

Advisory Commission	Intergovernmental responsibilities [mass trans.]	TSG-5
Army	Army operation [RRs]	US-1
	Cable ways, tramways, etc.	C-8
	Military railway service	MIL-1
	Operation and maintenance [diesel-electric]	LD-13
	Operation [steam locomotives]	MIL-2
	Organization and operation of railroads	RA-16
	Outloading of diesel locomotives	LD-14
	Question and answer [operating rules]	MIL-3
	Railroad map [United States]	MAP-3, 6
	Railway operating rules	OP-7
	Standard plans	MIL-4
	Unnecessary costs [commercial protective service]	US-3
Commerce, Dept. of	Railroad trackage	TK-4
Comptroller-General	Administration [Metroliner, etc.]	GO-1
	Follow-up examination [assistance to Turkey and Iran]	US-2
	Improved guidance [relocating railroad facilities]	GO-7
	Improvements in [budget presentation]	CO-4
	Potential savings [railway post offices]	RAP-4
	Problem areas [railroad retirement]	RET-6
	Review [railway post office requirements]	RAP-6
Defense, Dept. of	[Sect. 22–ICC Act]	WA-2
Defense Transportation Adm.	U.S. [freight car study]	CAR-7
	U.S. [locomotive study]	LG-12
Geological Survey	United States Railroads	MAP-8
Government Post Office	Railroad coal leases	LA-5
	Railroad retirement and unemployment	RET-1
High Speed Transportation, Office of	Statistical analysis [N.Y.– Wash. passenger svc.]	STA-1
ICC	See Interstate Commerce Commission	
Interior, Dept. of	The Alaska Railroad	CO-2
Internal Revenue Service	Regulations 114	T-4
Joint Study Com.	Study of REA Express	CO-233
National Archives	Preliminary inventory	BI-6

National Mediation Board	Administration [RR Labor Act]	LAW-1
	Administration [RR Labor Act]	L-29
	Interpretations [Nation Med. Bd.]	L-22
	Twenty years [Railway labor act]	L-30
National Park Service	Activities	WDT-15
Public Health Service	Handbook [sanitation of dining cars]	SAN-2
	Handbook [sanitation passenger cars]	SAN-4
	Handbook [sanitation servicing areas]	SAN-3
Railroad Retirement Board	Actuarial valuation [RR Ret. Act]	RET-3
	Field operating manual	RET-4
	Legal opinions	RET-5
	Questions and answers [RR Ret.]	RET-2
	The railroad retirement and unemployment	RET-9
	Railway pension plans	EMP-5
	RRB-SSA financial interchange	RET-7
	Twenty-five years [social insurance]	RET-10
Transportation, Dept. of	Highway-railway [crossing safety]	S-3
	Western railroad mergers	ME-11
United States Congress (Joint Committee)	National Capital transportation act of 1960	WDT-32
	Organization for transp. [national capital]	WDT-10
	Transportation plan [National Capital]	WDT-33
	Washington [transportation problems]	WDT-35
House of Representatives	Amending [ICC Act]	ICC-13
	Amend [Hours of Service]	L-24
	Amend [Nat. Capital Trans.]	WDT-23
	Amending [RR Ret.]	RET-19
	District of Columbia [Md., Va. transit]	WDT-42
	Emergency [legislation]	SE-2
	Environmental pollution	SAN-1
	Federal standard [safety]	S-2
	Guaranteed loans	F-12
	High-speed [transportation]	HI-1, 2, PAS-9
	Hours of service act	L-25
	Income tax exemption [employees]	T-1
	Guaranteed loans [carriers]	F-13
	ICC employee boards	ICC-17
	Interstate Comm. Comm. operations [safety]	S-5, 6
	Merger in a regulated industry	CO-165
	Metropolitan mass transportation	TSU-26, 27
	National freight car shortage	CAR-25
	1971 railway labor-management dispute	L-12
	Passenger train abandonment	PAS-7
	Passenger train discontinuance	PAS-6
	Passenger train service	PAS-13, 15, 18
	Port of New York Authority	NY(P)-2
	Railroad accounting procedures	ACT-6
	Railroad accounting procedures	ACT-7
	Railroad car shortage	CAR-35

House	Railway labor act amendments	L-33
	Railroad labor-management dispute	L-14
	Railroad passenger train	PAS-8
	Railroad problems	PR-6
	Railroad retirement act amendments	RET-23
	Railroad retirement [annuities]	RET-17
	Railroad retirement benefit increase— 1971	RET-12
	Railroad retirement [increase]	RET-14
	Rapid rail transit [Nation's Capital]	WDT-25
	Reorganization plan [locomotive inspection]	LS-28
	Return of subpoenas, Port of N.Y. Auth. inquiry	NY(P)-3
	Review [Emergency rail services act of 1970]	SE-3
	Section-by-section [mass trans. act 1962]	TSU-19
	Study [amortization]	T-5
	Surface transportation [safety]	S-12
	Technical amendments [retirement]	RET-22
	Transit development [National Capital]	WDT-28
	Transit program [National Capital]	WDT-29
	Transportation planning [urban]	WDT-19
	Urban mass transportation assistance act [1970]	TSU-7
	Urban mass transportation assistance act [1969]	TSU-10
	Urban mass transportation act [1963]	TSU-13, 16
	Urban mass transportation act [1962]	TSU-18, 20
	Urban mass transportation	TSU-8
	Urban mass transportation, 1961	TSU-24
	Use and disposition [grants]	LA-8
	Washington [Transit Authority]	WDT-36
	Washington [transit problem]	WDT-38
Senate	Accident reports to ICC	AC-2
	Alaska coal lands	CO-3
	Amending [ICC Act]	CAR-32
	Amendments to [ICC Act]	ICC-12
	Amendment to [ICC Act]	ICC-14
	Amendment to Section 20B	ICC-15
	Amend [Ry. Labor Act]	L-23
	To amend [Ry. Labor Act]	L-34
	Amend [Nat. Capital Trans.]	WDT-22
	Amending [RR Ret]	RET-15
	Amendments to Transportation Act	TT-6
	Atlantic and East Carolina	CO-23
	Causes of unemployment	L-35
	Contracts [forwarders & RRs]	FT-2
	The crisis in passenger [service]	PAS-9
	Hugh W. Cross [ICC]	ICC-16
	Commuter transportation	NY(M)-1
	The current [Ry. labor dispute]	L-15
	Curtailment [Ry. post offices]	RAP-7

Senate

District of Columbia [Md., Va.— transit]   WDT-41
Effect [mergers on commuter transportation]   COMM-14
Extension [high speed trans. act]   HI-4
Failing railroads   PAS-19
Financing subway [Nation Capital]   WDT-20
Freight car shortages   CAR-26
Freight car shortages   CAR-27
Freight car shortage   CAR-29
Freight car shortage   CAR-30
Freight car shortage   CAR-33
Freight car supply   CAR-24
Freight car supply   CAR-31
High-speed ground transportation   HI-3, 5, 6
Hours of service   EMP-1
Judicial review of ICC orders   ICC-18
Loan guaranty authority [ICC]
Mass transportation, 1970   TSU-6
Mass transportation, 1969   TSU-9
Mass transportation act of 1960   TSU-28
Midwest High Speed [Transit]   HI-9
Montana freight rates   MON-2
National Capital transit development   WDT-31
National freight car supply   CAR-28
Oregon and California railroad grant lands   LA-3
Payment for improvements, Red Rock Resevoir   LA-4
Passenger train discontinuances   PAS-10, 24
Passenger train service   PAS-11
Passenger train service   PAS-16
Preservation of competitive through trail routes   COMP-6
Problems of the railroads   PR-5, 7
Public assistance [D.C. Transit]   WDT-21

Public transportation [District of Columbia]   WDT-37
Rail merger legislation   ME-7
Rail passenger service act of 1970   PAS-17
Rail rapid transit [National Capital]   WDT-27
Rail rapid transit [National Capital]   WDT-26
Railroad industry overview—1971   A-13
Railroad rates [Alaska]   RAT-29
Railroad retirement act   RET-18
Railroad retirement amendments   RET-13
Railroad retirement [annuities]   RET-16
Railroad retirement annuity increase— 1971   RET-11
Railroad retirement benefits   RET-21
Railroad safety   S-8
Railroad unemployment insurance act   L-38
Railroad work rules dispute   RU-3, 4, 5
Railway labor-management dispute   L-13

Senate	Railway labor-management negotiations	L-10
	Railway shopcraft dispute	L-16, 17
	Reorganization plan (ICC)	ICC-20
	Regulation of Alaska Railroad	CO-6
	Regulation of track motorcars	MR-1
	Repeal ["round-trip" mail pay]	RAP-8
	Review of ICC policies and practices	ICC-21
	Review of the Penn Central condition	CO-213
	RFC loans [Baltimore & Ohio]	CO-33
	Safety regulation [track motorcars]	S-7
	Section-by-section [mass trans. act]	TSU-12
	Shortage of boxcars [grain]	CAR-34
	Stewardship of the ICC	ICC-22
	Study [passenger service]	PAS-12
	Subversive influence	EMP-9
	Surface transportation	ICC-23
	Train discontinuances	ICC-24
	Transportation act of 1958	TT-5
	Union Station train accident	WDC-1
	Urban loan mass transportation act [1963]	TSU-11
	Urban mass transportation act [1963]	TSU-14
	Urban mass transportation, 1963	TSU-15
	Urban mass transportation, 1963	TSU-17
	Urban mass transportation, 1962	TSU-21, 23
	Urban mass transportation 1962	TSU-22
	Urban mass transportation, 1961	TSU-24
	Voluntary modification [financial structures]	F-14
	Washington [transit]	WDT-39
	Washington [transit compact]	WDT-24
	Washington [transit compact]	WDT-40
	Widow's pensions	RET-20
United States Steel Corp.	Biography of a business [TCI&R]	CO-269
	USS trackwork	TK-5
United Transportation Union		UT-1
Urban Land Inst.	Crowded street	TSG-1
Use of Cybernetics		RES-2
Utley, Robert M.	Golden spike	HT-13

V

Van, Melvin	The big heart	C-4
Van Doren, C. S.	South Dakota interstate rail shipments	SOU(D)-3
Van Fleet, James A.	Rail transport and the winning of wars	WA-2
Van Trump, James D.	Railroad stations of Pennsylvania	TER-3
Van Zant, Lee	Early economic policies [Texas]	TEX-1
Vincent, Phillip E.	Fiscal impact [commuters on cities	COMM-3
Vickrey, William S.	The revision [transit fare structure]	NY(C)-6
Virginia	Certain health problems	SAN-5
	The economic situation [VA. passenger]	VA-4
	Interim report	VA-6
	Taxes [car line companies]	VA-7
Voorhees, Alan M. & Assoc., Inc.	Traffic, revenue and operating costs	WDT-13

W

Wagner, Charles M.	A pictorial history [WB&A Electric RR]	CO-301
Wagner, F. Hol, Jr.	Mile-high trolleys	D-1
Wagner, Jack R.	Short line junction	BR-3
Wagner, Richard H.	Practical guide to model railroading	MOH-6
Wakefield, Manville B.	Coal boats to tidewater	CP-87
Walden, Charles F.	Fundamentals of transportation	TT-2
Waling, Joseph L.	Least-weight proportions [bridge]	BRI-1
Walker, James B.	Fifty years of rapid transit	NY(C)-1
Walker, James, Jr.	Glendale & Montrose	CO-127
Walters, William K.	Handbook [model]	MOH-3
Wampler, Joseph	Ferrocarril de Chihuahua al Pacifico	MEX-1
Wardwell, W. W.	From horse trails to steel rails	NED-3
Warne, Colston E.	The Pullman boycott of 1894	CO-231
Warner, Paul T.	Baldwin locomotives	CO-26
	Locomotives of the Pennsylvania RR	CO-218
Warner, Sam B.	Streetcar suburbs	BO-6
Warren, Bob	764 helpful hints [model]	MOG-11
Warren, J. G. H.	A century of locomotive building	LS-6
Warren, John T.	Study of railroad motive power	LG-14
Washington	Statistics of railroad companies	WAS-2
Wash. (State) Univ.	Seattle monorail	MO-4
Washington Metro Study	Metro	WDT-7
Washington Transit Comm.		WDT-17
Washington Transit Auth.		WDT-18
Waters, Lawrence L.	Steel rails to Santa Fe	CO-13
Watson, Jane	The golden book of trains	JLT-8
Wayne County Hist. Soc.	The gravity railroads [Del. & H.]	CO-85
Wayner Publications	All time index [RR mags.]	PER-1
	Amtrack car spotter	AM-1
	Car names, etc.	CAR-18
	4-8-4 Pictorial	LS-14
	Great poems from Railroad Magazine	PO-1
	New York Central cars	CO-189
	Pennsy car plans	CO-216
	The Pullman scrapbook	CO-227
	Pullman private car service of 1939	CO-228
	The run of the Twentieth Century	CO-193
	Santa Fe Passenger [consists 1937]	CO-18
Weaver, John C.	The American railroads	HT-4, RA-2
Webb, Robert N.	The illustrated true book [RRs]	RA-12
Webber, Thomas	The Northern railroads in the Civil War	WA-1
Webster, Henry C.	Railway motive power	LG-13
	2750	LG-15
Weisgard, Leonard	The big book [stories]	STO-1
Weiss, George H.	Port differential rates	RAT-22
Weissenborn, Gustavus	American locomotive engineering	LG-1
Weller, John L.	The New Haven Railroad	CO-198
Westcott, Linn H.	HO primer	MOG-5
	The HO railroad that grows	MOC-1
	How to wire [model]	MOC-5
	Model railroader cyclopedia	MOE-2
	Practical guide to model railroading	MOH-6
	Small railroads you can build	MOC-10

Westing, Frederick	Apex of the Atlantics	LS-4
	Erie power	CO-113
Westing, Fred	The locomotives that Baldwin built	CO-25
Wetenkamp, Harry R.	The effect [brake shoe action]	BR-2
Wheeler, Robert	Steam on the Sierra	N-5
Wheelock, Walt	Angel's Flight	C-2
White, Edward	Famous subways and tunnels	SUB-1
White, John H., Jr.	American locomotives	LG-2
	Intro. [loco. safety truck]	LG-7
	The "Pioneer"	LS-26
White, Leslie T.	Scale model railroading	MOG-9
White, Lynne L.	The Nickel Plate Road	CO-187
White, William	The Lackawanna	CO-89
Whitman, Frederic B.	Western Pacific—its first forty years!	CO-304
Wiener, Lionel	Articulated locomotives	LS-5
Williams, Alfred	Life in a railway factory	EMP-3
Williams, E. W.	The regulation [rail-motor rate]	RAT-26
Williams, Ernest W.	The regulation [rail-motor rate]	COMP-10
Williams, Ernest W., Jr.	Freight transportation in the Soviet Union	FT-7
	Freight transportation in the Soviet Union	FT-8
Williams, Geo.	Life on a locomotive	LO-1
Wilson, George L.	Special railroad freight services	FT-13
Williams, Guy R.	The world of model trains	MOG-10
Williams, Harold A.	The Western Maryland	CO-302
Wilson, Edward A.	The building [first transc. RR]	HT-6
Wilson, George L.	Fundamentals of freight traffic	TRF-4
Wilson, G. Lloyd	Making [freight rates]	RAT-20
Wingo, Lowdon	Transportation and urban land	TSP-4
Wilgus, William J.	The railway interrelations [U.S. and Canada]	CAN-23
Winsten, Christopher B.	Studies [economics of transportation]	EC-8
Winther, Oscar O.	The transportation frontier	WE-7
Wisconsin	Summaries [motor vehicle accidents]	WIS-2
Wohn, M.	The urban transportation problem	TSU-5
Wojtas, Ed	Steam, wide and narrow	LS-33
Wolf Management Eng. Co.	Survey of [Interstate Commerce Commission]	ICC-9
Wolfe, Louis	Clear the track	STO-3
Wood, Charles R.	Lines West	CO-129
Wood, Charles and Dorothy	Milwaukee Road West	CO-69
Wood, Dorothy	Long Eye and the iron horse	JLR-3
Wood, E. V.	Working on the railroad	EMP-10
Wood, Helen	Employment outlook [RRs]	EMP-12
Wood, Norman J.	Restriction of output [RR unions]	PRO-2
Wood, Robert Tees	Rail freight [tri-state region]	TTG-3
Woods, Jim	Bradford, Bordell & Kinzua	CO-40
Worley, E. D.	Iron horses of the Santa Fe Trail	CO-15
Wornom, Douglas C.	Description list [Pullmans]	CO-227
Worsfeld, F. H.	Complete index to [rosters]	LG-3
Wright, Frank J.	Transfer values [transit systems]	PIT-2
Wright, Richard K.	Southern Pacific daylight	CO-261
Wright, Roy J.	Cincinnati streetcars	CI-1
Wright, Roy M.	An economic investigation [bearings]	TE-2

| Wurm, Theodore G. | The crookedest railroad | CO-178 |

Y

Yabroff, Bernard	Employment [& occupational patterns]	L-36
Yates, Raymond F.	The Boy's book [model RRs]	MOT-2
	How to improve [model]	MOC-4

Z

Zaffo, George J.	The big book [locos]	JLL-1
	Your freight trains	JLT-25
Zarchy, Harry	Model railroading	MOG-7
Zettel, Richard M.	Urban transportation [San Francisco]	SA-3
Ziel, Ron	Steam in the sixties	LS-30
	Steel rails to the sunrise	CO-153
	Steel rails to victory	WA-5
	Southern steam specials	CO-255
	The story [Steamtown and Edaville]	MU-2
	The twilight of steam locomotives	LS-36
Zwick, Charles	The economics of transportation	COMP-3

SECTION 5

TITLE INDEX

TITLE INDEX

Short Title	Author	Location

A

Short Title	Author	Location
About the engineer	Johnson	JLR-1
Abstracts of Supreme Court decisions [ICC]		ICC-1
The Accessible City	Owens	TSP-1
Accident reports to ICC	Senate	AC-2
Activities	National Park Service	WDT-15
Actual track capacity	Mostafa	TK-1
Actuarial valuation [RR Ret. Act]	RR Ret. Bd.	RET-3
Adhesion between rails and wheels.	Cabble	TE-1
Adjustment of retired railroaders	Tomlin	L-1
Adirondack railroads	Hochschild	E-1
Adirondack steamboats	Hochschild	E-2
Administration [Metroliner, etc.]	Comp. General	GO-1
Administration [RR Labor Act]	Nat. Med. Bd.	LAW-1
Administration [RR Labor Act]	Nat. Med. Bd.	L-29
Advanced model railroading	Hertz	MOG-1
Aerial tramways and funicular Rys.	Schneigert	C-1
The age of steam	Beebe	STE-1
Agenda	AAR, Acct. Div.	ACT-1
Air view [Boston]	Metro. Trans. Auth.	BO-1
Alaska coal lands	Senate	CO-3
The Alaska Railroad	Fitch	CO-1
The Alaska Railroad	Dept. of Int.	CO-2
Alaska-Ry-highway crossings	Dept. of Highways	CR-1
ALI-ABA course of study	Am Law Inst.	LAW-2
All aboard [Michigan]	Dunbar	HT-1
All aboard	Elting	JLT-1
All time index [RR mags]	Wayner	PER-1
Alphabetical index [tokens]	Kotler	CAN-13
Amend [Hours of Service]	House	L-24
Amend [Nat. Capital Trans.]	Senate	WDT-22
Amend [Nat. Capital Trans.]	House	WDT-23
Amend [Ry. Labor Act]	Senate	L-23
To amend [Ry. Labor Act]	Senate	L-34
Amending [ICC Act]	Senate	CAR-32
Amending [ICC Act]	House	ICC-13
Amending [RR Ret]	Senate	RET-15
Amending [RR Ret]	House	RET-19
Amendments to [ICC Act]	Senate	ICC-12
Amendment to [ICC Act]	Senate	ICC-14
Amendment to Section 20B	Senate	ICC-15
Amendments to Transportation Act	Senate	TT-6
American locomotive engineering	Weissenborn	LG-1
American locomotives	White	LG-2
American locomotives	Alexander	LS-1
American locomotives	RR Gazette	LS-2
The American railroads	Rando	RA-1
The American railroads	Saunders	AD-1
American railroads	Stover	HT-3
The American railroads	Weaver	HT-4, RA-2
American railroad journal	Golden West	RA-4
The American railroad network	Taylor	HT-2
American railroad politics	Kerr	GO-2
American railroads	AAR	RA-3
American railroads	AAR	DEV-1
American RRs [antebellum economy]	Fishlow	DEV-2

The American Ry. industry	Corliss	RA5, 6
American Ry. Eng. Assoc.		ENG-1
American Short Line Assoc.		SHO-1
American Soc. Mech. Engs.		LD-1
The American steam locomotive	Swengel	LS-3
The American [transportation token]	Logsdon	SJR-1
Amtrack car spotter	Wayner	AM-1
An acquaintance with Alco	Olmstead	CO-8
An analysis [loco dynamics]	Kamat	DY-1
Analysis [Port of N.Y. Auth obligation]	Stichman	NY-9
Andrews raiders	Feuerlicht	CO-55
Angel's Flight	Wheelock	C-2
Annals [great strikes]	Dacus	STRI-1
Annapolis Short Line	Merriken	CO-300
Annual green book	Nat. Safety Council	S-1
Ante bellum studies	Russel	HT-5
Apex of the Atlantics	Westing	LS-4
Arcade & Attica	Lewis	CO-11
The archaeology [cable car]	Hanscom	C-3
Arco RR series [employment]		EMP-17
The Argentine Central	Hollenback	COL-2
Argument [Manitoba]		CAN-27
Arid domain	Greever	CO-16
Army operation [RRs]	U.S. Army	US-1
AAR	Faricy	AS-1
The Assoc. of Am. RRs	AAR	AS-2
Associations [RR officers]	Bu. Ry. Econ.	AS-4
ASTM manual		LD-2
At the RR station	Reck	JLT-2
Atlanta and West Point	Prince	CO-20
Atlantic Coast Line	Prince	CO-21
Atlantic Coast Line	Davis	CO-22
Atlantic and East Carolina	Senate	CO-23
Articulated cars	Charlton	EL-1
Articulated locomotives	Wiener	LS-5
Atwood's catalog [tokens]	Atwood	GO-1
Automotive [transmissions]	Giles	LD-3

B

Backwoods railroads	Steinheimer	WE-1
Balance of trade [Mississippi]	Noblin	MIS-1
Baldwin locomotives	Taber	CO-26
Baldwin locomotive [catalog]	Specialty Press	CO-27
Baldwin locomotive [catalog]	Howell-North	CO-28
Baldwin [construction]	Golden West	CO-27
Baltimore [mass trans.]	Parson, etc.	BA-1
The Baltimore & Ohio	Bateman	CO-30
Baltimore [rapid transit]	Daniel, etc.	BA-2
Bangor and Aroostook RR	Nat. Survey	CO-35
BART at mid point	Demoro	SA-1
Basic study [traffic]	Polakoff	TRF-1
Benchmark survey [park and ride]		NJ-1
The Berkshire era	Rehor	CO-186
The Bessemer and Lake Erie	Beaver	CO-36
Bibliography [1893]	Cotterell	BI-1
Bibliography	ARR	BI-2, 3
The big book [locos]	Zaffo	JLL-1
The big book [streamliners]	Stewart	JLT-3
The big book [trains]	Cameron	JLT-4
The big book [stories]	Weisgard	STO-1
The big heart	Van	C-4

Biography of a business [TCI & R]		CO-269
The Birney car	Cox	STR-2
The bituminous coal [rates]	Campbell	EC-1
Blackhawk Films [movies]	AA	MP-1-61
Blue book [hobbies]	Polk's	MOE-1
Blue Ridge Trolley	Harwood	CO-134
Bonanza RRs	Kneiss	CA-1
Boston capitalists and western RRs	Johnson	F-1
Bradford, Bordell & Kinzua	Barber	CO-40
Bradshaw's railway annual	Kelley	GU-2
Bridges & buildings [models]	Anderson	MOS-1
Bridge and trestle handbook [models]	Mallery	MOS-2
Bridgton & Saco River	Baggage Car	CO-41
Brill 250 hp gas-electric	Old Line	CO-43
British Columbia		CAN-25
British investment [Am. Rys.]	Adler	F-2
Brotherhood RR Trainmen		RA-7
The Boy's book [model RRs]	Yates	MOT-2
The Boy's book [model Rys.]	Carter	MOT-3
Buffalo & Susquehanna	Pietrak	SHO-2
Building a RR [SAL]	Smith	CO-245
The building [first trans. RR]	Wilson	HT-6
Building out to sea [FEC]	Miss. Valley	CO-118
Building the Canadian West	Hedges	CO-51
Bulletin	Nat. Ry. Hist Soc.	HT-23
The Burlington in transition	Corbin	CO-59
The Burlington strike	Salmons	L-5
Burlington West	Overton	CO-60
Busted and still running	Mead	CO-42

C

Cab-in-front	Hungerford	CO-264
Cable car carnival	Beebe	C-5
The cable car in America	Hilton	C-6
The cable cars [SF]	Palmer	C-7
Cable ways, tramways, etc.	U.S. Army	C-8
Canada's Railways	Phillips	CAN-15
Canadian guide	Int'l Ry. Publ.	CAN-1
Canadian National Rys.	Stevens	CO-49
Canadian National Rys. [mag.]		CAN-33
Canadian National steam power	Clegg	CO-50
Canadian Pacific [map]		CAN-36
Canadian steam	Morgan	CAN-14
Canadian transportation [freight class]	Johnston	CAN-39
The capacity and capital requirements [RQs]	ICC	F-3
Capital Transit [mag.]		WDT-2
Car and locomotive cyclopedia	Simmons-Boardman	CAR-4
Car names, etc.	Wayner	CAR-18
Cars of Sacramento Northern	Swett	CO-239
The car-builder's dictionary (1906)	Gregg	CAR-1
The car-builder's dictionary (1888)	Gregg	CAR-2
The car-builder's dictionary (1879)	Gregg	CAR-3
Careers [RRs]	Morgret	MA-1
The case of train 3	Ridgway	WK-1
A case study [balloting]	Masson	CO-39
Catalogue [British stamps]	Potter	RAP-1
Causes of unemployment	Senate	L-35
The cavalcade of RRs [Colo.]	Everett	COL-3
Centennial map	Rand, McNally	MAP-1
Certain health problems	Va.	SAN-5
Central Pacific & Southern Pacific	Beebe	CO-258

A century of Chicago street cars	Johnson	CH-7
A century of locomotive building	Warren	LS-6
A century [SP steam]	Dunscomb	CO-262
Chalk talk [brakes]	Drennan	BR-1
Change at Jamaica	Goodrich	CO-154A
Chapters of Erie	Adams	CO-112
Chapters of history [SP]	Daggett	CO-259
Charter [Pan Am. Ry. Cong.]		CONG-1
Chessie's road	Turner	CO-57
Chicago [elevateds consolidation]	Davies	CO-254
Chicago's mass [trans.]	CTA	CH-2
Chicago today	Stead	L-6
The Chicago Transit Auth.	DeCamp	CH-1
Chili line [D & RGW]	Gjevre	CO-99
Chief engineer's [IC]		CO-142
Chief factors [rates]	Bu. Agr. Econ.	RAT-8
A chronological list [Fla. RRs]	AAR	RA-8
A chronology [Am. RRs]	AAR	CI-1
Cinders and timber	Harrison	LOG-1
City and interurban cars	Brill Co.	CO-44
City of little bread	Burbank	STO-2
City makers	Nadeau	HT-8
Civil Service Publishing Services [emp]		EMP-18
Civil War RRs	Abdill	SOU-1
Earl Clark's directory (electric RRs)		EL-3
Clear the track	Geer	STO-3
Clear type map [Ala.]		AL-1
Clear type map [Ark.]		ARK-1
Clear type map [Calif.]		CA-2
Clear type map [La.]		LA-1
Cleveland, Cincinnati, Chicago & St. Louis	Pabst	CO-78
Climax	Taber	LS-7
C & O Power	Shuster	CO-58
Coaches and trains	Cadfryn-Roberts	ART-1
Coal boats to tidewater	Wakefield	CO-87
The coal viewer	Curr	MIN-1
Collecting model trains	Hertz	MOT-1
Collective bargaining	Kaufman	L-19
Colorado Midland	Calky	CO-80
Colorado Mountain railroads	Le Massena	COL-4
Colorado rail annual	Colo. RR. Mus.	COL-5
Colorado & Southern	Ehernberger	CO-82
The commission and common law	Bennett	ICC-3
Commodity RRs	Dorin	COMM-1
Commuter transportation	Senate	NY(m)-1
The comparative efficiency [trucks]	Lowstuter	TER-6
Comparison of average rates	Horton	RAT-28
The complete book [model RR]	Sutton	MOG-2
The complete book [model RR]	Hertz	MOG-3
Complete guide [model RR]	Sutton	MOH-1
Complete index to [rosters]	Worsfeld	LG-3
Competition and [price discrimination]	Hillman	COMP-2
Competition [rail & truck]	Charles River	COMP-1
The composite report [BART]	Parsons, etc.	SA-5
Concordance [Ry. Act]	Bd. of Trans. Comm.	CAN-10
Concrete crossties	Polden	TI-1
Conducting transportation	AAR	ACT-2
A congressional history [RRs]	Haney	HT-9
Consolidated cross index [ICC]		ICC-26
Constitutional provisions [Va.]	Michie Co.	VA-2, 3
Contracts [forwarders & RRs]	Senate	FT-2

Contributory health plans	BR & SC	EMP-11
Jay Cooke and Minnesota	Harnsberger	CO-206
Consolidated bus-rail services [NY]	Tri-State	COMM-2
Costs	Poole	COS-1
Costs and decision making	Ry. System & Mgt.	FT-3
Cost standards [& rates]	Edwards	RAT-1
Coudersport & Port Allegheny	Pietrak	SHO-3
Cripple Creek RRs	Feitz	COL-6
The crisis in passenger [service]	Senate	PAS-9
The crookedest railroad	Wurm	CO-178
Hugh W. Cross [ICC]	Senate	ICC-16
Crosstie industry facts	Ogden	TI-2
Crossties through Carolina	Gilbert	NOC-1
Crowded street	Urban Land Inst.	TSG-1
The Crystal River Pictorial	McCoy	COL-7
The current [Ry. labor dispute]	Senate	L-15
Curtailment [Ry. post offices]	Senate	RAP-7

D

Delaware & Hudson	Shaughnessy	CO-85
The Delaware & Hudson Canal	LeRoy	CO-86
The demand for transportation	Perle	TT-1
Demise [iron horse]	Rainey	LG-4
Denver, South Park & Pacific	Poor	CO-103
Dept. of Defense [sect. 22–ICC Act]		WA-2
A description [canals & RRs]	Tanner	HT-10
Description [guided transport]	Grimble	CAN-2
Descriptive list [Pullmans]	Wornom	CO-227
Design in transit		ART-2
Destination Topolobampo	Kerr	CO-147
Destination Valley	Richardson	EL-2
Determination [maximum flow–RRs]	Boldyreff	OP-2
Detroit expressway & transit	Andrews	DE-1
The developing transportation revelation	Ry. Sys. & Mgt. Assoc.	FUT-1
Development of the locomotive engine	Sinclair	LG-5
Development [RR transportation]	Corliss	DEV-3
The development [transcotinental rates]	Gillett	RAT-5
A discussion [RR bond analysis]	Grinell	F-17
Dictionary of Ry. slang	Sheppard	GO-3
Digest of Awards	Nat. RR Adj. Bd.	L-18
Diesel locomotives	Draney	LD-4
Diesel spotter's guide	Pinkepank	LD-7
Diesel-electric 4030	Billings	JLL-2
The diesel-electric [dictionary]	Craig	LD-8
Diesel-electric [handbook]	McGowan	LD-9
Diesel-electrics [repairs]	Simmons-Boardman	LD-10
Diesel locomotives [productivity]		LD-5
Diesel power [mines]	East	LM-1
Diesel railway traction		LD-6
Diesels west	Morgan	CO-63
The dilemma [regulation]	Friedlaender	PR-1
Dinner in the diner	Hollister	DI-1
Directory [rates]	Leonard's	RAT-2
District of Columbia [Md., Va.–transit]	Senate	WDT-41
District of Columbia [Md., Va.–transit]	House	WDT-42
Domestic transportation	Sampson	FT-4
Down at the depot	Alexander	ST-1
Down brakes	Shaw	AC-1
Downtown Atlanta transit	Georgia Tech.	AT-1
Due process	Lazar	L-20, 26
Duluth, South Shore & Atlantic	R & LH Soc.	CO-106

The dynamics [trade]	Ry. Sys. & Mgt. Assoc.	DY-2
Dynamics [transit structures]	Parsons, etc.	TSE-1

E

Early American steam locomotives	Kinert	LS-8
Early electric cars [Phila.]	Cox	PH-1
The early history [AA ferries]	Frederickson	CO-10
Early history [LI RR]	Smith	CO-154
Early economic policies [Texas]	Van Zant	TEX-1
Early RR days [N. Mex]	Tice	EX-1
Easy to build [model structures]	Anderson	MOS-3
Eastern steam pictorial	Pennypacker	LS-9
Economic analysis [freight car mfg.]	Marshall	MAN-1
The economic effects [regulation]	MacAvoy	EC-2
The economic history [C & EI]	Teweles	CO-67
An economic history [GN Div.]	Thompson	CO-130
An economic investigation [bearings]	Wright	TE-2
The economic position [Pittsburgh commuting]	Schusler	PIT-1
The economic situation [Va. passenger]		VA-4
The economics of competition	Meyer	COMP-3
The economics and control [road-rail comp.]	Kolsen	FT-5
The economics [incentive rates]	Lundy	RAT-6
Economics [NY full crew laws]	Backman	RU-1
Economics of transportation	Locklin	EC-3
Editorial comment [LIRR plan]		CO-156
Edwards Ry. Motor Co. [model 10]		CO-109
The effect [brake shoe action]	Wetenkamp	BR-2
Effect [mergers on commuter transportation]	Senate	COMM-14
Effect [earthquake−Alaska RR]	McCulloch	CO-5
Effects [RR design]	Chang	TRF-3
The effects [weather on operation]	Hay	OP-10
VIII Pan Am. Ry. Conference		CONG-2
1877: year of violence	Bruce	STRI-2
The electric interurban rys. [Am.]	Hilton	STR-3
Electric railroads	NY Electric RR Assoc.	EL-4
Electric RRs [Indiana]	Marlette	IA-1
Electric Ry. [cars & trucks]	Stephenson	CO-249
Electric traction [eq.]	Hinde	EL-5
Electrical handbooks [model RRs]	Mallery	MOH-2
Electronics in business	Klingsman	PL-1
Elements of railway signaling	GRS Co.	SI-1
Eleventh report [RR Taxes−N.J.]	Tax Policy Comm.	NJ-4
Frank Ellison on model RRs		MOG-4
Emergency [legislation]	House	SE-2
Employment [& occupational patterns]	Delano	L-36
Employment outlook [RRs]	Wood	EMP-12
End o' steel	Dines	JLH-1
End of track	Kyner	WE-2
Engineer's operating manual [F-7]		LD-11
Engines, rails and roads	Popular Science	MP-O
Enterprise denied	Martin	GO-3
Environmental pollution	House	SAN-1
Epic of the overland	Fulton	CO-283
Equalization [rates]	Bd. of Trans. Comm.	CAN-40]
Erie to Conneault by trolley	Springirth	CO-79
The Erie-Lackawanna RR	N.J. Trans. Div.	CO-114
Erie power	Westing	CO-113
Essays [rys. advantages]	Lyne	SE-1
Essays [rates differentials]	Simmons-Boardman	RAT-3
Exercises [ICC 75th year]		ICC-25
Extension [high speed trans. act]	Senate	HI-4

Extra south	Reid	SOU-3
Evans [car forecast]	Evans	CO-115
Experience [disability insurance laws]	Dahm	L-37
Explanation [cost finding]	ICC	ACT-3

F

Factors affecting freight rates	Leavens	RAT-7
Factors influencing safety [grade crossings]	Schoppert	S-4
Facts about modern transit		TSG-2
Facts and arguments [railways]	Arno Press	COMP-4
Failing railroads	Senate	PAS-19
The failure [labor leadership]	Kerley	L-7
The Fairlie locomotive	Abbot	LS-10
The fall of a railroad empire	Staples	CO-194
Famous cableways of the world	F.E. Dean	C-9
Famous locomotives of the world	Ellis	LG-5A
Famous railroad stations	Nathan	ST-2
Famous subways and tunnels	White	SUB-1
Far wheels	Small	RA-9
Fares, please [trolleys]	Miller	STR-4
Farewell to steam	Plowden	LS-11
Farewell to steam in Canada	Mika	CAN-16
Feasibility [Richmond Br. for rapid trans.]		SA-4
Federal aid [urban transportation]	Hankerd	TSG-4
The Federal interest [passenger service]	Saunders & Co.	GO-4
Federal laws [governing employees]	B.R.T.	LAW-9
The federal [land subsidy] Canada]	Hedges	CAN-9
Federal standards [safety]	House	S-2
The Federal valuation of railroads	Moore	F-19
Ferrocarril de Chihuahua al Pacifico	Wampler	MEX-1
Fiddletown & Copperopolis	Fallberg	STO-4
Field operating manual	RR Ret. Bd.	RET-4
Fifteen years [Railway labor act]	N.M.B.	L-31
Fifty years of rapid transit	Walker	NY(C)-1
The financial community [RR treasurer]		F-7
A financial study [N.H. RR]	Edwards	CO-197
Financing subway [National Capital]	Senate	WDT-20
Find a career in railroading	Harrison	EMP-13
Finding list [Canadian Ry. campanies]	Butlin	CAN-30
The first book of trains	Hamilton	JLT-5
The first book of trains	Tatham	JLT-6
The first quarter-century [steam locos]	Oliver	LS-12
First steam west of the Big Muddy	Guise	LS-13
The first transcontinental railroad	Galloway	HT-11
Fiscal impacts [commuters on cities]	Vincent	COMM-3
A five-year forecast [commuter cars]	Sewall	CAR-19
Henry M. Flagler, 1830-1913	Martin	CO-117
Focus	Carper	PI-1
Follow-up examination [assist. to Turkey & Iran]	Comptr. Gen.	US-2
The formation [New Engl. RR sys.]	Baker	HT-36
Formula [rail terminal]	ICC	COS-2
Fort Wayne's trolleys, 1870-1963	Bradley	STR-5
4-8-4 Pictorial	Wayner	LS-14
4-8-0 tender locomotives	Carling	LS-15
400,000 miles by rail	Blanton	EXP-1
The Franco-Texan Land Company	Taylor	CO-170
Free transit	Domencich	TSG-3
Freight car disbribution	Coughlin	OP-3
Freight car lettering [model]	Champion Decal	MOD-1
Freight cars rolling	Sagle	CAR-12
Freight car shortages	Senate	CAR-26

Freight car shortages	Senate	CAR-27
Freight car shortage	Senate	CAR-29
Freight car shortage	Senate	CAR-30
Freight car shortage	Senate	CAR-33
Freight-car trucks	Bowes	CAR-16
Freight car supply	Senate	CAR-24
Freight car supply	Senate	CAR-31
Freight rates in Canada	MacMillan	CAN-41
Freight rates [New England and central]	Randolph	RAT-31
Freight rates [Western]	Randolph	RAT-34
Freight train	Bunce	FT-6
Freight train	Reichert	JLT-7
Freight transportation in the Soviet Union	Williams	FT-7
Freight transportation in the Soviet Union	Williams	FT-8
The freight yard	Stever	JLO-1
Frisco folks	Bain	CO-242
From cab to caboose	Noble	EN-1
The fun and work of railroading	Murphy	JLO-2
Fundamentals of freight traffic	Wilson	TRF-4
Fundamentals of transportation	Walden	TT-2
The future of rail transport	Lemly	FUT-3
FWD railroad equipment	Old Line	CO-122

G

John W. Garrett [B&O]	Catton	BIO-3
The Garret locomotive	Durrant	LS-16
Gateway to the Northwest	Donovan	CO-171
General development plan [National Capital]	Adams, etc.	WDT-3
General rail [rate changes]	ICC	RAT-11
General grade crossing survey	Calif. P.U.C.	CA-3
Geographia Map Co. [Illinois]	Gross	I-1
Geographia Map Co. [Maryland and Delaware]	Gross	MAR-1
Geographia Map Co. [Ohio]	Gross	O-2
Geographia Map co. [Virginia and W. Virginia]	Gross	VA-5
The Georgian locomotive	Bryant	LS-17
Ghost railroads of Indiana	Sulzer	IA-2
Ghost railroads of Kentucky	Sulzer	KE-1
The giant's ladder	Boner	CO-91
The Gilpin gold tram	Ferrell	CO-126
Glendale & Montrose	Moreau	CO-127
Gold rush narrow gauge	Martin	CO-309
The golden age of railroads	Holbrook	JLH-2
The golden book of trains	Watson	JLT-8
Golden rails	Kratville	PI-2
The golden spike	Harriman	HT-12
The golden spike	Littledale	JLH-3
Golden spike	Utley	HT-13
Government promotion [canals & RRs]	Goodrich	GO-5
Grade crossings in Ohio		O-1
The Grand Trunk Railway of Canada	Currie	CAN-37
The Granger laws	Miller	LAW-4
The Granger movement	Buck	GO-6
Grape belt trolleys	Springirth	NY-1
The gravity railroads [D&H]	Wayne Cty. Hist Soc.	CO-85
The great Burlington Strike of 1888	McMurry	CO-66
The great iron trail	Howard	HT-14
Great Lakes car ferries	Hilton	HT-35
Great poems from Railroad Magazine	Wayner	PO-1
The great railroad conspiracy	Hirschfeld	SO-1
Great railroad photographs	Beebe	PI-3
Great railroad stories	Moskowitz	STO-5

Great railway journeys	Jones	RA-10
The great Richmond terminal	Klein	TER-5
Great trains of all time	Hubbard	TRN-1
Great trains of the world	Coggins	JLT-9
Great train robberies of the West	Block	RO-1
The great third rail	C.E.R.A.	CH-8
Growth and travel [Toronto]		CAN-5
G-R-S carrier control	G.R.S. Co.	CO-124
G-R-S centralized traffic control	G.R.S. Co.	OP-1
G-R-S automatic train control	G.R.S. Co.	SI-2
G-R-S model 9 switch machine	G.R.S. Co.	SI-3
Guaranteed loans	House	F-13
Guaranteed loans	House	F-12
Guide to Burlington archives [Newberry Libr.]	Jackson	CO-61
Guide map [Kansas Pacific]		CO-148, 149
A Guide [to planning a trans. sys.]	Clark	WDT-4
The Gulf, Mobile and Ohio	Lemly	CO-132
Gulf to Rockies	Overton	CO-81, 121

H

Hall of History railroad	Beal	NOC-2
The handbook of American railroads	Lewis	RA-11
Handbook [model]	Walters	MOH-3
Handbook [sanitation of dining cars]	Pub. Health Ser.	SAN-2
Handbook [sanitation passenger cars]	Pub. Health Ser.	SAN-4
Handbook [sanitation servicing areas]	Pub. Health Ser.	SAN-3
Hawaiian railroads	Hungerford	HA-1
He built Seattle	Nesbit	BIO-1
Headlights and markers	Donovan	STO-6
Hear the train blow	Beebe	PI-4
To hell in a day coach	Lyon	PR-2
The Hiawatha story	Scribbins	CO-71
High finance in the sixties	Adams	CO-7
Highlights [railroad history]	AAR	HT-15
High-speed [transportation]	House	HI-1, 2, PAS-5
High-speed ground transportation	Senate	HI-3, 5, 6
Highway-railway [crossing safety]	Dept. of Trans.	S-3
A history and analysis [labor-mgmt. relations]	Roberts	PH-2
A history of American railroads	Stover	HT-17
History [Baldwin Locomotive Works]	Old Line	CO-24
History [Canadian National]	Stevens	CO-48
A history [Cleveland streetcars]	Morse	CLE-1
History of the Grange movement	McCabe	HT-18
A history [Kansas Central]	Crimmons	CO-284
History [Louisville & Nashville]	Klein	CO-161
History [Niagara, St. Catharines & Toronto]	Mills	CAN-38
The history [railway emergency boards	Schurman	EM-1
A history of Perry County railroads	Chandler	PE-2
History [railroads and canals]	Poor	HT-19
A history [transportation in Canada]	de Glazebrook	CAN-17
A history of transportation [east. Cotton Belt]	Phillips	HT-20
A history of travel	Dunbar	HT-34
History [Union Pacific]	Trottman	CO-281
Historic Alpine Tunnel	Helmers	TU-2
Historic cars [Seashore Museum]	Cummings	CO-246, 247
Historical sketches	Schultz	HT-17
HO primer	Westcott	MOG-5
The HO railroad that grows	Westcott	MOC-1
Holding [company ownership RR securities]	Berger	F-9
Hoot, toot & whistle	Carman	CO-136
Horny Toad man	Dils	NM-2

From horse trails to steel rails	Wardwell	NED-3
Hours of service act	House	L-25
Hours of service	Senate	EMP-1
The how and why wonder book	Scharff	JLG-1
How to build [model]	McClintock	MOC-2
How to build [model]	Yates	MOC-4
How to wire [model]	Westcott	MOC-5
How they travelled in Engine whistles		JLT-10
How we built [Union Pacific]	Dodge	CO-279, 280
The human side of railroading	Corliss	EMP-2
Henry Huntington [Pacific Electric]	Crump	BIO-5

I

I want to be a train engineer	Greene	JLR-2
ICC employee boards	House	ICC-17
ICC practice and procedure	Anderson	ICC-4
I'll take the train	Liddell	CAN-3
The Illinois Central RR [colonization]	Gates	CO-141
The Illinois Central heritage	Johnston	CO-138
Illinois Central Railroad Co.	Richardson	CO-139
Illinois Central Railroad	Sunderland	CO-143
Illinois Terminal RR Co.	Johnston	CO-144
The illustrated true book [RRs]	Webb	RA-12
The impending breakthrough in trans.	Palmer	NJ-2
Implementation requirements [urban trans.]		TSE-2
Import traffic [Chicago]	Draine	TRF-6
Improved guidance [relocating railroad facilities]		GO-7
Improved methods [track constr.]	U.N.	TK-2
Improvements in [budget presentation]		CO-4
In pursuit of the General	Pittenger	CO-56
Income tax exemption [employees']	House	T-1
Indexes [rates]	ICC	RAT-18, 19
Index of the Valuation reports	Rice	F-20
Indiana's abandoned RRs	Sulzer	IA-3
Industrial potentialities [Wabash R. Valley]	Longini	IA-4
Inland Empire	Fahey	BIO-2
Inside railroading	AAR	R-1
Integral train systems	Kneiling	OP-4
Interagency rate adj.	Bukovsky	RAT-17
Interborough Rapid Transit	IRT	CO-146
The intercity electric railway [Canada]	Due	CAN-19
Intercity passenger miles	ICC	STA-6
Interdisciplinary research		TSE-3
Intergovernmental responsibilities [mass trans.]		TSG-5
Interim report [Virginia]		VA-6
An international exhibition [aluminum stock]		CAR-8
International locomotives	Le Fleming	LG-6
Intermountain RRs	Beal	MT-1
International ropeway review		C-10
The interpretation [tariffs]	Starr	RAT-12
Interpretations [National Med. Bd.]		L-22
Interpretations system of accounts	ICC	ACT-4
Interstate Comm. Comm. jurisdiction [fin. statem.]	Andersen	ICC-6
The Interstate Comm. Comm.	Scharfman	ICC-5
The Interstate Comm. Comm. Act	ICC	ICC-28
Interstate Comm. Comm. activities	ICC	ICC-29
Interstate Comm. Comm. operations [safety]	House	S-5, S-6
The interurban era	Middleton	STR-6
Interurbans magazine		EL-6
Interurbans to the loop	Olmsted	EL-7
Intro. [loco. safety truck]	White	LG-7

Investment in transportation	Harrison	F-10
Iowa [assessments]		IO-1
The Iowa pool	Grodinsky	COMP-5
The iron horse	Comstock	LS-18
The iron horse	Kelley	JLL-5
Iron horse to diesel	Snow	JLL-3
Iron horses [men who rode]	McCall	JLL-4
Iron horses of the Santa Fe Trail	Worley	CO-15
Iron horses to Promontory	Best	HT-21
Iron ponies	Lionel	MOT-4
Iron road to empire	Hayes.	CO-77
It was never easy, 1908-1958	Greening	CAN-6

J

Jane's world railways, 1970-71		H-1
The Japanese National Railway	N.J.	HI-8
Journey to Amtrack	Edmonson	AM-2
Journey to work		NY(C)-4
Journey-to-work	N.Y.	NY(M)-3
Journey-to-work	Tri-State	TTC-1
Judicial review of ICC orders	Senate	ICC-18

K

Kansas City and the RR	Glaab	K-2
Kansas West	Anderson	CO-95
"Katy,"	Fraser	CO-175
The Katy Railroad	Masterman	CO-174
Minor C. Keith	Hatch	CIO-7
Kendall & Eldred	Stout	CO-150
Krauss-Maffei [manual]	Old Line	CO-151

L

Labor relation [New York transit]	McGinley	NY(C)-2
The Lackawanna story	Casey	CO-88
The Lackawanna	White	CO-89
The Lake Superior iron ore RRs	Dorin	MID-1
The last broad gauge	Brown	CAN-20
The last of steam	Collias	LS-19
Last of the 3-foot loggers	Krieg	CO-307
Late history [Ann Arbor ferries]	Frederickson	CO-9
The lateral distribution of loading bridges	Sanders	BRI-2
Law and locomotives	Hunt	LAW-7
Laws [Oregon]	Flagg	OR-1
Laying panel track [Morenci]	Lawson	MIN-2
Least-weight proportions [bridge]	Waling	BRI-1
Legal opinions	RR Ret. Bd.	RET-5
Let's go [build the first transcontinental]	Rosenfield	JLH-4
Let's go to a freight yard	Rosenfield	JLO-3
Let's look ahead	Transportation Facts	FUT-2
Let's look at trains	Carter	JLT-11
Let's operate a railroad	Roxbury	OP-5
Lettering guide [Colorado narrow gauge]	Cohen	COL-8
Library serv. for commuting students	Gocek	COMM-4
The life and decline [RR]	Stover	RA-14
Life and times [Central Pac.]	Myrick	CO-54
Life on a locomotive	Williams	LO-1
Life in a railway factory	Williams	EMP-3
The life of George Stephenson	Smiles	BIO-20
Lima locomotives, 1911 catalog	Golden West	CO-152
Lines West	Wood	CO-129
List of maps	AAR	MAP-2

A list of postage stamps	Cornish	CAT-1
List [typical RR occupations]	ICC	EMP-15
Little engines and big men	Lathrop	COL-9
Little railways of the world	Shaw	N-1
Abraham Lincoln [Illinois Central]	Sunderland	BIO-8
Lincoln's RR man [Haupt]	Lord	BIO-4
L&N	Tilford	CO-162
Loan guaranty authority [ICC]	Senate	F-11, IU-19
Local RR promotion in Kansas City	Glaab	K-3
Loco 1, the diesel	Carstens	LD-12
Locomotives and cars since 1900	Lucas	LG-8
A locomotive engineer's album	Abdill	LO-2
The Locomotive engineer		LG-11
The locomotive engineer	Richardson	LAW-3
Locomotive 4501	Morgan	LS-20
Locomotives in our lives	Pennoyer	JLL-6
Locomotives [Dickson Mfg. co.]	Best	CO-104
Locomotives of the empire builder	Martin	CO-131
Locomotives of the Pennsylvania RR	Warner	CO-218
Locomotives of the Reading	Pennypacker	CO-236
Locomotives of the Southern Pacific	Best	CO-265
The locomotives that Baldwin built	Westing	CO-25
Locomotive, trolley, and rail car bldrs.	Arnold	BU-1
Logging along the Denver & Rio Grande	Chappell	CO-07
Logging railroads of the west	Adams	LOG-2
Long Eye and the iron horse	Wood	JLR-3
Long Island journey-to-work report	N.Y.	NY-10
Long Island RR 1914 map	Camelback	CO-155
A long look at steam	Olmsted	LS-21
The lore of the train	Ellis	TRN-2
Uriah Lott	Allhands	BIO-10
Louisiana [street rys.]	Hennick	LOU-2
Louisiana's transportation revolution	Reed	LOU-3
Louisville & Nashville steam	Prince	CO-163
Louisville & Nashville steam	Prince	CO-164

Mc

McKeen Car scrapbook	Old Line	CO-167

M

Mack railcars	Old Line	CO-168
Maine two-footers	Moody	M-1
Mail by rail	Long	RAP-3
Main Line of Mid-America	Corliss	CO-137
Mail line to oblivion	Carson	NY-2
The mainliner program [mail carrier]	Macomber	RAP-2
Maintenance of way employment	Haber	EMP-16
Making [freight rates]	Wilson	RAT-20
Making your model railroad	Hertz	MOC-6
Man-hours expended [freight cars]	ICC	STA-5
Manitoba's submissions [rates]		CAN-29
Manitou Beach trolley days	Gordon	C-128
Manpower utilization	Horowitz	RU-2
Mansions on rails	Beebe	CAR-20
Manual of practice	Anderson	ICC-7
Map [transport Co.]	Milwaukee and Suburban	CO-169
Map [North Carolina]	N.C.	NOC-3
A map [New York]	N.Y.	NY-1
Map of the West	CB&Q	CO-65
The market structure [West Va.]	Clark	WEV-1
Mary takes a trip	Long Filmslide	TRN-3

Maryland's influence [land cessions]	Adams.	CO-34
Mass transportation act of 1960	Senate	TSU-28
A mass transport integral	Metropolitan Planning	WDT-5
Mass transportation in Massachusets	Maloney	MAS-1
Mass transportation−1970	Senate	TSU-6
Mass transportation 1969	Senate	TSU-9
Mass transit study	[Parson, etc.]	FLA-3
Mass transportation survey [Planning Comm.]	De Leuw, etc.	WDT-6
Mass transportation survey.	Smith	TSU-1
Mathematical physics and selected papers	Herapath	ENG-2
The measurement [unionization on wages]	Lurie	L-27
Mechanical refrigerator car equipment	Rodgers	CAR-11
Memories of [Pullman porter]	Turner	POR-1
Men, cities, and transportation	Chase	NED-1
Men of vision	DeButts	CO-256
Merchants, farmers & railroads	Benson	LAW-10
Merger in a regulated industry	House	CO-165
Message from the President [Panama Railroad]		PAN-2
Methods [trip destinations]	Sato	CH-3
The methods of [RRs promoting development]	Scott	EC-4
Methods [rate indexes]	Reese	RAT-21
Metro	Washington Metro Study	WDT-7
Metropolitan area pilot [study]	Day	WDT-8
Metropolitan mass transportation	House	TSU-26, 27
Metropolitan rapid transit financing	Port Authority	NY(M)-4
Metropolitan transportation	Lazarus	TSG-6
Metropolitan transportation politics [N.Y.]	Doig	NY(M)-5
The metropolitan transportation problem	Owens	PR-3
Mexican narrow gauge	Best	MEX-3
Midwest High Speed [Transit]		HI-9
Mile-high trolleys	Jones	D-1
Mileposts on the prairie	Donovan	CO-170
Military railway service	Army	MIL-1
Milwaukee Road freight cars	Martin	CO-70
Milwaukee Road locotives	Martin	CO-72
Milwaukee Road West	Wood	CO-69
From mine to market	Lambie	CO-200
Mine transportation	Pierce	LM-2
Minisink Valley express	Best	NY-3, CO-172
The Missabe Road	King	CO-105
Missouri [map]		MIS-2
Mixed train daily	Beebe	SHO-4
Modern railroad structures	Disney	ENG-3
The model railroad book	Morgan	MOG-6
Model railroader cyclopedia	Westcott	MOE-2
The Model railroader cyclopedia	Kalmbach	MOE-3
Model railroad handbook	Kalmbach	MOH-4
Model railroad track and layout	Kalmbach	MTL-1
Model railroading	Lionel	MOT-5
Model railroading	Trend	MOC-7
Model railroading	Zarchy	MOG-7
Model railroading	Lionel	MOT-6
The model railway encyclopaedia	Carter	MOE-4
The Moffat Road	Bollinger	CO-92
Moguls and iron men	McCague	HT-22
Monorails	Harvey	JLG-2
Monorails	Botzow	MO-1
The Moreleys	Cleaveland	BIO-12
Montana freight rates	Senate	MON-2
Montana [grade crossing]	Mont. Hwy. Comm.	MON-3
More unusual railways	Day	RA-15

Morristown and Erie	Taber	CO-173
Motive power [Union Pacific]	Kratville	CO-294
Mount Washington Railway	Teague	CO-180
The move toward railroad mergers	Keyserling	ME-1
My little library	Andes	JLG-3
My railroad saga	Tigrett	CO-133
The myth of a progressive reform	Caine	WIS-1

N

N scale [track plans]	Larson	MTL-6
Names and nicknames [freight trains]	AAR	TRN-4
Narrow gauge in a kingdom	Conde	CO-135
Narrow gauge in the Rockies	Beebe	N-3
Narrow gauge nostalgia	Turner	N-2
Narrow gauge to the redwoods	Dickinson	CO-201
Narrow gauge to Silverton	Hungerford	CO-100, 101
Narrow gauge railways in America	Hardy	N-4
Nashville, Chattanooga and St. Louis	Prince	CO-182
National Capital transit development	Senate	WDT-31
National Capital transportation act of 1960		WDT-32
National Capital Transportation Authority		WDT-34
The national dream	Berton	CAN-21
National freight car shortage	House	CAR-25
National freight car supply	Senate	CAR-28
Passbook for civil service examinations (series)	National Learning	EMP-19
National Model RR Assoc.	Directory	MOH-5
Nationalization of railways	Richardson	BI-5
National Railway Historical Society		NB-1
The national, regional, and metropolitan relationships [Tulsa expressway]	Sadler	OK-1
National survey of public opinion		PU-1
NCTA technical report		WDT-9
Nebraska C.B. & Q. depots	Rapp	ST-3
The Negro in the urban transit industry	Jeffress	TSG-7
NEMA standards publications		LE-1
Nevada County Narrow Gauge	Best	CO-184
Nevada Northern	Allen	CO-185
A new and dynamic concept for growth	Evans	CO-225
The New England railroads	Lindahl	NED-2
The New Haven Railroad	Weller	CO-198
New Haven [station and line improvements]	Tone	CO-195
New ideas in railroad modeling	Mourning	MTL-5
The New Jersey short line railroads	Johnston	NJ-3
New loose-leaf atlas	LaSalle	TRE-7
New Mexico's railroads	Myrick	NM-1
New Mexico and the Santa Fe	Gurley	CO-17
New Orleans and the railroads	Reed	HT-24
New roads to adventure in model railroading	Hertz	MOG-8
New shares for old	Masson	CO-38
New tracks in North America	Bell	SUR-1
New York Central cars	Wayner	CO-189
The Nickel Plate Road	White	CO-187
Nickle Plate Road		CO-188
Night train	Duke	PI-5
1971 railway labor-management dispute	House	L-12
1966 thru 1972 steam passenger service directory		PAS-4
1925 Shay locomotive catalog	Old Line	LS-22
The Norris locomotives	Dewhurst	LS-23
The North Arkansas line	Fair	CO-176
North Dakota	McGill-Warner	NOD-1
North Shore	Middleton	CO-73

The Northern Indiana Railway	Bradley	CO-202
Northern Ohio Traction revisited	Blower	CO-203
The Northern Pacific Railroad	Cooke	CO-205
The Northern railroads in the Civil War	Webber	WA-1
The Northwestern Pacific Railroad	Stindt	CO-207
The NOT&L story	Blower	CO-204

O

Obsolescence [tax assessments]	Thatcher	T-2
Obstacles to railroad unification	Sampson	ME-3
O & C counties		LA-2
The O & C lands	Basler	LA-1
The Official list [ticket agents]		GU-4
Official map, Chicago Terminal District		CH-9
Official map of Montana	McGill-Warner	MON-1
Ohio trolleys	Morse	O-3
Oil lamps and iron ponies	Shaw	CAN-22
On the "White Pass" payroll	Graves	CO-308
100 years of railroad cars	Lucas	CAR-6
Open throttle	Fenner	STO-7
Operating manual for model railroaders	Kalmbach	MOO-1
Operation [steam locomotives]	Army	MIL-2
Operation and maintenance [diesel-electric]	Army	LD-13
Operation of railroad yards	Roxbury	Y-1
Opinions and orders [Nevada]		NE-1
Organization and operation of railroads	Army	RA-16
Organization for transp. [national capital]	Congress	WDT-10
Oregon and California railroad grant lands	Senate	LA-3
Oregon rail and water [trends]	Sampson	TRF-8
Origin-destination survey		COMM-5
The Original 1879 Car-builder's Dictionary		CAR-5
Our GM scrapbook	Kalmbach	CO-123
Outloading of diesel locomotives	Army	LD-14
Outlook for the railroads	Tyler	EC-5
Over the hills to Woodstock	Mead	CO-310
Over the railroad air waves	Missouri Pacific	COM-1
Over the rails by steam	Thurlow	STE-2
The Overland Limited	Beebe	CO-287
O & W	Helmer	CO-199

P

Pacific coast Shay	Ranger	LS-24
Pacific Electric	Duke	CO-209
Pacific Electric's big red cars	Long	CO-210
Pacific Great Eastern Railway		CO-211
Pacific railways and nationalism	Irwin	PAC-1
Pacific slope railroads	Abdill	PI-6
The Pacific tourist	Shearer	CO-52
General Wm. Jackson Palmer	McCarthy	BIO-13
Park 'n ride rail service	Tri-State	COMM-7
Passenger terminals and trains	Droege	TER-1
Passenger train abandonment	House	PAS-7
Passenger train discontinuance	House	PAS-6
Passenger train discontinuances	Senate	PAS-10, 24
Passenger train service	Senate	PAS-11
Passenger train service	House	PAS-13, 15, 18
Passenger train service	Senate	PAS-16
Passenger transport annual		TSR-1
Pattern of distribution [fruits and vegetables]	Reeves	TRF-9
Payment for improvements, Red Rock Reservoir	Senate	LA-4
PCC cars of Boston	Anderson	BO-2

PCC cars of North America	Cox	STR-7
Penn Central investigation report	N.J.	CO-214
Pennsy, A to T	Carleton	CO-220
Pennsy car plans	Wayner	CO-216
Pennsy power	Staufer	CO-219
Pennsylvania Railroad	Brooks	CO-215
Pennsylvania RR K-4s	Golden West	CO-217
Percent of empty to loaded freight car-miles	ICC	STA-11
"Percent variable" study	Hansbury	COS-3
Perhaps I'll be a railroad man	Bethers	JLR-4
PCE, railway to the north	Ramsey	CAN-34
A pictorial catalog [steam locomotive]	Long	LS-25
A picture history of B & O motive power	Sagle	CO-31
The pictorial history of electric locomotives	Haut	LE-2
A pictorial history [W, B & A Electric RR]	Wagner	CO-301
Piggyback transportation [Northwest]	Bouser	FT-9
The Pike's Peak Cog Road	Abbott	CO-222
Pine across the mountain	Hanft	CO-166
Pino Grande	Polkinghorn	CO-224
The "Pioneer"	White	LS-26
Pioneer locomotives	Brown	LS-27
Pioneer railroads	Bowman	HT-25
Pioneer railways of central Ontario	Michaud	CAN-35
Pioneering the Union Pacific	Ames	CO-274
Pittsburg, Shawmut & Northern	Pietrak	HT-37
Plan for the Long Island Railroad		CO-159
Plan of reorganization	Long Island Transit Auth.	CO-158
Pocket guide to American locomotives	Lucas	LG-9
The politics of railroad coordination	Latham	ME-2
Policy formation in railroad finance	O'Neil	F-15
Henry Varnum Poor	Chandler	BIO-14
Popular picture and plan book	Lucas	LG-10
Port differential rates	Weiss	RAT-22
Port of New York Authority	House	NY(P)-2
Potential savings [railway post offices]	Comptroller General	RAP-4
Practical covers [crossties]	Huffman	TI-3
Practical guide to model railroading	Westcott	MOH-6
Practice and procedure [rate-making assoc.]	Lowe	RAT-23
Preliminary abstract [railway statistics]	ICC	STA-7
Preliminary [report metro. transportation]		WDT-11
Preliminary inventory [cartographic records—Secretary of the Interior]	Kelsay	MAP-7
Preliminary inventory [Comm. of RR]	Johnson	GO-8
Preliminary inventory	U.S. Nat'l Arch.	BI-6
Preliminary inventory [Dept. of Transport]	Ottawa	CAN-12
Preliminary report [BART]		SA-9
Preservation of competitive through trail routes	Senate	COMP-6
Principles of inland transportation	Dagget	LAW-11
Principles of urban transportation	Mossman	TSG-8
Prize model railroad layouts	Kalm bach	MTL-4
Problem Boston's Transit	Deem	BO-3
Problem areas [railroad retirement]		RET-6
Problems of the railroads	Boston College	COMM-8
Problems of the railroads	Senate	PR-5, 7
Proceedings	Ry. Sy. & Mgt. Assos.	MA-3
A productive monopoly	Taylor	COMP-7
Productivity, supervision, and morale	Katz	PRO-1
Profiles of American railroading	GEC	R-4
Progress report [roadbeds and embankments]	U. of Ill.	RI-1
Progress reports [rails and joint bars]	U. of Ill.	TK-3
Property atlas [Main Line, Penna.]	Franklin	PH-3

Proposal [Superail transit]	Bingham	MO-2
Proposed legislation [L. I. Transit Auth.]		CO-160
The pros and cons [compulsory arbitration]		L-8
Prospects [railfreight statistics as a mktg. tool]	McPhee	MA-2
Prospectus [Tri-State Trans. Comm.]		TTC-2
Protection [shipments of fruits and vegetables]	Redit	FT-10
Public assistance [D.C. Transit]	Senate	WDT-21
Public Service Commission laws of Indiana	Stuckey	IA-5
Public transit	Cincinnati	CI-2
Public transportation in Detroit	Dahlheimer	STR-8
Public transportation [District of Columbia]	Senate	WDT-37
George M. Pullman, 1831-1897	Harding	BIO-15
Pullman	Buder	CO-232
The Pullman boycott of 1894	Warne	CO-231
Pullman Company [instruction book]	Old Line	CO-230
Mr. Pullman's elegant palace car	Beebe	CO-226
The Pullman scrapbook	Wayner	CO-227
Pullman private car service of 1939	Wayner	CO-228
The Pullman strike	Stein	L-9

Q

Quest for crisis	Sites	AN-1
Questions and answers [RR Ret.]		RET-2
Question and answer [operating rules]	Army	MIL-3
A quick review [East Broad Top]	Mannix	CO-108
Quiz, Jr.	AAR	JLG-4

R

Rail Book Bibliography	Specialty	BI-7
Rail carload cost scales	ICC	COS-4
Rail freight [Tri-State region]	Bick	TTG-3
Rail merger legislation	Senate	ME-7
Rail passenger service act of 1970	Senate	PAS-17
Rail rapid transit [National Capital]	Senate	WDT-27
Rail-water rate adjustments	Bukovsky	RAT-24
Rail rapid transit [National Capital]	Senate	WDT-26
Rail transport and the winning of wars	Van Fleet	WA-2
Rail and water routes	Johnson	RAT-25
The Railfan		PER-3
Railroad accounting and statistics	Edward H. Bunnell	ACT-5
Railroad accounting procedures	House	ACT-6
Railroad accounting procedures	House	ACT-7
Railroad album	O'Connell	RA-20
The railroad and the space program	Maxlish	DEV-4
Railroad avenue	Hubbard	STO-8
Railroad books checklist	Ladd	BI-8
The railroad caboose	Knapke	CAR-10
Railroad capitalization	Ronright	F-4
Railroad car shortage	House	CAR-35
Railroad coal leases	GPO	LA-5
Railroad consolidations and the public interest	ICC	ME-5
Railfoad consolidation [Transportation Act of 1920]	Leonard	ME-4
Railroad decisions [ICC]	Bishop	LAW-6
Railroad employees' benefits		EMP-4
Railroad engineering	Hay	ENG-4
Railroad equipment financing	Street	F-6
Railroad freight classification	Randolph	CL-1, 2
Railroad freight rate indexes [farm]	Smith	RAT-13
Railroad freight tariffs	Baxter	RAT-14
Railroad financial modifications	Chamberlin	F-8
Railroads and the Granger laws	Miller	LAW-5

Railroad industry overview—1971	Senate	RA-13
Railroad-labor dispute	Kennedy	L-3
Railroad labor-management dispute	House	L-14
Railroads, lands and politics	Desker	LA-7
Railroad land grants		LA-6
Railroad leaders, 1845-1890	Cochran	CIO-16
Railroad map [Oklahoma]	Oklahoma	OK-2
Railroad map [United States]	Army	MAP-3, 6
Railroad materials and facilities research	AST&M	RES-1
Railroad men	Kalisher	BIO-17
Railroad mergers and abandonments	Conant	ME-6
Railroad mergers [economy of New England]	Nelson	ME-8
The railroad monopoly	Shott	COMP-9
Railway operating and signaling techniques		SI-5
The railroad passenger car	Mencken	CAR-21
The railroad passenger deficit		PAS-1
Railroad passenger [costs]	Berge	PAS-2
Railroad passenger train	House	PAS-8
The railroad police	Dewhurst	POL-1
Railroad problems	House	PR-6
The railroad question	Larrabee	PR-4
Railroad rates [Alaska]	Senate	RAT-29
Railroad reading rooms [Ohio]	Richie	O-4
Railroad reorganization	Daggett	RE-1
Railroad retirement act amendments	House	RET-23
Railroad retirement amendments	Senate	RET-13
Railroad retirement act	Senate	RET-18
The railroad retirement and unemployment	RR Ret. Bd.	RET-9
Railroad retirement and unemployment	GPO	RET-1
Railroad retirement annuity increase—1971	Senate	RET-11
Railroad retirement benefits	Senate	RET-21
Railroad retirement benefit increase—1971	House	RET-12
Railroad retirement [increase]	House	RET-14
Railroad retirement reporter		RET-8
Railroad retirement [annuities]	Senate	RET-16
Railroad retirement [annuities]	House	RET-17
Railroad safety	Senate	S-8
The railroad scene	Middleton	PI-7
Railroad shipments [Northwest]	Sampson	RAT-32
The railroad station	Meeks	TER-2
Railroad stations of Pennsylvania	Van Trump	TER-3
The railroad story of San Diego County	Phillips	CA-4
Railroad suburban equipment	Tri-State	NY(M)-7
Railroad terminal strategy		TER-4
The railroad that died at sea	Parks	CO-116
The railroad that lighted Southern California	Johnston	CO-251
The railroad that ran with the tide	Feagans	CO-145
Railroad trackage		TK-4
Railroad transportation		FT-11
Railroad transportation		JLT-12
Railroad transportation	Bu. of Ry. Econ.	STA-8
Rail transportation proceedings	ASME	CONG-3
Railroad trends	Parmelee	AN-2
Railroad unemployment insurance act	Senate	L-38
Railroad wages and labor relations, 1900-1952	Jones	EMP-6
Railroad work rules dispute	Senate	RU-3, 4, 5
The Railroad yardmaster		PER-4
Railroading around the world	Farrington	R-2
Railroading the modern way	Farrington	R-3
Railroads	Am. Geo. Soc.	JLG-5
The railroads	Potter	ME-10

The railroads [first big business]	Chandler	RA-17
Railroads and American economic growth	Fogel	EC-6
Railroads and regulation, 1877-1916	Kolkoe	LAW-12
Railroads and the Rockies	Ormes	COL-10
Railroads at work	AAR	JLO-4
Railroads down the valleys	Mills	SHO-5
Railroads in defense and war	Richardson	BI-10
Railroads in the days of steam	McCready	JLL-7
Railroads in the U.S.A.	ECC	RA-22
Railroads in the U.S.A.	ECC	RA-23
Railroads in the woods	Labbe	PI-8
Railroads, land and iron	Morgan	BIO-11
The railroads of America	Armitage	RA-21
Railroads of the Black Hills	Fielder	SOU(D)-1
The railroads of the Confederacy	Black	HT-26
Railroads of the hour	Farrington	HT-27
Railroads of Nevada and eastern California	Myrick	WE-3
Railroads of New York	Pierce	NY-7
Railroads of New York	O'Conner	NY-8
The railroads of Pennsylvania	Saylor	PE-1
The railroads of the South, 1865-1900	Stover	Sou-2
Railroads to the Rio	Allhands	SOU(W)-2
Railroads, today and yesterday	Beuhr	JLG-6
Railroads, Tri-State	NY(M)-6	NY(M)-6
Rails across the continent	Johnson	HT-28
Rails across the midlands	Cook	PI-9
Rails across Panama	Schott	PAN-1
Rails around Gold Hill	Calfy	COL-11
Rails from the West	Hinckley	BIO-6
Rails, mines, and progress	Pletcher	MEX-4
Rails, sage brush, and pine	Ferrell	CO-268
Rails that climb	Stedman	CO-102
Rails through Dixie	Krause	PI-10
Rails to the North Star	Prosser	MINN-1
Rails west	Abdill	PI-11
Railway and transit equipment, 1940-45	McColley	WA-4
Railway Association [Special Agents and Police]		POL-2, 3
Railway conductors	Robbins	CON-1
Railway developments in Maine	Corliss	M-2
Railway economy	Lardner	EC-7
Railway freight traffic		CAN-42
The railway [grade crossing problem]	Beggs	CR-2
Railways [years of pre-eminence, 1905-1919]	Nock	RA-18
The railway interrelations [U.S.] and Canada]	Wilgus	CAN-23
Railway labor act amendments	House	L-33
Railway labor-management negotiations	Senate	L-10
Railway labor-management dispute	Senate	L-13
Railway [clearances and car dimensions]		OP-6
Railway monopoly and rate regulation	McFall	COMP-8
Railway motive power	Webster	LG-13
Railway operating rules	Army	OP-7
Railway operating statistics		CAN-11
Railway operating statistics	ICC	STA-9
Railway passenger lists of overland trains	Rasmussen	TRN-5
Railway pension plans		EMP-5
Railway progress		PER-5
Railway revenue freight loadings		CAN-43
Railway shopcraft dispute	Senate	L-16
Railway statistical manual	AAR	STA-2
Railway supply industry yearbook	Simmons-Boardman	MAN-2
Railway to the moon	Kidder	CO-179

Railways	AAR	RA-24
Railways: a readers guide	Bryant	BI-9
The railways of Canada for 1870-1	Trout	CAN-31
Railways in the cinema	Huntley	MP-00
The railways of Mexico	McNeely	MEX-5
Railways the world over	Allen	RA-19
A ramble into the past [East Broad Top]	Kyper	CO-107
Rand McNally handy railroad atlas		MAP-5
Rand, McNally & Co.'s [New Hampshire]		NH-1
Rand McNally's pioneer atlas [West]		MAP-4
Rapid rail transit [Nation's Capital]	House	WDT-25
Rapid transit Boston	Clarke	BO-4
Rapid transit in Canada	Boorse	CAN-4
Rapid transit [six metropolitan areas]	Gottfeld	TSR-2
Ratios [empty to loaded car-miles]	ICC	STA-3
Rates or return	Miller	F-16
Read aloud train stories	Seiden	JLT-13
The real book about trains	Elting	JLT-14
Reading steam pictorial	Carleton	CO-235
The Reading's heritage	Fisher	CO-234
The real book about trains	Cole	TRN-6
Reasonable freight rates	Shinn	RAT-15
Rebel of the Rockies	Athearn	CO-93
Recommendations [rail passenger service]	Pa.	PE-3
Recommended [transit plan]	Mass.	MAS-2
Recorded depreciation and amortization	ICC	F-5
Redwoods, Iron Horses, and the Pacific	Crump	CO-45
Redwood railways	Kneiss	CA-5
Reestablishing the link	Sloan	COMM-9
A reference guide to metropolitan transportation	Northwestern U.	TSP-2
Reference list [writings Charles Sherrington]	Cullen	BIO-21
Regional rapid transit [S.F.]	Parsons	SA-6
Reign of the rabble	Burbank	STRI-3
Regulated property	Stuart	T-3
Regulation of Alaska Railroad	Senate	CO-6
The regulation [rail-motor rate]	Williams	RAT-26
The regulation [rail-motor rate]	Williams	COMP-10
Regulation of railroads	Denniston	LAW-13
Regulation of track motorcars	Senate	MR-1
Regulation of transport innovation	MacAvoy	ICC-8
Tegulations 114	IRS	T-4
Reorganization plan (ICC)	Senate	ICC-20
Reorganization plan [locomotive inspection]	House	LS-28
Repeal ["round-trip" mail pay]	Senate	RAP-8
Report	AAR	RES-3
Report [High Speed Rail Transit Commission]	Illinois	HI-7
Report	Car Service Div., AAR	CAR-9
Report [N.Y. Central and New Haven commuter]		COMM-10
Report [New York transit]		NY(C)-5
Report [San Francisco Bay]		SA-8
Report	N.Y.-N.J.Trans. Agcy.	NY(M)-8
Report [commuter service]	Mass. Bay T.A.	BO-5
Report on N.J. Assembly bill No. 692	Jones	NJ-6
Report [Railroad Insurance Rating Bureau]	Cardi	I(N)-1
Report [financial aspects S.F. transit]	Allen	SA-7
Report [District of Columbia]		WDT-12
Report [utilizing Old Colony Line]	Mass.	MAS-3
Report of accidents	Calif. P.U.C.	CA-6
Report [financial condition N.Y. railroads]		NY-12
Report [National Transport Association]		RAP-5
Report [Presidential Railroad Commission]		L-28

Report [tax and relief commuter railroads]	Mass.	MAS-4
Report [employment of firemen]	Ottawa	CAN-8
Report [ski lift and tramway safety]	Mass.	S-10
Report [zone fares]	Mass.	TSG-9
Report	Task Force RR Safety	S-9
Report	Tenn. Publ. Svce. Comm.	TEN-2
Report	AAR, Commun. Sec.	COM-2
Report to RFC ½Baltimore & Ohio]	Smith	CO-32
Report [Old Colony Area]	De Leuw	MAS-5
Report [National Capital]		WDT-16
Report [Washington Transit Comm.]		WDT-17
Restriction of output [RR unions]	Wood	PRO-2
Return of subpoenas, Port of N.Y. Auth. inquiry	House	NY(P)-3
Revenue-cost relationships	Dodge	RAT-9
A review [freight rates South Dakota]		SOU(D)-2
Review [railway post office requirements]	Comptroller General	RAP-6
Review of ICC policies and practices	Senate	ICC-21
Review [Emergency rail services act of 1970	House	SE-3
Review of the Penn Central condition	Senate	CO-213
The revision [transit fare structure]	Vickrey	NY(C)-6
RFC loans [Baltimore & Ohio]	Senate	CO-33
Richard learns about railroading	Braude	JLO-5
Ride the big red cars	Crump	CO-208A
Ride down memory lane	Stevens	MU-1
Rio Grande	Beebe	CO-94
The Rio Grande pictorial	Sundance	CO-98
The Rio Grande Southern story	Crum	CO-237
Rip Van Winkle railroads	Helmer	NY-4
Rights of railroad workers	Robb	L-21
Rights of trains	Josserand	DIS-1, 2
Road movement of trains	Roxbury	TRN-7
The road to Paradise	Moedinger	CO-266, 267
The robber barons	Josephson	BIO-18
The robber barons revisted	Jones	BIO-19
Rochester Transit work stoppage		ROC-1
Route location and design	Hickerson	SUR-2
Route surveying and design	Meyer	SUR-3
The Royal Blue line	Gordon	NY-5
RPM	Cascio	GU-5
RRB-SSA financial interchange		RET-7
Rules for construction [boilers]	ASME	LS-29
Rules governing [classification of employees]	ICC	EMP-8
Rules governing [expenses]	ICC	ACT-8
Rules [freight classification]	Randolph	RAT-16
Rules, standards, and instructions [automatic block signal]	ICC	SI-6
The run of the Twentieth Century	Wayner	CO-193
The Rutland Road	Shaughnessy	CO-238

S

Safe railroader		PER-6
Safety regulation [track motorcars]	Senate	S-7
The St. John's Railroad	Bathe	CO-240
The St. Joseph Valley Railway	Galloway	CO-241
Saint Louis cable railways	Elect. Ry. Hist. Soc.	C-11
San Francisco's golden era	Beebe	SA-2
San Francisco Grip	Perini	C-12
The Sandley story	Rooksby	CO-243
Santa Fe	Duke	CO-12
Santa Fe	Marshall	CO-14
Santa Fe Passenger [consists 1937]	Wayner	CO-18

Scale model railroading	White	MOG-9
Scenery for model railroads	McClanahan	MOC-8, 9
Scenes from the Shore Lines	Olmsted	CO-74
Seaboard Air Line Railway	Prince	CO-244
Seattle monorail	Wash. (State) U.	MO-4
Seattle monorail demonstration study	Alexander	MO-3
Section-by-section [mass trans. act]	Senate	TSU-12
Section-by-section [mass trans. act 1962]	House	TSU-19
Segregation in [railway travel]	Long	PAS-3
A selected bibliography [Port of N.Y. Auth.]		NY(P)-1
Selected elements of value	ICC	F-21
Selected financial and operating statistics	ICC	EL-8
Selected financial and operating statistics	ICC	STA-4
Selected impacts [mergers]	Brandes	ME-9
Selected reading [principal laws]	Assoc. of ICC Pract.	ICC-2
Selected special freight statistics	Ambelang	FT-12
Self-propelled [cars and M.U.s]	Berge	CAR-23
SEPACT III final report		PH-5
Separable suburban costs [New York]	Banks	COS-5
The 7-foot model train book	Rigby	MTL-7
764 helpful hints [model]	Warren	MOG-11
Ships and narrow gauge rails	Best	CO-208
A short haul to the bay	Henwood	CO-181
A short history [railways]	Thompson	HT-29
Short Line to Paradise	Johnston	CO-311
Short line juncion	Wagner	BR-3
Shortage of boxcars [grain]	Senate	CAR-34
Shortline railroads of Arkansas	Hull	ARK-s
Show me the way	Beatty	ANE-2
Sierra railway	Deane	CO-250
Signature reproductions [commissioners]	ICC	ICC-30
The slim princess	Hungerford	CO-265A
Slim rails through the sand	Turner	CO-53
The Silverton train	Hunt	COL-12
Simulation of railroad operations	Ry. Sy. & Mgt. Assoc.	MA-4
Six units to Sycamore	Olmsted	CO-68
Sketch map [central and western]		MID-2
The Skokie Swift		CH-5
Skokie Swift	Buck	CH-4
The Skunk Railroad	Crump	CO-46
Small railroads you can build	Westcott	MOC-10
Smoke across the prairie	Ehernberger	CO-290
Smoke above the plains	Ehernberger	CO-289
Smoke along the Columbia	Ehernberger	CO-291
Smode down the canyons	Ehernberger	CO-288
Smoke over the divide	Ehernberger	CO-292
Snowplow	Best	SN-1
A socio-economic [worders families]	Millican	L-4
Some classic trains	Dubin	TRN-8
Some social aspects [mass transit]	Smith	TSG-10
Some rules of evidence	ICC	ICC-27
South Dakota interstate rail shipments	Van Doren	Sou(D)-3
South Pacific Coast	MacGregor	CO-253
South Shore	Middleton	CO-75
South Side [terminal for Chicago]		CH-10
Southern New Jersey [mass transportation]	Parson	NJ-5
Southern New Jersey [transit]		PH-6
Southern Pacific daylight	Wright	CO-261
Southern Pacific steam locomotives	Duke	CO-263
Southern steam spacials	Ziel	CO-255
Southwestern [rates]	Randolph	RAT-33

Soviet transport experience	Hunter	OP-8
Special railroad freight services	Wilson	FT-13
Specifications [bridges]	Fenton	BRI-3
Spirit of the rails	Brin	STO-9
Standard and special flatcars	Marshall	CAR-13
Standard plans	Army	MIL-4
Standard time	Allen	OP-9
Standards [fire protection]		S-11
The State [investor, and railroad]	Salsbury	CO-37
The station agent's blue book	Kirkpatrick	TER-7
Statistical analysis [N.Y.-Wash. passenger svc.]		STA-1
Statistical report	Iowa	IO-2
Statistics of railroad companies	Washington	WAS-2
Steam and electric locomotives [N.Y. Central]	Edson	CO-191
Steam and trolley days [F, J & G]	Gordon	CO-119
Steam's finest hour	Morgan	LS-34
Steam in the Rockies	Colorado RR Museum	CO-96
Steam in the sixties	Ziel	LS-30
Steam locomotives and boats [Southern]	Prince	CO-257
Steam locomotives and history [Georgia & W.P.]	Prince	CO-125, 305
The steam locomotive in America	Bruce	LS-31
The steam locomotives in 1838	Tredgold	LS-32
Steam locomotives [Burlington]	Corbin	CO-64
Steam on the Sierra	Allen	N-5
Steam power [New York Central system]	Staufer	CO-190
Steam railway employees compensation	Ottawa	CAN-7
Steam, steel & limiteds	Kratville	PI-12
Steam, wide and narrow	Wojtas	LS-33
Steamcars to the Comstock	Beebe	CO-298
Steel gondola and hopper cars	Castles	CAR-14
Steel rails to the sunrise	Ziel	CO-153
Steel rails to victory	Ziel	WA-5
Steel trails to Santa Fe	Waters	CO-13
Steel trails and iron horses	Buchanon	HT-30
Stewardship of the ICC	Senate	ICC-22
Stock cars, refrigerators, and cabooses	Castles	CAR-15
Stories and history [Erie]	Gordon	CO-111
The story of "Labor"	Keating	L-2
The story [Canandaigua Street Railway]	Gordon	CO-47
The story of a mountain railroad	Langsdale	CO-223
The story of the Florida railroads	Pettengill	FLA-2
Stories of the railway	Hibbard	STO-10
The story [Steamtown and Edaville]	Ziel	MU-2
The story of the Virginia Central	Coleman	CO-295
The story of trains	Simmons	JLT-15
The story of the western railroads	Riegel	WE-4
Straddling the Isthmus of Tehuantepec	Glick	MEX-2
Street cars and interurbans of yesterday	Davies	STR-10
Street map [Philadelphia]	PTC	CO-221
The street railway era in Seattle	Blanchard	STR-9
Streetcar suburbs	Warner	BO-6
Strikers, communists, tramps and detectives	Pinderton	HT-31
Strike control proposals	Marsh	L-11
Structural fatigue	Munse	BRI-4
Studies [economics of transportation]	Beckmann	EC-8
Studies [tax problems]	Tenn.	TEN-1
Study [marine lighterage]	Tri-State	NY(M)-2
Study [passenger service]	Senate	PAS-12
A study [grade crossing collisions]	St. Martin	CR-3
Study of railroad motive power	Warren	LG-14
Study of REA Express		CO-233

Study [amortization]	House	T-5
Submissions [on transportation]		CAN-28
Suburban service adjustment [N.Y.C.]	Tri-State	COMM-11
Suburbs to Grand Central		COMM-12
Subversive influence	Senate	EMP-9
Suggestions for books	Cullen	BI-11
Summaries [motor vehicle accidents]		WIS-2
Summary presentation	Pres. Cabinet Comm.	AS-3
Summary [freight station costs]	ICC	COS-6
Summary [freight station costs]	ICC	COS-7
Super power steam locomotives	Cook	LS-35
Super-railroads	Barringer	FUT-4
Surface cars of Boston	Cox	BO-7
Surface cars of Philadelphia	Cox	PH-4
Surface transportation	Senate	ICC-23
Surface transportation [safety]	House	S-12
Survey [Texas Western Railroad]	Gray	CO-260
Survey of [Interstate Commerce Commission]	Wolf	ICC-9
Survey [car shops]	Simmons-Boardman	SH-1
A survey [rate discrimination]	Shearer	RAT-30
A survey [taxation]	Dambrun	T-6
Susquehanna trolleys	Gordon	PE-8
Symposium [diesel maintenance]	Alco	LD-15
Symposiums [materials 9and0 oils]	ASTM	CONG-4
System of accounts [Pullman]	ICC	CO-231
The system of wire-cable railways	Pac. Cable Ry. Co.	C-13
The Switzerland trail of America	Crossen	CO-90

T

Tales of the rails	Hutchinson	STO-11
Taxes [car line companies]		VA-7
Taxes levied and chargeable		T-7
Technical amendments [retirement]	House	RET-22
Technical analysis [rehabilitation of LIRR]	Bingham	CO-157
Technical report	Wash. T.A.	WDT-18
Techniques of transport pricing	Meyer	RAT-4
Technological change and labor	Cottrell	TE-4
Technological change and [future]	Nelson	TE-3
The technology of urban transportation	Berry	TSE-4
Tedrow's regulation of transportation	Tedrow	ICC-10
The telegraphers	Ulriksson	TEL-1
A tentative check-list [Euro. lit.]	Cole	BI-4
Texas railroad map	Dodge	TEX-2
Then came the railroads	Clark	SOU(W)-1
They built the West	Quiett	WE-5
They felled the redwoods	Johnston	LOG-4
Thirty pound rails	Choda	COL-14
36 miles of trouble	Morse	CO-306
This was railroading	Abdill	NW-1
Three little lines	Crum	CO-252, COL-1
Throttling the railroads	Carson	GO-9
Through covered bridges to Concord	Mead	CO-83
Thunder in the mountains	Johnston	LOG-3
The time of the trolley	Middleton	EL-9
The Toledo, Port Clinton and Lakeside	Hilton	CO-271
Tooooot!	La Well	JLT-16
Track design [model]	Carstens	MTL-2
The track going back	DeGolyer	WE-6
Track planning	Armstrong	MTL-3
The trackless trolleys of Boston	Clarke	BO-8
Traction planbook and photo album	Carstens	STR-12

220

Trade cases		ICC-11
Traffic, revenue and operating costs	Gilman	WDT-13
Tragedy at Eden	Helmers	WK-2
Trail of the Zephyrs	Olmsted	CO-62
Train and engine books for children	AAR	JLT-17
Train collectors quarterly		MTL-8
Train discontinuances	Senate	ICC-24
Train wreck	Griswold	WK-3
Train wrecks	Reed	WK-4
Trainman news		PER-7
Trains	Day	TRN-9
Trains	Smith	JLT-21
Trains	Henry	JLT-18, 19
Trains	Scarry	JLT-20
Trains abbum of photographs	Kalmbach	TRN-10
Trains and how to draw them	Hogeboom	TRN-11
Trains at work	Elting	JLT-22, 23
The trains of Lionel's stnadard gauge era	Carstens	MTL-9
Trains [Pennsylvania Dutch country]	Denney	PE-4
Trains rolling	McBride	STO-12
The trains we rode	Beebe	PI-13
Trains work like this	Thomas	JLT-24
Transcontinental railway strategy	Grodinsky	PL-3
Transcript of proceeding [wage increase]		L-23
Transfer values [transit systems]	Wright	PIT-2
Trans-Hudson rapid transit	De Leuw	NY(M)-9
Transit development [National Capital]	House	WDT-28
Transit modernization and street traffic	Bauer	TSP-3
Transit program [National Capital]	House	WDT-29
Transport and economic integration [S. Am.]	Brown	EC-9
Transport and national goals	Haefele	GO-10
Transport input [urban sites]	Marble	TSU-2
Transport investment and [development]	Fromm	PL-4
Transportation	Tryon	HT-32
Transportation		PER-8
Transportation act of 1958	Senate	TT-5
Transportation and traffic management	Knorst	TRF-12
Transportation and logistics education	Cherington	TT-3
Transportation and urban land	Wingo	TSP-4
Transportation demand projection	Lawson	FT-14
The transportation econ. [soybean processing]	Hedlund	EC-10
The transportation frontier	Winther	WE-7
Transportation [National Capital]		WDT-30
Transportation [New York]	Tobin	NY(M)-10
Transportation needs of the poor	Ornati	COMM-13
Transportation of grain [Southwestern	Smith	TRF-11
Transportation plan [National Capital]		WDT-14
Transportation plan [National Capital]	Congress	WDT-33
Transportation planning [urban]	House	WDT-19
Transportation rates [South Dakota]	Poth	SOU(D)-4
Transportation to the Seaboard	Schonberg	TT-4
The Traveling Engineers' association		H-2
Trends and cycles [capital formation	Ulmer	F-18
Trolley car treasury	Rowsome	STR-11
Trolley days in Seattle	Blanchard	CO-248
Trolleys down the Mohawk Valley	Gordon	CO-120
Trolleys of Berks County	Goesig	PE-5
Trolleys of lower Delaware Valley	Schieck	PE-6
Trolley lines of the Empire State	Reifschneider	NY-6
Trolleys of the Pennsylvania Dutch country	Denney	PE-7
Trolley through the countryside	Chandler	K-1

True adventures of railraoders	Morgan	JLR-5
20th Century	Beebe	CO-192
Twenty years [Railway labor act]		L-30
Twenty-five years [social insurance]		RET-10
2750	Webster	LG-15
The twilight of steam locomotives	Ziel	LS-36
Two trains to remember	Beebe	CO-196

U

Uintah Railway	Bender	CO-272
The Ulster & Delaware	Best	CO-273
Uniform system of accounts	ICC	ACT-9
Uniform system of accounts	ICC	ACT-10
Uniform system of accounts	ICC	ACT-11
Uniform system [accounts for persons furnishing cars	ICC	ACT-12
The Union Pacific	Carson [Best]	CO-277
Union Pacific	Hogg	CO-275, 278
Union Pacific in Colorado	LeMassena	CO-286
Union Pacific locomotives	Kratville	CO-293
The Union Pacific Railroad	Fogel	CO-282
Union Pacific railroad	U.P.RR	CO-285
Union Station train accident	Senate	WDC-1
Unnecessary costs [commercial protective service]	Army	US-3
United States. Railroads	U.S. Geol. Surv.	MAP-8
The United States RAilway Mission in Mexico	Linden	MEX-6
United States rugulations [locomotives]	Gibson	LAW-8
United States safety appliances	Gibson	S-13
United Transportation Union		UT-1
Updating the opportunity [trans. planning]	Curry	CH-6
Urban mass transportation	House	TSU-8
Urban mass transportation, 1961	House	TSU-24
Urban mass transportation, 1961	Senate	TSU-24
Urban mass transportation, 1963	Senate	TSU-15

Urban mass transportation, 1962	Senate	TSU-21, 23
Urban loan mass transportation act [1963]	Senate	TSU-11
Urban mass transportation act [1963]	House	TSU-13, 16
Urban mass transportation, 1963	Senate	TSU-17
Urban mass transportation act [1963]	Senate	TSU-14
Urban mass transportation act [1962]	House	TSU-18, 20
Urban mass transportation act [1962]	Senate	TSU-22
Urban mass transportation assistance act [1970]	House	TSU-7
Urban mass transportation assistance act [1969]	House	TSU-10
Urban rail transit	Lang	TSU-3
Urban transit development		TSP-5
Urban transportation dilemma	Paranka	TSU-4
Urban mass transportation [Colorado]		COL-1
Urban transportation [San Francisco]	Zettel	SA-3
The urban transportation problem	Meyer	TSU-5
U.S. [freight car study]		CAR-7
U.S. [locomotive study]		LG-12
U.S. railroads [capacity]	Ullman	MAP-9
U.S. steam locomotive directory	Koenigsberg	LS-37
Use and disposition [grants]	House	LA-8
Use of Cybernetics		RES-2
User-furnished freight cars		CAR-17
Using precast [concrete sets]	Parsons	TU-3
USS trackwork		TK-5

V

Valuation of railroads	Gronouski	T-8
Valuation study [Pottawatomie lands]		CO-19
Value of service	ICC	RAT-10
Victory rode the rails	Turner	WA-6
Henry Villard [Northern Pacific]	Macfarlane	BIO-22
Henry Villard [Northwest]	Hedges	BIO-23
Vintage steam	Roberts	STO-13
Virginia railroads [Civil War]	Johnston	VA-1
Virgina & Truckee	Beebe	CO-296
The Virginian Railway	Reid	CO-199
Voluntary modification [financial structures]	Senate	F-14

W

Wages, earnings, and employment	Fels	CO-183
War materials reparation cases	ICC	RAT-27
The war of the gauges	Palmer	G-1
Washington and northern Idaho	McGill-Warner	WAS-1
Wahsington [Transit Authority]	House	WDT-36
Washington [transit compact]	Senate	WDT-24
Washington [transit problem]	House	WDT-38
Washington [transit]	Senate	WDT-39
Washington [transportation problems]	Congress	WDT-35
Washington [transit compact]	Johnson	WDT-1
Washington [transit compact]	Senate	WDT-40
Waybill analysis		CAN-44
Waybill statistics	ICC	STA-10
We were there [golden spike]	Shepard	JLH-6
The Weeks Mills "Y"	Thurlow	N-6
Wellsville, Addison & Galeton	Lewis	SHO-6
The Western Maryland	Williams	CO-302
Western rail trail	McKillup	CAN-24
Western Pacific	Crump	CO-303
Western Pacific—its first forty years!	Whitman	CO-304
Western railroad mergers	Dept. of Trans.	ME-11
The Western traction quarterly	Pacific Bookwork	PER-9
Western trains	Steinheimer	PI-14
Westward to Promontory	Combs	CO-276
Wheels, wings, and water	Coombs	FT-15
When beauty rode the rails	Beebe	PI-15
When the railroad was king	Elliott	MI-1
When the rails ran west	McCague	JLH-7
Whistle in the night	RKO	TRN-12
Widows' pensions	Senate	RET-20
Will not run Gebruary 22nd	Stinett	ANE-1
With a cinder in my eye	Downing	TRN-13
The wonder book of trains	Carlisle	TRN-14
A work of giants	Griswold	HT-33
Work staggering for traffic relief	Cohen	NY(C)-3
Workin' on the railroad	Reinhardt	STO-14
Working in the shops	AAR	ACT-13
Working on the railroad	Stagner	EMP-10
Working on the tracks	AAR	ACT-14
The world of model trains	Williams	MOG-10
World steam in action	Edmonson	LS-38
The wreck of Old 97	Fox	WK-5
The wreck [Penn Central]	Daughen	CO-212
The WW & F two-footer	Thurlow	N-7

X

"X," symbol [progress]	Spencer	CAR-22

Y

Yearbook of railroad facts 1965–	AAR	RA-25
Yonder comes the train	Phillips	TRN-15
Robert R. Young	Borkin	BIO-24
Your freight trains	Zaffo	JLT-25
Your future in railroading	Goodfellow	EMP-14
Your future in traffic management	Heine	TRF-5
Your world	Pope ·	JLG-7

BIBLIOGRAPHY

Card Catalog—Subjects, Library of Congress, Washington, D.C.
Card Catalog—Authors, Library of Congress, Washington, D.C.
Library of Congress Catalog—Books: Subjects, 1950-1954. Ann Arbor, J. W. Edwards, Inc., 1955.
Library of Congress Catalog—Books: Subjects, 1955-1959. Paterson, N. J., Pageant Books, Inc., 1960.
Library of Congress Catalog—Books: Subjects, 1960-1964. Ann Arbor, J. W. Edwards, Inc., 1965.
Library of Congress Catalog—Books: Subjects, 1965-1969. Ann Arbor, J. W. Edwards, Inc., 1971.
Library of Congress Catalog—Books: Subjects, 1970, Washington, 1971.
Library of Congress Catalog—Books: Subjects, 1971, Washington, 1972.
Library of Congress Catalog—Books: Subjects, 1972 (through June), Washington, 1972.
AMS Press, Inc., 56 E. 13th St., New York, N. Y. 10003.
Arno Press, 330 Madison Ave., New York, N. Y. 10017.
Arco Publishing Co., 219 Park Ave. South, New York, N. Y. l0003.
The Baggage Car, Box 87, Arcade, N. Y. 14009.
Bordertown Publishing, 3491 W. 37th Ave., Vancouver 13, B. C., Canada.
The Brookings Institution, 1775 Massachusetts Ave., N.W., Washington, D. C. 20036.
Camelbach Publishing Co., 37 Edgemere Ave., Mt. Arlington, N. J. 07856
Columbia University Press, 562 W. 113th St., New York, N. Y. 10023
Drake Publsihers, 381 Park Ave., New York, N. Y. 10016
The Eastin-Phelan Corp., 1235 W. 5th St., Davenport, Iowa 52808
Empire State Railroad Museum, Box 666, Middletown, N. Y. 10940
Glenwood Publishers, Box 194, Felton, Calif. 95018
Golden West Books, Box 8136, San Marino, Calif. 91108
Stephen Greene Press, Box 1000, Brattleboro, Vt. 05301
Greenwood Press, Inc., 51 Riverside Ave., Westport, Conn. 06880
Grosset & Dunlap, Inc., 51 Madison Ave., New York, N. Y. 10010
Harvard University Press, 79 Garden St., Cambridge, Mass. 02138
Howell-North Books, 1050 Parker St., Berkeley, Calif. 94710
Johnson Reprint Co., 111 5th Ave., New York, N. Y. 10003
Kalmbach Publishing Co., 1027 N. 7th St., Milwaukee, Wis. 53233
A. M. Kelley, 305 Allwood Rd., Clifton, N. J. 07012
Ladd Publications, Box 137, Jacksonville, Ill. 62650
The Macmillan Co., Riverside, N. J. 08075
National Learning Corp., 20 DuPont St., Plainview, N. Y. 11803
Normandie House Publishers, 1236 Chase Ave., Chicago, Ill. 60626
Old Line Publishers, Box 123, Milwaukee, Wis. 53201
G. P. Putnam's Sons, 200 Madison Ave., New York, N. Y. 10016
Specialty Press, Inc., Box 2187, Ocean, N. J. 07712
Sundance, Ltd., Box 6385, Denver, Colo. 80206
Superior Publishing Co., 708 Sixth Ave. N., Seattle, Wash. 98111
Trans-Anglo Books, Box 38, Corona del Mar, Calif. 92625
Wayner Publications, Box 871, Ansonia Station, New York, N. Y. 10023